SWORDS CASTLE: DIGGING HISTORY

SWORDS CASTLE: DIGGING HISTORY:
Excavations 2015–17

Christine Baker

with contributions from
Ruth Carden, Siobhán G. Duffy, Linda G. Lynch, Margaret McCarthy, Meriel
McClatchie, Clare McCutcheon, Ellen OCarroll and Joanna Wren

Wordwell

First published in 2022
Wordwell Ltd
Unit 9, 78 Furze Road, Sandyford Industrial Estate, Dublin 18
www.wordwellbooks.com

ISBN: 978-1-913934-69-9

British Library Cataloguing-in-Publication Data.
A catalogue record for this book is available from the British Library.

Cover image: Plate of Swords Castle from F. Grose's *Antiquities of Ireland*. (NLI)

Typeset in Ireland by Wordwell Ltd
Copy-editor: Emer Condit
Cover design and artwork: Wordwell Ltd
Printed by Printrun Ltd, Ireland

The authors and publisher would like to acknowledge that research reported in this publication was funded by the Heritage Council and Fingal County Council. The content of this publication is solely the responsibility of the authors and does not necessarily represent the official views of the Heritage Council.

Contents

Foreword

Swords Castle is now recognised as one of the major monuments of north County Dublin, a welcome development for those who remember the castle's neglected and forlorn condition in days gone by. Driving north to Drogheda, long before the building of the Swords bypass and motorway, there was a brief glimpse of the walls and gatehouse but no indication of the importance of the place. In those days much of the fabric was obscured from view and visitors were not encouraged to venture inside. It was hard to appreciate that this was once a major administrative centre, the headquarters of a vast estate belonging to the archbishop of Dublin, one of the wealthiest and most powerful men in the country. It was especially fitting that in 1996 Fingal County Council selected Swords as its headquarters, the splendid new offices now overlooking this ancient seat of authority.

The year 2021 marks the 50th anniversary of the first serious investigation of the castle, when the late Tom Fanning excavated a highly decorated tiled floor, leaving us in no doubt that this was the site of a stylish medieval residence as well as the headquarters of a manorial estate. In the decades that followed, attention turned to the architecture of the castle, with various programmes of restoration and reconstruction. It is only in the last decade, however, that our understanding of the site has been dramatically expanded, thanks to a series of excavations, the most important being those carried out under the direction of Christine Baker between 2015 and 2017. Over the course of 50 years the discipline of archaeology has been transformed, and at Swords the latest scientific techniques have been employed to unlock the past in a most exciting way, producing all manner of information about those who lived and worked within the castle boundaries. One of the great merits of this volume is that it goes far beyond the recent excavations. There is an account of the early history of Swords, along with valuable summaries of earlier excavations, providing a complete picture of what archaeology has achieved in recent years.

Among the highlights of the excavation was proof that the site was inhabited for at least two centuries before the founding of the castle in about 1200, a settlement that included an extensive burial-ground. The examination of the skeletal remains underlines just how far archaeology has progressed in modern times. Every bone was scrutinised for clues, with the skills of the forensic pathologist brought to bear. As readers will discover, the results are quite remarkable. It turns out that many of the early inhabitants of Swords suffered from degenerative joint disease, enduring spinal problems and back pain. Others suffered from gallstones, and their diet was so rough that in some cases teeth were ground down to the gums—a reminder of how much our own age owes to modern medicine and dentistry. Nutrition was poor; life was hard, brutish and very physical.

Later in the Middle Ages, those dwelling within the castle were healthier and more prosperous. The excavations recovered a wealth of information about the type of agricultural produce collected at the site, along with the diet of the inhabitants, much of the information coming from pits—a precious source for the archaeologist. The menu for the archbishop, as well as for those living more permanently within the castle walls, included beef, mutton, pork and rabbit, along with peas and beans. As Swords is close to the coast, it is no surprise to discover that this menu was supplemented by cod, plaice and haddock, along with oysters, cockles, periwinkle and whelk. One of the more surprising finds was music, in the form of a slate engraved with 30 musical notes, a relic of the fifteenth century. Unexpected discoveries continued into modern times, including children's toy bubble pipes from around 1900 and a lead seal with the date 1903, showing that Dunne's Bakery, situated just outside the walls, was using flour imported from Paris. The volume is in fact a veritable encyclopaedia, its relevance extending far beyond the town of Swords itself.

The sheer quantity of material extracted is quite dazzling—many thousands of items, all of which had to be cleaned, identified and catalogued. Equally impressive is the way the whole operation was carried out by communal archaeology, with an army of over 300 volunteers drawn from the local area. Scores of people have now gained an insight into archaeological practice and no doubt feel, quite justifiably, that they have part-ownership of the information that has come to light. Community archaeology has the capacity to spread our understanding of the past and provides a spectacular demonstration of the simple fact that heritage belongs to everyone. Whenever those who were involved in the excavations pass by the castle walls, they will surely recall their own part in uncovering—and, indeed, making—history.

The task of directing the excavations, especially ones with so many participants, required formidable organisational skills on the part of Christine Baker, the success of the project being carried along by her infectious enthusiasm. Her comprehensive report is ably supported by a series of specialist contributors, who have dealt with such matters as human remains, floor tiles, pottery and molluscs. The volume provides an accurate and comprehensive record of the excavation, while offering innumerable insights into how our forebears lived and died over a period of 1,000 years. In view of all their hard work, the many participants in the *Swords Castle: Digging History* project deserve our thanks as well as our hearty congratulations.

Roger Stalley

Acknowledgements

Many thanks are due to my archaeological colleagues—Stephen Johnston, Siobhán Duffy, Laura Corrway, Ian Kinch and Kim Rice—and to all those who volunteered: Agineska Czyzowicz-Janiszewska, Aaron Jennings, Audrea Juinfare, Aidan Giblin, Alan Keogh, Alan O'Malley, Aleksanders Haidurov, Aleksei Haidurov, Alexey Gishchenko, Aileen Donnelly, Ailish Durney, Andrew Fosonu, Angela Thornton, Angela Lodge, Ann Kilmeade, Ann McNamee, Ann Lynch, Anne Reumann, Ann Marie O'Shea, Aine O'Connor, Antoinette Madden, Anthony Neville, Antje Renner, Aoife Foley, Aoife Higgins, Aonghus McGovern, Audrey Rossa, Austin Fennessy, Barry Rellis, Beatrice Augustyniak, Betty Boardman, Brigit Berkenkoff, Brian Madigan, Brian McCabe, Brian Simpson, Brian O'Connor, Brid Barnes, Breege Casey, Brendan Black, Brendan Murphy, Caoimhe Smith, Carmel Mahon, Caroline O'Malley, Carija Ihus, Catriona Chuinneagain, Chris Clements, Christine Flood, Ciaran Mathews, Ciaran McDonnell, Ciaran O'Connor, Ciara O'Leary, Ciarrai O'Sullivan, Clare Bradley, Claire Ferris, Clare O'Conor, Clare Ryan, Cormac Smith, Colm Diamond, Daniel McEvoy, Daniel Withero, Daire O'Shea Brady, Nessa O'Shea Brady, Danny Cummins, Damien Farrell, Dave McKeon, Dave Weldon, Dean Rossa, Derek O'Brien, Diane Clarke, Deirdre O'Neill, Eamonn Flanagan, Edward Mullarkey, Eileen Connolly, Eileen Keelan, Eilis Young, Elaine Brennan, Eoin Bairéad, Eoin Cotter, Etain Feeley, Eunan Gaffney, Fergus Finch, Fergus O'Donnell, Fiona Daly, Finola O'Carroll, Fionnuala McGinley, Frank Duffy, Gabriel Byrne, Gabrielle Smyth, Gareth Casserly, Georgia Leonard, Geraldine Clarke, Gerda O'Donovan, George O'Carroll, Gerry Stanley, Grace Monaghan, Glenn Delves, Grainne Donoghue, Grainne Moussally, Grainne Smith, Guenaell Saidlear, Hans Visser, Helen Weldon, Helen Corrway, Hilary Klompenhower, Hugh Deery, Ian Brown, Iongla Visinoae, Irena Haidurov, Irina Pavlivkova, Jacqui Brennan, Jackie Flanagan, Janine Merry, James Lindsay, James Walker, Jessica Fitzsimons, Joan Murphy, Joe Foy, John Drinane, John Kennedy, Jolita Garliene, Joe Newman, Joe Foley, Joseph Fletcher, Josephine Ennis, Judith Finlay, Julia Grishchenko, Kate Drinane, Katee Lawlor, Katelyn Hoffart, Karen O'Toole, Ken Byrne, Kelvin Osotutu, Kevin Jenkinson, Kieran Campbell, Kestutis Gelatis, Larry Arnold, Lesley Donohoe, Len O'Donnell, Liam Roche, Linde Lunney, Linda Jago, Louise Boughton, Loraine Kenny, Loraine Morgan, Mairead O'Byrne, Margareta Grunenwald, Margaret Kirwan, Maighread Medbh, Mari Carpenter, Marian Kelly, Mairin Ní Cheallaigh, Mark Henry, Mark Kilmartin, Martin Walsh, Mary Finch, Mary Lynch, Mary Sims, Mary Clare Walsh, Mary Scanlon, Michael Scanlon, Michael Scullion, Mick Farrell, Mick Kelly, Mick Mongey, Molly Devlin, Monica Lindsay, Maureen Lambert, Nessa Earley, Niamh Kelly, Niall Casey, Nichola McGrattan, Nicola Mullooly, Nicholas Keyes, Nicholas McGrattan, Nicholas Mulloolly, Nina Peier, Noel Mahon, Noel Young, Noreen Lynch, Olwyn Moyne, Paddy O'Byrne, Pat O'Donovan, Pat Quinlan, Paddy McKittrick, Patricia Graham, Patricia Lyons, Paul Corcoran, Paul Feeley, Paul Kennedy, Paul O'Flaherty, Pauline Collins, Paulene Cunningham, Pauline O'Riordan, Phil O'Flaherty, Philip Costello, Peter O'Toole, Rachel

Scahill, Reamonn McLoughlin, Roisin Mead, Raymond Daly, Raymond Feerick, Richard Coplen, Rivolta Pierlivio, Robert Woods, Robert Cox, Ross Creed, Ronan Kelly, Rory Corian, Rosaire Dunne, Ryan Carter, Sandra Murphy, Seán Byrne, Seamus Canty, Seamus Cashman, Seamus Murray, Seán MacDomhnaill, Shannen Smith, Shay Kelly, Siobhán Keely, Simon Brennan, Stella Giblin, Stephen Phillips, Susan Lynch, T.F. Bradshaw, Tara McLoughlin, Terry Hurrell, Tony Howley, Tom McErlean, Tracy Lanigan, Treasa Kerrigan, Therese Foster, Veronica Walsh, Vlad Vasildov.

Thanks to the post-excavation team for their input and expertise: Dr Meriel McClatchie, Dr Linda Lynch, Mags McCarthy, Clare McCutcheon, Joanna Wren, Siobhán Duffy, Dr Ruth Carden, Dr Ellen OCarroll, Susannah Kelly and the [14]CHRONO Centre, Queen's University Belfast.

Many thanks to the staff of the National Museum of Ireland, especially Judith Finlay and her colleagues in the Collections Resource Centre, for their support and participation in the project. Thanks also to the National Monuments Service, Department of Housing, Local Government and Heritage, especially Martin Reid, for their support of the project.

Thanks are due to Fingal County Council, not least for funding the project, and specifically to my colleagues and former colleagues who helped in a myriad of ways: Dr Gerry Clabby, Niall McCoitir, Gilbert Power, AnnMarie Farrelly, Coilin O'Reilly, Fionnuala May, Brian O'Connor, Paul Smyth, Billy McClean, Colm Connell, Alex Graham, Ray Lambe, Niall Nevin, Greg O'Mahony, Damian Ryan, Noeleen McHugh, Cormac O'Sullivan, Michelle Burnett, Fergal Duignan, Martin Daly, Deirdre Sinclair, Duncan Henderson, Mary Dwyer, Valerie Geddes, Ciara Monahan, Shay Barker, Darragh Sheppard, Maeve Egan, Fergal Duignan, Seán Healy, and Swords Castle caretaker Paddy Duffy. Thanks are also due to the Heritage Council, who funded the Community Archaeologist position, and to Ian Doyle and Professor Gabriel Cooney for their support.

Bringing a publication to press is a lengthy process, and I'd like to thank Dr Linda Lynch, Mags McCarthy and Siobhán G. Duffy for their assistance. I am grateful, too, to Mark Moraghan, Katherine Daly, Anthony Corns, Rob Lynch and his team at IAC Ltd, and Lisa Courtney and Siobhán Deery of Courtney Deery Ltd for their help in sourcing images.

I would especially like to thank Professor Roger Stalley for taking the time to read this volume, for providing the foreword and for his encouragement and kind words. This volume was published with the financial sponsorship of Fingal County Council and the Heritage Council and I am grateful for their generous support. Thanks also to Nick Maxwell, Emer Condit and all the Wordwell team for their patience and professionalism. Finally, many thanks to Conor, Katie and Oisín Dinneen, who make everything possible.

PART I: SWORDS CASTLE

Introduction

S words Castle is not a castle in the accepted sense but rather the best remaining upstanding example of a medieval episcopal palace in Ireland. Attributed to the first Anglo-Norman archbishop of Dublin, John Comyn, it was founded in the later twelfth century as the administrative centre of an extremely wealthy manor.

Swords, which is *c.* 15km north of Dublin, is the county town of Fingal. This publication describes the results of the three seasons of archaeological excavation carried out at the castle under Ministerial Consent C450/E004619 as part of the *Swords Castle: Digging History— Fingal Community Excavation Project 2015–2017*. The project was designed to address the research and knowledge gaps identified in the *Swords Castle Conservation Plan* (Fingal County Council 2014) and to inform the urban identity of the developing *Swords Castle Cultural Quarter Masterplan* (Fingal County Council 2015).

Pl. 1.1—Aerial photograph taken c. *2001.*

LOCATION, TOPOGRAPHY AND GEOLOGY

Swords Castle, which is a National Monument (No. 340), a recorded monument (DU011-034001-) and a protected structure (No. 351), is located at the northern end of Swords Main Street (ITM 718195/ 747010) at its junction with North Street and Bridge Street within the historic town of Swords (DU011-035----). It is set on high ground above the Ward River, which lies to the west, and is situated within Swords Town Park. The castle was strategically located west of the head of the Malahide estuary, surrounded by a fertile rolling hinterland, at the confluence of the roads to the north and west, with views towards the ecclesiastical centre of Swords on the high ground west of the Ward River.

The site consists of curtain walls that form an irregular polygon enclosing over an acre of land that slopes down from east (18m OD) to west (15m OD). The solid geology of the area that forms the parent material is Carboniferous limestone, and the soil in the general area is part of the grey/brown podzolic group. Sands and gravels derived from Carboniferous material are mapped along the path of the Ward River and there is made ground in Swords town (Fay *et al.* 2007, 1–12). Local knowledge has it that the Main Street of Swords is stone and that beyond it is gravel (Des Gallagher, pers. comm.).

This complex of buildings saw many phases of reuse and redesign, and latterly reconstruction in the 1990s. A programme of consolidation and enabling works commenced in April 2016. This involved the removal of a set of portacabins that had been in place since

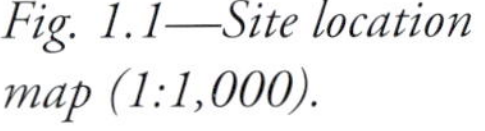

Fig. 1.1—Site location map (1:1,000).

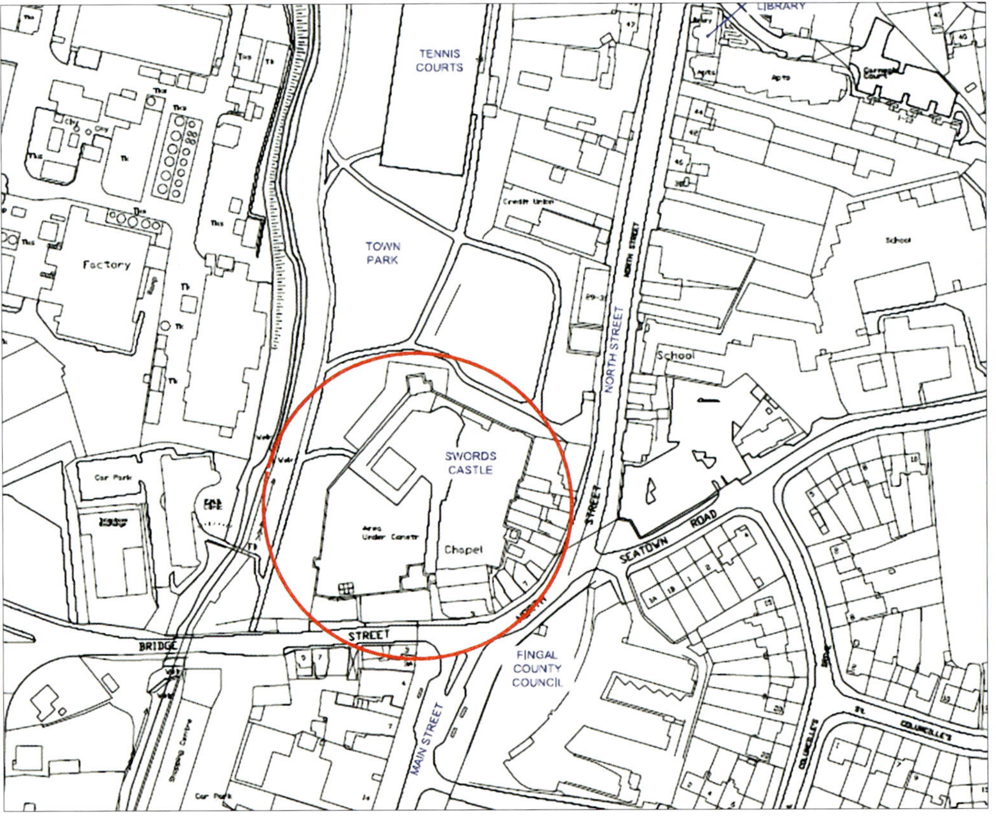

the mid-1990s, the insertion of paths into the precinct space and the consolidation of the Gatehouse, the East Tower and the eastern curtain walls. Phase 2 enabling works were undertaken between November 2018 and December 2019 and encompassed the stabilisation of the East Tower and replacement of the wall-walk.

There are well-established apple trees on the higher ground to the east. The area to the south-west was previously used as an equipment compound and is currently under gravel. The access way and carpark are under compacted asphalt. The remaining open spaces within the site are under grass.

HISTORICAL BACKGROUND

Pre-Anglo-Norman Swords

The place-name Swords is derived from *Sord*, meaning 'pure' or 'clear' (Joyce 1920). It has been associated with a spring reputedly blessed by St Columcille (d. 597), known as Sord Colm-Cille or St Columcille's Well, which is located to the south of the Ward River and west of the Main Street. St Columcille is said to have appointed Fínán Lobur Suird ('Finian the leper/invalid of Swords') as the first abbot, although it is believed that St Fínán died within Colmcille's lifetime. Another theory is that the church was originally founded by St Fínán and transferred to the Columban monks at a later date (Gwynn and Hadcock 1970, 44). It is unclear whether Fínán was the founder of a male community at Swords, a distinguished early member or a saintly figure (MacShamhráin 2016, 56).

There is, however, an earlier association between St Brigit and Swords. The Old Irish Life of St Brigit, the *Bethu Brigte*, written in the ninth century, refers to *Cell Suirdd i ndesciurt Bregh* ('Cell Suirdd in south Brega'), where Brigit performed one of her miracles, and one of her community, Caimell, is referred to as being *i nDisiurt Brigte i Cill Suird* (Bhreathnach 1999, 7; MacShamhráin 2016, 54). Dísert Brigte was probably a hermitage site or an enclosed community of virgins, but its exact location is unknown. Veneration of Brigit continued despite the strength of the Columban foundation at Swords, and her association with Swords is mentioned in the mid-thirteenth century in a list of feoffees in the *Liber Niger* of Christ Church, Dublin, stating that the canons of St Patrick's 'have in pure and perpetual alms the whole of Bream[ore] where St Brigid's chapel was in the manor of Swerdes from the house of the Balniator to the wall of Walter Cumin, along with 4a, in the land of Warenne' (Bhreathnach 1999, 7). In the nineteenth century Dalton (1838a, 140) makes references to three churches at Swords, dedicated to St Fintan, St Brigit and St Catherine. St Fintan's church was purportedly to the south of Swords, while St Brigit's was described as being on the north side of the town, 'not far from the gates of the old palace'.

Whatever the truth of its origin, the church at Swords grew as a powerful ecclesiastical centre to become a *plebia* or mother church. The ecclesiastical centre would have followed the schema as outlined in the seventh century. The core of each site contained the 'holiest of holies', where the church and the dead were, surrounded by enclosures of decreasing sanctity. As described in a manuscript from the *Collectio Canonum Hibernensis*,

'there ought to be two or three termini around a holy place: the first in which we allow no one at all to enter except priests … the second, into its streets the crowds of

common people, not much given to wickedness; the third murderers, adulterers and prostitutes …' (Doherty 1985, 59).

The ecclesiastical centre of Swords is located on high ground bounded to east and south by the River Ward, which doubtless acted as a boundary for the site, the line of the enclosures (DU011-034002) now fossilised in the present street layout of the Brackenstown, Church and Rathbeale roads. The round tower or *cloig teach* (DU011-034005) probably dates from the tenth/eleventh century. Another surviving element of the early church is a lunette cross-incised slab (DU011-034007), originally a pillar stone, that has been incorporated into the base of the medieval residential tower. The cross with expanded terminals probably dates from the eighth/ninth century. In the nearby rectory garden, a beehive chambered souterrain (DU011-034022) has been uncovered. Souterrains were used variously for food storage, for shelter in times of attack or for securing goods or slaves; they also date from the early medieval period.

Such ecclesiastical sites were not only centres of spirituality but also major centres of economic power. Granted land and amassing benefices from the secular septs, the churches were in a position to produce surpluses and thus become centres for trade, exchange and craftsmanship. At the time of the founding of the early ecclesiastical establishment of Swords this area probably lay within the petty kingdom of Gailenga Becca, which extended from the Tolka River in the south to the Broad Meadow River in the north. By the eighth century, or possibly earlier, the Síl nÁedo Sláine, part of the southern Uí Neill dynasty, had established the kingdom of Brega in this area (MacShamhráin 2016, 39). Two Viking raids on the monastic settlement at Swords are mentioned in the annalistic material included in the *Cogad Gáedeil re Gallaib*, in the early 830s and *c.* 841–5, but there is no mention of Swords in the mainstream annals for over 150 years after these references (Bhreathnach 1999, 7). According to the Annals of Ulster, in 994 Swords was attacked by Máel Sechnaill, the king of Clann Cholmáin, who was then vying for the high-kingship of Ireland (MacShamhráin 2016, 50). The eminence of Swords is attested to in the Annals of Ulster, where it is recorded that in 1014, after the Battle of Clontarf, the body of Brian Boru was given over to Máel Muire mac

Fig. 1.3—Ecclesiastical centre, Swords, c. 1014: artist's reconstruction by Johnny Ryan.

Eochada, *comarba Pátraic*, at Swords on the first stage of Brian's funeral procession to Armagh (Bhreathnach 1999, 11).

The eleventh century saw a shift in political power from the Hiberno-Scandinavians to native Irish dynasties, which resulted in ongoing conflict in Dublin and its hinterland. The burning of Swords by the Vikings is recorded in the Annals of the Four Masters in 1012, and it was burned again by the Vikings in 1016, according to the Annals of Ulster. Swords came under attack again in 1035, this time by Conchobar úa Máel Sechnaill, the king of Meath, in revenge for an attack by Sitric mac Amlaíb on Ardbraccan (*ibid.*). This would seem to indicate that Swords was seen as part of the Scandinavian kingdom of Dublin at this time (Bradley 1998, 138). In 1059 both Swords and Lusk were burned (MacShamhráin 2016, 51), and Swords was repeatedly attacked by the O'Melaghlin kings of Meath, in 1069, 1130, 1135, 1138, 1150 and 1160, probably because of its close ties to the Vikings of Dublin (Bhreathnach 1999, 13).

Despite the influence of the Dublin Vikings in Swords, however, all the recorded churchmen at Swords are from native Irish families. The first recorded bishop of Swords and Lusk, Ailill mac Máenaig, who died in 965, was from a local family who were possibly even part of the Gailenga, and throughout the eleventh century the holders of senior offices at Swords all appear to have belonged to ecclesiastical lineages with Columban connections (Bhreathnath 1999, 13; MacShamhráin 2016, 60). Ecclesiastical reform, initially led by the Dál Cais overkings (who dominated Dublin from 1056 to 1116), took place throughout the eleventh and twelfth centuries, coinciding with an extended period of church construction as dynasties vied to endow ecclesiastical sites (MacShamhráin 2016, 62). It is likely that the round tower at Swords is associated with this development. It also appears that Swords emerged as a parish centre in the 1140s as the regional parish system was developed.

Fig. 1.4—View of the North Tower (Constable's Tower), Swords Castle, by Daniel Grose, 1792 (courtesy of the National Library of Ireland).

Medieval Swords

After the Anglo-Norman invasion of 1169, the property of the monastery of Swords formed part of the lands of the see of Dublin, confirmed to Archbishop Laurence O'Toole in 1179 (McNeill 1950). Swords Castle was founded by the first Anglo-Norman archbishop of Dublin, John Comyn, towards the end of the twelfth century. One of several manorial centres that encircled the principal residence of St Sepulchre's in Dublin, Swords Castle was also one of the wealthiest. As an administrative centre it had a constable and a court of justice, and it was granted an eight-day market in 1192. John Comyn not only founded the manor house at Swords but also, keen to expand the income of his estate, established a new town. The main street and its burgage plots were aligned on the castle. In order to attract settlers, the same trading and tax privileges enjoyed by the citizens of Dublin were offered. In return, the burgesses paid an annual rent of twelve pence and undertook certain labour services, such as harvesting the archbishop's hay and repairing the millpond. Swords grew to become one of Dublin's largest boroughs, and such was its wealth that it became known as the Golden Prebend.

A description in Archbishop Alen's Register depicts Swords Castle in 1326 (MacNeill 1950, 175):

> 'a hall, a chamber for the archbishop annexed to it, of which the walls are stone and crenellated like a castle and roof with shingles; and there was a kitchen there with a larder whose walls are stone and roof of shingle, a chapel with stone walls and a shingle roof; there was a chamber for friars with a cloister now thrown down; near the gate is

a chamber for the constable and four chambers for knights and squires roofed with shingles; under these a stable and bakehouse; there was a house for a deieria and carpenteria, now thrown down. In the haggard a grange of poles (*furcae*) thatched, a timber granary roofed with "bords", a byre for housing nags and kine; these easements they extend at no value, for nothing is to be got from them by either letting or otherwise, since they need great repair as they are badly roofed.'

This description was part of a formal inquisition into the dealings of the archbishop of the time, Alexander de Bicknor, who was accused of misappropriating finances for his own gain. There is a possibility that the dilapidated state of the castle was a deliberate attempt to downplay de Bicknor's assets, as it was occupied sporadically by the archbishops after this point. Records of Swords Castle over the next 300 years are scant.

The fifteenth century saw the enclosure of Swords Castle with crenallated walls and the beginning of its being referred to as a 'castle' or *castrum*. Ascribed to Archbishop Richard Talbot (1417–49), who had led military expeditions in defence of the marches, the curtain walls with their stepped battlements and interior wall-walk did not, however, have particularly strong defensive capabilities (Stalley 2006, 155). Dubious leasing practices resulted in loss of control over some manorial lands and in 1522 Swords is listed as being 'in the king's hand by reason of vacancy' (Griffith 1991, 4). The late Archbishop Walter Fitzsimons, however, had granted the office of constable of his castle of Swords to Thomas Fitzsimons, whose fee was fixed 'owing to the poverty of the bishop' (*ibid.*). The office of constable at Swords Castle continued to be granted by the archbishop, with Robert Eustace appointed in 1540 and the Barnewall family thereafter in perpetuity, thus indicating a tenancy if not of Swords Castle then of the manorial lands. In 1583 Sir Henry Sydney, lord deputy of Ireland, housed 40 Protestant families fleeing from persecution in the Low Countries in Swords Castle. He wrote that it did his heart good to see how they repaired the 'quite spoiled old castell' (Smiles 1889).

Relationship between castle and town
From the time of Archbishop Comyn, when the high street of Swords was laid out with burgages to either side and the incentives of the liberty were offered to settlers, the fortunes of the town and castle seem to have been intertwined. Grants such as that made by Nicholas Russell of a 'burgage in Swerdes situated on the south way to the church … for rent of one clove of garrofili' in 1295 to Archbisop Fulk, or that by Archbishop Walter to William Fureter of 'land beside the mill' in 1255, demonstrate the interlinkage between the archbishops and the borough. The archbishops who took up sporadic residence in Swords Castle were generally English and well-travelled. The settling of the English borough was a process of acculturation of what had previously been the 'land of the Ocadesci' (McNeill 1950). Surviving grants offer glimpses of the people, places and activities of medieval Swords.

It appears that not only the English were encouraged to settle in Swords. In 1285 a John Folebourne was paid to carry Welshmen from Aberconway to Swords (Close Roll 14). There was also reference in 1326 to 'sixteen foreign burgesses' at Swords, the phrase *burgagii fornscei* being a term used to describe Ostmen or Viking settlements (Bradley 1998). By 1326 there were 122 burgesses and Swords was one of the largest and most enduring boroughs, functioning continuously until the sixteenth century. Medieval society was hierarchical and regimented. The lands of the manor were farmed by the betaghs, who were required to watch

Pl. 1.2—Burgage plots were still visible off Swords Main Street in the 1980s (© National Museum of Ireland).

the archbishop's 'nags and kine'. On the next rung were the cottars, who held small plots (< 1 acre) and, although free, were dependent on the archbishop and larger tenants. In the early fourteenth century there were 44 cottages and gardens 'built and unbuilt' in Swords. 'Gavellors' held their land at the will of the lord and could be ejected should the archbishop wish. In de Bicknor's time there were 28 gavellors who held one carucate, four score and three acres 'in diverse places about the town of Swords' (Murphy and Potterton 2010). Recent archaeological investigations have also revealed evidence for thirteenth/fourteenth-century settlement activity along the flood-plain of the Ward River to the south and west of the main street (McGlade 2017; McLoughlin 2019).

The markets and courts licensed and held by the archbishop were integral to the economic and social well-being of the town. The weekly Monday market confirmed in 1395 would have been located where the main street expands in front of Swords Castle. This and the annual eight-day fair held since Comyn's time would have attracted merchants and commerce from the large towns and ports of the region. There are records of 'beasts of the plough' and corn being bought at Swords in the early fourteenth century (Sweetman 1879, V, 10). In 1395 it was detailed how the archbishops kept a 'clerk of the market and keeper of the measures' and had 'assize of wine, bread and beer, of their standards and of ells, weights, bushels, gallons, yards and other measures and weights' (Patent Roll 18). By 1541 Richard Russel, a merchant of Drogheda, was trading in Swords, where a Powyll Fayoff of Lytle Egypt (a company of Egyptians apparently 'sojurning in Dublin') was accused of stealing black stain and black damask (Nicholls 1994, I, 32). Aside from merchants and farmers, Swords had Roger the cobbler and Peter Smith the faber (thirteenth/fourteenth century), shoemakers (Patrick Connaght) and tanners (Hugh Tallard and Patrick Morry) (sixteenth century) (Griffith 1991, 97).

Near the market-place, the old village stocks were still in position in front of the castle in the early nineteenth century (Dalton 1838a, 137), although there are no surviving records of the implementation of 'pillory, tumbrel and thew'. The administration of justice for the manor was an essential undertaking by the archbishops and their appointees at Swords Castle. As outlined in the grant of 1395, they could pronounce on 'pleas of manslaughter, murder, slaying of English men, all kinds of robberies, larcenies, trial by combat of Englishmen and all other within their manors; Abjurations of fugitives and felons fleeing the holy church', and had liberty to take fines and ransoms in their courts. They could also 'correct and punish artificers and labourers and take fines and corrections of their tenants' (Patent Roll 18). Cases that came before the episcopal courts were varied. In 1279 a payment was made to William de Folham for maintaining three hostages at Swords from September 1272 until St Patrick's Day (Sweetman 1877, II, 313). Sir Robert Bagod, who had undergone great expense in improving his land but had 'lost all he had spent by death of an infant, the only heir of his father' in 1277, was 'desirous that the bishop should provide him, if possible, with another ward and marriage in the manor of Swords' (*ibid.*, III, 264). Most of the surviving records are to do with land grants and compensations for burgages, although it is known that men found guilty of sheep-stealing were hanged on Gallow's Hill, located on the Brackenstown road.

There is very little record of the women of Swords. One exception is Joan Relawe. In 1459 Richard Ward, John Kerlan and John Foster were indicted by 'one John Yonge of Swords merchant' of taking seventeen pecks of salt, amongst other goods, before Alexander Ewer, 'Constable of the castle of Swords', and were ordered to make *replevia* to Joan Relawe of the seventeen pecks of salt (Berry 1910, 609).

The office of constable of Swords Castle seems to have been filled irrespective of the presence or absence of an archbishop, although it may not always have been the most rewarding of positions. Archbishop Comyn's constable, William Galrote, was murdered, and Samson de Crumba, who 'slew Laur. Bissop in the vill of Swerdes', for which he had to pay a fine to the archbishop, thereafter served as constable of Swords for a considerable length of time (McNeill 1950, 104). Archbishop Michael Tregury appointed Edmund Dudelay knight constable of the castle of Swords in 1474, but it transpired that Edmund was 'not in this land' and had 'no deputy in this land' to occupy the office (Morrisey 1939, 343). There also seems to have been some personal expense involved in the honour. William Smyth was appointed to the office of the serjeantry of Swords in 1450, to hold and exercise by himself, or by sufficient deputies for whom he is willing to answer (Patent Roll 28). In the sixteenth century Thomas Fitzsimons held that office for 6s, although at other times for 5s 4d and a robe (Nicholls 1994, I, 253), only for the archbishop of Dublin to license the office of the manor and castle of Swords from Fitzsimon's 'death or surrender' in trust for the use of Patrick Barnewall of Gracedieu (Morrin 1861, 131).

The fortunes of the castle and the town appeared to decline in the face of the upsurge of the Gaelic Irish. In the mid-fifteenth century, when the castle was undergoing fortification, it was recorded that Irish enemies and English rebels were 'coming at night … into Fingal … [to] rob, kill and destroy the liege people of the king so that parts of Fingal are likely to be finally destroyed'. Barriers were ordered on bridges and at the 'Cross of Swords … shall stop fords and raise trenches …' (Berry 1910, 315). Furthermore, it seems that the fortunes of the town fell along with those of the archbishops in the sixteenth century. In his resettling

of the Dutch Protestants in 1583 Sir Henry Sydney had referred to the town of Swords as 'ruinous' and the castle as 'quite spoiled'. Only five years earlier Swords had been granted a new charter by Elizabeth I; serjeants-at-law were appointed to measure two miles from the town of Swords to indicate the bounds of the liberties of the town. The queen had also incorporated Thomas Molyneux, his wife, children and family and as many strangers as he could induce within five years to inhabit Swords (Nicholls 1994, II, 454).

Post-medieval to modern Swords

In 1603 James I granted the archbishop of Dublin a confirmation of the privileges of the town, including the weekly market on Monday in the archbishop's manor of Swords. Two additional fairs were granted in 1699. Swords was one of the few free boroughs in Ireland, the franchise being vested in what was called the 'potwalloper': a man who qualified as a householder, and therefore as a voter, by virtue of his ownership of a fireplace at which to boil pots—or, in the case of Swords, Protestants resident for six months. In the eighteenth century, however, the borough of Swords was 'of notorious fame in the annals of bribery and corruption'. By 1791 it was noted that the voters in Swords 'sell themselves to the highest bidder' (Forbes 2021). The 1727 election was particularly hotly disputed. One witness described a group of 24 men arriving into the borough in March 1727 with their wives and children and 'Furze on their Back to potwallop with, or Boyle their pot'. Some witnesses claimed to have been in a position to choose between bribes from opposing candidates, while others claimed to have accepted payments in exchange for their vote (*ibid.*). The negative reputation continued into the nineteenth century, when it was asserted that voters in Swords 'were of the meanest class of citizens … whose venality was as black as the pots that qualified them' (Walsh 1888).

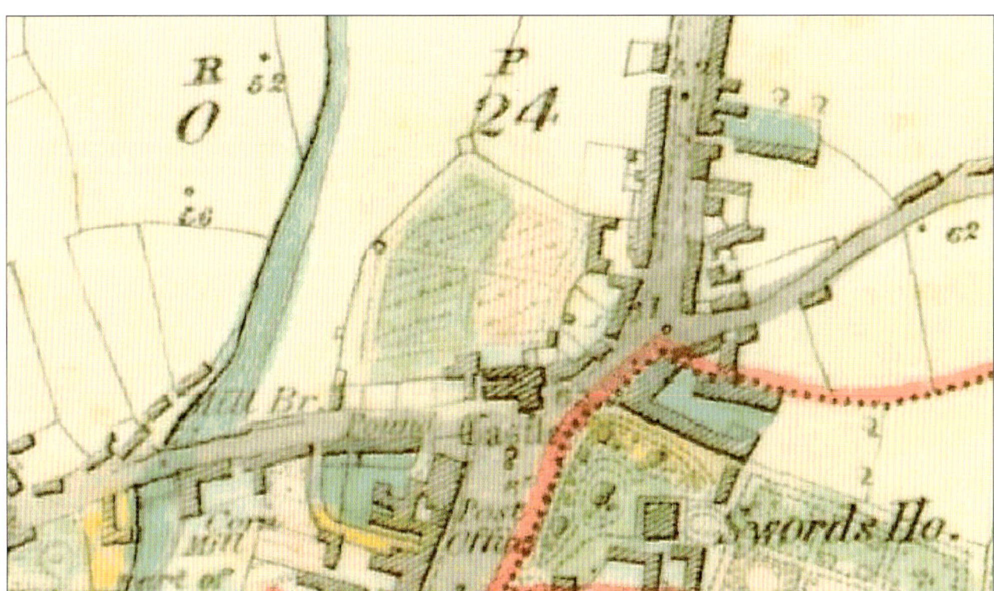

Fig. 1.5—First-edition Ordnance Survey map, 1838.

On 14 December 1831 Richard, Archbishop of Dublin, signed a lease giving 'The Castle of Swords … together with all and singular the Houses, Edifices, Building and Lands therein contained and all and singular other the rights and privileges and appurtenances thereabouts belonging or appertaining formerly in the possession of the Reverend John Wynee or his under tenants and containing in the whole one acre and 15 perches plantation measurement be the same more or less' to Charles and George Cobbe for a term of 40 years at a rent of £2-6s-2d (Cobbe Papers).

The 1836 first-edition Ordnance Survey (OS) six-inch map for Swords (Fig. 1.5) shows the castle in the townland of Townparks, and the familiar irregular pentagon plan of the precinct is accurately mapped for the first time. By this time the interior of the castle was well established as a garden and this is shown with diagonal hatching, which indicates cultivation, and subdividing paths.

The Griffith Valuation of *c.* 1844 lists the 'Old Ruins and the Castle garden', with a note that 'this garden belongs to John McCann of 67 Main St.'. A tenement valuation of George Cobbe's holdings in the town of Swords, dated May 1869, also ascribes the 'Old ruins and Castle Garden' to John McCann. Although there was a garden within the castle in the archbishop's time, it was not until the eighteenth century that Swords Castle was described as possessing an orchard. Although details of the type of orchard are unknown, demesnes of the time grew cherries, pears, damsons and plums as well as apples. The oldest surviving apple tree is near the Chapel; it is an Old Bramley dating from the 1890s.

Restoration works began at Swords Castle in the 1990s. The curtain walls, the Constable's Tower and the Chapel were reconstructed as part of a FÁS scheme which provided training in masonry and carpentry for local people. Fingal County Council published the *Swords Castle Conservation Plan* in 2014. This details the history and development of the castle, explains its significance and provides a policy framework for its future care and management.

2

Previous works

PREVIOUS WORKS TO SWORDS CASTLE

Like any buildings of such an age, Swords Castle has undergone a myriad of changes to its fabric, including repairs and reconstruction. The earliest repairs recorded are those undertaken by the Dutch settlers in the sixteenth century which were described by Sir Henry Sydney in a letter of 1583:

> '… it would have done any man good how diligently they wrought, how they re-edified the quite spoiled old castell of the same town and repayred [repaired] almost all the same' (Smiles 1889).

The nineteenth century saw several breaches of the curtain walls and subsequent repairs. The segment of wall between the East Tower and the Great Hall, the so-called link wall, is a nineteenth-century garden wall rebuilt along the presumed line of the previously robbed-out

Pl. 2.1—Internal façade, doorway in south wall, 2001.

curtain wall. There are the remnants of a doorway in the south wall not far from the Pound public house. Removal of the overburden internal to this doorway in 2001 revealed a retaining wall or possible step.

Also in the nineteenth century, a doorway into the castle grounds was inserted along the northern section of the eastern curtain wall from Dunne's Bakery, which stood outside it. The Cobbes, who owned Swords Castle at the time, took great exception to the 'illegal' doorway and insisted that it be blocked up forthwith (Bernadette Marks, pers. comm.).

In early 1899 Joseph Hill, the Cobbe family's estate manager, alluded to repairs in correspondence with Sir Thomas Newenham Deane of the 'Board of Works':

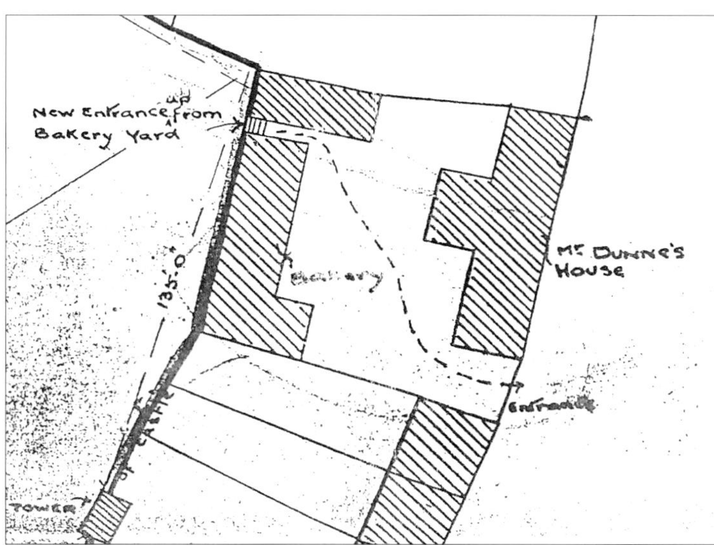

Fig. 2.1—Drawing of the new entrance c. 1860s (courtesy of Bernadette Marks).

'I may mention here Mr Cobbe threw down a house he received £8 8 shillings a year for in order the front of the castle might be seen to advantage from the main street. He also spent over £100 on improvement close to the front entrance where the buildings were degrading very fast. Looking over the accounts I find that there was 119 pounds 19 shillings spent on repairs to the ruins between the years 1867 and 1880. In the latter years there was 82 pounds spent.'

While no details of the earlier works survive, there are receipts dating from 1880 in the Cobbe papers. Between May and July 1880, a total of nine weeks of 'repairs to old castle Swords', including 'masons and horse labour', were undertaken by the Westons of Corduff. While a description of the actual works is lacking, an 'account of Material and Horse labour at the Castle Gardens Swords' survives and includes tonnes of lime, flags, gravel, sand and Portland cement. Flags were drawn from McCormack and Thomas Brien, while the sand and gravel was drawn from Mr Baker's pit. An intriguing entry was for 'Blue Black and Umber for Colouring'. Also notable is that 27 tonnes of 'waste stones' from the castle were sold to McCormack.

In 1937 the Office of Public Works commenced repairs to the extensive walls and buildings of Swords Castle, which had been 'lately placed in our guardianship' (OPW 1937, 39). The annual report for 1938 described the works for that year:

'Repairs which were commenced last year were continued. Large masses of ivy were removed from the walls which were thoroughly repaired and made secure. The vaultings of the building at the entrance, the north tower and two other turrets were cleared, secured and covered with concrete and the very defensive eastern wall-tower overhanging some adjoining premises was thoroughly repaired and made secure.'

Repairs were recorded as completed in 1939.

Prior to the present project, the most extensive works to the Castle were those undertaken between *c.* 1995 and *c.* 2011. In 1994 the Swords Castle Development Consortium created a vision for the repair, reconstruction and use of the castle. Under the auspices of the Parks

Top:
Pl. 2.2—1980s (left) and modern view (right) of the Constable's Tower.

Above:
Pl. 2.3—The West Tower in 1999 (left) and 2016 (right).

Department and led by architect David Newman Johnson, a FÁS training scheme was developed to realise the vision through repair and reconstruction. To accommodate these works, a large area was gravelled and shipping containers were used as offices, later augmented by the insertion of workshops and storage areas.

The North Tower, which has since been renamed the Constable's Tower, was rebuilt as a fifteenth-century tower-house. The upper parts of the walls (mainly above the string-course) and crenellations have been reconstructed; new chimneys, floors and roof have been added. New limestone surrounds to windows and doors have been added and the ground level lowered immediately in front of the entrance. Unfortunately, some original elements of the historic

Pl. 2.4—The interior of the Chapel in 1971 (left) (©National Monuments Service) and currently, looking east (right).

Pl. 2.5 —The Chamber Block in 2001 (left) and 2019 (right).

Pl. 2.6—Interior of Swords Castle after enabling works in 2018–19.

fabric were removed to accommodate the new vision (Stephen Johnston, pers. comm.).

From the available photographic evidence, work on the west curtain wall, the West Tower and the northern curtain wall appears to have taken place between 1998 and 2001. This included the rebuilding of the West Tower and the provision of a new arch and entranceway to a newly built wall-walk (Pl. 2.3). The wall-walk extends from the Constable's Tower along the west wall to the south-western corner tower and along the northern curtain wall to the junction with the northern mural tower. Repointing was carried out to the internal and external façades of the curtain walls, while battlements were constructed.

The building interpreted as the Chapel and the adjoining Chamber Block were also reconstructed. The walls of the Chapel were built up in height and crenellations reconstructed, while a new slate roof topped with red ridge tiles was added. The partially infilled east window was opened up; a window was reconstructed and new quatrefoil window openings were inserted in the north façade, as were three new Gothic-style pointed-arch windows in the south façade. A concrete undercroft was inserted into the Chamber Block, the walls rebuilt upwards and new parapets added. A new stone stairway and roof were added. In both buildings, new window surrounds, floors, doors and decoration were added. Services were also inserted, and the exterior was finished with concrete and paving.

Two phases of enabling works (in 2016 and 2018–19) have resulted in the removal of the works buildings; the insertion of paths; the consolidation of the curtain walls; repair of the Gatehouse; repairs to the Chapel roof; widening of the eastern doorway; the replacement of the wooden wall-walk; provision of access to and lighting of the wall-walk; the stabilisation and rendering of the East Tower; and the opening of the external space along the junction of North Street and Main Street through the demolition of buildings (Baker 2016; 2020).

GEOPHYSICAL SURVEY

An electrical resistivity survey undertaken in 1991 highlighted locations of collapsed masonry and possible boundaries (McGarry 2001). Conductivity geophysical survey by Whiteford Geoservices was carried out to locate any unknown foundation footings or features within the castle grounds, ahead of the removal of overburden by ADS Ltd. Ground conductivity survey was carried out using an EM38 ground conductivity meter between 18 and 25 October 2000.

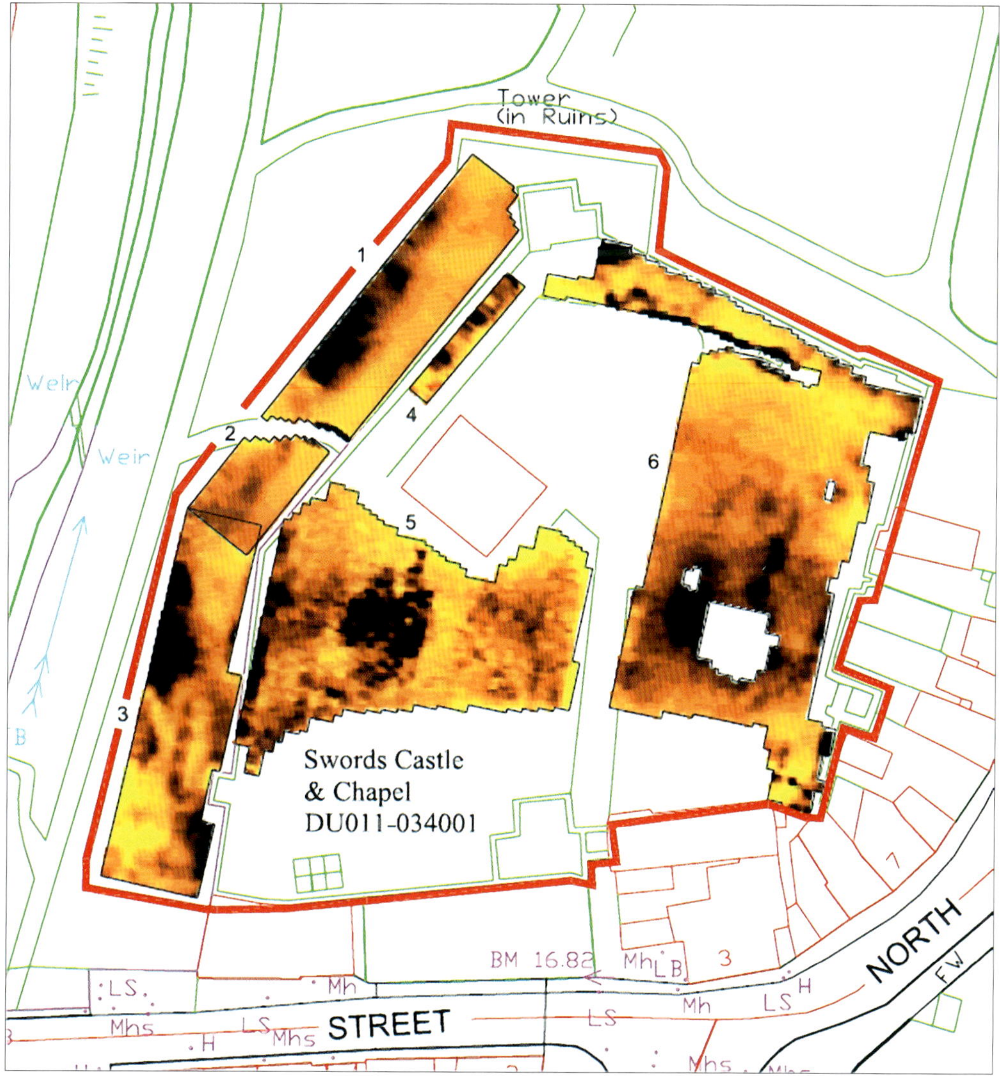

Fig. 2.2—Resistivity results and interpretation (Nicholls 2011).

Several anomalies were identified, the most obvious features being close to the south-west and south-east walls. These features are linear in nature and are suggestive of foundations or wall footings (Whiteford Geosciences 2000).

A geophysical survey was undertaken by Target Survey (Licence no. 11R0038) for the Swords Conservation Plan. It consisted of resistivity survey (of an area totalling 0.4ha) internally and external to the west wall of the castle, and GPR survey (of an area totalling 0.14ha) both internally and for a small section externally south of the Knights and Squires.

The resistivity results indicated no evidence for a moat west of the wall of Swords Castle, although there is a suggestion of underlying material associated with the perimeter wall to the south-east. On the lower ground south of the portacabins a subrectangular response, *c.* 6m by 10m, was identified. High-resistance responses on the higher ground to the east indicated a grouping extending *c.* 22m north–south by 10m east–west which may represent foundations associated with buildings (Nicholls 2011, 10–11).

PREVIOUS EXCAVATIONS

Several licensed archaeological investigations, both internal and external to the castle, have been previously undertaken. Unlicensed archaeological monitoring was also carried out of the restoration works and services insertions in 1996–7.

Excavation of the south-eastern area of the castle was undertaken by Tom Fanning in 1971 (E101). The Chapel and Chamber Block were located and what became known as the Archbishop's Apartments were excavated. The original level of the Chapel floor was found to be disturbed by the reuse of the structure as stables in the eighteenth and nineteenth centuries. A silver *denier tournois* dated to 1310 was found in a post-hole next to the north wall, and skeletal remains were identified. Excavation within the Archbishop's Apartments revealed an *in situ* decorated medieval tiled pavement laid out on an east–west axis. Consisting of stamped and line-impressed decoration, the motifs had parallels with those from Mellifont Abbey, Co. Louth, and Christ Church, Dublin. Burials were uncovered in the raised area north of the Chapel and within the Archbishop's Apartments. Fanning interpreted these as being relatively late in date, possibly suggesting that the bawn was reused as a graveyard when the castle was no longer occupied (Fanning 1975).

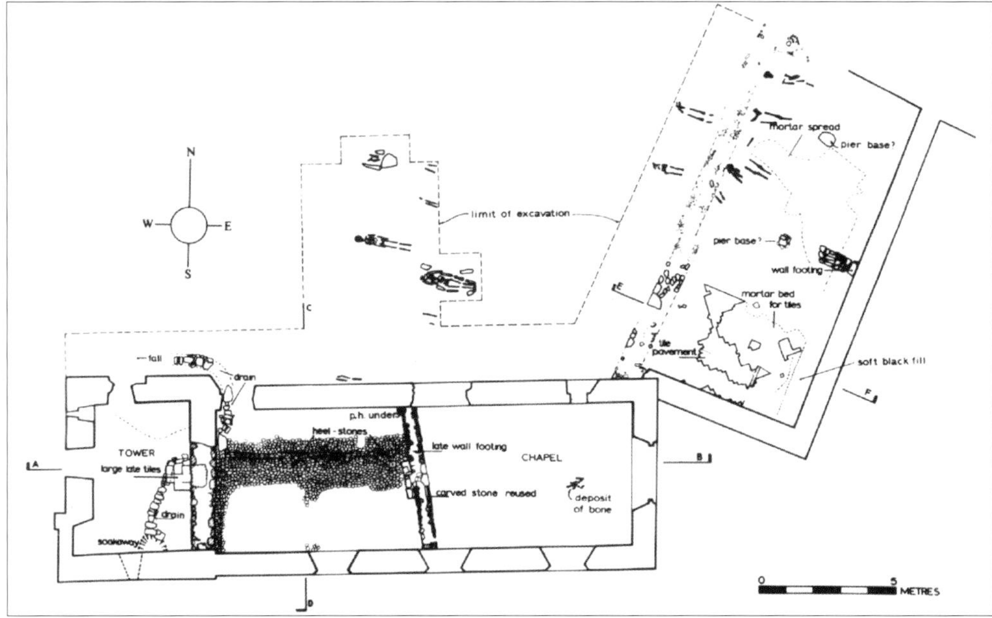

Fig. 2.3—Fanning's 1971 excavation (after Fanning 1975).

The removal of overburden from an area to the north and west of the Knights and Squires Chamber was carried out by Eoin Sullivan in 2001 (Licence no. 01E002). The top of wall footings, paths and ground surfaces were exposed and subsequently preserved *in situ*. In 2014 (C450/E4376) Mark Moraghan opened a single trench to enable stabilisation works within the Gatehouse. A total of seventeen skeletons pre-dating the construction of the Gatehouse were identified. Towards the base of the trench a wattle screen, lime render and part of a stone structure were excavated.

Immediately outside the Gatehouse, archaeological monitoring (C450/E4376) of services insertions in 2011 revealed a wall 0.8m wide and two narrower parallel walls running east–

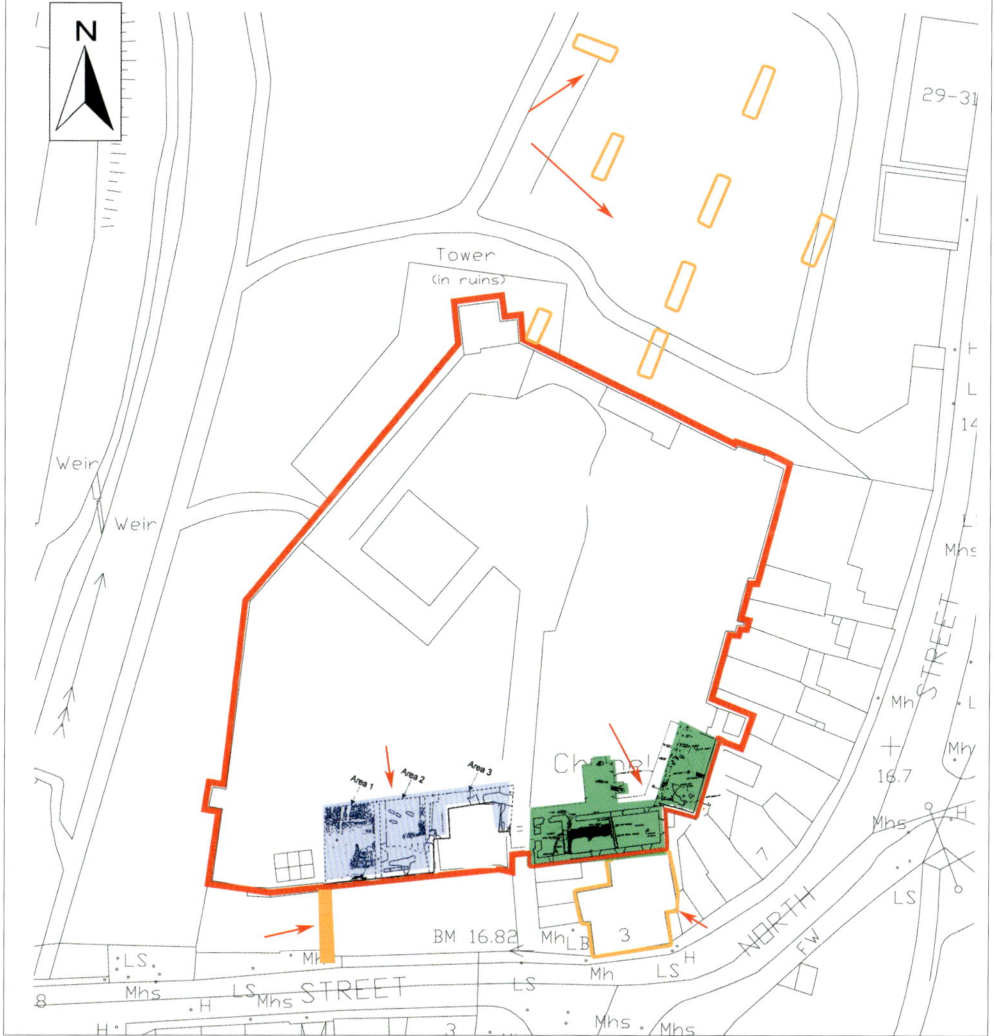

Fig. 2.4—Composite of previous excavations prior to 2011 (Swords Castle Conservation Plan).

west across the entrance.

Monitoring of the foundation trenches at the Pound to the south of the castle wall was undertaken in 1993 by Leo Swan. A ditch was identified and was interpreted by the excavator as part of a moat (Swan 1994). Test excavation in 1994 to the north of the castle by John Channing (94E0191) did not identify any remains of archaeological significance. Nor did an investigation by Margaret Gowen (95E0243) adjacent to the castle on North Street.

Claire Walsh tested (02E1279) the area external to the Chapel wall in 2002 and identified almost 1m of medieval deposits that may be deeper, as bedrock was not reached. In June 2016 Christine Baker (C450/E4676) undertook a test excavation along the external walls of the east range. The wall footing of the Archbishop's Apartments was identified, as was a ditch pre-dating its construction. The curtain wall between the East Tower and the Double Gable was confirmed as a nineteenth-century rebuild, the link wall. The junction between it and the Double Gable was examined. Trenches within the footprint of the demolished terrace identified natural subsoil into which a drain of medieval date had been cut.

Pl. 2.7—Monitoring undertaken by ADS Ltd, 2011.

Fig. 2.5—Archaeological investigations 1971–2016, East Wall, Swords Castle.

3

Community archaeology

THE *SWORDS CASTLE: DIGGING HISTORY* PROJECT

Despite the restoration works of the 1990s/early 2000s, Swords Castle had been closed to the public for over a decade prior to 2015. *Swords Castle: Digging History* was developed not only as a means to answer the research questions posed in the *Swords Castle Conservation Plan* (Fingal County Council 2014) but also as a means of re-engaging the local community with the castle itself. It is also fitting, given the symbiotic relationship between the castle and the townspeople of Swords throughout history, that the response to the call for volunteers on the community archaeology project was so positive. The initiative to involve local people directly in uncovering their heritage and to provide them with an opportunity to take part

Pl. 3.1—Watching Swords Castle—*participation in the Chapel.*

in an archaeological excavation was something of a departure not just locally but also nationally. The concept was based on bringing the archaeological experience to new audiences and to those who had always wanted to try archaeology but had never had the chance. Over 300 individuals participated directly by volunteering on the excavation. Participants (who were all over eighteen) have included locals, teenagers, retirees, members of the new communities, tourists, members of the National Learning Network, the Dublinia Training programme, Tourism Ireland, local authority staff members and family groups. The majority were from Swords and its environs and County Dublin, although some travelled from across Ireland or even from abroad (Germany, Switzerland). Interaction with visitors was encouraged, and volunteers enthusiastically explained the complexities of 'their' trench or showed 'their' find. Somewhat surprisingly, the sieving stations proved popular—and not just with those not inclined towards the more physically demanding trench-digging—as was the finds-washing tent, which also allowed for visitors, especially children, to see and touch what had been found.

It was important to encourage engagement at different levels and so the project encompassed several elements. The child-focused *Swords Archaeofest* took place as part of the Swords Festival, which proved a fruitful opportunity to raise awareness of the project. *Swords Castle: My Castle* was a means of involving those who might not be interested in excavation. People were requested to submit their memories, images and photographs of the castle— what it meant to them, how they saw it, how they painted it. These were then collated by local artist Andrew Carson in an exhibition in the Chapel that ran concurrently with the excavation during Season 1. The exhibition included a film piece in which Andrew interviewed local people about their memories of Swords Castle to create a film that was shown in the Chapel (https://www.youtube.com/watch?v=Rnyz5ioOWmU). For Season 2, Andrew Carson created a companion piece by filming the excavation and interviewing the participants and supporters of the project. The result (https://www.youtube.com/ watch?v=1id9diAgPlM) was shown on the last day of the excavation in the Chapel and emailed to participants. Season 3 saw the art project *All Bread is Made of Wood*, an artistic interpretation of the archaeobotanical remains that had been analysed by Dr Meriel McClatchie. This took the form of an exhibition by Sabrina MacMahon within the Chapel which involved nail art based on seeds, and an interactive piece by Fiona Hallinan in which food prepared with plants identified through the environmental analysis was served to participants (Crowley *et al.* 2020).

Most of the participants had little or no previous experience of archaeological excavation, and it was important to introduce the range of professionals and specialisms that are involved in the archaeological process. To that end, processing of artefacts and ecofacts took place on site. Dr Meriel McClatchie of UCD conducted an Environmental Day on site each season, teaching participants about wet sieving. Dr Steve Mandal conducted a Geology Day during Season 2. This was apposite, given the ongoing repointing and consolidation of the east range and Gatehouse of Swords Castle. Season 3 saw a Post-medieval Pottery Day with Rosanne Meenan, which was of particular interest given that nearly all participants had either found or washed such pottery.

Interaction with the post-excavation process was via the National Museum of Ireland, who held a Behind the Scenes Day with conservation staff at the Collections Resource Centre, and through a 'First Findings' seminar each spring in which post-excavation specialists would

Pl. 3.2—Post-medieval Pottery Day with Rosanne Meenan.

Pl. 3.3—First Findings seminar, 2016.

update attendees on their work. Wider dissemination took place in seminars and conferences, including the Space and Settlement Conference, Trinity College Dublin; the Irish Conference of Medievalists, NUI Maynooth; the Royal Society of Antiquaries of Ireland; Fingal Rotary Club; the National Monuments Service Annual Conference; the Institute of Archaeologists of Ireland conference; and the European Association of Archaeologists conference. The first Culture Night event was held in Swords Castle, where some of the artefacts were on display to the public, and there is a section on the Fingal County Council website for the preliminary excavation reports. Pieces on the excavation were published in local newspapers and in magazines from *Archaeology Ireland* to *Ireland's Own*.

Analysis of participants from their feedback sheets has shown the plurality of individuals and communities involved, something also evident in the various responses and outcomes. Some wish to be committed stakeholders driving the process and continue to participate in recent community excavations; others are content simply to turn up and enjoy the event. For many the opportunity just to experience an archaeological dig was enough, while other participants have taken the experience further—returning to college to study archaeology; volunteering at the National Museum of Ireland; or developing art projects or language pieces in response to the dig. Analysis has shown that the majority of participants were in the 30–65-year age bracket, which has had a greater ripple effect in the community, with requests for engagement through schools so that their children can benefit and there can be more intergenerational family involvement.

Swords Castle: Digging History was the first excavation financed directly by a local authority under the auspices of a Community Archaeologist. From an archaeological perspective, it proved a real success in terms of answering research questions, engaging people with their local heritage and encouraging visitor participation and interaction with Swords Castle. From a local authority perspective, its success lay in the provision of a service to the community, but also in attracting tourism and publicity. Most important, however, has been the development of a 'Swords Castle' community of diverse ages, backgrounds and experiences who have spread their enthusiasm for their archaeological heritage beyond the gates of the castle.

IN THEIR OWN WORDS …

'What a great experience! This is community archaeology at its very best. It's a very enjoyable project with a lovely atmosphere and high professional standards. Well done!'

'I'd give my eyeballs to do it again.'

'I liked to have the chance in this project to come in contact with Irish people and Irish culture.'

'Best fun I've ever had in a totally unglamorous role. I was educated, amused and fab conversations. Who knew digging could be so much fun!'

'Great experience. It is usually very difficult to get involved in an archaeology dig so this is a great idea.'

'This is a fantastic project. Great to have the local community engaged with and enjoying archaeology. You need more community digs in various areas to give people this opportunity and break down the feeling archaeology is only for professionals.'

'The dig in Swords Castle has been tremendous. Working under the supervision of the patient professional archaeologists we peeled back the past, looking at the objects they used and the surfaces they walked on, worked and perhaps died. Not the wars or great events but the ordinary everyday lives of our ancestors, perhaps emigrants to these shores years ago. We were allowed to see instances in their lives across the centuries. Would I do it again? In a heartbeat.'—*Brendan Black*

'I grew up in Swords, under the shadow of its iconic castle, and spent many a twilight in my formative years scaling the great walls and playing within its boundaries. The opportunity to become involved in the "Dig", therefore, was not one to be passed up. To be able to uncover some of the mysteries we had pondered as young children was truly exciting. I learned so much fascinating knowledge from the professionals who were involved in and those supporting the dig. I can now look at my beloved castle in a new, more insightful light.'—*Grace Monaghan*

'After watching the six o'clock news and the feature on the Dig in Swords Castle I became involved with the project. I was asked to number and bag the finds. No one would believe the care and work that is done behind the scenes on a dig and for me to be part of all the process was an honour and privilege.'—*Caoimhe Ní Fhearghail Smith*

'It was a very interesting and novel experience being involved in the Swords Castle Dig. I was unable to do any actual digging and so concentrated on the cleaning of the artefacts. Some very interesting items were unearthed and gave a surprising insight into the history of the castle. Though I live in Swords I was not aware of the extent of the work and study that has been done by Fingal County Council. The experience re-ignited my interest in the castle and its history. It was great to share the work experience with neighbours and friends.' —*Seán Mac Domhnaill*

'The archaeologists and volunteers were all very like-minded people, all with their own tale to tell, there was great camaraderie and fun had by all. As Swords is now cosmopolitan, there were volunteers from all over Europe and of course locals. A lot of foreign visitors ventured into the castle during the dig. This is encouraging for tourism in Swords and paints a bright future for Swords.' —*Monica Lindsey*

'We were sitting at home one night and my husband saw a notice for the community dig and said I should go along, but I thought I was too old to join. The following year I saw the notice again and thought to myself this is something I have always wanted

to see and be part of. When I walked through the Castle gates it was everything I had dreamed about and what a dig would look like. I decided I would love to wash what was discovered in the ground, and soon I was cleaning a piece of a broken wooden comb, bits of clay pipe and fish bones that all had been discarded so many years ago. I had achieved my lifelong ambition to take part in history of times gone by in Swords Castle.'—*Linda Jago*

PART II: EXCAVATION

4

Phase I—Pre-Anglo-Norman

INTRODUCTION

Excavation was carried out over three seasons centred on National Heritage Week in August of 2015, 2016 and 2017. The project was designed to address the research and knowledge gaps identified in the *Swords Castle Conservation Plan* (Fingal County Council 2014). This included investigating specific geophysical anomalies; gathering environmental samples for analysis and dating; ascertaining the extent of burials; and establishing the preservation levels between higher and lower ground. A total of ten trenches were excavated, measuring from 8m by 2m to a maximum of 6m by 5.5m and averaging 1.1m in depth. Trenches 1–4 were located to investigate geophysical anomalies, while Trench 5 was opened in an area that had not produced significant geophysical results to determine the accuracy of the geophysical survey. Trenches 6–8 were located to answer specific questions in regard to the previous seasons. Trench 9 was located immediately west of the East Tower in order to investigate the

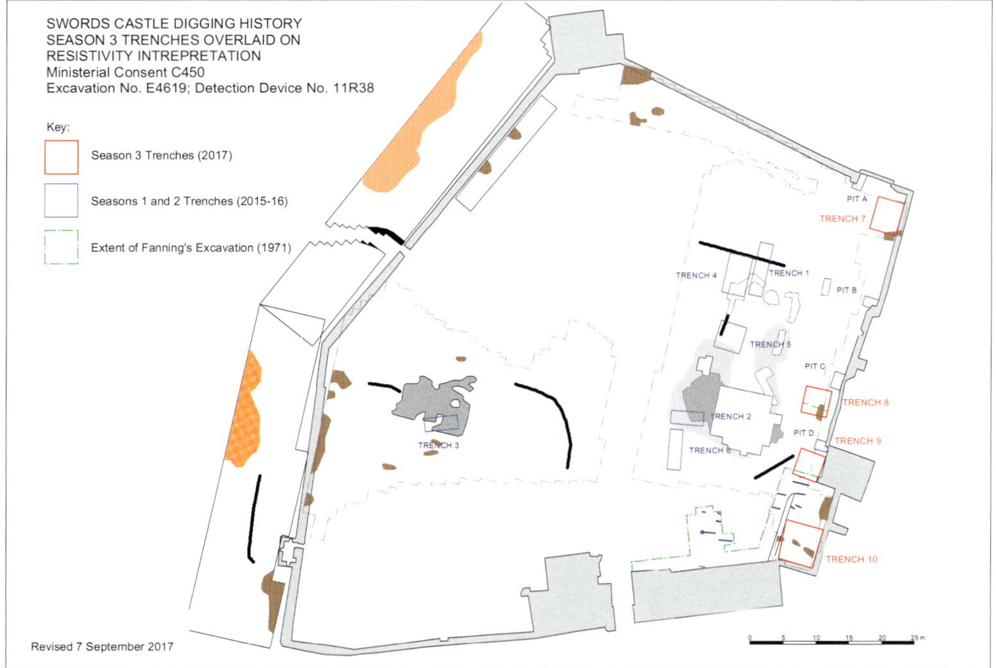

Fig. 4.1—Layout of Trenches 1–10 and pits A–D.

confluence of the 'missing' west wall of the East Tower and the limit of burials identified by Fanning. The recovery of burials in this trench meant that it was excavated to a maximum of 0.64m below current ground level. Owing to the identification of tile remnants along the south wall of the Archbishop's Apartments, Trench 10 (6m north–south by 5.5m east–west) was located over the remains of the medieval tile pavement identified by Fanning in 1971 to ascertain whether the tile pavement had indeed been removed. Pits A–D, excavated during

Fig. 4.2—Trench 9, upper layer of burials.

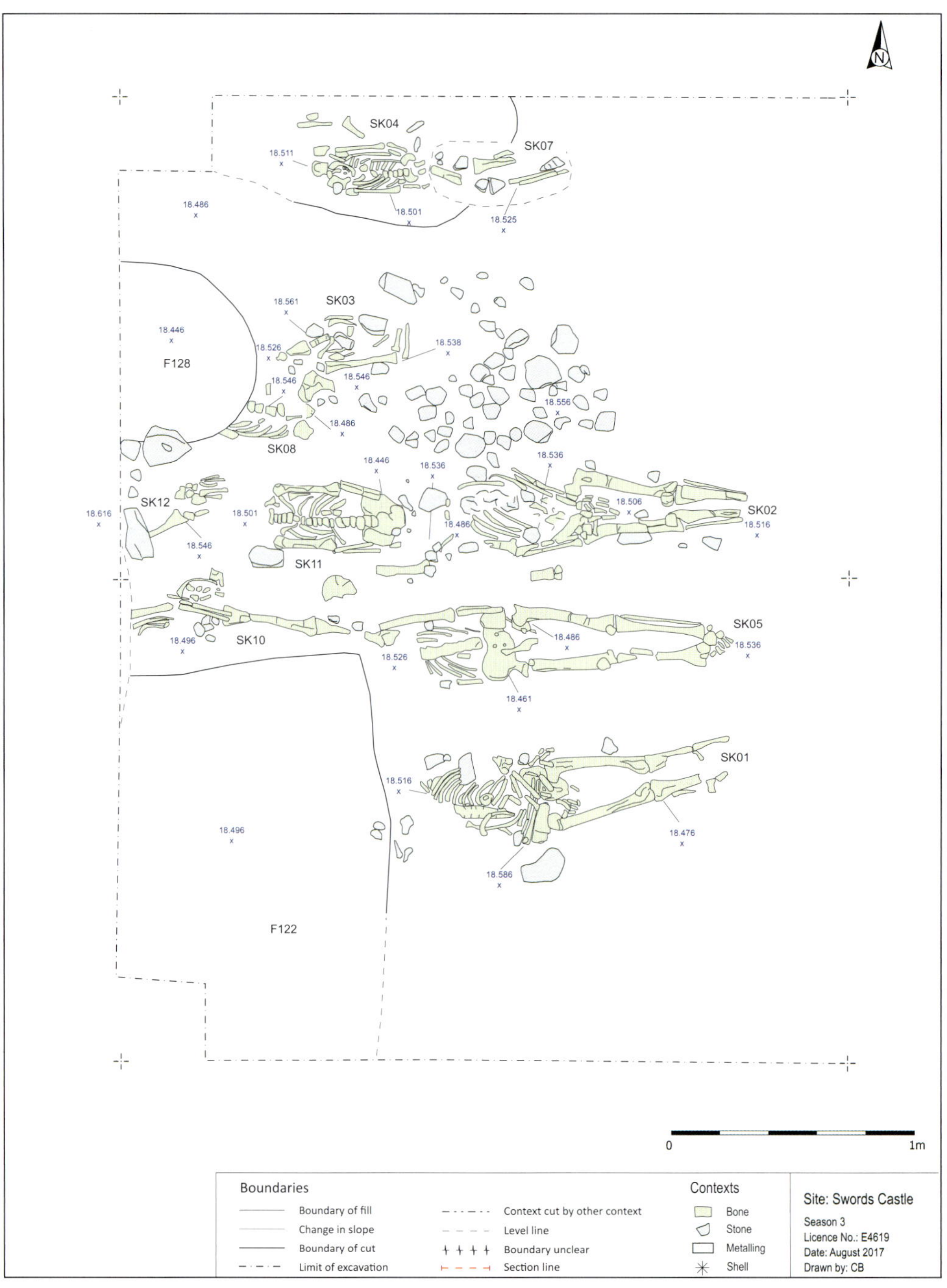

Season 1, were located at key junctions of upstanding buildings to investigate their relationship and to inform the development of the subsequent enabling works.

The overall stratigraphy consisted of grey-yellow stony natural subsoil overlain by medieval layers and features truncated by post-medieval and modern disturbance. The depth of topsoil in all trenches was substantial and highly disturbed owing to the presence of orchards and previous cultivation. Three main phases of activity were identified, ranging from the eleventh century to the twentieth century: pre-Anglo-Norman, medieval, and post-medieval to modern.

PHASE 1—PRE-ANGLO-NORMAN

Evidence for pre-Anglo-Norman activity was concentrated to the south-east of the precinct, contiguous to where the burials had been uncovered in 1971. This activity was characterised by a series of burials (Trench 9), an enclosure ditch (F85), and a series of pits (F11, F19, F103, F88, F92, F93, F95) and post-holes (F101A, F101B) cut into natural subsoil.

Burials
The remains of at least fifteen burials were uncovered, as well as the disarticulated remains of possibly eight individuals within Trench 9. Burials were identified less than 10cm below the current ground level. Aligned east–west, these were in poor condition, many exhibiting evidence of having been crushed. There had been significant disturbance in and around the burials, with pits having been dug through them and tree roots from the later orchard

Pl. 4.1—Trench 9, upper layer of burials, looking west.

Pl. 4.2—SK15 truncated by west wall of East Tower, looking south.

planting having become intertwined with the skeletal remains. There were two distinct horizons of soil, both of which contained burials. The soil horizon F163 was disturbed by the insertion of the west wall of the East Tower and contained a fragment of DT2 crested ridge tile, garden snail and seashell. In addition, domestic animal (cattle, sheep and pig) bones with eroded surfaces characteristic of disposal were found in this layer. F127 was characterised as redeposited natural that directly underlay topsoil. From this interface Leinster Cooking Ware (dating from the late twelfth century to the mid-fourteenth century) and unglazed red earthenware (from the eighteenth–nineteenth century), red earthenware pantile and modern pottery were recovered. Disarticulated human bones (E4619:127:8) included hip, fibula, tibia, patella, cranial, tarsal, metatarsal and foot phalanx (Lynch, this volume).

Analysis of the human bone by Dr Linda Lynch has shown that all but one of the *in situ* burials were of adult individuals; the exception was SK04, the remains of an individual aged approximately 6–8 years at the time of death. Poor preservation ensured that it was only possible to determine the age at death of four of the twelve adults. All four were female and were aged over 26 years at the time of death. Likewise, it was possible to determine the sex of nine of the twelve adults (75%), the overwhelming majority of whom were female. The plan of the burials indicates the density and, indeed, the order of burial, with SK01, SK05 and SK03 appearing to form at least one approximate row, suggesting ordered burial. Others, however, intercut older burials, which suggests that any type of grave-markers may have been quite transitory. All were buried supine and extended with the head to the west in what may be considered the traditional mode of Christian burial. A pillow stone was recorded with one burial, SK09 (possible male, adult). In most cases the lower arm bones were crossed slightly over the abdominal area. The exceptions appeared to be SK10 (female, adult) and SK11 (possible female, adult), whose arms were placed parallel to the body. The significance, if any, of this variation is unknown.

Three burials were selected for radiocarbon dating. Despite being recovered from different levels, they showed a degree of similarity in date range, indicating that the burial-ground was in use between the tenth and twelfth centuries AD. SK15 was at a lower level than the other burials and survived as a cranium within layer F163. A fragment of the cranium returned a date range of AD 994–1059 (UBA-38842); the remainder of the burial was left unexcavated. SK14 (possible female, adult) survived as a truncated supine burial within a concentration of burials that had been disturbed by the insertion of SK09 (possible male, adult). These burials were associated with disarticulated burials, which may correlate to the pushing aside of its lower limbs to accommodate the later burial. SK14 extended into the western baulk

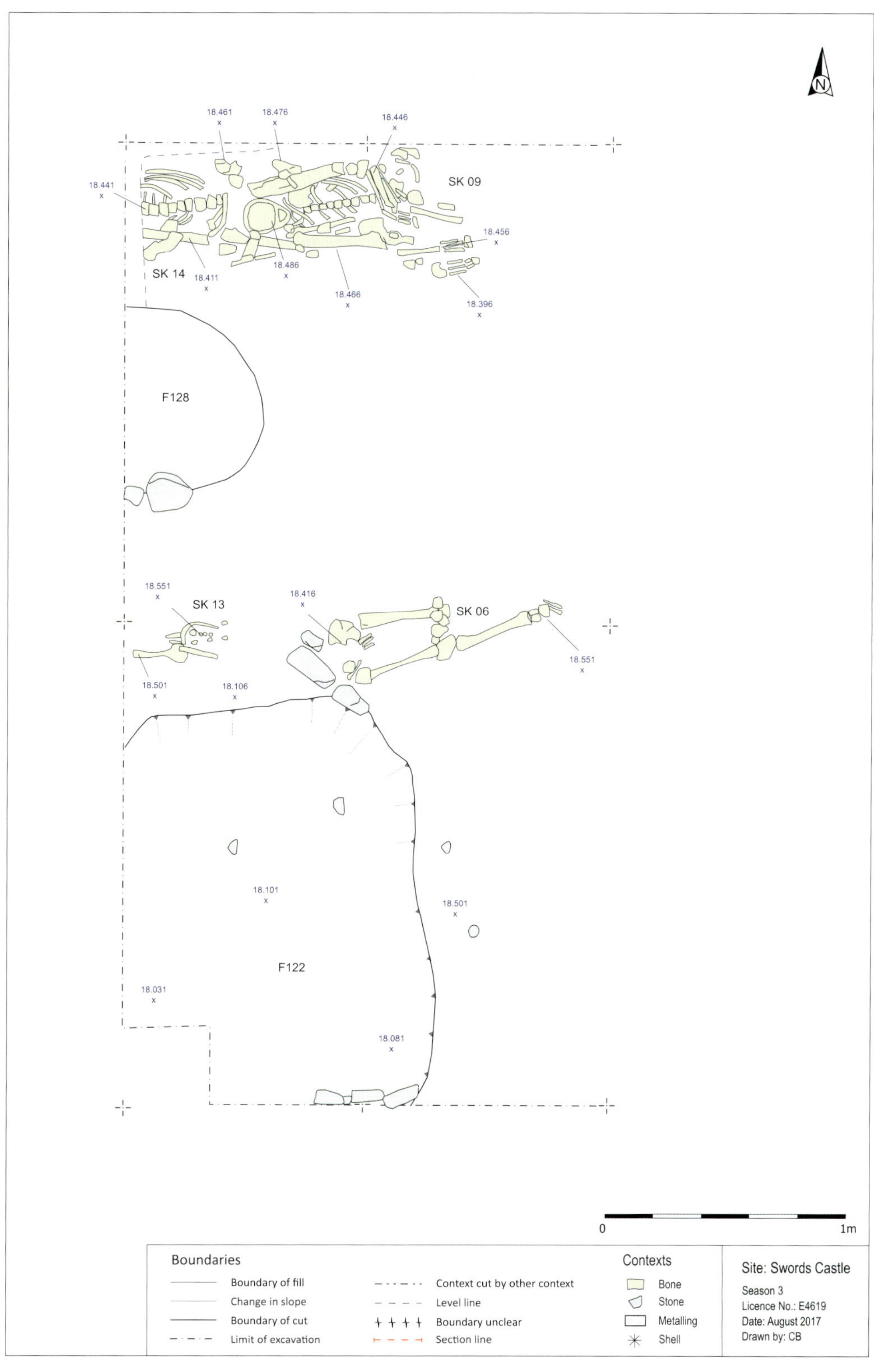

Fig. 4.3—Trench 9, lower layer of burials.

Fig. 4.4—Trench 5, enclosure ditch F85, west-facing section.

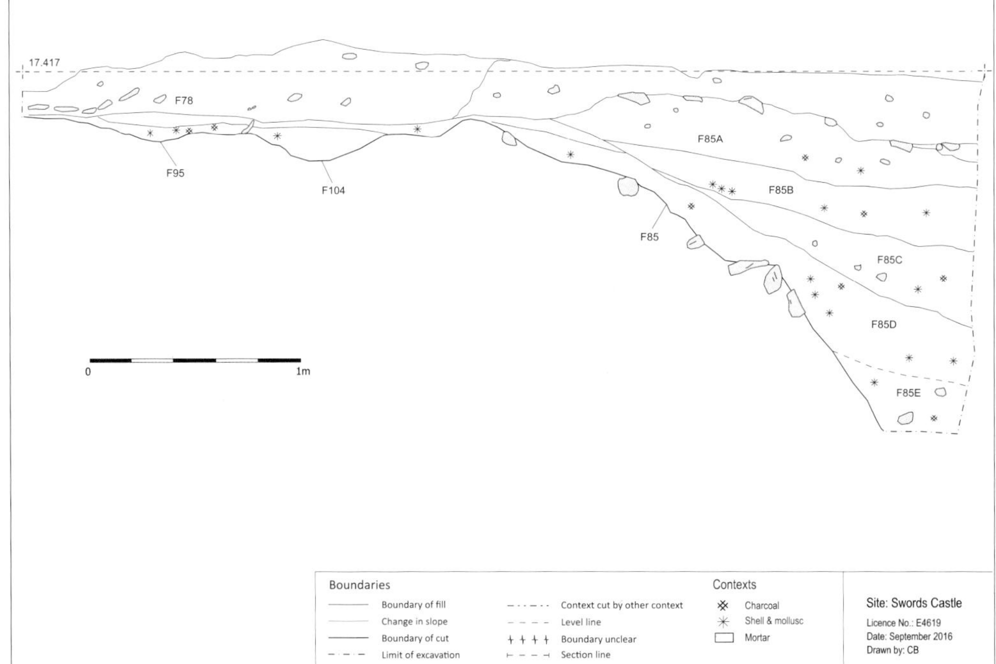

and returned a date range of AD 995–1185 (UBA-38840). SK01 (possible female, adult 45+) was identified just 0.05m below the current ground level, which in this area consisted of patchy sod and wood chips. Aligned east–west, it survived as an extended supine burial with arms flexed across the pelvis, a truncated torso (no cranium) and truncated legs (no feet). It returned a date range of AD 996–1185 (UBA-38840).

In terms of the disarticulated remains, the vast majority (96.9% of fragments) were recovered from Trench 9, the same trench in which the only *in situ* burials were uncovered. Disarticulated remains were recovered from almost every trench, however, the exception being Trench 7. A single vertebra (E4619:29:1) from Trench 3 returned a date range of AD 1065–1154 (UBA-3252). It was recovered from redeposited clay associated with a pit where medieval activity dominated, inferring a disturbed origin. In contrast, a fragment of cranial vault (E4619:101:3) of an adult (45+) recovered from a post-hole in Trench 4 returned a date range of AD 936–1013 (UBA-34515), similar to that recovered from plant material in a nearby pit (F103) of similar stratigraphical position, inferring *in situ* tenth- and eleventh-century activity.

Enclosure ditch (F85)

Located within Trench 5, this ditch was exposed for 4m east–west and for 2.04m north of the southern baulk. It was rock-cut, with a sharp break of slope at the top and relatively sharp sides; the base could not be fully determined within the excavated areas, but the ditch is at least 1.2m in depth with a projected width of 4m. The basal fills were analysed for plant remains and a small number of oat grains and hazelnut shells were identified (McClatchie, this volume). A grain of oat (F85e) submitted for AMS dating returned a date range of AD 975–1037 (UBA-34517). Animal bones recovered from the ditch fill included two individual cattle—a cow older than 4.5 years at death and another *c.* two years old at slaughter. Sheep

Pl. 4.3—Enclosure ditch during excavation.

bones represented prime meat-bearing joints, while a pig was less than a year old at death. A young chick was also identified among the animal bone assemblage (McCarthy, this volume). Some fragments of Dublin-type ware (thirteenth century) and Dublin-type cooking ware (late twelfth–thirteenth century) were recovered from the upper fill.

Pits

Trench 2 and Trench 6 were positioned close to the 1971 burials in the hope of identifying an enclosure or the limit of those burials. Instead, a number of pits were identified cut into natural subsoil. These were sealed by a medieval yard surface but were dated to an earlier period. A radiocarbon date from the pit (F19) in Trench 2 returned a date range of AD 937–1019 (UBA-32456). The pit contained 30 grains of possible bread wheat, occasional grains of oat and barley and a wide variety of weeds (McClatchie, this volume), along with a gnawed fragment of cow femur, a sheep bone and seashell.

The fill of pit 95 in Trench 6 contained mainly oat, with occasional grains of hulled barley, hazelnut shell and a variety of wild plants. An oat grain returned an AMS date range of AD 1023–1154 (UBA-34518). The pit also contained an assemblage of 128 bones, including a pig bone that had been gnawed by a dog, a newborn piglet, and cattle, sheep and chicken bones, as well as a range of periwinkles and cockles. Fragments of calcined bones also recovered here were interpreted as the result of roasting over a spit (McCarthy, this volume). A human tooth (E4619:93:3) was recovered from this fill, as were a number of later objects, including a sherd of green-glazed Saintonge ware (thirteenth to mid-fourteenth century) and a medieval long pin, indicating a level of disturbance.

Fig. 4.5—Trench 2, Season 1, and Trench 6, after excavation.

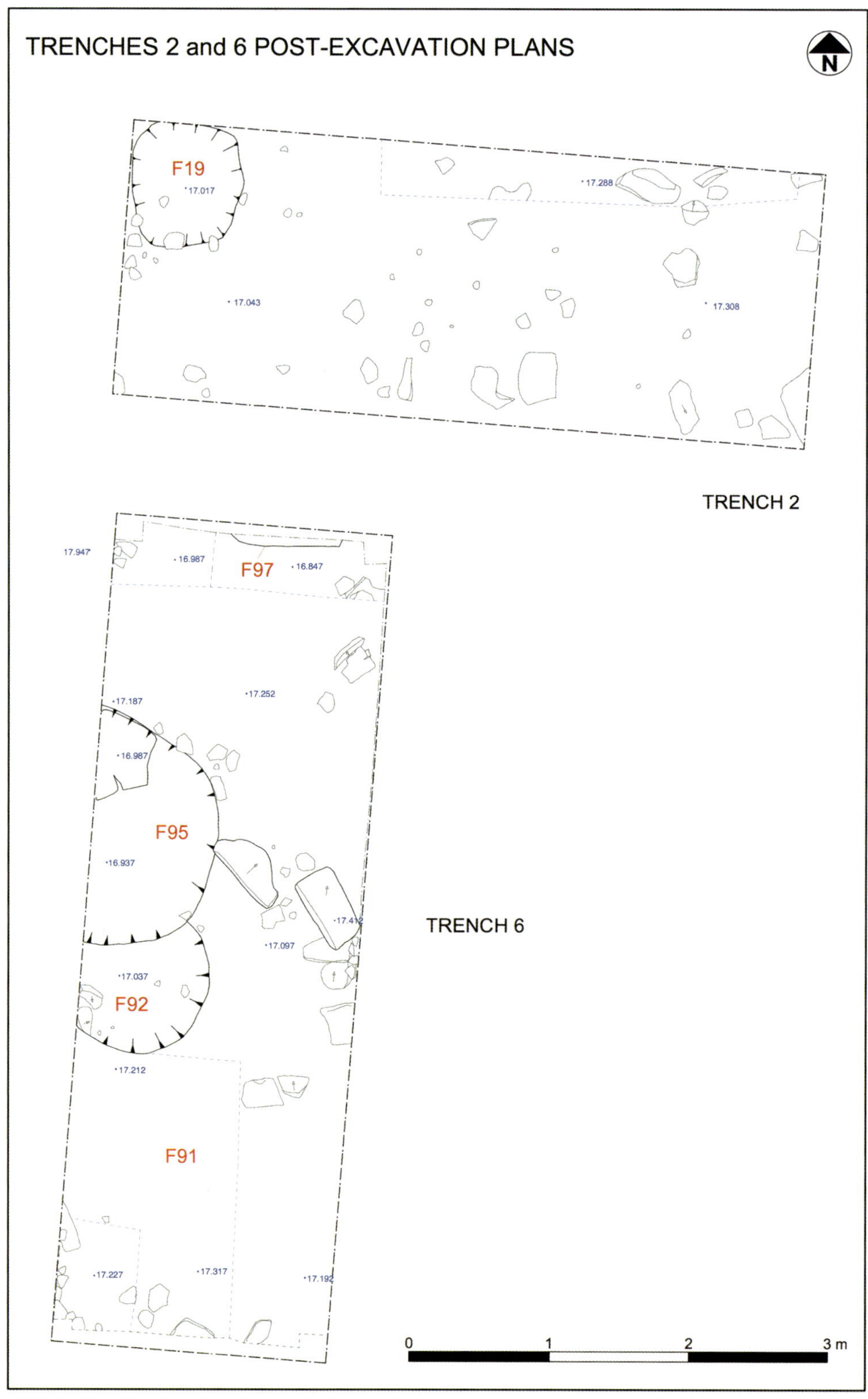
TRENCHES 2 and 6 POST-EXCAVATION PLANS
N
F19
17.017
17.288
17.043
17.308
TRENCH 2
17.947
16.987
F97
16.847
17.252
17.187
16.987
F95
16.937
17.412
17.097
17.037
F92
17.212
F91
17.227
17.317
17.192
TRENCH 6
0
1
2
3 m

Post-holes

Two large post-holes in Trench 4 (which may relate to a relatively large post-hole (F40) in Trench 1) could indicate the presence of a timber building at an early stage in the site's history. A fragment of human cranium was retrieved from the base of the eastern post-hole (F101B). The presence of a suture line with some obliteration indicates an older adult of 45+ years, and a date range of AD 936–1013 (UBA-34515) was returned. Located nearby was pit F103, where *in situ* burning had taken place. It contained oat grains, a barley grain, grass culm and a range of arable weeds, as well as a hazelnut fragment and a sloe stone (McClatchie, this volume). AMS dating of an oat grain returned a date range of AD 1029–1159 (UBA-34519).

Pl. 4.4—Trench 4, F101, during excavation, looking north.

5

Phase II—Medieval

INTRODUCTION

Evidence for medieval activity was widespread throughout the precinct and can be divided into phases of construction and specified activities. The medieval activity often truncated the early pre-Norman activity, including burials. Radiocarbon dating indicates concentrations of activity in the fourteenth and sixteenth centuries. A number of built elements, some relating to extant structures such as the East Tower and the Archbishop's Apartments, were uncovered. In addition, remnants of walls of buildings long demolished and not previously recorded were identified.

EAST TOWER

The position of Trench 9 was selected in order to identify the 'missing' wall of the East Tower. Evidence for the western wall (F170) of the East Tower at the junction with the southern

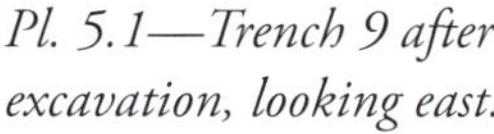

Pl. 5.1—Trench 9 after excavation, looking east.

Pl. 5.2—Trench 9, wall junction F154 during excavation, looking east.

Pl. 5.3—F151 after excavation, looking north.

Fig. 5.1—Trench 10, post-excavation plan, looking north.

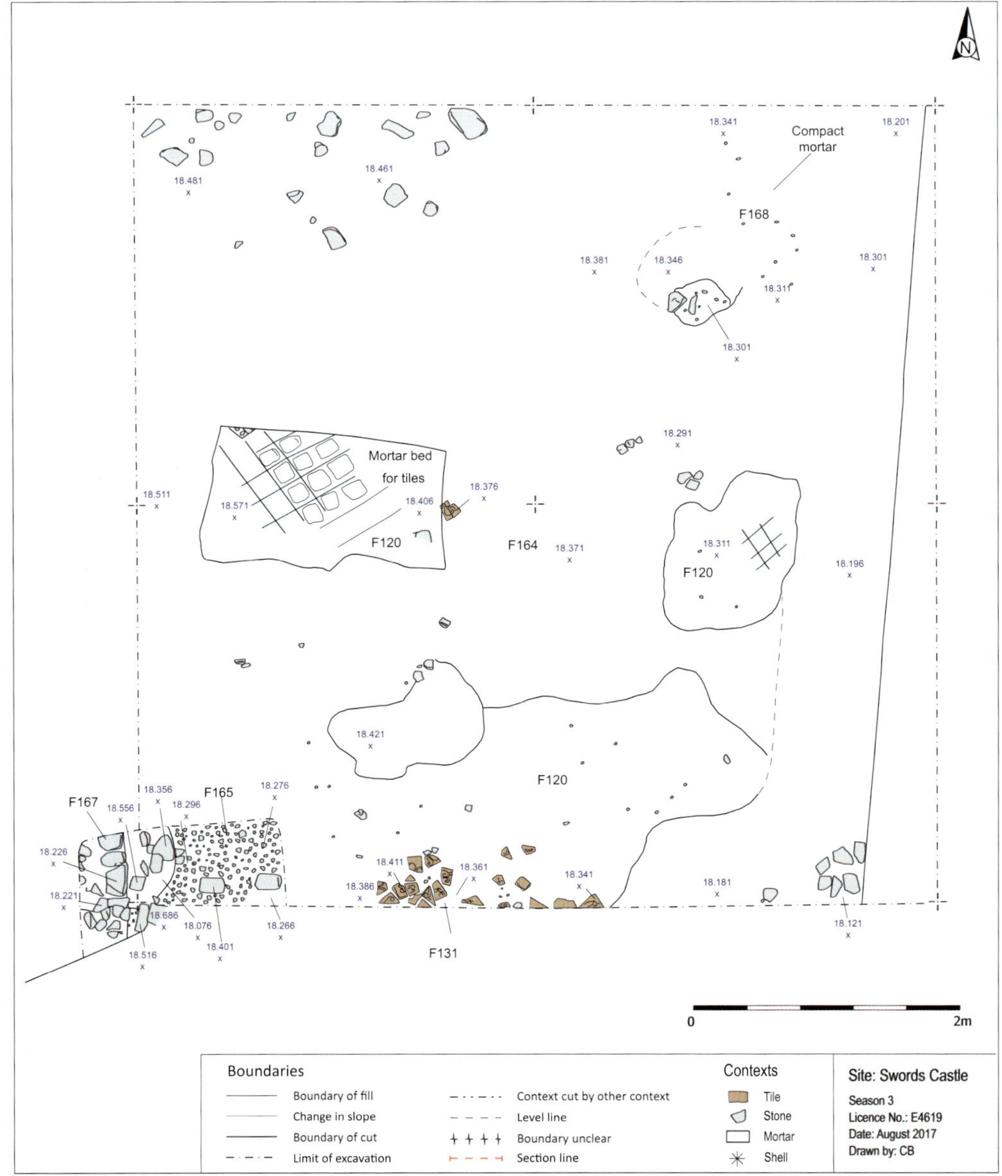

wall of the tower was uncovered, as well as a curved foundation (F154). The limestone foundation stones of F170 were exposed for 2.2m north–south within Trench 9. Apparently robbed out, the remaining large (0.4–0.7m in diameter), unshaped stones lay within a compact orange-brown stony clay deposit, *c.* 1.2m in width. The wall trench was backfilled with a mortar-rich silt (F153), which contained two fragments of cow scapula and a fragment of sheep pelvis. A sherd of thirteenth-century Dublin-type ware was also recovered from the backfill.

At the junction of the truncated southern wall of the East Tower and the removed western wall (F170) there was a rounded plinth of mortared stone (1.62m east–west by 1.6m north–south) that survived to three courses in height (0.35m). The base of the plinth (F154) was not exposed owing to the presence of human skeletal remains (SK15), the skull of which was identified *c.* 0.18m west of the face of wall F154, thus indicating pre-construction deposition of burials.

ARCHBISHOP'S APARTMENTS

Trench 10 was located within the structure known as the Archbishop's Apartments, which was built against the southern wall of the East Tower and was truncated to the south by the construction of the Chapel. The 1971 excavations uncovered the medieval tile pavement towards the south of the structure. The 2017 season of excavation returned to this area to ascertain whether all the medieval tiles had been removed. The relationship between the structural remains of the Archbishop's Apartments and the Chapel was investigated in an exploratory cutting at the south-western corner of Trench 10. The western wall (F167) of the structure, previously uncovered by Fanning, was identified. It survived as one course (exposed for 0.6m north–south by 0.35m east–west) of unmortared, unfaced limestone blocks (averaging 0.2m in diameter) and loose small stones. It was confirmed that the construction of the Chapel had truncated the southern wall of the Archbishop's Apartments.

In total, 85 fragments of medieval floor tile (F151) related to the medieval tile pavement were uncovered contiguous to the southern wall of the Archbishop's Apartments. Becoming more fragmented as they extended northwards, the tiles were set into mortar bedding (F120). Analysis of the tiles by Joanna Wren showed a range of motifs belonging to a group of designs that also occur in Chester. Close connections between the Irish line-impressed floor tiles and those in Cheshire suggest that some of the same tile-makers may have worked in both areas. The tile-makers would have carried with them their wooden stamps for decorating the tiles, but they would have set up kilns locally and used locally sourced clays. This theory is reinforced by the presence of 366 sherds of floor tile made in SCT1 fabric, most of which were recovered within the Archbishop's Apartments structure. The presence of a kiln waster among the SCT1 fabric (E4619:151:10) confirms that the floor tiles were manufactured on site using locally sourced clays. The presence of line-impressed tiles in the assemblage indicates an early fourteenth-century date, as comparisons can be drawn between decorative techniques used on the mosaic tiles at Swords and those found on tiles in England and Wales, where line-impressed mosaic is securely dated to the first half of the fourteenth century. A similar date is likely for the two-colour tiles recovered, as this form of decoration was largely obsolete in Ireland after *c.* 1330. A DT2 roof ridge tile datable to the thirteenth century and a sherd of thirteenth-century Dublin-type ware were also recovered from these contexts.

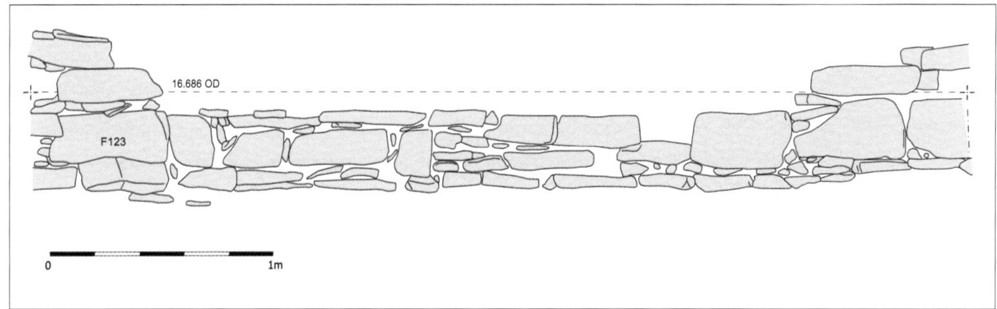

Fig. 5.2—Medieval wall F123, northern elevation.

In the sondage excavated at the south-west corner of Trench 10 it was demonstrated that the medieval tile pavement and its mortar bedding overlay a soft orange-brown silt (F164), which in turn overlay a rough cobbled metalled surface (F165) consisting of angular and sub-angular stones (0.02–0.06m in diameter) set into orange clay.

MEDIEVAL WALL, TRENCH 8

A previously unknown built element was uncovered within Trench 8. Located *c.* 4m north-west of the East Tower, the substantial medieval limestone wall (F123), which measured 1.5m in width, was exposed for 4m north-north-east/south-south-west. It stood to a maximum height of 0.7m at its eastern end, although it averaged three courses. The foundation course was uneven, consisted of small stones and appeared to overlie natural subsoil directly. The wall, which consisted of mortar-bonded large stones (0.23–0.36m in diameter) interspersed with smaller infill stones, was truncated by later activity (F171). This resulted in a surviving wall height of 0.56m at the western end and a higher central area (1.2m east–west by 0.6m north–south) along the southern baulk.

Abutting the medieval wall (F123) were a series of relatively thin layers and deposits, some of which extended over the entire east–west extent of the trench. As they were excavated within a sondage (1–1.2m wide), the full north–south extent was not ascertained. Overlying the footing of the wall was a sterile deposit (F169) which was abutted to the north by a loose, blackish-brown burnt deposit (4m east–west by 0.5m north–south). This burnt deposit overlay natural subsoil at a depth of 1.42m below current ground level. Analysis of the charcoal from this deposit indicated that it consisted of oak (aged 5–43 years), while the seed remains included possible naked wheat, oat and barley. Wild grasses were also present, as were vetch seeds and crab-apple (McClatchie, this volume).

Overlying these basal fills was loose, grey, stony sandy mortar (F152), interpreted as building or demolition debris. An architectural fragment (0.1m in height; 1m in max. diameter, 0.5m in min. diameter) of chamfered stone, with striations visible on carved surfaces and an indent that possibly formed part of the frame of a door or window, was recovered from this deposit (Pl. 5.5). Carved at one end and truncated at the other, it appeared to have been burnt. A

Pl. 5.4—Wall F123 after excavation and layer F159 before excavation, looking west.

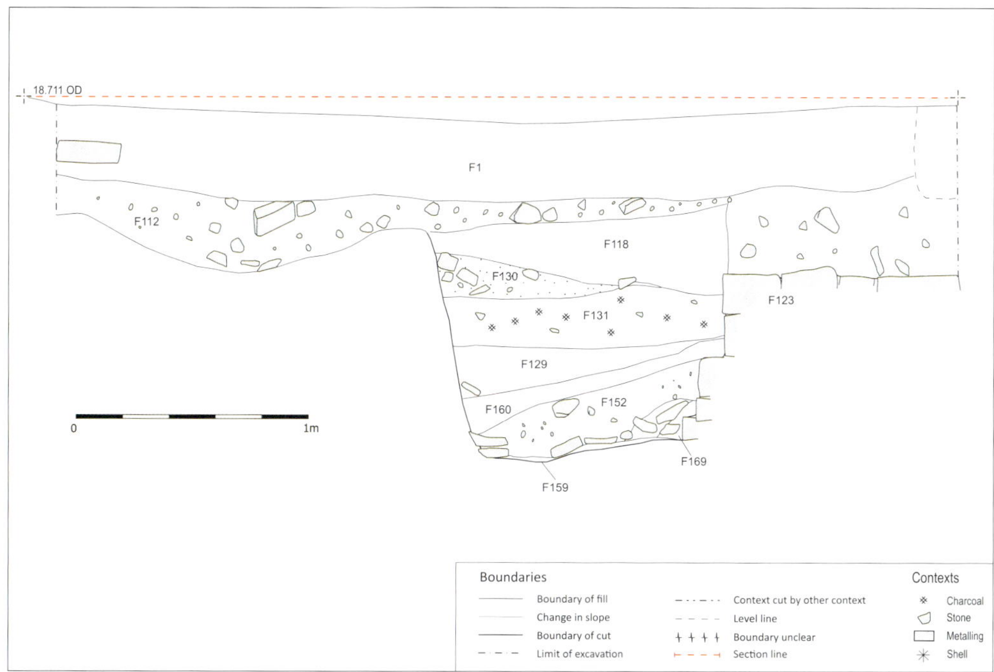

Fig. 5.3—Trench 8, west-facing section.

wedge-shaped fragment of possible Dundry stone (0.08m in height; 0.085m in max width; 0.055–0.15m thick; tool marks visible on one end face) was also recovered, as were fragments of Dublin-type fineware (of the late thirteenth–early fourteenth century), Dublin-type cooking ware (of the late twelfth–thirteenth century) and thirteenth-century Dublin-type ware (McCutcheon, this volume).

Pl. 5.5—Architectural fragment, photogrammetric model (courtesy of Mick Mongey).

This activity was sealed by a sterile layer (F160) which was overlain by a band of heat-affected soil (F129). This friable reddish-brown silt contained roof slates, plaster fragments and mortar as well as a range of environmental material, including the bones of cattle, sheep, pig, horse, rabbit, domestic fowl, woodcock and corncrake. European flat oyster, saddle oyster and common cockle were also recovered. Analysis of the charcoal from this layer identified birch, willow, ash, hazel, holly, oak and Pomoideae (OCarroll, this volume). Cereal grains recovered included naked wheat and barley. The only rye found at Swords Castle was identified in this deposit. The date ranges of the medieval pottery from F129—Dublin-type ware (thirteenth century), Dublin-type fineware (late thirteenth–early fourteenth century) and Leinster Cooking Ware (late twelfth–mid-fourteenth century)—corresponded with the radiocarbon date of AD 1298–1372 (UBA-38838) returned from a grain of wheat.

A similar layer (F131) overlay the fourteenth-century F129. Also reddish-brown, it contained frequent faunal remains characterised by cattle, sheep, pig, rabbit, hake, haddock, periwinkles, whelk, cockle and European flat oyster. F131 contained the same range of medieval pottery (Dublin-type fineware, Dublin-type ware and Leinster Cooking Ware), as well as examples of SCT1 floor tile. Mortar and plaster fragments were also recovered. In a similar stratigraphic position, extending eastwards for 2.78m from the western baulk, F142 consisted of compacted mid-grey gravel and sand, with frequent mortar flecks and angular stones. It contained medieval pottery (Dublin-type ware and Dublin-type fineware) and cattle, sheep, rabbit and plover bones, along with cod bones, cockle, whelks and European flat oysters. Iron nails, medieval pottery and tile and a possible fragment of human bone (E4619:142:36) were recovered from this feature.

A series of mainly sterile layers and deposits (F130, F174 and F173) were built up over the medieval activity and were overlain by more mixed deposits (F118 and F112) which may relate to the deconstruction of the medieval wall (F123). Similar faunal remains, including swan

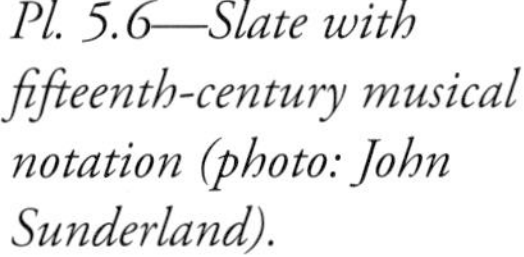

Pl. 5.6—Slate with fifteenth-century musical notation (photo: John Sunderland).

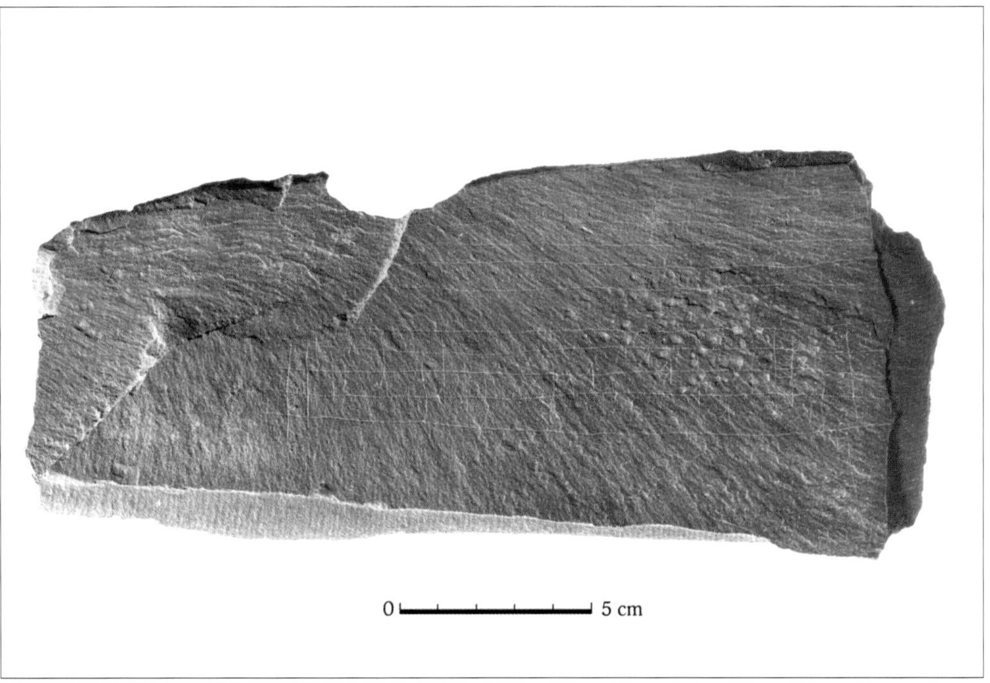

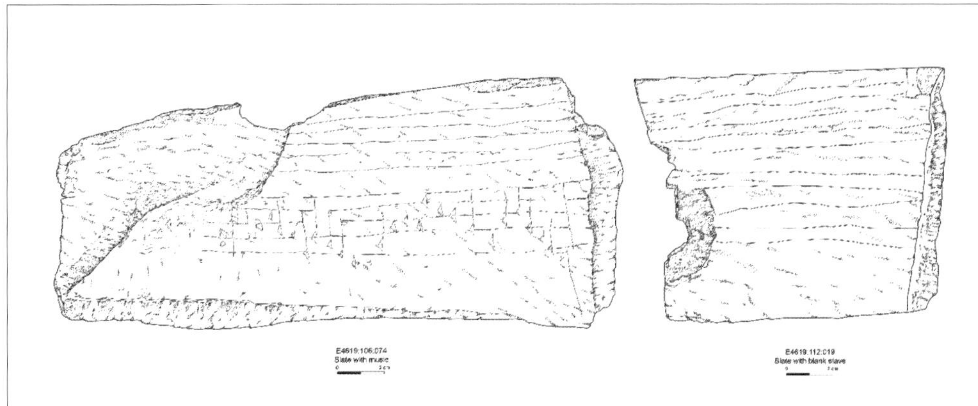

Fig. 5.4—Two fragments of incised slate, E4619:106:74 and E4610:112:019 (drawn by Sara Nylund).

bones, were recovered from deposits F118 and F112, both of which also contained blue mussel, European flat oyster, periwinkle, cockle, whelk and razor shell. Stone and slate, medieval pottery (thirteenth-century Dublin-type ware and late thirteenth–early fourteenth-century Dublin-type fineware), nineteenth-century pottery and eighteenth/nineteenth-century clay pipe fragments were recovered from these two deposits, along with an L-shaped socketed iron candle-holder (E4619:118:18), forged from a single piece of iron, from the lower of these mixed layers. Socketed candle-holders are typical of medieval times and were probably used for tallow candles, while the superior wax candles were held on iron prickets. Coincidentally, a candle-snuffer was recovered from a later deposit (E4619:106:28) within the same trench. It has been tentatively identified as part of a scissors-style candle-snuffer, a type known from the sixteenth century (Duffy, this volume).

A U-shaped cut extending down to the medieval wall F123 was identified in the south of Trench 8. It was filled with a mixed deposit, F106, which contained slate, mortar, medieval pottery (Dublin-type ware, Dublin-type fineware), North Devon gravel-tempered ware (dating from the seventeenth century) and nineteenth-century black-glazed and red earthenware. Two fragments of inscribed slate (E4619:106:74 and E4619:112:19) were recovered from deposits F112 and F106 (Pl. 5.6; Fig. 5.4). Although the fragments were recovered from separate (but adjoining) layers, they were found to fit together, forming a single slate that had broken vertically into two unequal parts.

Arranged as two sets of five, the inscribed lines were identified as staves, with musical notation identified on the lower stave of the larger fragment. In total, the notation comprised some 30 musical notes and symbols, formed by incised rectangles, triangles and vertical lines, and was entirely confined to the larger slate fragment. The notes are consistent with mensural notation, associated with the development of polyphonic music in the later medieval period (Duffy, this volume). This was confirmed by David Fallows, a musicologist specialising in fifteenth-century music, who identified the style of the line and major prolation as indicating composition in the 1420s or thereabouts. Although very short, it was felt that the longa on the last note is evidence that this was the end of the piece, which could have been the second half of a *chanson* by Binchois or someone of his generation (David Fallow, pers. comm.).

KITCHEN AREA

The remnants of a medieval wall (0.94m wide and exposed for 2m) running west-north-west/east-south-east within a vertical cut into natural subsoil were identified in Trench 1. The wall, F14, consisted of clay-bonded angular blocks of calp limestone and sandstone infilled with small stones and cobbles. Standing to a maximum height of 0.3m to the east, where three–four courses survived, it petered out to the west. There was considerable stone collapse (or demolition) to the north of the wall (F17). To the south was a single-course stone wall, F9, aligned north–south (1.2m north–south by 0.5–0.9m wide); it was set into a medieval layer (F23) and was of later construction than nearby wall F14.

Pl. 5.7—Walls F14 and F9, kitchen area, looking west.

There were two distinct dates for the activities that took place on either side of wall F14, which transected Trench 1. To the south were three deposits (F23, F51 and F8). The basal deposit (F23) contained Dublin-type coarseware (dating from the late twelfth–thirteenth century), some cattle and domestic fowl bones, oyster and periwinkles, as well as possible bread wheat, oat, peas, beans and vetches. The upper deposit (F8), which was characterised by oxidised clay inferring *in situ* burning, similarly contained Dublin-type coarseware and comparable faunal and plant assemblages, but a wheat grain submitted for AMS analysis returned a date range of AD 1011–1187 (UBA-32453). To the north of wall F14, a series of thin layers (F43, F42, F41, F37 and F39) overlay a compact metalled surface (F45) set into natural subsoil which encompassed a hearth setting (F44). The latter consisted of a series of heat-affected slabs (0.62m north–south by 0.5m east–west).

F43, the lowest of the series of thin layers (0.03–0.06m thick) confined to the northern end of Trench 1, was characterised by a high frequency of fish bones. Analysis of the faunal

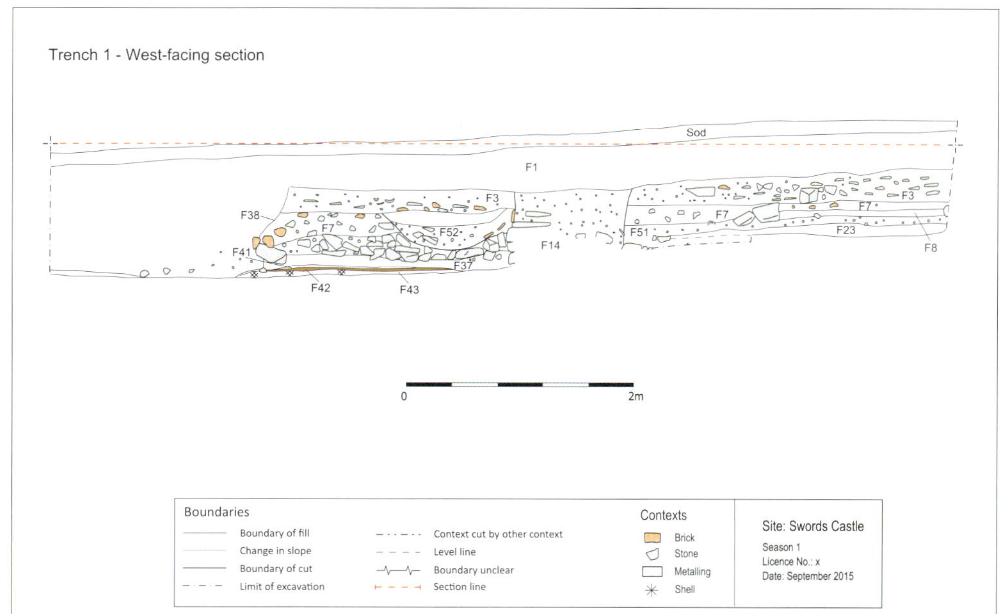

Fig. 5.5—Trench 1, west-facing section.

Pl. 5.8—Trench 1, metalled surface F45, hearth F44 and pit F40, looking north.

material identified clumps of fin rays, spines and scales associated with the preparation of fish for cooking. These fish included cod, pollock, hake, ling, haddock, whiting, conger eel, gurnard, plaice and red sea bream. There were also bird bones, including the largest number of snipe identified within the precinct, woodcock, plover, starling, finch, jay, duck (wild mallard and wild teal) and domestic goose, along with the remains of cattle, sheep, pig and rabbit (McCarthy,

Pl. 5.9—Pit A, western wall, north mural tower.

this volume). Blue mussel, whelk, cockle and European flat oyster were also recovered. An analysis of the plant remains identified bread wheat, oat and wild legume. A radiocarbon range of AD 1298–1373 (UBA-32454) was returned from a grain of wheat. Artefactual evidence from this layer consisted of a possible bone scoop (E4619:43:12) and Leinster Cooking Ware. It is not hard to imagine the gutting of fish beside the kitchen wall, not far from the Great Hall.

PIT A—WALL

The north–south wall (F48) that extended southwards from the extant arch of the possible mural tower of the north wall of Swords Castle was identified 0.48–0.7m below present ground level. It was recessed back 0.2m from the inner façade of the arch and consisted of large, mortar-bonded blocks of cut calp limestone. The basal 0.4m of the inner façade of F49 was heat-affected owing to the presence of burnt stone and material abutting it. This material (F30) consisted of red ashy silt with charcoal and mortar that contained bones of a cat and kitten and seashell. The sample taken for environmental analysis proved very seed-rich, with over 1,500 seed components identified. Dominated by bread wheat grains, it also included oat, Fabaceae and common sorrel (McClatchie, this volume). A wheat grain was submitted for AMS dating and returned a range of AD 1419–1512 (UBA-32458). Two medieval floor tiles (Pl. 5.10) were set at floor level. According to Wren, they have been reused from elsewhere.

Pl. 5.10—Medieval floor tiles, Pit A, looking east.

Pl. 5.11—Pit B, northern wall of the Great Hall (F36), looking south.

PIT B—WALL

Pit B was located at the northern junction of the curtain wall and the gable ruin of the eastern range of the Swords Castle precinct. An east–west wall (F36) was identified extending westwards from the gable. Built on natural subsoil, the foundation levels consisted of three–four courses of clay-bonded rough stone (averaging 0.12m in diameter). The uppermost course was topped by a mortar layer into which a course of cut stone (0.3–0.37m in diameter) was placed, 0.11m from the northern edge. Abutting it was a north–south retaining wall (F35), which consisted of a rubble base and one–three courses of clay-bonded stone. The space between the retaining wall and the castle curtain wall was filled with stones in a sandy matrix (F34).

DEMOLITION

Pl. 5.12—Architectural fragment, demolition debris (F77), looking west.

There was evidence for rapid demolition (F74 and F77) of a structure identified within Trench 4 which was located west of the food preparation area within Trench 1. This proximity was reflected in the extensive faunal and seashell assemblages recovered from these layers. Both layers contained wading species of birds found during summer and winter months (greenshank and bar-tailed godwit) and fish bones. Dog and cow bones were also found, the former the size of a modern Labrador, the latter possibly an elderly ox (McCarthy, this volume). An extensive range of shellfish was recovered, including European flat oyster, cockle, blue mussel, blunt tellin, periwinkles, whelk, limpet and razor shell, along with a fragment of coral (Carden, this volume). Both layers also contained Dublin-type ware and Dublin-type fineware.

Fig. 5.6—Trenches 1 and 4 after excavation.

Both layers contained significant quantities of building material, including stones, mortar fragments and slate. Architectural fragments such as a dressed window moulding and a roll and fillet fragment were recovered. These were heat-affected, indicating a burning event which may have been a factor in the subsequent demolition. Indicative of wooden elements of a structure were a range of carpentry nails and a partial clench bolt (E4619:74:2). Between demolition deposits was a compact surface (F87) interpreted as caused by foot traffic on a surface of rubble. Cattle, sheep, pig and rabbit bones were recovered, along with domestic goose and fowl. Fish bones included cod, hake, ling and gurnard. European flat oyster, blue mussel, periwinkle and cockle were identified, and Dublin-type ware and Dublin-type fineware were also recovered.

SURFACES AND YARDS

Within Trench 4 a series of surfaces and activities (F79, F80, F86, F87 and F99) were identified which may be associated with the demolished structure described above.

The basal surface within Trench 4 was a metalled surface (F100), set into natural subsoil, to the south-east of which was heat-affected clay (F98) and charcoal-rich silt (F99), perhaps representing a hearth and its contents. Cattle, pig and sheep bones, European flat oyster, periwinkle and blue mussel, Dublin-type ware and Dublin-type cooking ware were recovered, along with a small iron tanged object (E4619:98:1) that may be a fragment of a whittle-tanged blade. The stratigraphic position of surface F100 indicates that it is a continuation of metalled surface F45 within nearby Trench 1. A similar compact stony surface (F86) was noted in the south-east of the trench and somewhat patchily in the middle of the trench. Horse bone, cockle, periwinkle and European flat oyster were recovered from this layer, as were Dublin-type coarseware, Dublin-type ware and Dublin-type cooking ware. A fragment of a small polished bone tube (E4619:86:22;) was also recovered from this surface. Similar tubes recovered from other sites were identified as either handles, needle-cases or bobbins and were frequently decorated.

Two surfaces (F79 and F80) were identified in relatively similar stratigraphical position within Trench 4, both overlain by rubble activity (F71 and F74) and both later than an accumulation of material (F84) in the south of the trench. The latter was characterised by stone inclusions and the presence of cattle, sheep, pig, rabbit, domestic fowl, goose, woodcock and fish bones (hake, haddock, pollock, plaice) and seashell. A range of medieval pottery was also recovered, including Dublin-type ware, Dublin-type fineware, Leinster Cooking Ware and green-glazed Saintonge ware (dating from the thirteenth–mid-fourteenth century). A compact clay layer (F79) truncated to the north and south was interpreted as a deliberate surface and yielded a faunal shellfish and pottery assemblage similar to that from deposit F84. An untrampled ground surface, F80, which could be closely contemporary with surface F79, survived to the north of the trench, having been truncated by later activity to the south. It was rich in chopped and split animal bone, representing primary butchery, food-processing and kitchen preparation. A sample analysed for plant remains returned bread wheat with a small amount of oat and barley. Fabaceae, including garden pea, were identified, as was hazelnut and grass seeds. A wheat seed was sent for AMS dating and returned a range of AD 1299–1371 (UBA-34516). A small iron buckle (E4619:80:1) was also recovered. An upward-projecting hook indicates that the buckle was originally attached to a spur.

It appears that there was an extensive medieval yard surface laid over earlier activity that followed the sloping topography of the site and was identified in Trenches 5, 2 and 6 (F68, F72 and F5). Given the proximity of Trenches 2 and 6, it was unsurprising that the yard surface was identified in both. The surfaces (F5 and F72) consisted of small stones (0.02–0.03m in diameter) with occasional larger ones (0.2m in diameter) set in a gravelly silt matrix. Dublin-type ware, Dublin-type fineware, cattle, sheep and pig bone, oyster and cockle shells and slate fragments were recovered from both surfaces. Five fragments from a single antler comb (E4619:72:15) were recovered from the base of surface F72 in Trench 6. The overall morphology of the comb suggests that it belongs to Dunlevy's (1988b) Class G, datable to the twelfth/thirteenth century. The surface (F68) in Trench 5 appeared to have been consolidated (F78). Both sloping surfaces sealed the pre-Norman ditch F85 and yielded a similar assemblage of medieval pottery, with the addition of fragments of Leinster Cooking Ware and Saintonge green-glazed ware.

TRENCH 3

Located on low ground in the western quadrant of the Swords Castle precinct, Trench 3 contained pits (F33, F31 and F28) that extended beyond the western limits of the trench. East of the pits were metalled surfaces and compacted layers (F50, F27, F21, F20 and F18) that were defined by a low bank (F20).

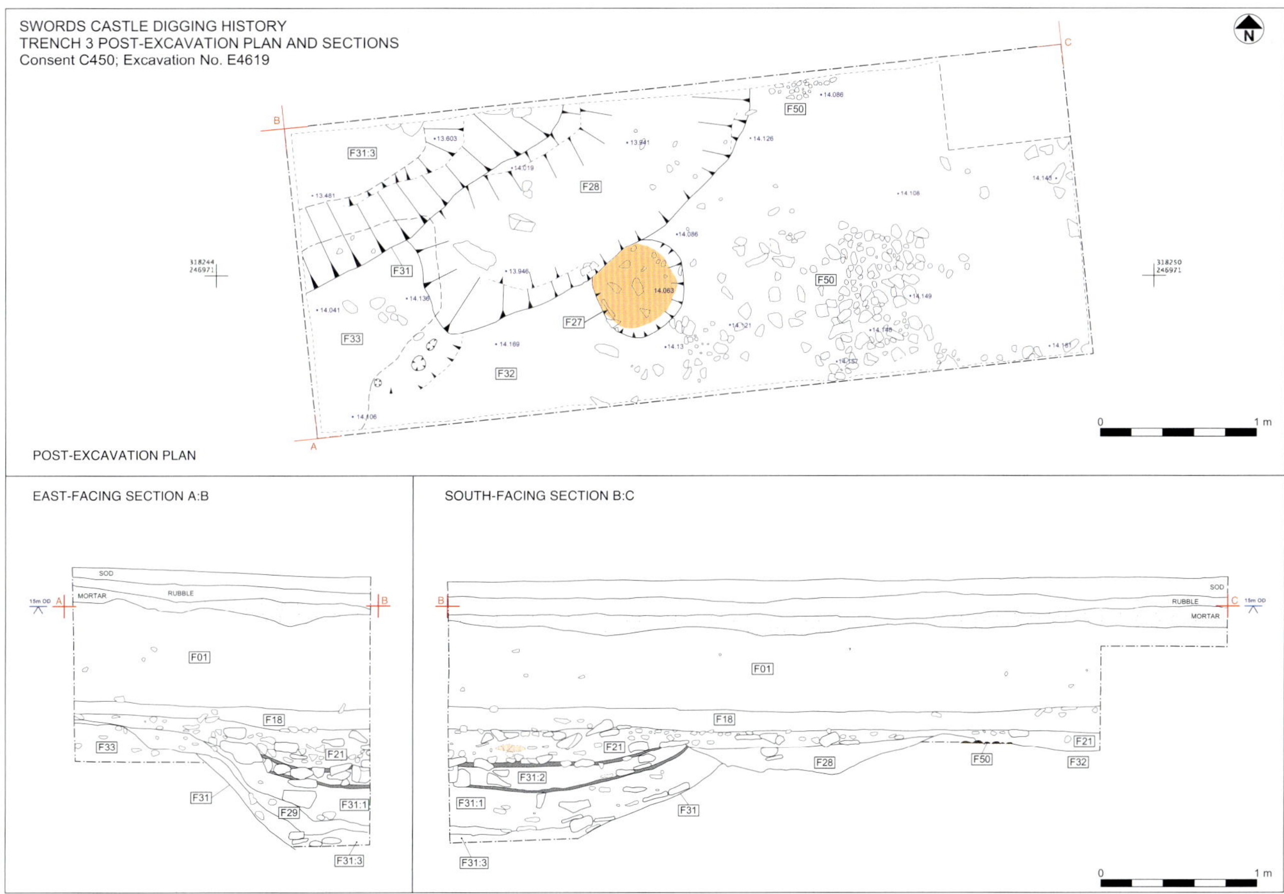

Fig. 5.7—Trench 3, post-excavation plan and east-facing and south-facing sections.

Pits

A mainly unexcavated pit (F33), cut into natural subsoil, was located in the south-west corner of Trench 3. Ten fragments of animal bone were recovered, which did not appear to be typical domestic meat waste. Possible bread wheat, oat, common vetch, fat hen, stinking chamomile and common sorrel were also identified. F33 was cut by a much larger, steep-sided pit, F31, which dominated the north-western quadrant of Trench 3 and contained four fills, all of which were rich in faunal and plant remains. Domestic livestock, horse, cat, dog, rabbit and stoat were identified, along with cod, whiting, gurnard and European flat oyster and periwinkle. Much of the faunal assemblage was calcined, suggesting the rakings of fires where meat was roasted on spits.

The plant assemblage contained bread wheat, oat grains and cereal straw, along with arable weeds such as corn-cockle, field gromwell and corn marigold. A wheat seed from the lower fill

Pl. 5.13—Trench 3, pit F31, after excavation, looking west.

(F31:c.3) was submitted for AMS dating and returned a range of AD 1021–1186 (UBA-32457). A human seventh cervical vertebra was recovered from a redeposited layer (F29) within this pit and returned a date range of AD 1065–1154 (UBA-3252). Pit F31 also contained medieval pottery, including Dublin-type coarseware, Leinster Cooking Ware, Dublin-type ware and Dublin-type fineware, as well as an incomplete, jaggedly broken tuning-peg (E4619:31:15) that may have belonged to a smaller instrument such as a lyre, lute or fiddle.

The upper fill of pit F31 was partially cut to the east by pit F28. Animal bone (including cattle, sheep, pig, horse and rabbit) and oyster shell were recovered from the fill, as were several hundred plant components which consisted of bread wheat rachis, bread wheat grains, oat and barley, as well as brambles, hazelnut, common sorrel and possible garden pea. Dublin-type coarseware and green-glazed Saintonge ware were recovered from pit F28. On the base of a fragment of Saintonge ware was an 'owner's mark' (Pl. 5.14). Found almost exclusively on Saintonge green-glazed jugs, these crude marks were scratched onto fired pot. In a society with low levels of literacy, these marks would have been easily recognisable. In a study of those from Wood Quay, Waterford and Cork, no real pattern has emerged for the marks, which suggests that the designs were the result of individual choice rather than emanating from a single source (McCutcheon 2006, 114–15).

F28 also yielded a pair of iron tweezers (E4619:28:4) consisting of two flattened arms,

Pl. 5.14—A basal sherd of Saintonge ware with an owner's mark was recovered from the base of a medieval pit, F28, in Trench 3.

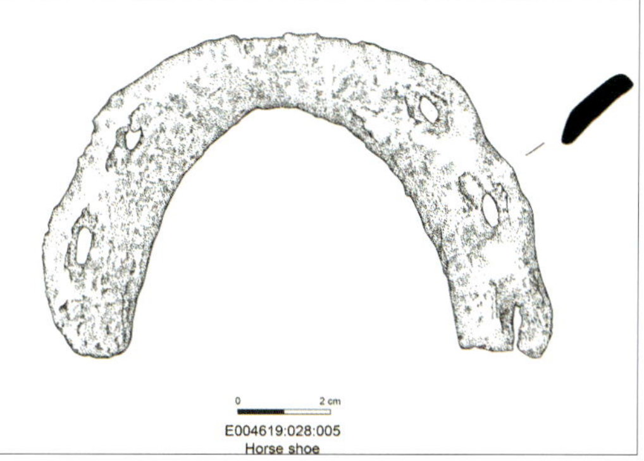

Fig. 5.9 (left)—Partial horseshoe (E4619:28:5) (drawing: Sara Nylund).

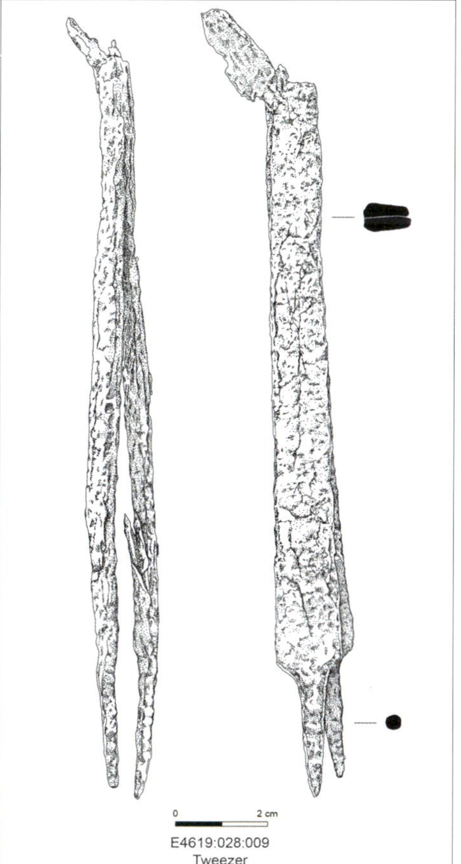

Fig. 5.8 (left)—Possible burling tweezers (E4619:028:009) (drawing: Sara Nylund).

broken at the head where the arms join (Fig. 5.8). Larger and more robust than would be expected of personal tweezers, they may have been associated with craftworking; similar tweezers from thirteenth- and fourteenth-century levels in York and London were interpreted as tools used in a process known as 'burling' in the cloth-making industry. Another find was a partial horseshoe (E4619:28:5) with a wavy outer edge (Fig. 5.9), consistent with Clark's (1995) Type 2B, a form predominantly used in the period *c.* 1150–1225.

Identified within the cut of pit F28 but extending eastwards beyond the limit of the cut and across a stony layer (F21) was deposit F22, a soft, black, charcoal-rich silt with a very high proportion of charcoal/carbonised seeds. A similar animal bone and seashell assemblage to that within F28 was recovered (cattle, sheep, pig, cod and oyster). Likewise, seashell and medieval potsherds (Dublin-type fineware and Dublin-type ware) were also recovered from this deposit. A very seed-rich sample turned out to contain more than 10,000 plant components, the majority being bread wheat, oat and barley grains. Also identified were cereal straw and small numbers of garden pea, broad bean, common vetch and sorrel. A wheat seed sent for AMS analysis returned a date range of AD 1032–1217 (UBA-32456).

Layers and deposits

A series of deposits were interspersed between pit cuts and appear to have been used to seal the pits or to consolidate the areas around them. There was a differentiation in activity between the western (pit-rich) end of Trench 3 and the eastern end, which was reflected in the layers immediately above. A discontinuous layer of small stones (F50) pressed into natural subsoil formed a firm surface, through which the pits described above were cut. A small hearth (F27) consisted of black silt retained by stones over compact metalling (F50) and heat-affected subsoil. Small quantities of bread wheat and possible barley were recovered. Rake-out (F46) from the hearth was also spread over surface F50.

Used as a consolidating layer to fill in the soft pit area, stony surface F21 extended over the majority of Trench 3, delineated to the east by a concentration of stones (F20). In addition to the usual domestic animal assemblage (cattle, sheep and pig), bones of rabbit, domestic fowl, a large dog (equivalent to a modern Alsatian) and a cat were recovered, along with seashell, cod and haddock. Possible bread wheat, oat, barley, possible broad bean, Fabaceae, wild redshank and goosefoot were identified. Artefacts recovered from this layer include seventeen sherds of medieval pottery (Dublin-type ware, Dublin-type coarseware and Leinster Cooking Ware).

One of the most personal items recovered from Swords Castle is a copper-alloy stick-pin

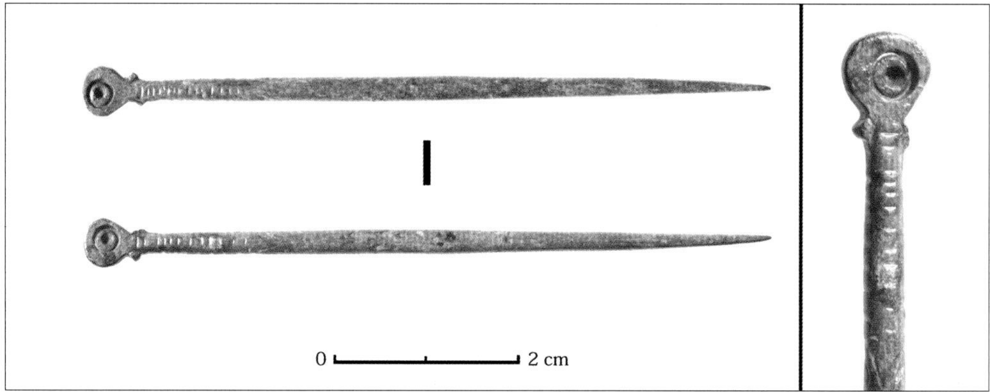

Pl. 5.15—Copper-alloy stick-pin (E4619:21:41) (photo: John Sunderland).

(E4619:21:41) (Pl. 5.15). Stick-pins were used as clothes-fasteners and are considered to date from the tenth to thirteenth centuries. The example from Swords Castle accords with O Rahilly's (1998) Type 13B, characterised by an upright, rounded, spatulate head. Pins of this type recovered in Dublin dated from the late twelfth to the mid-thirteenth century, putting them quite late in the stick-pin chronology.

Also recovered from this layer was a sandstone hone (E4619:21:43) (Fig. 5.10). It is likely to have been used to sharpen knives or larger blades, although no wear patterns or striations from use were visible; its surface was uniformly smooth, apart from one damaged corner. A range of nails were recovered from Trench 3, but Type A and Type B were recovered from surface F21. Type A (or 'fiddle keys') and Type B were associated with horseshoes, and their typology suggests a thirteenth–early fourteenth-century date for their deposition. A possible smith's punch (E4619:18:20) was recovered from the compacted layer immediately above.

Some building materials, including fragments of slate, were associated with surface F21. A small,

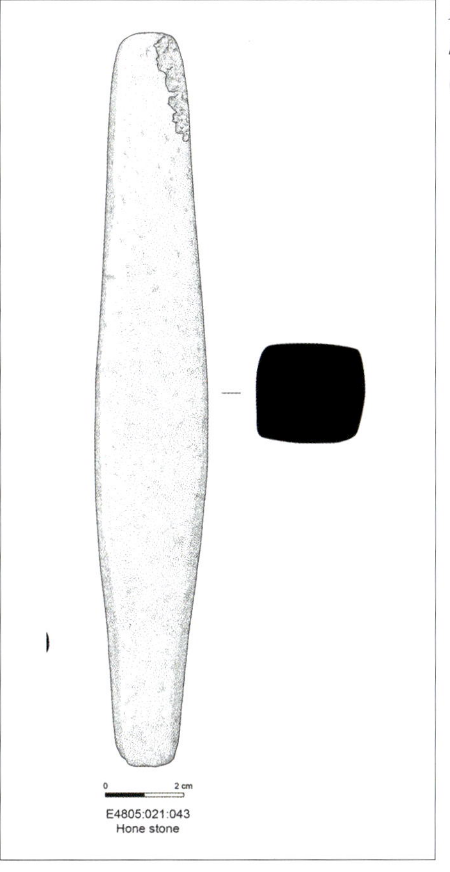

Fig. 5.10—Sandstone hone (E4619:21:43) (drawing: Sara Nylund).

Pl. 5.16—Trench 7, kiln and flagged floor, looking north.

subrectangular fragment of limestone (E4619:21:44) was interpreted as a corner broken off a larger item such as a stone flag or tile, or possibly a very shallow step. A complete clench bolt (E4619:21:30), which would have been used to join overlapping planks of timber together, may have been used in a door.

KILN AREA

Located in the north-eastern corner of Swords Castle, Trench 7 was positioned near the north mural tower in order to identify its southern limit and with a view to understanding the effect of the breach of the curtain wall by the proprietors of Dunne's bakery in the nineteenth century. A kiln (F143, F161, F162, F146 and F158) cutting through flagged flooring (F147, F145 and F149) and its associated deposits (F126, F144 and F125) were identified as indicative of sixteenth-century activity in this area.

Three elements of a flagged floor were identified. To the north-west was a level floor surface of mortared slabs (average dimensions 0.3m by 0.2m) with a clearly defined northern edge. In the southern half of Trench 7, the flagged surface consisted of large limestone flags (0.4m by 0.6–1m in diameter) with decayed rounded edges; the stones were not mortared and gaps were infilled with smaller, irregular stones (0.2m in diameter). The eastern quadrant was contained within a trapezoidal setting of vertically set stones (0.25m in length and projecting 0.05–0.12m above the level of the stones) of the same material defining a gently sloping surface that formed part of drain F149.

This drain feature, which extends through the eastern curtain wall, was integrated with the

Pl. 5.17—Floor leading into drain (F145 and F149) in curtain wall.

Pl. 5.18—Flagged floors F147 and F145, looking north.

flagged surface. The drain consists of a well-made mortared opening in the eastern wall; it measures 0.65m at its inner face, narrowing to 0.35m over its east–west extent of 0.7m. There was no obvious point at which this feature was inserted into the eastern wall and it may represent an original feature, which implies that the flagged surface represents ground level at the time of the construction of the curtain wall in this area of the precinct.

Although likely contemporary, there was a different usage of the flagged floor to the north (F147), which was heat-affected and had an overlying deposit (F126) consisting of a series of occupation floors of heat-discoloured clay and loose charcoal and grit. The basal layer (F126:3) consisted of dark grey and red clay of firm compaction (0.1m thick) that came off onto heat-affected slabs but extended beyond their northern edge into the baulk. Environmental sampling of the basal layer identified oat grain with germination; grass culm node, which may represent cereal straw; and large and small Fabaceae (peas, beans, legumes). Charcoal analysis identified hazel, birch and furze. An oat grain was sent for AMS analysis and returned a date range of AD 1461–1636 (UBA-38837). Above this was a mottled dark grey and red clay (F126:2) of similar dimensions to the layer below (0.05–0.1m thick) which contained a subrectangular patch of *in situ* mortar (0.8m by 0.6m by 0.7m thick). This coarse sandy mortar may have been an attempt to create a surface, perhaps for a post-pad. The upper surface (F126:1) consisted of pale yellowish-brown clay, heavily mottled with red orange patches and black staining (0.05–0.1m thick). It contained naked wheat, occasional possible oat, vetch, bedstraw and Fabaceae.

Pl. 5.19—Elizabeth I sixpence (E4619:126:12) (photo: John Sunderland).

A silver sixpence from the reign of Elizabeth I (Pl. 5.19), dating from 1569, was recovered from the upper surface of these occupation layers, providing a *terminus ante quem* for the flooring. The crown mint mark, just discernible above the monarch's head, indicates that the coin was issued from the London mint and for circulation in England rather than Ireland (Irish coins carried a harp as mint mark). This easy distinction was perhaps necessary, as officially circulated coins in Ireland continued to be of lesser value than their English counterparts: the silver Irish coins struck in 1561, for example, contained only three-quarters the weight of silver of their English equivalents. A small, rectangular, copper-alloy mount (E4619:126:11) was also recovered from these layers. It is uncertain whether this would have adorned an item of clothing or a horse harness, although its small size and fragility may suggest the former. Sherds of Leinster Cooking Ware and a DT2 ridge tile were also recovered from here. The faunal and shell assemblages were extensive, with cattle, sheep, pig, rabbit, mallard and woodcock identified, alongside cod, hake, European flat oyster, whelks, and rough, common and flat periwinkle.

Partially overlying the remainder of the flagged surface was a deposit of pale brown clayey silt that extended part-way into drain F149. The faunal assemblage contained more fish remains—cod, hake, ling, plaice/flounder and members of the gadid family—alongside cattle, sheep, pig, rabbit, domestic fowl, greenshank, dog and seashell. A sherd of Dublin-type ware was recovered from F144, as was a tapering copper-alloy tube (E4619:144:2), identified as a lace-tag or aglet. The edges of the tube fold inwards towards the centre, thus gripping the lace without the need for rivets; this is consistent with a design form identified as mid-sixteenth- to seventeenth-century in date.

Kiln

The northern (F147) and southern (F145) flagged floors and the overlying deposits (F126, F144 and F125) were all truncated by the insertion of the kiln, F143. The northern bowl of F143 consisted of a tapering oval defined to north and east by an earth-cut face rendered with mortar and to the south and west by a mix of large and medium stones in a random rubble bond (0.5m north–south by 2m east–west, 0.5–0.6m in height). Curiously, there is no real indication of burning/heating of the mortar surface, but as it was left *in situ* it is possible that it represents a final clean use and that earlier layers of burnt material lie beneath. The basal fill, friable mid-greyish-brown silt with charcoal inclusions, appeared to represent the initial post-use fill of the kiln bowl. Animal and fish bone, including cattle, sheep, pig, rabbit, greenshank, cod and hake, and a range of seashell were recovered. Analysis of the kiln fill identified fragmented and barely identifiable bread wheat, occasional oat, possible pea and vetch,

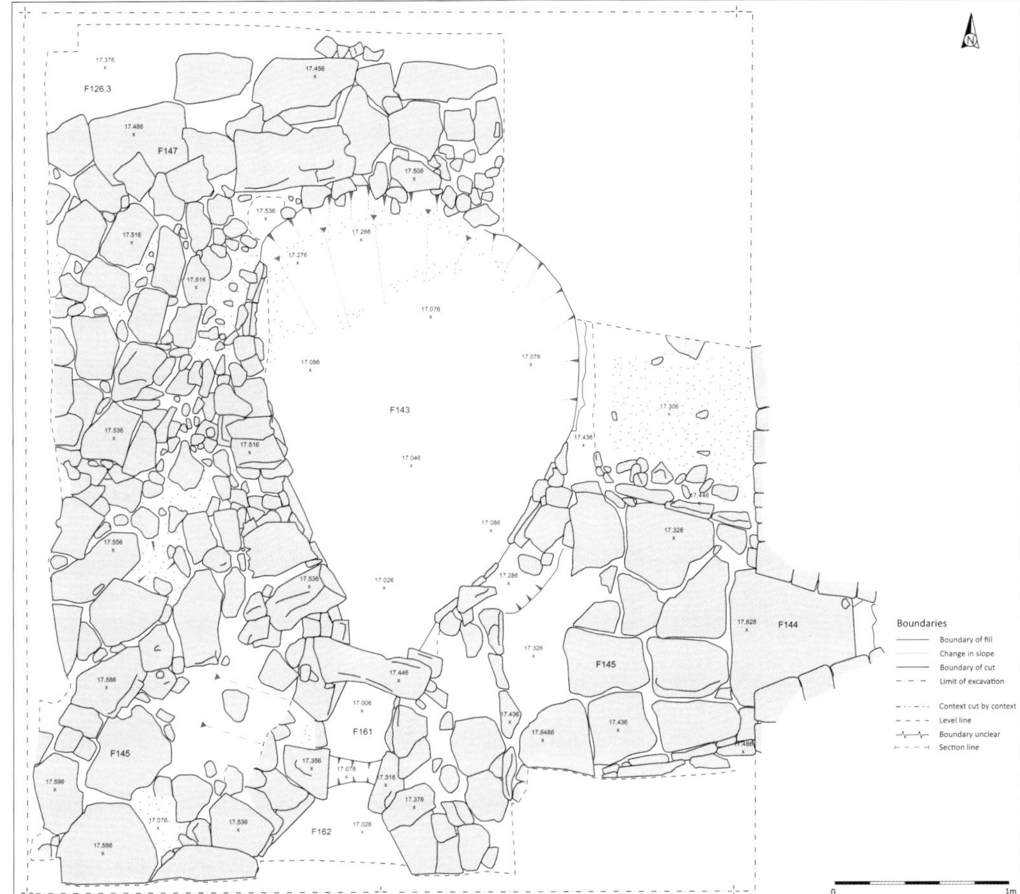

Fig. 5.11—Trench 7, post-excavation plan.

occasional Fabaceae and bedstraw. A grain of hulled barley was sent for AMS dating and returned a range of AD 1451–1528 (UBA-38839). In addition, a range of medieval pottery (Dublin-type ware, Dublin-type fineware and Saintonge green-glazed ware) was recovered from this feature alongside two examples of DT2 ridge tile, one of which was crested.

The bowl led into a fine orthostatic flue (F161) with side walls generally made of a single upright (two–three in a row on each side) and with one surviving lintel at the northern end. Two infill deposits were noted. The basal fill was almost pure charcoal, apparently representing a single large timber of oak set transversely across the flue. The upper fill was an ashy deposit mixed with mortar which filled the flue almost entirely. This contained oak and a small number of indeterminate seeds. The flue led into a southern kiln bowl or fire-pit, which consisted of a finely made stone-walled chamber or bowl. In contrast to the flue, the walling of the chamber was of coursed stone rather than orthostatic. No mortar was identified between the stones but was exposed on the upper surface at both sides. Two fills were noted. The lowest fill was stony, dark, friable clayey silt. It was not fully excavated (owing to time constraints) but appeared to overlie a layer of mortar similar to that in the kiln bowl. The upper fill was loose, reddish, clayey silt and sand, 0.2m thick and dished in profile, with occasional small stones and frequent charcoal inclusions. A single sherd of Dublin-type ware was recovered from this feature. A small number of cattle, sheep, pig and domestic fowl bones and European flat oyster shells were noted.

Pl. 5.20—Kiln bowl F143 during excavation, looking south-west.

Pl. 5.21—Flue F161 and southern bowl F162, looking west.

6

Phase III—Post-medieval–modern

INTRODUCTION

Evidence for later activity that truncated medieval layers or resulted in mixed-date assemblages was identified across all excavation trenches and can typically be divided according to pits (F6=F38, F52, F69, F76 and F81), deposits (F148, F114, F106 and F112), layers (F117, F63, F82, F64, F66 and F127) and drains (F4, F73 and F94).

PITS

A number of pits truncated medieval layers and tended to contain both medieval and later material. A large pit cut through the medieval kitchen layers in Trench 1. It contained animal bones, 33 of which were identified as a mixture of meat-bearing bones and waste of cattle, sheep and pig, and seashell. A commercial token (E4619:6:4) issued by the Hibernian Mining Company (HMC) was recovered from this pit (Pl. 6.1). The date of issue was 1794 and the 'Halfpenny' could be exchanged for official coinage or goods in Dublin or in Ballymurtagh, Co. Wicklow, where the mining company was based. Clay pipe fragments, including a seventeenth-century stem (E4619:6:5), were also recovered.

Pl. 6.1—Commercial token (E4619:6:4) (photo: John Sunderland).

There were four pits in the nearby Trench 4. One (F69) contained a partial pig skeleton. Aged between one and 2.5 years at death, the pig had severe degenerative joint disease and had been discarded rather than processed. Cattle bones, a sheep aged over 3.5 years and a small lamb were also identified. A range of medieval pottery (late twelfth–mid-fourteenth-century Leinster Cooking Ware and thirteenth-century Dublin-type ware) was recovered, along with post-medieval pottery, brick and slate fragments. A nearby subrectangular pit (F76) yielded a similar mixture of meat-bearing animal bones, seashell and pottery; it also contained an iron tool with a long tang (E4619:76:4) that appears to be a woodworker's auger or gouge.

Cutting through a rubble layer, pit F81 contained a moderate amount of butchered bone, including cattle bone, both meat-bearing and peripheral, and sheep bone, indicating a mixture of primary butchery and domestic refuse. A piglet and a chicken leg and wing were also identified. Like the other pits in Trench 4, F81 also contained European flat oyster, cockle, periwinkle and razor shell. Medieval pottery recovered included thirteenth-century Dublin-type ware and late thirteenth–early fourteenth-century Dublin-type fineware.

DEPOSITS

Activity interpreted as deposition over medieval material was notable in Trench 7 (F148, F114 and F124) and Trench 8 (F106 and F112). The deposit (F114) resulting from the demolition of the kiln was characterised by large angular stones dipping into the chamber of the kiln. Seashell, Dublin-type ware, Dublin-type fineware and fragments of SCT1 floor tile and DT4 roof tile were recovered. A clay pipe bowl (E4619:114:1) displaying the name of the Dublin United Trades Association around a pair of clasped hands and the word 'Trademark' was also recovered. This Association, a precursor to the trade union movement, existed from 1863 until *c.* 1877. Concentrated in the south-west corner of Trench 7, F124 partially overlay slabs and contained a similar mix of material, including pottery ranging from late twelfth–mid-fourteenth-century Leinster Cooking Ware to glazed earthenware and transfer-printed ware of the eighteenth–nineteenth century. An incomplete knife with scale tang thought to be sixteenth-century or earlier was also recovered.

Within Trench 8, the stone deposit F112 that extended over the north of the trench contained swan bones; swans were held in high regard as prestige birds. Blue mussel, periwinkle, cockle, razor shell and European flat oyster were also identified. Dublin-type fineware and DT2 ridge tile were recovered, along with eighteenth–nineteenth-century pottery and red earthenware (REW) pantile. A decorated pipe stem (dating from the eighteenth–nineteenth century), a Type I iron nail and a late eighteenth–early nineteenth-century 'treble gilt' button from a man's coat were also found, indicating the disturbed nature of the deposit. The adjoining deposit, F106, contained a similar mix of material. Widgeon (wild duck) and rock dove were identified, along with European flat oyster, cockle, periwinkle, blue mussel, razor shell, needle shell and grooved carpet shell. Dublin-type ware, Dublin-type fineware, seventeenth-century North Devon gravel-tempered ware, and black-glazed and glazed earthenware (of the seventeenth–nineteenth century) were recovered, along with SCT1 floor tile, DT2 ridge tile, DT4 crested ridge tile and REW pantile. The disturbed nature of deposits in this area was demonstrated by the variety of artefacts from a single deposit: a possible candle-snuffer (E4619:106:28), tentatively identified as part of a scissors-style candle-snuffer, a type known from the sixteenth century; an incomplete knife with scale tang, a type developed in the thirteenth century; and a copper-alloy pin (E4619:106:1) from a large buckle. The pin has a series of raised lateral ridges at the base of the loop, a feature noted on pins from large, annular buckles of the mid-thirteenth to mid-fifteenth centuries. A button (E4619:106:2) with a surviving gilt finish was also recovered. The surviving decoration on the front is typical of buttons from the early to mid-nineteenth century. A fragment of human cranium (E4619:106:96) was also identified. Quite an extensive quantity of grey and purple slate fragments, some with nail holes and mortar adhered, were recovered, indicating a collapsed roof of a structure in the vicinity.

Pl. 6.2—Duck bill retrieved from layer F3.

LAYERS

A number of layers within the excavation trenches were stratigraphically above medieval activity or mixed by later disturbance. A consolidation layer, F3, was evident within Trenches 1 and 2. In the latter it overlay a medieval yard surface. Of the 1,124 animal bones recovered only 280 could be identified. Cattle (35%) and sheep (37%) dominated the assemblage, with twice as many individuals of sheep, both meat- and non-meat-bearing. Three pigs and two piglets were identified, as well as two adult rabbits. There were fine knife marks on the rabbit bones, indicating pelt removal. A single duck bill (Pl. 6.2) and swan bones were also identified. Molluscs recovered included periwinkle, whelk, blunt tellin, blue mussel, European flat oyster and cockle. The range of pottery from F3 comprised Dublin-type ware, Dublin-type coarseware (from the late twelfth–thirteenth century), Leinster Cooking Ware, Frechen ware (of the seventeenth century) and other stoneware. A complete clay pipe bowl (E4619:3:64) from this layer corresponds to Oswald's (1975) Type 20G, dated to 1690–

1730. Four Type I and one Type VIII iron nails were recovered, as well as a poorly preserved forked iron object (E4619:3:58) which may represent a spacer from a strap-end. A human tooth (E4619:3:68), a second molar, was recovered from F3 within Trench 2, which was located close to known burials.

Within Trench 4, layer F65 formed an interface between the underlying rubble and the improved soil above. Animal bone included dog and rat, while the shell identified comprised European flat oyster, saddle oyster, dog whelk, grooved carpet shell, limpet, whelk, periwinkle, razor shell and cockle. The range of pottery recovered was similar to that in nearby Trench 1, with Dublin-type ware, Dublin-type cooking ware (of the late twelfth–thirteenth century), Leinster Cooking Ware, North Devon gravel-tempered ware, Frechen stoneware and unglazed earthenwares (of the eighteenth–nineteenth century). A fragment of copper-alloy mount (E4619:65:31) comprised the angular, polygonal terminus of a rectangular strip mount, with a rivet hole close to the end, and is likely to have formed part of the decoration on a casket or coffer. Four clay pipe bowls and two stem mouthpieces were recovered from this layer. One of the clay pipe bowls was datable to 1600–60 and the remainder were from the nineteenth–early twentieth century.

Within Trench 5, contemporary layers F64 and F66 overlay a yard surface and contained a mix of material. Bones of cattle, sheep, pig, dog, rabbit, domestic fowl, goose and duck were identified, along with cod, hake, periwinkle, cockle, blue tellin, blue mussel, European flat oyster and king scallop. The pottery recovered from these layers ranged from late twelfth–thirteenth-century Dublin-type cooking ware to twentieth-century domestic wares and included North Devon gravel-tempered ware and Westerwald stoneware. Four clay pipe bowls and stem fragments dating from the late eighteenth century to the early twentieth century were also recovered.

Trench 6 also contained a consolidation layer (F63) above a medieval surface. Bones of

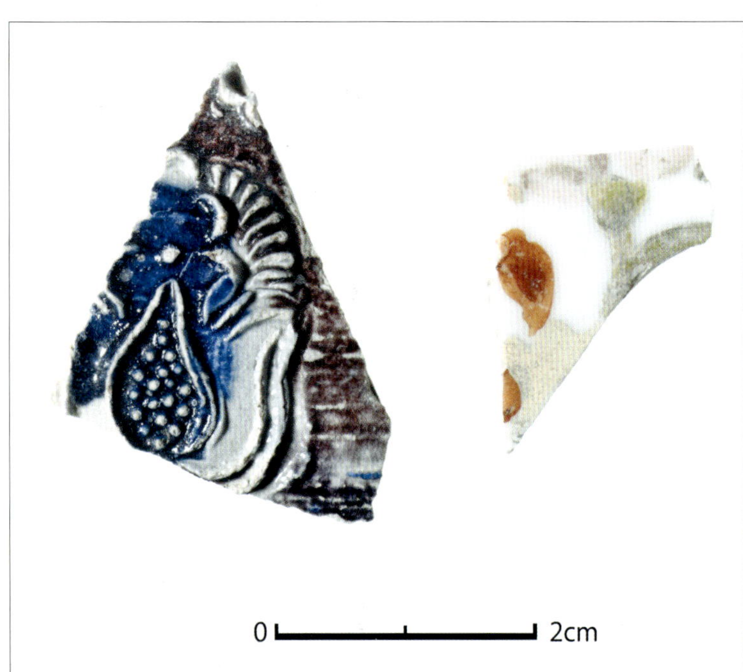

Pl. 6.3—Westerwald stoneware and porcelain sherd.

cattle, sheep, pig, dog, rabbit, rat, domestic goose, mallard, cod and hake were recovered, along with European flat oyster, periwinkle, dog whelk, grooved carpet shell, blunt tellin and cockle. The pottery assemblage included Dublin-type ware, Dublin-type fineware, North Devon gravel-tempered ware, seventeenth-century Seville coarseware, unglazed earthenwares and transfer-printed wares (of the eighteenth–nineteenth century). Clay pipe bowls and stem fragments dated from the early–mid-nineteenth century. Metal objects recovered include a range of iron nails and objects associated with structures. A small, complete wall hook (E4619:63:2) is comparable to wall hooks from twelfth/thirteenth- and fifteenth-century levels in York and from late fourteenth-century levels at Trim Castle. A small length of lead window came (E4619:63:54) was also identified. This was a relatively uncommon find, as lead was often melted and reused (meaning that it was generally recycled). An iron mount (E4619:63:49) resembles examples recovered from fourteenth- and fifteenth-century sites in London and may once have formed part of a fleur-de-lis shape or the end of a strap-hinge from a chest or coffer. Two small fragments from the rim of an iron vessel (E4619:63:5; E4619:63:6) suggest a thin-walled vessel of unknown size and shape. A single small fragment of olive-green bottle glass (E4619:63:56) was retrieved. Glass fragments of similar colour and patina recovered in Dublin were dated to the seventeenth century. In addition, fragments of disarticulated human remains (E4619:63:55), consisting of cranial fragments, vertebrae, foot phalanx, femur and two teeth, were identified in this layer.

Sealing the occupation layers overlying the flagged floor in Trench 7 was a post-medieval topsoil layer, F117. To the north of the trench there was a sharp transition to the underlying charcoal-rich surface (F126:1), which was characterised by a concentration of slate. Cattle, sheep, pig, rabbit, curlew, cod, hake and plaice/founder bones were identified, along with

Pl. 6.4—Doorway (F175) through the eastern curtain wall to Dunne's bakery, Trench 7.

European flat oyster, periwinkle, grooved carpet shell, blue tellin and common cockle. The medieval pottery identified included Dublin-type ware, Dublin-type fineware and Leinster Cooking Ware, as well as ST1 floor tile. Type I, Type IV and Type XII iron nails were also retrieved, and a fragment of disarticulated human bone (E4619:117:14) was identified.

The use of the precinct of Swords Castle as an orchard and gardens throughout the nineteenth century and into the twentieth century has had a significant effect on the archaeological strata. This is perhaps most obvious in the disturbance and spread of human burial material across the site (and recorded in all excavation trenches) owing to extensive ploughing. A number of furrows (F67, F115, F116 and F121) and drains (F4, F70 and F107) most probably associated with the site's use as an orchard were identified. A breach of the curtain wall (F175) and the entrance and pathways (F108, F110 and F111) associated with Dunne's bakery in the late nineteenth century were recorded in the north-eastern corner of the site.

Within Trench 1, a linear feature, F4, was cut into consolidation layer F3. F4 contained two cattle scapulae (one with modern saw marks), cockle, periwinkle and whelk shells. Dublin-type fineware, North Devon gravel-tempered ware and eighteenth–nineteenth-century earthenwares and delph were recovered, along with iron nails and a large oval clay pipe stem fragment (E4619:4:8).

Nearby Trench 4 contained a modern east–west trench or gully (F70); this yielded 295 animal bones, mostly eroded or abraded, some of which displayed gnaw-marks. They comprised cattle, sheep, pig, rabbit, chicken, goose and duck. European flat oyster, periwinkle, cockle, grove snail and garden snail were also identified. The pottery retrieved was a mix of Dublin-type ware, Dublin-type fineware, unglazed red earthenware and whiteware (of the eighteenth–twentieth century). An incomplete copper-alloy key from a pocket watch (E4619:70:4) of probable nineteenth-century date was also recovered from this feature. A mortared wall shore and slate-floored lintelled drain (F73 and F94) truncated the northern limit of Trench 4. European flat oyster and periwinkle were recovered, along with a sherd of Dublin-type coarseware.

Pl. 6.5—Lead bag seal E4619:109:1 (photo: Siobhán Duffy).

Within Trench 5 was a gully or furrow (F67) that contained 23 animal bones, unidentifiable except for a cattle rib with a modern saw mark. European flat oyster, cockle, periwinkle and garden snail were identified. A single sherd of Dublin-type ware was recovered. In the south-east corner of the trench was a sharp-sided, flat-based pit (F83) with a mix of inclusions. A total of 72 domestic livestock bones were retrieved, along with European flat oyster and cockle. The pottery was a mix of whiteware and a small number of medieval sherds (Dublin-type ware and Dublin-type fineware).

Three possible furrows or drainage

features (F115, F116 and F121) were identified within Trench 7. All contained a mixture of modern pottery and occasional medieval sherds, seashell (periwinkle, blue mussel and European flat oyster), clay pipe fragments and iron nails. F121 also contained SCT1 line-impressed floor tile and SCT1 floor tile. An incomplete branch of a horseshoe with a narrow web (E4619:121:1), suggesting a seventeenth-century or later date, was recovered, as was a partial double-sided fine-toothed comb (E4619:121:8). This appeared to be a mass-produced nit-comb, probably of nineteenth-century date.

An old topsoil of probable nineteenth-century date extended across Trench 7 and was cut by the step and path (F110 and F111) associated with the doorway (F175) leading to Dunne's bakery, suggesting that this layer represents the ground level during the use of the doorway. The recovery of a lead seal (E4619:109:1) lent credence to this interpretation. Stamped with inscriptions on both faces, it was identified as a flour-bag seal from the *Grands Moulins de Corbeil* mill in Paris, and it carried the date of March 1903 (Pl. 6.5). The presence of the seal at Swords Castle almost certainly relates to the adjacent bakery, owned by Patrick Dunne in the early 1900s. The Dunnes at this time appear to have been using imported French flour, which may have been considered superior to the local produce. A very worn coin (E4619:109:2) from here was identified as a farthing from the reign of William III (Pl. 6.6). The figure of Britannia narrows the range of minting to 1698–9. The obverse of the coin has been defaced by a countermarked 'SS' over the head of the monarch. From the nineteenth century onwards, slogans, initials and messages were stamped on coins as a means of protest or advertising or to create a personal token. The style of the countermark on the Swords example suggests that it is of a much later date than the coin, most probably nineteenth-century. As the coin would have been long out of circulation at that point, it would have had no use as either a form of protest or advertising. It is more likely, therefore, to have been a way of personalising the coin, either for use as a token or as a memento.

Pl. 6.6—William III farthing (E4619:109:2), countermarked 'SS' (photo: John Sunderland).

A wide range of pottery was recovered from this layer: Dublin-type cooking ware, Dublin-type ware, Dublin-type fineware, North Devon gravel-tempered ware, Seville coarseware, black-glazed earthenware (seventeenth–nineteenth century), unglazed red earthenware (eighteenth–nineteenth century) and modern white ware (nineteenth–twentieth century). Medieval DT2 ridge tile and SCT1 line-impressed floor tile and REW pantile were identified. A clay pipe mouthpiece fragment and iron nails were also recovered from this layer.

A three-sided wall formalising the step down to the threshold of the doorway (F175) to Dunne's bakery was set into a roughly dug pit which was infilled with mortar, trampled

cinders and a looser mortar-rich top (F110). A well-defined compacted path (F111) led to the blocked-up doorway. From here tin-glazed earthenware, a sherd of Leinster Cooking Ware, an unglazed marble/bottle-stopper and a clay pipe bowl (E4619:111:10) of Oswald's (1975) Type G17/G (1610–70) were recovered. A modern concentration (F108) of material was cut into the step feature F110. The deposit comprised a dump of shell, glass bottle fragments, nineteenth-century ceramics and clay pipe bowls. REW seventeenth-century narrow brick was also identified. A fragment of disarticulated human remains (E4619:108:9) was recovered from this deposit.

Within Trench 8 a modern gully aligned north–south contained a mix of plastic, modern pottery, Dublin-type ware, a decorated clay pipe stem (E4619:107:7) and disarticulated human remains (E4619:107:9). In the south-west corner of Trench 9 was a rectilinear pit (F122) which contained a mix of modern pottery, Dublin-type ware, Dublin-type cooking ware, Leinster Cooking Ware, and glass and iron detritus. Unsurprisingly given the presence of burials, the insertion of the later pit had disturbed the human remains. A range of disarticulated human remains (E4619:122:13) included femur, cranial, tooth, mandible, clavicle, tarsal, tibia, fibula, metatarsal, foot phalanx, radius, metacarpal, hand phalanx, vertebrae and rib fragments. Another pit (F128) located along the western baulk of Trench 9 cut into SK08. The pit contained roots and brick and was probably connected with orchard activity. Modern pottery, clay pipe and REW pantile were recovered, along with some disarticulated remains (E4619:128:7).

TOPSOIL

The topsoil (0.3–0.5m deep) across the site reflected the cultivation that had taken place within the precinct of Swords Castle into the early twentieth century. Friable and well-ploughed, it contained a mix of modern and medieval material. Some 2,959 fragments of animal bone were recovered from topsoil across the site and were assessed in terms of overall species frequency. Cattle (44%) and sheep (40%) were the dominant species, with pig (13%) the least well represented. Rabbit, dog, horse, domestic fowl, goose, duck and fish were present but generally modern in date. All parts of the skeleton were represented, suggesting local slaughter and dismemberment during the most recent phase of agricultural activity in the castle grounds. The range of ceramics retrieved from topsoil included medieval pottery (Dublin-type ware, Dublin-type fineware, Dublin-type coarseware, Leinster Cooking Ware, Ham Green ware, Saintonge green-glazed ware), post-medieval and early modern pottery (North Devon gravel-tempered ware, Anglo-Netherlands slipware, mottled ware, Frechen and other stoneware) and common wares (black-glazed, unglazed red earthenware, whiteware, transfer-printed wares and tin-glazed wares), as well as high-status ware (porcelain). The pottery assemblage represents a mix of local and imported medieval wares typical of contemporary sites, with the later wares reflecting use on site and manuring practices for cultivation.

The artefacts retrieved represented the mundane and the occasional and included items associated with personal attire, labour and leisure activities. It is difficult, however, to distinguish between artefacts initially disposed of at the castle and those introduced from elsewhere (for example, in manure brought in as fertiliser). Artefacts from the modern era associated with personal attire were primarily to do with men's clothing. These included eight buttons, three of which had surviving gilt or an inscription implying that they originally had gilt surfaces. All are likely to be from the nineteenth century and to have originally fastened waistcoats or coats. A decorated copper-alloy strap-adjuster (E4619:1:307) with a tinned surface was probably associated with men's braces in the late nineteenth or early twentieth century. Likewise, a range of buckles were recovered from topsoil. Although it was not always possible to distinguish those used in personal attire from those associated with horse equipment, a total of four buckle frames, a strap-loop and five loose buckle pins were identified. Among these was a shoe buckle (E4619:1:1037) of mid–late eighteenth-century date.

The clay pipe assemblage recovered appears to be predominantly nineteenth-century in date. This is perhaps unsurprising, as the bulk of the assemblage was recovered from the topsoil layer, associated with the use of the site as a garden and orchard throughout the nineteenth century. Other items reflect literacy and the presence of children. Two decorated clay pipe bowls (E4619:1:568 and E4619:1:331), featuring a ship and cockerel respectively, were identified as bubble pipes by virtue of their small size and design (Pl. 6.8). In the later nineteenth and early twentieth centuries, the use of clay pipes by children to blow bubbles is known from contemporary sources. Miniature pipes were also made especially for the purpose, particularly in England and Germany, and were even included with bags of sweets. A lead pencil-sharpener (E4619:1:1043), with blade still *in situ*, was of a style indicative of the late nineteenth century. A toy cap-gun was recovered from Trench 4, the mechanism for which was still largely intact. As with the sharpener, the design of the gun dated it to the late

Pl. 6.8—Children's bubble pipes (right and below) (E4619:1:331 and E4619:1:568) (photo: John Sunderland).

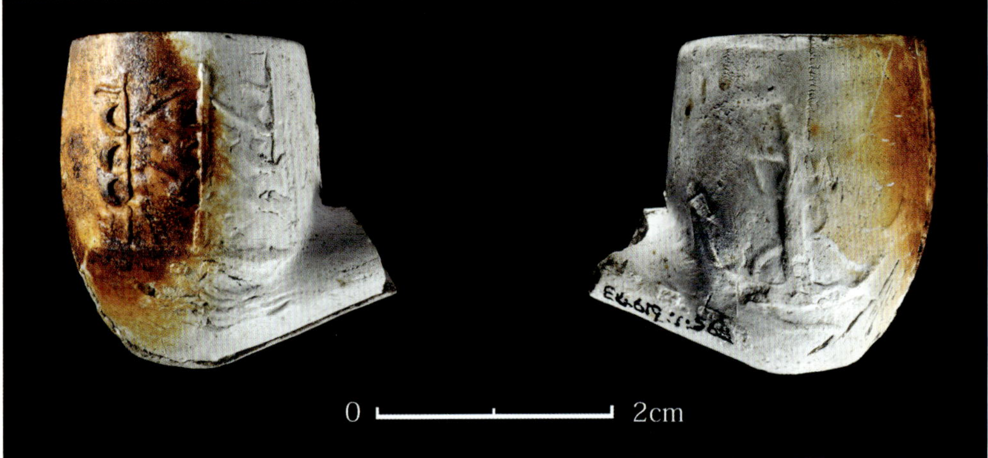

Pl. 6.9—Bone die (E4619:1:1045) (photo: John Sunderland).

Pl. 6.10—Trench 10 with 1971 plastic exposed.

nineteenth century. While both these items may have been stray losses at the site, it is more likely that they arrived at the site within refuse material intended for manure.

A small bone die (E4619:1:1045) was recovered from the topsoil in Trench 6 (Pl. 6.9). This was cut from a single piece of bone and is irregularly cuboid in shape, with evenly spaced 'dot-in-circle' roundels denoting values. The values on opposite faces add up to seven: this is known as the 'standard arrangement', found on dice since Roman times. The use of 'dot-in-circle' values appears to be characteristic of medieval dice both in England and Ireland, which suggests a potential medieval date for the die recovered from Swords, although owing to its unstratified provenance this cannot be stated with certainty.

In Trench 10 the upper layer consisted of overburden (F119), owing to one of the more recent activities on site—the backfilling of the Archbishop's Apartments with the spoil heaps created during Fanning's 1971 excavations. Given that this was the site of the medieval tile pavement, the presence of hundreds of small fragments of SCT1 floor tile was unsurprising. As elsewhere, the assemblage was mixed, with DR2 crested ridge tile and DT2 ridge tile, DT3 ridge tile and REW pantile recovered. The pottery was both medieval and modern, with Dublin-type ware, Frechen and other stoneware recovered alongside nineteenth- and twentieth-century earthenwares and white wares. As in all excavation trenches, disarticulated human remains (E4619:119:251), including vertebrae, rib, carpal, radius, hand phalanx, foot phalanx, metatarsal, tarsal and teeth, were recovered. Modern finds included nineteenth-century clay pipe fragments and the head of a toothbrush (E4619:119:2).

7

General discussion and conclusions

PHASE 1—PRE-ANGLO-NORMAN

Excavations uncovered evidence for activity from the late tenth century onwards, pre-dating the construction of Swords Castle. This evidence consisted of an enclosure ditch, burials, pits and post-holes, indicating structures and some agricultural activity taking place in eleventh- and twelfth-century Swords.

The ecclesiastical centre of Swords was surrounded by lesser foundations, either documented in the historical records or uncovered during archaeological investigations. As outlined above, there is an association with St Brigit and the *Dísert Brigte*, a hermitage or foundation for women. MacShamhráin posits that there may have been a cluster of women's foundations in and around Swords. The foundresses of *Tech Ingen mBáiti*, Eithen and Sodelb, were listed among the 'Holy Virgins of Ireland' and mentioned in the late eighth-century Martyrology of Tallaght. Another manuscript notes that their foundation was *taeb Suirt* (beside Swords) (MacShamhráin 2016, 56). A site mentioned in the historical record but with a disputed location is that of Glás Mór. Associated with St Crónán, the church was recorded in the Martyrology of Óengus as being attacked and the entire community slaughtered in one night by 'the foreigners of *Inber Domnann*' (*ibid.*, 58). Glás Mór is recorded as being located south of Swords, unlike the building with medieval inserts that is known as Glasmore Abbey (DU011-019) to the north-west of Swords. The foundation at Glás Mór appears not to have recovered from the Viking attack and was described in the ninth century as a 'desolate church' (Stokes 1905).

Archaeological investigations uncovered an extensive early medieval site (DU011-144001) bordering the townlands of Oldtown and Mooretown, consisting of a large (200m in diameter) enclosure, centred on burials, and a field system. The site is not associated with any of the historical documentation regarding religious foundations (Baker 2010) and may fall into the contemporary category of cemetery settlement. These, like ecclesiastical sites, were laid out with central burial enclosure, radial divisions, outer enclosures and associated field systems but are secular and generally have left no folkloric, hagiographic or cartographic record. Within Swords town, on the high ground to the east of the River Ward, was a burial place at Mount Gamble (now the Pavilions shopping centre). There were no historical indications of a burial site prior to excavation. In use from *c.* AD 550 to 1150, it appears to represent the burial place of a small local population, perhaps several generations of a family or members of a tribal group. Analysis of the graves showed a variety of grave types and body positions, which may reflect the different status of individuals buried there. The burials represented a broad spectrum of the local population, with all ages and sexes identified. No clear divisions were identified to distinguish where men or women were buried. Interestingly, six men between the ages of 23 and 44 displayed evidence of weapon-related injuries. All were robust, tall (5cm taller than the average male population of the period) males who had suffered stab wounds. Three had been subjected to sword blows and two had been decapitated. Radiocarbon dating revealed, however, that these burials were not contemporary but that the men had met their respective ends during the eighth and ninth centuries in separate violent incidents (O'Donovan 2009).

Three areas of *in situ* burial have been identified within Swords Castle. In 1971, excavations by Tom Fanning uncovered a total of 25 burials in an area that extended northwards from the current Chapel almost to the East Tower. On the basis of the shallow nature of the interments, Fanning (1975, 60) suggested that the 'bawn had been re-used as a graveyard when the castle was no longer occupied'. A total of seventeen burials were identified under the Gatehouse arch during excavations in 2015. This was an area of dense stratigraphy, although dating evidence suggests burials occurring within a 200-year period from the early eleventh century to the late thirteenth century. Season 3 of the *Swords Castle: Digging History* excavations identified a total of fifteen *in situ* burials immediately west of the East Tower and north of Fanning's burials. They were uncovered just 10cm below the current ground level and ranged in date from the late tenth century to the late twelfth century. A substantial enclosure ditch (F85) of contemporary date was also identified, although not immediately enclosing the burials. There was evidence for tenth- and eleventh-century settlement activity between the ditch and the burials. Clearly there was an enclosed burial site at the northern end of a high ridge that overlooked the River Ward within view of the main ecclesiastical centre of Swords Colm-Cille and the familial burial-ground of Mount Gamble, in use during the latter centuries of the early medieval period.

What the burials tell us

Fanning's excavation, 1971

While Fanning published the results of his 1971 excavation, the references to the burials are limited. Unfortunately the archive is also incomplete, although Fanning's site notebook and finds catalogue survive. From these and the surviving photographs it can be ascertained that at least 25 burials were uncovered. Those up to Burial VIII are described, a Burial 14 is referenced, and then there is an allusion to '11 more burials'. Described as being orientated on an east–west axis, the burials were considered highly disturbed, with three within slab-lined graves. Burial VIII could be identified on plan and in photographs. It was described by Fanning in his notebook as 'full skeletal remains—in situ—arms extended by the side, all leg bone complete. The cist had no covering and was supressed by the slabs laid on edge. Feet together. On the south a stone missing. The S lower leg bone broken. Slightly south of the cist at a higher level are the remains of a child—orientation more NW (skull frags). Further uncovering has revealed adult remains probably female in south baulk.'

Burial X was also identifiable from photographs. It was described as the 'most complete skeleton recovered'; 'a number of extraneous bones (leg) lie northwards beyond the skull and to the west. Beside this body directly south lies another skeleton Burial XI part disarticulated particularly the skull with only a small portion of the big bones remaining. NB. A feature of these burials is the presence of shells—mainly cockle with some oyster.'

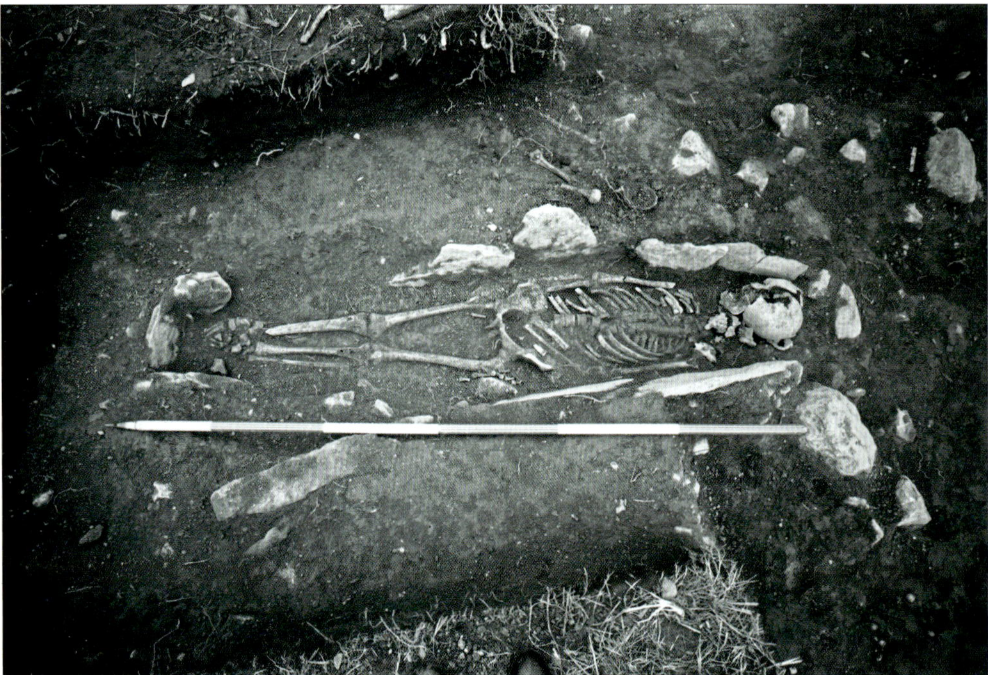

Pl. 7.1—Burial VIII, looking south (courtesy of the National Monuments Service).

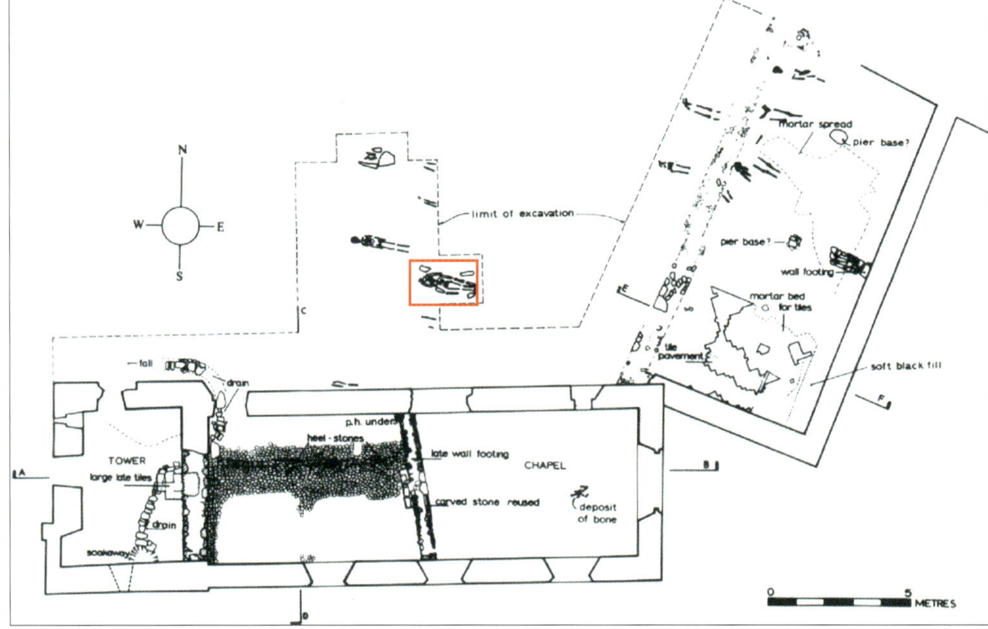

Fig. 7.1—Burial VIII highlighted in Fanning's 1971 post-excavation plan (after Fanning 1975).

Fanning noted that the burials and 'collections of bone' which were uncovered about 25–30cm below the present ground level lay in the yellow clay identified as natural subsoil and that this subsoil sloped upwards appreciably, reflecting the topography of the site. The investigation being of its time, no analysis of the skeletal remains was undertaken. There are three references to a 'child being involved' and one to a possible female skeleton. None of the burials were accompanied by grave-goods. One of the objectives of the *Swords Castle:*

Pl. 7.2—Burial X (right) and Burial XI, looking west (courtesy of the National Monuments Service).

Pl. 7.3—SK.15 under Chamber Block wall (courtesy of Mark Moraghan).

Digging History project was to locate Fanning's burials and submit the remains for analysis. To date, however, this has not proved possible, as neither the National Museum of Ireland nor the National Monuments Service has any record of the burials. Nor did surviving visitors to the site at the time have any memory of them. Indeed, it has been surmised that the burials were left *in situ* and reburied (Con Manning, pers. comm.).

Gatehouse excavations, 2014 (after Tobin 2015)
In contrast, the seventeen burials identified during the 2014 excavation undertaken by IAC Ltd (C450/E4376) were subject to osteological analysis and radiocarbon dating. Located under the Gatehouse arch, the 2015 burials appeared to be a continuation of the burials identified by Fanning in the 1970s *c.* 30m to the north-east within the castle yard. Of the eleven burials fully excavated at this time, four were subject to radiocarbon dating. While the dense stratigraphy of the burial area would indicate a long period of use, the dating evidence suggests that the burials occurred roughly between the early eleventh century and the late thirteenth century. The latest-dated burial, Skeleton 5, a late adolescent/adult, returned an AMS result of AD 1190–1281 (784±34 BP; UBA-29339). Sk. 5 was identified securely below the western wall of the Gatehouse, providing a *terminus post quem* for the construction of that structure and indicating that burial was still taking place here even as elements of Swords Castle were being constructed.

The individuals identified at the Gatehouse comprised seven juveniles and ten late adolescents or adults. The juveniles appeared to fall into two broad 'age at death' categories: young child (*c.* 3–6 years) and young adolescent (*c.* 12–15 years). It was only possible to accurately age and sex three adult individuals, who were identified as middle adult females. Stature was estimated for these three females (Sk. 8, Sk. 10 and Sk. 12, dated to AD 1022– 1182; 935±36 BP; UBA-29341) and ranged from *c.* 153.4cm to 154.1cm (± standard deviation), which falls significantly short of the mean results from the known population in Mount Gamble. The burials largely conformed to a rough east–west pattern, but three deviated from this norm. Sk. 14, a young child, was aligned north–south high/late in the stratigraphy, possibly indicating a later clandestine insertion. Sk. 15, another young child, lay north-east/south-west and had been truncated by the east wall of the Chamber Block (Pl. 7.3).

Most interesting was the prone burial of Sk. 8, dated to AD 1043–1222 (9879±29 BP; UBA-29340), which had the appearance of a careless, rushed interment. This middle adult female displayed evidence for general non-specific infection (active at the time of death) and a long-standing trauma to the left elbow joint. A possible token or coin (E4376:70:3) appeared to have been placed in or by her right hand. The coin had degraded and survived as an impression in the soil. The remains of Sk. 7, an adolescent, had been removed from his or her grave to facilitate the burial of Sk. 8 and was then reinterred with the body of the middle adult female. It was clear that the remains of Sk. 7 had been skeletonised at the time of their disturbance, indicating a significant passage of time between the two burials. Intermingled with the disarticulated remains of Sk. 7, in the fill of the grave for Sk. 8 a twelfth–thirteenth-century copper-alloy stick-pin (E4376:70:2) and a copper-alloy riveted plate (E4376:70:1) were retrieved. Another interesting case was that of a young child, Sk. 9, dated to AD 1034–1204 (909±30 BP; UBA-29341). Two sheep scapulae (shoulders) appeared to have been placed on either side of the body in a grave cut that was wider than necessary. An adult fibula appears to have been placed directly across the neck of the body

Pl. 7.4—SK14 and SK09, looking north.

during burial. If this was a deliberate action, it may perhaps have been an attempt to connect this juvenile with a predeceased adult relative.

Swords Castle: Digging History excavations (after Lynch, this volume)
In total, fourteen burials (including one unexcavated) and 3,524 fragments of disarticulated human bones and teeth were excavated over the course of the three seasons of archaeological investigation. Unfortunately, the level of preservation of the *in situ* skeletons was very poor. The majority were adult individuals; just one juvenile individual was present, aged between six and eight years at the time of death. No young adults (18–25 years) were present and many were aged between 26 and 44 years at the time of death. The sex of 75% of the observable adults could be determined, showing a possible bias towards females (77.8%). It was only possible to estimate the stature of a single adult: the stature of one female, AMS-dated to the first half of the eleventh century, was estimated as 166.3cm. This limited evidence suggests that she was taller than her average contemporary.

Unusual biological artefacts were recovered with two of the burials. Multiple small, relatively smooth nodules were recovered with SK11 (?sex, adult), and at least one large and another much smaller mass of globular bone-like formation or calcification were recovered with SK01 (female, 45+ years). These were tentatively identified as some form of calcification associated with the lungs, possibly linked with tuberculosis. All of the disarticulated skeletal remains from the three seasons were considered together in order to establish an overall minimum number of individuals (MNI). The evidence indicates an MNI of eight individuals: four juveniles (<18 years) and four adults (18+ years), with the remains of at least one infant (<1 year), one young juvenile (1–6 years), one older juvenile (7–12 years), and one possible adolescent (12–17 years).

Three burials were subject to radiocarbon dating. Despite being recovered from different levels, the burials showed a degree of similarity in date range, indicating that the burial-ground was in use between the tenth and twelfth centuries. Skeleton 15 (E4619:163:41) was at a lower level than the other burials and returned a date range of AD 994–1059 (UBA-38842); Skeleton 14 (E4619:157:1) survived as a truncated supine burial (possible female, adult) and returned a date range of AD 995–1153 (UBA-38841). SK01 (possible female, adult 45+) (E4619:132:1) was identified just 0.05m below the current ground level and returned a date range of AD 996–1185 (UBA-38840). The dating of two fragments of disarticulated bone correlated with the *in situ* burials: a single vertebra (E4619:29:1) from Trench 3 returned a date range of AD 1065–1154 (UBA-32452), and a fragment of cranial vault (E4619:101:3) of an adult (45+) recovered from a post-hole in Trench 4 returned a range of AD 936–1013 (UBA-34515).

The analysis of the 2017 burials and the Gatehouse burials, while recognising the limitations of a very small sample size, indicated a possible bias towards female burial, with most of the identifiable skeletons from both excavations being female. Another possible ambiguity was the lack of infant (<1 year) burials. A single infant bone was identified among the 3,424 disarticulated bones in the 2015–17 excavations; none were identified in the Gatehouse excavations and Fanning's report only refers to 'children' in the burials uncovered in 1971. Based on the current data, it is possible that infants were excluded from burial areas of the cemetery or that a specific area of the cemetery was designated for such burials.

The date ranges from both modern excavations reveal a burial-ground active between the late tenth century and the late twelfth century, with later burial activity taking place downslope at the Gatehouse. While heavily constricted by the small sample size of 24 excavated skeletons (thirteen in 2017, eleven in 2014) and an assemblage of disarticulated remains, the following observations were made. The majority were women aged between 26 and 44 years at the time of death. Many were smaller than average for the period, perhaps reflecting poor nutrition during childhood. There was one exception (166.3cm or 5ft 5in.) who was considerably taller than the females buried (154cm or 5ft) at the Gatehouse (and, indeed, most of her peers), which could suggest less physiological stresses and perhaps higher status. Dental health, where it could be assessed, was very poor and was indicative of poor general health and nutrition. One middle-aged woman had lost four teeth in her lifetime, as well as suffering cavities and a large abscess. Another adult had tooth defects which indicated periods of stress and possibly starvation in early childhood, while there were examples of gum disease, cavities and lesions. Many teeth, particularly in the disarticulated assemblage, were worn down to their roots, reflecting the coarse dietary intake of the early medieval period. The population also suffered degenerative joint disease, with the spine in particular being affected. This was generally the result of repetitive work such as lifting and carrying. Traumas were minor: a healed broken finger, a stress fracture in the spine, a healed fracture to a toe bone and a displaced elbow. Infectious disease indicators were generally not noted but this may have been due to the state of preservation of the skeletons. The exception was the rarely found biological inclusions that indicated that at least one woman had suffered a pulmonary disease, possibly TB, and that another had kidney stones. Overall, the burials, including the observed skeletal and dental pathological indicators, are largely what might be expected from an early medieval cemetery, revealing the trials of life with hard work, poor nutrition and without modern medicine.

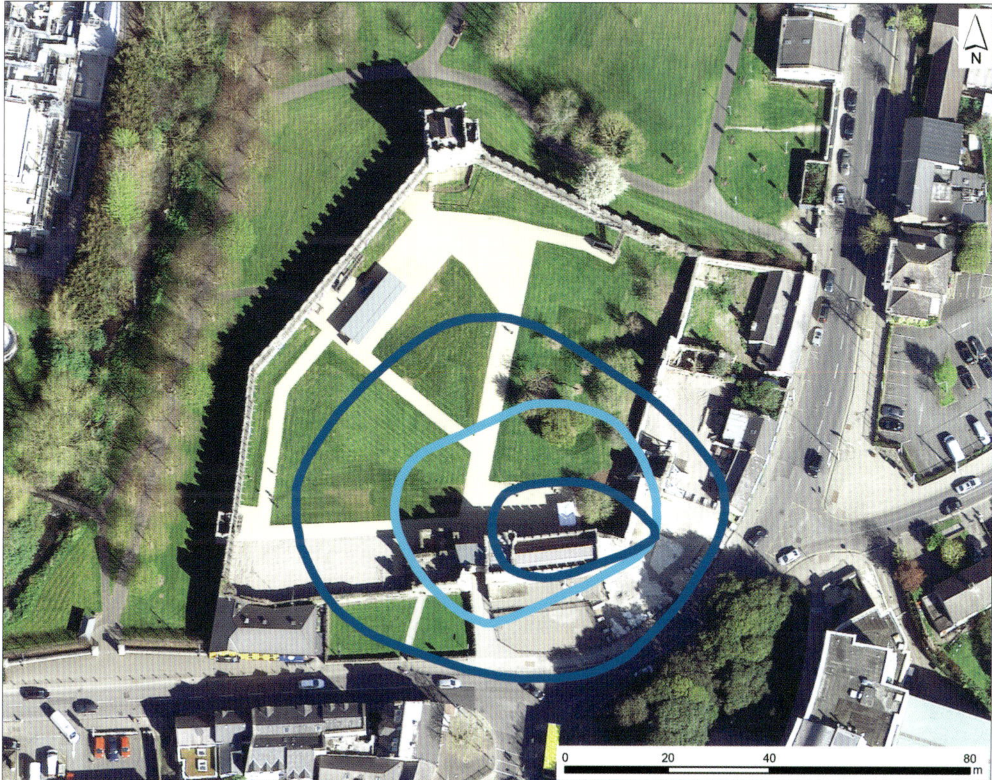

Pl. 7.5—Suggested early medieval enclosure layout, based on archaeological results and townland boundary.

Cemetery settlement or St Brigit's Church?

Until the Church reorganisation that began in the eleventh century there was significant diversity in the layout of burial-grounds. Archaeological evidence shows that they could be enclosed, unenclosed, liminal or centralised, either with ecclesiastical communities or within the secular sphere. The latter, categorised as cemetery settlements, were similar in layout to the ecclesiastical sites, with a number of enclosures centred on burials but with evidence for settlement and habitation and none for religious associations. Excavations at Swords Castle uncovered a large (*c.* 4m wide) rock-cut enclosure ditch dating from the same period as the burials, although at some remove. Between the ditch and burials was evidence for contemporaneous activity, exemplified by a number of pits. There was also evidence for similar activity, post-holes and deposits, beyond the enclosure ditch, indicating that this ditch possibly formed the middle enclosure of a large site. Further west on Bridge Street, a rock-cut ditch had been identified *c.* 2.2m south of the Swords Castle curtain wall (Swan 1992). It was *c.* 4.5m wide but was not excavated and was interpreted by Swan as a moat. Could this have been part of an enclosure ditch instead?

The extent of the *in situ* burials defined by the excavations—and, more tellingly, their absence—infers an inner enclosing element extending from just north of the East Tower downslope to west of the Gatehouse, a diameter of *c.* 30m. Intriguingly, below the burials at the Gatehouse was a subrectangular structure, cut though subsoil down to bedrock. Ash roundwoods dated to AD 1026–1166 (928±30 BP; UBA-29345) appear to have been laid on the bedrock and deliberately charred before being covered in lime mortar. There was a stepped entrance by which a timber revetment had been erected, near which were the remains of a wall. The formation layer for the wall returned an AMS result of AD 1029–1183 (919±28 BP; UBA-29344). To the north were boundary ditches which contained animal bone, shell and a silver 'bracteate' coin (E4376:122:1) dating from between the twelfth and fourteenth centuries (Moraghan *et al.* 2016). The date ranges for the structure and the burials are relatively contemporary, although the structure was stratigraphically below the burials in this area.

As both ecclesiastical and cemetery settlements have a similar morphology, attempts have been made to define both beyond just their burials and enclosures. Swan (1983) listed criteria such as a founder's tomb, church structures and crosses, a holy well, a place-name associated with an ecclesiastical element, the incorporation of a townland boundary, a souterrain and folk ritual as defining elements of an ecclesiastical site (all of which can be applied to the main ecclesiastical site of Swords). Others, such as Stout and Stout (2008), have assigned common features such as low-lying locations (less than 50m OD), proximity to rivers, streams or waterlogged areas, and enclosures averaging 50–70m in diameter to cemetery settlements. The location of the burial and enclosure site at Swords Castle is beside the River Ward and less than 20m OD. The extent of the site cannot be defined, as the ground beyond the castle walls to the east and south has been scarped and truncated. The townland boundary coincides with the curved roadway south-east of Swords Castle, which could have formed part of an enclosing element, and there is a tentative association with the church of St Brigit in the form of a description of the latter's having been located to the north of the town, close to the gates of the old palace.

The archaeological evidence indicates a burial site, enclosure and associated activity dating from the tenth century and into the transition period of Anglo-Norman settlement. Historical sources tell us that this was a period of extended conflict with the Irish dynasties, as the Scandinavian kingship sought to consolidate its territorial kingdom centred on Dublin. As an ecclesiastical and economic centre in the hinterland of Dublin, Swords was subject to repeated attacks throughout the eleventh century. It is within this context that we see a population of hard-working, poorly nourished women and children being buried at the site where Swords Castle was constructed.

PHASE 2—MEDIEVAL

After the Anglo-Norman invasion of 1169, the property of the ecclesiastical centre of Swords formed part of the lands of the see of Dublin, confirmed to Archbishop Laurence O'Toole in 1179 (McNeill 1950). The extensive lands attached to the archbishopric were administered through manorial centres, of which Swords was one, the principal manor being that of St Sepulchre's, close to St Patrick's Cathedral in Dublin. John Comyn was appointed archbishop of Dublin in 1181 and is generally credited with the building of Swords Castle in 1200 (Dalton 1838b; Reeves 1970 [1860]). As outlined above, there is evidence that burial at Swords Castle continued into the late twelfth and thirteenth centuries in parts of the cemetery while construction was taking place over other parts of the site. Just how deliberate was the siting of the castle? Was this a very definite attempt by the newly established Anglo-Normans to stake their claim by literally building their manorial centre over an Irish burial-ground of significant size? It is interesting to note that drainage works at Comyn's other foundation, St Sepulchre's, in 1926 unearthed three human burials (two adults and a child), and disarticulated human remains were recovered from redeposited subsoil there during excavations in 2019, leading the excavator to conclude that 'the site was a burial ground at an early stage before building works in the late twelfth century' (Hayden 2020, 295).

The recognition of the proximal distribution of mottes and pre-Norman high-status sites, both secular and ecclesiastical, points to a deliberate consolidation of pre-existing territories. Primarily military, administrative and cultural, Anglo-Norman influence was based on installing a knight in pre-existing territories. Integral to the granting of land was a devotion to the Church and a commitment to the development of the parish system, and there are examples of sites being chosen beside 'old ruined churches' (Baker 2010). In the context of Swords, this pattern may be seen in the founding of the archbishop's manorial centre on or near what was perhaps the old church of St Brigid. The site was also of strategic importance. Located at the end of a high ridge above the River Ward, the site of Swords Castle was near a fording point and a source of building stone, within sight of Malahide estuary and at the confluence of the road north and the road into Meath. It was also a physical and visual counterpoint to the long-established ecclesiastical centre on the high ground on the other side of the river, and thus an effective statement of administrative power.

Influence of John Comyn, archbishop of Dublin 1181–1212

John Comyn, often characterised as an English Benedictine monk, was primarily a court official and administrator, and it was for these talents that he was rewarded with the archbishopric of Dublin. A clerk, judge and court official for twenty years, he had been ordained an archdeacon of Bath in 1167, without being ordained a priest, and spent his time in the service of King Henry II in the courts of Europe (O'Donovan 2003, 254). Elected archbishop of Dublin at Evesham on 6 September 1181, Comyn was a cosmopolitan figure who proved to be in no hurry to take up his office, not arriving in Dublin until 1184. In the meantime he had consolidated his position, both spiritually and politically, by being ordained a priest, and he was consecrated archbishop by Pope Lucius III, who also, 'by a bull dated the 13th of April, 1182, took under his especial protection, and confirmed to this see, the manor of Swords, with its church and other appurtenances' (Dalton 1838b, 71). On the occasion of Prince John's visit and Comyn's arrival, the king conferred upon Comyn the lands of Coillagh 'in barony tenure'. By this right he became a lord of parliament and was the first Irish archbishop to be invested with feudal and baronial rights (*ibid.*).

In 1186 Archbishop Comyn held a provincial synod in Dublin, the extents of which included directions on altars and the placement of baptismal fonts but also on taxes and tithes. It was directed that 'tithes be paid to the mother churches out of provisions, hay, the young of animals, flax, wool, gardens, orchards, and out of all things that grow and renew yearly, under pain of an anathema after the third monition' (*ibid.*, 75). Grants made to the archbishop by Prince John as lord of Ireland gave Comyn further independence so that he could rule the manor of St Sepulchre (which included the manor of Swords) as a liberty. This meant that the archbishop exercised both temporal and spiritual authority over the citizens of the liberty (O'Donovan 2003, 255). As a way of expanding both the income of the archiepiscopal manor and the influence of the 'English', Comyn established a new town along what is now Main Street, Swords. In 1197 King Richard I granted a charter to Swords

whereby each burgess was to pay 12d per annum. Burgages were laid out on either side of the street leading to Swords Castle. Prospective burgesses were offered the same liberties and free customs as those of the citizens of Dublin. Comyn had also been granted a patent to hold an annual fair lasting eight days from the feast of St Columcille on 9 June; revenue from the stallholders would have contributed to the archbishop's income (Stalley 2006, 164).

Although there is no explicit reference to the construction of Swords Castle, the murder of the archbishop's constable, William Galrotte, is recorded 'at the gate of the court of Swords', confirming the presence of an enclosure. As the main street is aligned with the castle, it seems likely that the manor's administrative centre, court and town were planned by Comyn, the most likely date of its foundation being between 1185 and 1190 (*ibid.*; O'Donovan 2003, 269).

The story of the stone

Most of the stone found in the buildings of Swords Castle is a Dublin calp limestone. Used extensively in Dublin, it would have been quarried from the underlying bedrock in the vicinity of the site. Bedrock is recorded less than 2m below the surface in Swords. Close inspection of the extant structures has shown that the stone used varied in quality, that of the East Tower being of particularly low quality and workmanship. Analysis has also found that the mortar used in the East Tower, unlike the surrounding buildings, does not contain pozzolan fragments (crushed ceramic), which may indicate a different phase of construction.

Pl. 7.6—Archbishop's Apartments, East Tower and Great Hall: external view prior to 2016 enabling works.

All mortars except that used in the Double Gable (Great Hall) contained crushed shell. The mortar used to construct the walls was a lime mortar using a coarse grit as a binder and had been poorly mixed in the construction of the eastern range of buildings (Bolton 2016). The stone is mid-grey when dry, turning darker when wet, although it is important to remember that at the time of use the limestone would have been rendered to prevent water ingress. Remnants of sandy render are visible on the south wall of the Gatehouse.

Several sources for the limestone used to construct the castle are known within the town of Swords. The first-edition Ordnance Survey map records numerous quarries in use in the early nineteenth century along the River Ward towards the base of the stone ridge that forms the main street. Excavation at Church Road near the site of the old vicarage revealed two phases of medieval outcrop quarrying (O'Carroll 2008), but a more convenient location was on Bridge Street, across from the south wall of the castle. Here archaeological investigations identified a bedrock scarp which may have been exposed to weathering for some time, a layer of shattered bedrock under a layer that produced thirteenth–fourteenth-century pottery and backfilling through to the nineteenth century (Halpin 1999).

The remainder of the stone used around window and door opes was for decorative purposes; it included Dundry stone and yellow and red sandstones, which were not sourced locally. Waterman in his 1970 work on foreign building stone in medieval Ireland had identified Dundry stone dressing within the Gatehouse block, the building west of the entrance and in the Constable's Tower. The dressings of the Chapel and Double Gable were identified as red sandstone. Occasional pieces of oolite were incorporated into the walls of the Gatehouse and Chapel, while Cotswold oolite and possible Painswick stone occur in the entrance block (Waterman 1970, 72).

Dundry stone was sourced at Dundry Hill near Bristol. An Inferior Oolite, it is composed of minute fragments of shell, coral and algae with a distinctive creamy or yellowish colour

Pl. 7.7—Dundry stone, Gatehouse, Swords Castle.

(*ibid.*, 63). The distribution of Dundry stone in Ireland reflected the heart of the Anglo-Norman colony on the south-east coast and in Dublin. The use of imported stone at Christ Church may be associated with the arrival of Archbishop John Comyn, who was familiar with the architecture of western England (O'Donovan 2003, 254). His connections with Glastonbury, in particular, provided him with an accessible supply of oolitic limestone, as the monks of Glastonbury used the quarries in Somerset. Given Comyn's association with Swords Castle, it is therefore unsurprising that Dundry stone should also have been used there.

Apart from their working properties, these stones held some ritual and symbolic significance for the Anglo-Normans (Moss 2006, 75). Dundry stone, with its yellow-golden colour, is believed to have been in essence a symbol of Heaven, representing physical light in the world, and it was used throughout the thirteenth century in doorways, chancel arches and the windows of churches. It was also reflective of wealth and social status. Its use in the Gatehouse of Swords Castle is therefore not coincidental but rather a display of the power of the Anglo-Norman administration. Imported stone was undoubtedly a display of Anglo-Norman wealth, power and prestige, besides reflecting the close trade links between Bristol and the south-east coast of Ireland. The Anglo-Normans, however, were also aware of the propaganda value of an impressive new structure, and the use of imported stone contributed to this (O'Brien 2014).

Red, too, was a symbolic colour in religious iconography, as it represented the blood of Christ and the Pentecostal fire. In the Christian calendar, red is also the liturgical colour used for feasts of the Apostles and martyrs. At Dunbrody, Co. Wexford, the mixture of red sandstone and Dundry stone may have represented the light of heaven, the blood of Christ

Pl. 7.8—Gothic window, double ope, internal view and detail.

and the Resurrection (Van Leeuwen 2011, 16). At Swords a similar combination of red sandstone and Dundry stone at the Gatehouse has been interpreted as a later repair. During the enabling works, the erection of scaffolding allowed for an examination of the window in the Double Gable (or Great Hall). The upper tracery was separated from the upright elements by slate. Although predominantly red sandstone, there were occasional blocks of yellow sandstone or possible Dundry stone, again reflecting this mixture of red and yellow stone.

Fragments of carved and dressed stone had been recovered on site at Swords Castle during the 1990s works, and further examples (including roll and fillets etc.) were recovered during excavation. Three examples of carved stone from the castle were subject to analysis (Sevastopulo 2014). The results showed that they were probably from similar beds in a source quarry which almost certainly contained rocks of Mesozoic age. This type of rock is limited to the north-east of Ireland but is widespread in England. The Swords examples were consistent with Sherwood Sandstone; the closest source to Dublin is the Cheshire Basin, but the formation is widespread in the midlands, south Wales and south-west England. The distribution of imported stone in Ireland highlights the reliance on water-borne transport for the haulage of heavy materials, thus reducing costs to the Anglo-Normans during a period of expansion. Carved stone may have been delivered directly to the sites, and any transportation over land would have covered only a short distance. Swords Castle was next to the River Ward and within sight of Malahide estuary. Owing to the great demand for stone during the building campaigns, dimensions and templates would have been provided by the master mason to the banker mason at the quarry. It is quite possible that the likes of Dundry stone were worked and dressed to specific measurements and styles with the use of templates and shipped to their destination in Ireland in their finished state (O'Brien 2014).

In the absence of documentation or historical sources, the reasons for the use of imported limestone in Ireland can only be presumed. Aesthetic reasons may have perhaps been one of the main factors, associated with the desires of both mason and patron. Imported Dundry and other types of stone are connected to a variety of individuals and in certain areas, such as William Marshal on the south-east coast and Archbishop Comyn in the Dublin region. The decline of the importation of stone into Ireland began during the latter half of the thirteenth century and continued throughout the fourteenth century. This was in no small part due to the decline in the Anglo-Norman colony resulting from the Bruce invasion and pressure from the Gaelic Irish. The Black Death, in the mid-fourteenth century, took a heavy toll on masons and resulted in the decline of imported products (O'Brien 2014). The imported stone at Swords Castle may have been 'reused or cannibalized' (Stalley 2006, 165), but the presence of Dundry stone does indicate buildings of style here from the late twelfth or early thirteenth century.

Layout of Swords Castle

Swords Castle is not a castle in the accepted sense and was not referred to as such until the fifteenth century. Contemporary sources referred to it as the 'court' or 'manor' of Swords. Although also termed an episcopal or bishop's palace, it was in reality a manor house. John Comyn, who founded the manor of Swords, is also credited with the construction of St Sepulchre's, the main residence of the archbishops of Dublin, as he 'planted the palace down beside the collegiate church' (O'Donovan 2003, 255). Both St Sepulchre's and Swords Castle were built at a similar time for the same archbishop, and both fulfilled similar functions as a residence and as an ecclesiastical and temporal court. Swords Castle was, however, a fortified manor house, built as an administrative centre for the archbishop's northern estates, something reflected in its layout.

O'Donovan (2003, 263) put forward the theory that St Sepulchre's was planned using a geometrical method known as *ad quadratum*. It is believed that medieval builders laid out buildings using rope and pegs, and set down a general plan based on ratios and proportions to achieve rectangular building ranges. Using this technique, St Sepulchre's may have been laid out around a rectangular courtyard in a single campaign. Archaeological investigations at the site revealed, however, that the proposed southern range did not exist and that medieval buildings were present within the courtyard. Instead, there appears to have been a range of buildings south of the present palace, which were demolished probably in the late fifteenth century (Hayden 2020, 315).

It is clear that Swords Castle was constructed in different phases, expanding from what is considered the earliest stone structure, the East Tower. As it survives, Swords Castle consists of a group of buildings forming the eastern and south-eastern ranges and a polygonal ward made by the curtain walls. Within the site, the ground slopes down towards the Ward River with an overall fall of 4.3m. The area enclosed by the curtain walls and building ranges is 5,730 square metres, the substantial size underlining the extent of administrative activities. Three seasons of excavation and investigations undertaken for the 2016 enabling works revealed evidence for structures within the enclosed area.

East Tower

The earliest structure appears to be the East Tower, on the highest point of the north–south

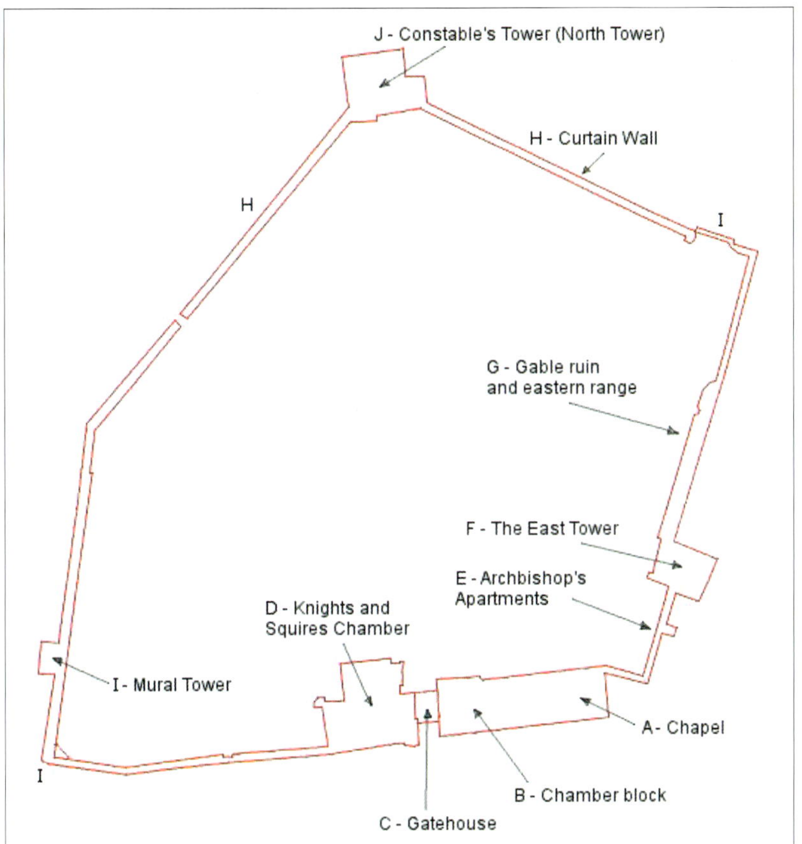

Fig. 7.3—Current layout of Swords Castle.

ridge, above the Ward River. The placing of the tower in line with the Main Street probably dates from the earliest stages of development during Comyn's time (1181–1212) (O'Donovan 2003, 269). The width of the walls (1.05m thick) is suggestive of an early date for the structure (Fingal County Council 2014, 58). Analysis has also found that the mortar used in the East Tower, unlike that in the surrounding buildings, does not contain pozzolan fragments, which may indicate a different phase of construction. Standing two storeys in height over a barrel vault at ground level, the tower is missing its west wall, while the north wall is severely truncated owing to collapse after Hurricane Charlie in 1985. At first-floor level there are two windows with embrasures and distinctive 'keyhole'-shaped opes. Investigations to inform the 2016 enabling works comprised the excavation of two small test trenches at the northern façade of the tower. The footings of the East Tower were identified and the foundation of just three courses was exposed. This means that the exterior base of the East Tower is between just 20cm and 40cm below current ground level. Along the southern façade, an arch at the base of the tower at its junction with the Archbishop's Apartments, and partly concealed by the latter, was exposed. As part of the 2015 season of excavation, Pit D was excavated at the north-western corner of the East Tower, where the undercroft arch abuts a wall of later construction. The foundation of the arch was 0.9m high and consisted of mortared stone, becoming increasingly rubble-like towards its base.

During Season 3, Trench 9 was positioned so as to identify the 'missing' wall of the East Tower. The foundation stones of the west wall of the East Tower were exposed for 2.2m

Pl. 7.9—Arch at base of East Tower, southern façade.

north–south, truncating the earlier tenth–twelfth-century burials within the trench. Apparently robbed out, the remaining large, unshaped limestone blocks were within a compact orange-brown stony clay deposit, *c.* 1.2m in width. The backfill of the wall trench contained animal bone and a sherd of Dublin-type ware. At the junction of the truncated southern wall of the East Tower and the removed west wall there was a rounded plinth of mortared stone (1.62m east–west by 1.6m north–south) that survived to three courses in height (0.35m). The base of the plinth was not exposed owing to the presence of human skeletal remains, specifically the remains of SK15, which returned a radiocarbon date of AD 994–1059 (UBA-38842). Also present before the construction of the East Tower was a ditch. Identified in the test excavation for the enabling works, it extended south-south-eastwards to the exterior of the castle and was exposed for a width of 0.7m. It contained animal bone and detritus consistent with demolition and was defined by the arch in the southern façade of the East Tower.

Archbishop's Apartments

The interior of the Archbishop's Apartments, as this building which constitutes the 12m-long south-eastern section of Swords Castle is now called, was excavated by Tom Fanning in 1971. It was within the southern section of this building that Fanning uncovered the early fourteenth-century medieval tiled pavement. Externally the structure is characterised by two relieving arches, the tops of which are also visible internally. The contrast in present ground level internally and externally is most marked here, with a difference of approximately 1.8m. The building was 6m wide, and the foundation layer of the west wall was uncovered by Fanning. Also identified by Fanning (1975, 62) was an east–west wall footing which probably

Pl. 7.10—Ditch under Archbishop's Apartments aligned with arch of East Tower.

formed part of an internal partition. Corbel stones at first-floor level suggest that the floor consisted of timber beams and planks. There is considerable evidence for alteration and additions in this building, such as the insertion of a fireplace and chimney, probably in the fifteenth or sixteenth century. An ogee-headed window in the south gable is typical of the fourteenth century.

As described above, test excavation outside the castle identified a ditch. The east wall of the Archbishop's Apartments was built directly over the ditch towards its northern end. This may account for the expansion of the width of the wall in this area (from 0.82m at the south to 1.2m at the north), for greater stability. Analysis of animal bone deposits indicates redeposition and suggests backfilling. The presence of large quantities of render and burnt timber is also suggestive of relatively rapid backfilling, probably to facilitate the construction of the structure. The relieving arch constructed over this ditch to assist in load-bearing would also indicate knowledge of unsound ground in the area, such as a relatively recently infilled ditch. The recovery of stratified sherds of medieval pottery, and specifically a sherd of imported Saintonge ware directly under the building's walls, implies that the construction of the Archbishop's Apartments must post-date at least the twelfth century. This building was also constructed against the southern façade of the East Tower across the earlier ditch and partially obscuring the arch at the base of the East Tower. A stone arch in the southern façade of the East Tower at first-floor level is a form described as a 'Caernarfon arch'. This arrangement suggests that, although constructed at different dates, the Archbishop's Apartments and the East Tower were in use together at some point.

Trench 10 of the 2017 excavation was located within the southern end of the Archbishop's Apartments, where the 1971 excavations uncovered the medieval tile pavement. The presence of a kiln waster among the SCT1 fabric (E4619:151:10) indicated that the floor tiles were manufactured on site using locally sourced clays. The presence of line-impressed tiles in the assemblage indicates an early fourteenth-century date for the tiles, as comparisons can be drawn between decorative techniques used on the mosaic tiles at Swords and those found on tiles in England and Wales, where line-impressed mosaic is securely dated to the first half of the fourteenth century. A similar date is likely for the two-colour tiles recovered, as this form of decoration was largely obsolete in Ireland after *c*. 1330. This indicates that the construction and primary use of the Archbishop's Apartments took place within the first three decades of the fourteenth century.

The Chapel, Chamber Block and Gatehouse
The Chapel was subject to considerable reconstruction during the 1990s, having been excavated by Fanning in 1971. The interior measures 15.3m east–west and 5.2m in width. A fragment of sandstone canopy over a decayed niche survived in the east wall (Pl. 7.11). The excavations uncovered evidence for the use of the interior of the Chapel for gardening, as a stable and for burial. A *denier tournois* of Philip IV of France, dated to *c*. 1310, was recovered from a post-hole along the north wall, leading to an accepted date in the early fourteenth century for the building of the chapel (Fanning 1975, 59).

The architectural and archaeological evidence shows, however, that the Chapel was an 'infill' building. The east wall of the Chapel is clearly later than the southern wall of the Archbishop's Apartments, as the Chapel wall truncates the latter. The relationship between the structural remains of the Archbishop's Apartments and the Chapel was investigated in an exploratory cutting at the south-west corner of Trench 10. The western wall of the Archbishop's Apartments, previously uncovered by Fanning, was identified. It survived as one course (exposed for 0.6m north–south by 0.35m east–west) of unmortared, unfaced limestone blocks (average diameter 0.2m) and loose small stones. It was confirmed that the construction of the Chapel truncated the southern wall of the Archbishop's Apartments—or, as Fanning had put it in his site notes (for 4 October 1971), 'where the probable earlier S wall of the bishop's quarters seems to have been interrupted for the insertion for the N chapel wall'. How could the

Pl. 7.11—Canopy in east wall of Chapel, c. 1994.

Pl. 7.12—South and west wall foundation of Archbishop's Apartments.

Archbishop's Apartments have remained in use to at least the fifteenth century, when the chimney was inserted, if its south-western corner had been taken out by the Chapel building?

The recovery of more than 500 sherds of floor tile from the eastern end of the Chapel building during the 1971 excavations was interpreted by Fanning (1975, 59) as the remains of a tile pavement here. Based on this, Wren has consistently interpreted the floor tile deposits as representing 'a single planned building project at the castle, involving the laying of floors in at least two locations'. This idea is reinforced by the fact that the same decorative motifs occur in both the oratory (the southern end of the Archbishop's Apartments) and the Chapel. 'The evidence from both buildings indicates that they were either built or renovated at some time in the fourteenth century' (Wren, this volume). Although on Fanning's evidence the two buildings couldn't be standing at the same time, is it possible that they were? Stalley (2006, 157) draws attention to the re-entrant angle, 'a large triangle of space', that interrupts the line of the buildings, created by the angle of the southern end of the Archbishop's Apartments and the eastern end of the Chapel, leaving this area of the castle exposed. It was also noted in the 2014 architectural assessment that the south wall of the Archbishop's Apartments was not parallel to the north wall and that part of the south wall had been reconstructed out of line. Could modifications to the south wall, specifically its south-west corner, have been undertaken to accommodate the construction of the Chapel?

Fanning exposed the foundations of the east wall of the Chamber Block at the west end of the Chapel, which confirmed that the Chapel was built against it. 'For it is now clear that the line of this wall was broken for the construction of the Chapel wall—note broken wall face and the upper tie in (or lack thereof) on the outside. Note also on the interior face the obvious vertical joint and where the roof line of the Chapel has been set into the E wall of the Tower (Chamber Block). Note also the south wall the vertical joint and the old tie stone' (Fanning's notebook entry for 28 October 1971). Waterman (1970, 72) and Fanning (1975,

58) have suggested a mid-thirteenth-century date for the Chamber Block on the basis of the two-light window in the south façade. The indicative dating is confirmed by the next sequence of construction. The Gatehouse is built against the west wall of the Chamber Block and is therefore later. O'Donovan (2003) suggests that it dates from the time of Archbishop Fulk de Sanford or his brother John (1256–94). This would tally with the radiocarbon dates from the burials over which the Gatehouse was built, one of the latest of which returned a range of AD 1190–1281 at 2 sigma (784±34 BP; UBA-29339). To the west of the Gatehouse is a network of chambers, barrel-vaulted at ground level. At a south-east angle to the entrance is a polygonal stair turret, which was not common in Ireland in the thirteenth century (Stalley 2006, 160). Now known as the Knights and Squires, this range has undergone extensive reworking and alterations. Removal of overburden to the west of the upstanding range in 2001 revealed evidence, including the remains of a barrel vault and wall foundations, that this range of buildings had extended westwards (Sullivan 2001).

Pl. 7.13—Removal of overburden west of the Knights and Squires in 2000.

The Great Hall

Located north of the East Tower, the Double Gable indicates the presence of a substantial hall. A large window with the remains of tracery cut in red sandstone dominates the high gable wall (1.05m in width). At ground level are two recessed opes. In 2015 Pit B was excavated at the northern junction of the Double Gable and the curtain wall, and Pit C at the southern junction with the nineteenth-century rebuilt wall that extends to the East Tower. Excavation at the northern junction of the towering east gable and the curtain wall uncovered the foundations of a wall extending westwards from the gable, the northern wall of the Great

Pl. 7.14—Curved foundation, exterior of the Double Gable, in 2016.

Pl. 7.15—North mural tower, Pit A, looking north.

Hall. The foundation levels of this wall consisted of three–four courses of clay-bonded rough stone (averaging 0.12m in diameter) which stood to a height of 0.47m. The upper course of this wall foundation was topped by a mortar layer into which a course of cut stone (0.3–0.37m in diameter) was placed. Above this the wall consisted of mortar-bonded cut calp limestone. In addition, it was established that the curtain wall was of later date. A small north–south wall at the foundation level of the eastern gable building wall appears to have been used as a retaining wall while construction of the curtain wall was undertaken.

Pit C did not locate the southern wall of the building, but excavation on the outside of this junction in 2016 revealed a curved foundation at the southern end of the Double Gable where the gable is truncated and intersects with the nineteenth-century wall. The curved foundation contrasted with the angular layout of the walls above ground, and particularly with what is being interpreted as a later repair and buttress above it. The level of truncation is high in this area, but the foundation may represent an earlier structure or the base of a construction technique similar to that identified in the south-west corner of the East Tower.

The north mural tower
The remains of the tower are visible in the line of the barrel vault in the north-east corner of the site. A centrally placed corbel indicates the presence of a supporting central rib. It is believed, however, that the tower was derelict by the fifteenth century (or deliberately removed), as the crenellated north curtain wall was built over the top of the vault (Stalley 2006, 163). Excavation (Pit A) under the arch spring of the remnants of a barrel vault established the base of the arch, from which a recessed wall extends southwards. Within the building, above a foundation layer was a clay floor, which, given the remains of two decorated floor tiles, appears to have been tiled at one point. Wren believes that these early thirteenth-century tiles were not *in situ* but had been reused at a later date, which was confirmed by the radiocarbon date range of AD 1419–1512 (UBA-32458) for activity in Pit A. Burnt stone associated with a thick layer of heat-affected soil was the result of demolition, or perhaps a fire that resulted in roof collapse.

The Constable's Tower
The North Tower or Constable's Tower, as it is now known, is located at the north-west corner of the site. This is a substantial three-storey structure which projects to both the inside and the outside of the curtain wall and dominates the low ground of the castle precinct. Its construction has been assigned to the fifteenth century, and in the late 1990s it underwent significant reconstruction as a tower of that date. There was evidence, however, including the use of Dundry stone and the pre-reconstruction arrangement of elements, that this tower had been constructed at an earlier date.

Enclosing Swords Castle
There was a gate and, by definition, an enclosure at Swords Castle from Archbishop Comyn's time. A ditch under the Archbishop's Apartments contained mortar render and fragments of demolition material. This was also uncovered during a test excavation on the outside of the Chapel (Walsh 2002), where a demolition layer containing fragments of lime plaster or render was revealed. Located beneath a medieval soil layer, this demolition layer overlay a grey-brown soil and indicated a drop in ground level to the east, interpreted by Walsh as a ditch

or local quarrying relating to the castle entrance. The presence of a significant amount of lime mortar in all features and large chunks of charcoal indicative of burnt timbers may indicate demolition of earlier structures or perhaps a rendered palisade, delineating land ownership, in these areas prior to the construction of the extant buildings. Evidence for intersecting ditches that indicate subdivision or boundaries was identified below features and later burials at the Gatehouse. These ditches contained ash and charcoal and a silver bracteate coin of a type that appears in Ireland in the final phase of Hiberno-Norse coinage between 1100 and 1160 and disappears from circulation around the time of the Anglo-Norman colonisation (Moraghan *et al.* 2016).

The extant masonry curtain wall is approximately 300m long and varies significantly in height (3.1–7.2m) and width (0.6–1.2m) along its length. Putlog holes for the timber scaffolding indicate that they were raised in sections of about 2m at a time (Fingal County Council 2014, 44). This stone structure may have replaced the earlier ditch and timber palisade or may have represented an enlargement of the castle, taking in the meadows beside the river. The crenellated parapets indicate a likely fifteenth-century date for the construction of the curtain walls. It is also likely that Archbishop Richard Talbot (1417–49) was responsible for the fortification of the archiepiscopal manor. Talbot, whose brother was the lord lieutenant, was known for leading military expeditions against the king's enemies and had held the offices of justiciar and chancellor. His successor, Michael Tregury (1449–71), was granted extra benefices to assist with the repair of the castle and may have undertaken works. He was known, however, to prefer Tallaght to Swords, and by this stage Swords was being referred to as a 'castle' or *castrum* (Stalley 2006, 155–6). The archaeological evidence uncovered in Trench 7 appears to confirm this sequence. As described above, the flagged floor surface sloped into a drain that extends through the curtain wall. As there was no evidence for its insertion into the wall, it appears to represent an original feature, which implies that the flagged floor represented ground level at the time of construction of the curtain wall in this area of the precinct. The radiocarbon dates from material overlying this floor returned a range of AD 1451–1528, indicating that the floor and, by extension, the curtain wall were present at this time.

Internal buildings

The three seasons of excavation uncovered new evidence for structures and their demolition within the precinct of Swords Castle. In Trench 8, which was located between the East Tower and the Great Hall, there was a substantial (1.2m wide) east–west wall, exposed for 4m. Immediately north of this wall was evidence for burning and building collapse or demolition, including architectural fragments. One example was a chamfered stone with striations visible on carved surfaces and an indent that possibly formed part of a door- or window-frame. Carved at one end and truncated at the other, it appeared to have been burnt. A wedge-shaped fragment of possible Dundry stone or yellow limestone, used elsewhere to decorate window or door openings, was also recovered, as were mortar and plaster fragments. Among the domestic debris—thirteenth–mid-fourteenth-century pottery, animal bone, and wheat, barley and rye seeds—was an L-shaped socketed iron candle-holder (E4619:118:18) (Fig. 7.4), which would have been fixed to a wall. The radiocarbon date range for this activity was AD 1298–1372 (UBA-38838).

There was similar evidence for structural remains and demolition within Trenches 1 and 4, located *c.* 20m west of the Great Hall. The remnants of a medieval wall (0.94m wide and

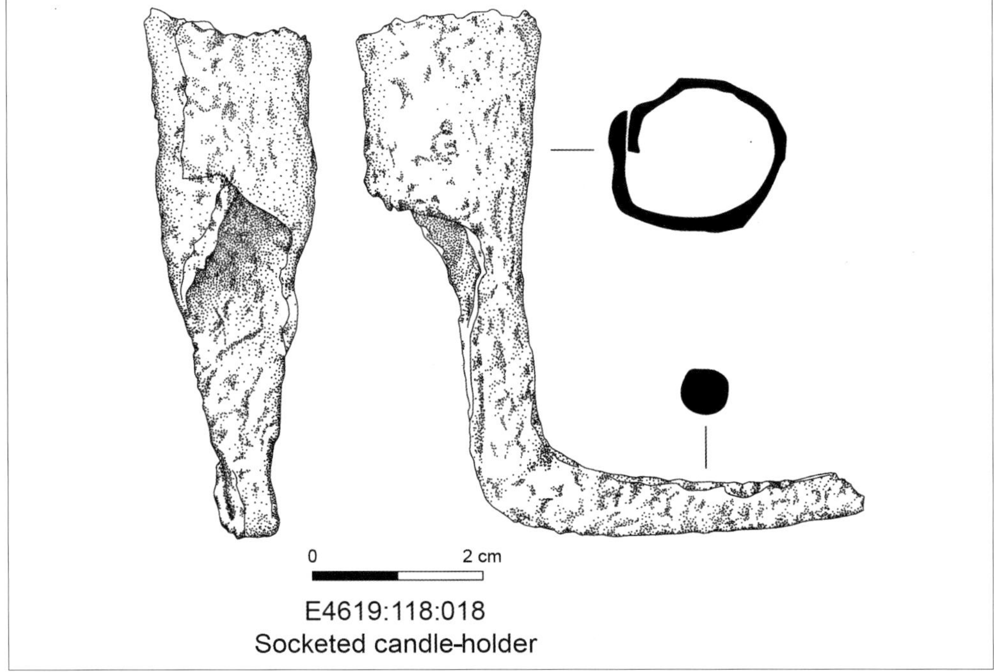

exposed for 2m) running west-north-west/east-south-east were identified in Trench 1. The wall consisted of clay-bonded angular blocks of calp limestone and sandstone infilled with small stones and cobbles. To the north of the wall was a metalled surface and hearth area. It was overlain by thin layers. Analysis of the faunal material contained within these layers identified clumps of fin rays, spines and scales associated with the preparation of fish prior to cooking. A radiocarbon date range of AD 1298–1373 (UBA-32454) was returned. Artefactual evidence from this layer consisted of a possible bone scoop (E4619:43:12) and Leinster Cooking Ware.

Evidence for rapid demolition (F74 and F77) of a structure was identified within Trench 4, which was located west of the food preparation area within Trench 1. This proximity was reflected in the extensive faunal and seashell assemblages from these layers. Significant amounts of building material, including stones, mortar fragments and slate, were also recovered. Architectural fragments such as a dressed window moulding and a roll and fillet fragment were found. These were heat-affected, indicating a burning event which may have been a factor in the subsequent demolition. Indicative of the wooden elements of a structure were a range of carpentry nails and a partial clench bolt, the latter often used in wooden doors. Among the artefactual evidence was a possible drop-handle from a casket or chest, a common item of furniture. A radiocarbon date range of AD 1299–1371 (UBA-34516), remarkably similar to that from nearby Trench 1, indicates contemporary activity. Given the evidence for food preparation, it seems likely that the kitchen was sited close to the north-west corner of the Great Hall.

This structural activity to the north-west, west and south of the Great Hall returned the same date range, indicating activity between 1298 and 1373. All areas showed evidence for *in situ* burning and architectural fragments that had been subject to burning. To the west and south was evidence for rapid demolition or collapse. Is it possible that there was a

Pl. 7.16—Worked stone (photo: John Sunderland).

destructive event that caused the Great Hall and its attendant buildings to burn down? Although there are no historical references, Fanning (1975, 48) posits that Swords could have been subject to attack during the Bruce invasion of 1317, 'which devastated the country south of Dundalk up to the walls of Dublin city'. As we have seen, however, the Bruce invasion coincided with a period of intense building on site in the early fourteenth century.

More evidence for conflagration and collapse was apparent at the northern mural tower with Pit A and towards the northern limit of Trench 7. Within the north-west corner of the tower there was evidence for burnt stone, ashy material and slate indicative of a fire and subsequent building collapse. A date range of AD 1419–1512 (UBA-32458) was returned from Pit A. Likewise, at the northern edge of the flagged floor within Trench 7 there were burnt deposits which returned a similar date range of AD 1461–1636 (UBA-38837). Large assemblages of seeds were found in both deposits, suggesting a grain store which may have burnt down in the first half of the sixteenth century.

Excavations within the lower ward of Swords Castle in Trench 3 also produced evidence for a possible structure. Although no built evidence remained, there was a metalled surface and hearth, similar to that in Trench 1, next to pits containing a faunal assemblage that suggested food preparation, including the roasting of meat over spits. Radiocarbon date ranges for this activity lay between the late eleventh and thirteenth centuries, although the artefactual evidence from the same activity included thirteenth–mid-fourteenth-century pottery. Subsequent use of this area may have included craftworking and the shoeing of horses, while a very seed-rich sample returned a date range of AD 1032–1217 (UBA-32456). An extensive range of nails, a whetstone and a possible smith's punch point to a possible workshop in this area, while some building materials, including fragments of slate and a stone flag or tile, were associated with an upper surface. A clench bolt (E4619:21:30) which would have been used to join overlapping planks of timber together may have been used in a door.

Comparative layouts

Descriptions from medieval inquisitions are similar in the type of buildings listed as contained within the archbishop's residences but not in layout. St Sepulchre's, although laid out around a courtyard, contained a stone hall, a chamber, a kitchen and a chapel. Colonia (Cullenswood) had a stone hall, a chamber for the archbishop with an adjoining chapel, a kitchen, a grange, a stable and a granary; Tallaght had no buildings left apart from a chamber, another small chamber for clerks and other small cellars; Clondalkin had a chamber, a chapel, a stone stable and two small houses; and Ballymore Eustace had a chamber, a chapel, a small chamber for clerks, a kitchen, a stable, a grange, a chamber for the constable and a granary (O'Keeffe 2015, 181–3). Similarly, Swords contained a hall, an adjoining chamber for the archbishop, a kitchen, a chapel, a chamber for the friars, a chamber for the constable and four chambers for the knights and squires, under which was a stable, a bakehouse, a dairy, a workshop, a grange, a granary and a byre (McNeill 1950, 175).

It is difficult to match the description to the standing remains, and Swords Castle has no direct surviving comparisons in Ireland. It may be, however, that it belongs to a typology that is inclusive of the manor houses and bishops' houses built in England and Wales in the medieval period. The archbishops and many of the senior functionaries in the see of Dublin for 300 years after the Anglo-Norman invasion were all born and educated in England/Wales. From these locations they brought with them all their cultural background in terms of law, systems of governance, religious practices etc. As the archbishops used their residences for administrative functions (both secular and ecclesiastical) and to collect rental income from their lands, it is unsurprising that they followed the form and layout of the contemporary secular manor houses (Fingal County Council 2014, Appendix C).

The typical arrangement of the essential elements of a manor house is seen in bishops' palaces at Wells, Boothby Pagnell, Lincoln, Mayfield, Lyddington, Bede and other locations. The more or less typical plan for the thirteenth/fourteenth-century manor house shows a hall at ground level, with the chamber block located transversely to the long axis of the hall at one end. The chamber block normally contained a solar (living room/bedroom/office) at upper level, with vaulted cellars below it on the ground floor. The kitchen was always kept separate from the main buildings in the earlier medieval houses because of smells and the risk of fire. In Swords, the buildings on the south range conform quite closely to a typical manor house plan of the period in England and Wales. This, however, raises a question as to the origins of the Chapel, which has taken the place usually occupied by the hall in the typical manor house plan (*ibid.*).

The designation of the structure next to the Chamber Block as a chapel has always been seen as problematic. Stalley (2006, 167) described it as 'surprisingly capacious, even for an archbishop'. In archbishops' residences in England and Wales, the chapels are universally a fraction of the size of the hall and are better described as oratories than as chapels. An archbishop would not need a chapel of this size, given that a monastic settlement and a parish church already catered for public worship in Swords. The archaeological and architectural evidence shows the Chapel to have been constructed later than the Chamber Block to the west and the Archbishop's Apartments to the east, although the floor tiles recovered in both buildings indicate contemporary use. In England the thirteenth century saw a move from the Continental style of vaulted ground floor with hall and chamber above to the ground-floor aisled hall. A new hall was often built next to the older, Continental-style hall block (O'Donovan 2003, 272).

What is clear is that the form and use of the buildings in Swords Castle have changed over time. That the Gatehouse is the latest in the sequence of construction from the East Tower to the southern range points to an intense period of building and rebuilding between 1280 and 1330. There were five archbishops appointed within this period. John de Sandford (1284–94) was tasked as one of those overseeing the collection of a tenth of all ecclesiastical rents, profits and oblations in Ireland, to be paid to the king towards the expenses of a proposed crusade (Dalton 1838b,108); William of Hotham (1296–8) was consecrated abroad and spent his time being an 'active organ of reconciliation between Philip the Fourth of France and Edward the First of England' before dying in Rome (*ibid.*, 112); Richard de Ferrings (1299–1306) resided abroad for the most part, having constituted Thomas de Chadsworth (whose election to the see the pope had previously twice annulled) his vicar-general, while John Lech (1311–13) was also lord treasurer of Ireland. It seems most likely, therefore, that Alexander de Bickford (1317–49) was responsible for the commissioning of many of the buildings at Swords Castle.

Life in Swords Castle

The manor of Swords was an agricultural administrative unit of the archbishopric that dealt with the lands, tenants and produce and the money generated from them. A plea of the Crown from 1310 describes how the archbishop had gallows, held pleas of bloodshed, kept Englishmen in prison and fined them for burglary and receiving usuries. The archbishop's court at Swords could try all crimes except 'forestalling, rape, arson and treasure-trove' (McNeill 1950, 162). An example of the power of the archbishops is revealed in a letter written to the mayor and citizens of Dublin in 1266. An inquisition on the archiepiscopal manor of Swords found that during the episcopacy of Archbishop Luke de Roches (1229–55) two of the king's sergeants had been excommunicated for entering the manor of Swords to serve a writ. The archbishop consented to lift the sentence only after the men had been publicly beaten around the church of Swords. This powerful public sanction was seen as a humiliating spectacle by the letter's author (Murphy 1989, 95). It was also noted that 'every seneschal of the archbishop of Dublin since John Darlington's death has chosen Englishmen and freemen to do the office of provost', reflecting the cultural differentiations. From an economic standpoint, the archbishop also had the 'correction of bred and ale' and 'ell pound and bushel and gallon by the king's standard' and all measures under his seal. He could therefore regulate the measures and weights, as 'his tenants take all measures under the archbishop's seal'. If there was a defect, then the 'archbishop and his bailiffs will make correction'. By the fourteenth century it was calculated that the archbishop's estates encompassed approximately 53,200 acres, with the manor at Swords yielding up to half of his entire income. It is unsurprising, therefore, that Swords was known as the 'Golden Prebend'.

Alexander de Bicknor (1317–49) was one of the most important archbishops in the history of Swords Castle. A native of Gloucestershire in England, he had served as an intermediary between King Edward II and the duchy of Lancaster, as an ambassador to France and as the king's chief treasurer in Ireland before being consecrated archbishop of Dublin in Avignon. It was his time in the Treasury, however, that led to a loss of much of his status. De Bicknor was accused of misappropriating funds for his own gain. He was found guilty of forgery and false accounting and his property was seized. As part of an evaluation of his lands in 1326 the following description of Swords Castle survives:

> '… a hall, a chamber for the archbishop annexed to it, of which the walls are stone and crenellated like a castle and roofed with shingles; and there are a kitchen there with a larder, whose walls are stone and roof of shingle; a chapel with stone walls and shingle roof; there was a chamber for friars with a cloister now thrown down; near the gate is a chamber for the constable and four chambers for knights and squires, roofed with shingles, under these a stable and bakehouse; there was a house for a dairy and workshop now thrown down. In the haggard a grange constructed of poles and covered with thatch, a timber granary roofed with wooden boards, a byre for housing nags and kine; these easements they extend at all no value, for nothing is to be got, since they need great repair, as they are badly roofed' (McNeill 1950, 175).

While Fanning (1975, 48) interpreted this description as the castle 'being abandoned *c.* 1326', the historical, architectural and archaeological evidence demonstrates that this was not the case. O'Donovan (2003, 258) notes that the inquisition of 1326 describes St Sepulchre's in the same formulaic language as a

> 'stone hall badly roofed with shingles and unsafe, a kitchen and chapel badly roofed of no value and in great need of repair … there is a prison there now broken and thrown down …'.

The hall and chamber at Swords are described in the same way as the buildings at St Sepulchre's even though the two sites are very different, indicating that their condition—and hence their value—may have been considerably downplayed by those surveying the lands. It was also documented that de Bicknor spent a significant amount of time at Swords Castle towards the end of his career. He was recorded as being resident there for the summer months of 1346, when Thomas Beuley, his clerk, and others had to visit the archbishop in Swords three times to obtain money from him. In April 1349 a deed was witnessed by the archbishop, again resident in Swords (Stalley 2006, 167). As the archaeological evidence demonstrates, the period that coincided with de Bicknor's archbishopric was, despite his financial woes, one of intense construction at Swords Castle.

The tile pavement dating from de Bicknor's time was just one of the signifiers of the wealth and status associated with Swords Castle. Many of the archbishops had been exposed to the royal and episcopal courts of England and Europe, consorting with kings and popes. When the archbishops took up residence, they brought with them a household of people and goods befitting their rank. This could include a retinue of 50–100 people, with furniture and linen in wagons. The will of Archbishop Michael Tregury (1449–71) details his goods, which included a basin and ewer, two salt cellars, standing cups and flat cups of silver; a chalice and paten of silver gilt; his scarlet robe with furred hood used for parliament, five habits, a black furred gown with a scarlet hood, a gown of russet furred with lambskins, a red gown and two habits cut for riding; two feather beds, three bed-coverings, a white bed with three curtains, two red beds, four mantles and a mattress; a banner called a *guidon*; one trunk and one coffer of spruce; four bankers and two candlesticks. In addition, there were his church effects (a missal, a 'grayle', two candlesticks for the altar, one blue cloth and five towels for the altar, two chasubles with three albs, and two organs) and his agricultural assets—40 acres sown in wheat, grain in the barns of Tallaght, Fingal and Swords, fourteen plough-horses, six cart-horses, two horses, four mares with their foals, 30 cows and fourteen calves (Murphy 1989). The few personal items recovered from the medieval activity were all related to dress and the fastening of clothes. They included a decorated stick-pin (E4619:21:41), a strap loop (E4619:98:4) and three buckle pins (E4619:106:1, E4619:20:18 and E4619:21:40), recovered from Trenches 3, 4 and 8. These were all dated, by typology or stratigraphy, to the twelfth to fourteenth centuries, and most probably the thirteenth and fourteenth centuries. With the exception of two iron buckle pins, all were made from copper alloys and suggest a well-to-do rather than opulent household during medieval times.

The archaeological evidence shows that fire, demolition or collapse and construction were happening in rapid succession, especially in the early decades of the fourteenth century. Craft and workshop activities appear to have been undertaken in the lower ward of the castle (Trench 3), downslope from the main habitation areas of the twelfth and early thirteenth centuries. A stone reused as a rubbing stone (E4619:13:1), perhaps in textile-making, and a whetstone (E4619:21:43) also provide evidence of the daily work at the castle; the latter was recovered along with a number of metal artefacts indicative of the workshop of a smith or carpenter. Iron tweezers from Trench 3, identified from their size and morphology as burling tweezers, suggest that cloth-making and wool-processing were carried out at the site. From other artefactual evidence these probably date from the mid-twelfth to mid-fourteenth centuries, consistent with thirteenth/fourteenth-century examples elsewhere. A lead spindle-whorl (E4619:1:316), also from Trench 3, may provide further evidence for textile-working at the site in medieval times: spindle-whorls were used with spindle and distaff until the advent of the spinning-wheel from the fourteenth century. There was also evidence for the shoeing of horses in this area, as horseshoe fragments and horseshoe nails were recovered.

Fig. 7.5—Medieval sheep-farming, from the Luttrell Psalter (1320–40).

Fig. 7.6—Medieval feasting, from the Luttrell Psalter (1320–40).

Excavation revealed at least two food preparation areas or kitchens within the precinct of Swords Castle. The first, located on low ground (Trench 3), was dated to the eleventh/twelfth century and contained charred seeds and evidence for the roasting of animals on spits. The second, on the eastern ridge close to the buildings and dating from the fourteenth century, demonstrated that the gutting and preparation of fish were being undertaken in (or outside) the kitchen. The study of the animal bones, molluscs, seed remains and pottery gives an insight into not only the diet of the occupants of Swords Castle but also the medieval economy and some of the pursuits being undertaken at the manorial centre.

The faunal evidence shows that the meat supply to the manor was mostly provided by cattle and sheep, which is unsurprising given that the episcopal manor possessed large tracts of agricultural land. The presence of butchery marks and all body parts suggests the procurement of animals on the hoof and their slaughter within the precinct of the manor. Beef would have constituted the greater part of the diet; mutton and lamb were also significant food items. Pigs, although relatively scarce, were reared in the castle and suckling pig was occasionally consumed. Domestic fowl and geese were common and would have provided variety to the diet, and a number of hens were raised for eggs. A wide range of birds were also consumed, and this is suggestive of a high-status site, with evidence for numerous species of wader, game birds, herons, swans and doves. Owing to their physical appearance, cranes and herons were used as centre-pieces on the banqueting table. The range of birds identified at Swords Castle is wider than at contemporary urban sites, which is suggestive of a socially élite community which perhaps had greater wealth than others. The presentation to the table of species such as partridge, teal, woodcock, snipe, heron and swan would certainly have impressed guests being entertained at the manor (McCarthy, this volume).

Another Anglo-Norman innovation was the introduction of rabbits in the thirteenth century as prestige food items for the very wealthy in society. In Britain they were introduced as domesticated or semi-domesticated animals, and were kept in small enclosures or warrens close to castles, monasteries or manor houses. The management of the animals was tightly controlled by powerful ecclesiastical and secular landlords, and live rabbits were bestowed as high-status gifts to others of rank who were setting up warrens. Rabbit fur was highly regarded and was commercially produced and marketed. There are warrens or coney boroughs documented within Fingal under the control of the archbishops, and rabbits seem to have been a particularly favoured delicacy at Swords Castle.

Exploitation of the surrounding resources is evident in the consumption of fish and shellfish, although the latter appears to have been an added extra rather than underpinning the diet of the residents. On occasion cockles, mussels, periwinkles and oysters graced the tables. Fish also appear to have made a relatively small contribution to the diet, despite this being an ecclesiastical site occupied at a time when there were many more fast days than in later centuries. The assemblage is dominated by the bones of large marine species, including hake and several members of the cod family (Gadidae), with a few examples of flatfish and gurnard. Element distribution indicates that fish were landed intact and brought from nearby ports to the manor in a complete state.

A very large quantity of charred cereal grains (wheat, oat and barley) as well as cereal chaff, cultivated legumes, weed seeds, and fruit and nut remains were identified at Swords Castle. Cereal grains could be used in a variety of food products, including breads, gruels and porridges, as well as in brewing and as animal fodder. Bread wheat was the main cereal recovered at Swords Castle; wheaten flour, when carefully processed, produced pleasant, light and fine-textured bread, compared to the heavy, coarse and dark breads of oat, barley and rye flours. Oats were used to make bread shaped into a broad, flat cake, in addition to porridge and oatmeal pastes, while barley was consumed in the form of breads, porridge and meal pastes, and in stews and pottages. Two types of cultivated legume—garden pea and broad bean—were recorded in deposits at Swords Castle, and condiments such as sorrel were important for nutrition and palatability. Fat hen (similar to spinach) and wild radish were also consumed at Swords Castle, while crab-apple, bramble, sloe and hazelnut trees were growing nearby (McClatchie, this volume).

It is also probable that oats and barley were used in the production of ale—especially barley, which was frequently malted for brewing. The pottery evidence from Swords Castle indicates, however, that wine was imported and consumed here. The Saintonge pottery from a region of south-west France is synonymous with the Bordeaux wine trade. Pottery was also

Fig. 7.7—Medieval threshing, from the Luttrell Psalter (1320–40).

something of a cultural signifier in that the style of locally produced pottery reflected that produced in England. This shows that the Anglo-Norman settlers not only wanted to maintain their connection with Anglo-Norman material culture but also had rejected the Irish practices of using wooden, leather and metal vessels (Curtin 2019, 153).

The archbishop's manor at Swords was primarily the hub of a thriving economic enterprise. The average demesne in the Dublin region *c.* 1300 was 427 acres (74% arable); Swords was over 800 acres. In 1325–6, at the time of the de Bicknor inquiry, the archbishop's annual income was £553, almost half of which, £242, came from Swords. Swords was also a centre for the collection of tithes, storage and distribution, the weekly market and eight-day fair forming an outlet for produce and crafts. The historical record of granaries, barns and stables is reflected in the archaeological evidence, with more than 16,000 charred seed remains recovered, mainly consisting of cereal grains. Cereals were recorded in almost all examined deposits from Swords Castle, from the eleventh/twelfth century up to the fifteenth/sixteenth century, highlighting their importance over several centuries at this location.

The cultivation of bread wheat became much more significant in Ireland after the arrival of the Anglo-Normans, related in part to the introduction of new farming techniques, such as crop rotation. The cultivation of bread wheat requires an increased input of labour and a better quality of soil than other cereals. Legumes are important not just as foodstuffs but also owing to their ability to fix nitrogen in soils, thus making cultivation plots more productive. The presence of legumes and the dominance of bread wheat at Swords Castle is striking; it is possible that legumes formed part of a crop-rotation system to improve soil quality. Farmers in medieval England recognised this potential, which led to legumes becoming an important component of intensive cropping regimes. Such regimes produced surpluses which could be traded. A glimpse of the nature of this trade was captured in a licence issued during the reign of Richard II to Robert Crull, prebendary of Swords, 'to load grain and fish pertaining to that prebend in ships … and transport them to England, Wales, Bayonne, Bordeaux and Portugal, and to sell them to others …' (Patent Roll 10).

Aside from the business of the manor there was evidence for other pursuits, such as hunting, music and games. Although there was no evidence in the main faunal assemblage, fragments of butchered red deer were recovered from the excavations at the Gatehouse (McCarthy 2015) and a deer tooth from the ditch during the enabling works (Duffy 2016), indicating hunting during the early years of the site's occupation. The remains of a sparrowhawk were retrieved from the ditch underlying the Archbishop's Apartments. The presence of the remains of a raptor in a medieval setting is generally accepted as evidence of hawking or falconry at the site, one of the clearest indicators of higher social status. Although sparrowhawks were of the lesser order of hawks used for hunting, they were still only the property of the upper strata of medieval society. A range of dogs, from medium to large-sized, were identified, including examples displaying evidence of extreme muscle strain from running activities, probably associated with hunting (*ibid.*).

A tuning-peg (E4619:31:15) from an instrument such as a lyre and a slate with incised musical notation (E4619:106:74; E4619:112:19) attest to the presence of musicians at the castle, at least on occasion. Slate has been used as a medium for writing since medieval times. The uneven finish of the Swords slate suggests that it was used because it was close to hand, rather than being acquired specifically for the task. Certainly, there are references to work being carried out at the castle in the fifteenth century and slate fragments may have been readily available there as a result. It conjures the image of a musician or student practising notation by taking down a *chanson* on a handy slate sometime in the early 1500s within Swords Castle.

Other leisure activities may be reflected in the presence of a die and gaming counters. Although not from a secure context, the bone die with evenly spaced 'dot and circle' roundels in standard arrangement bears comparison with late thirteenth–early fourteenth-century material at Trim Castle. A small disc of dolomitised limestone from Trench 3 is likely to have been a gaming counter. Another unusual item was an undecorated glazed body sherd of Dublin-type fineware that was modified for secondary use as a gaming counter. The use of such counters probably originated in Norse times, as did many of the table games played throughout the medieval period (Duffy, this volume).

PHASES 3–4—POST-MEDIEVAL–MODERN

The last phase of major construction at Swords Castle was its mid-fifteenth-century fortification and enclosure with crenellated walls. This was part of an increased fortification of the Pale in general and was reflective of a trend in Britain whereby it was normal for bishop's manors to be protected by curtain walls and the occasional flanking tower or turret (Stalley 2006, 175). Despite their appearance, however, the curtain walls were not of sufficient height to be effective and there was a lack of defensive elements such as a ditch or portcullis. It appears that their main function was to protect animals and livestock and provide security for the site rather than to withstand the onslaught of an army (*ibid.*). In 1484 Doctor Walton, the then archbishop of Dublin, 'being blind and infirm', retired to Swords Castle to live out his days, but within less than a century the castle was ruinous.

It does appear that the fortunes of both the castle and the town of Swords had deteriorated by the sixteenth century. Sir Henry Sydney wrote to Sir Francis Walsingham in 1583:

> 'I caused to plant and inhabit there about fortie families of the Reformed Churches of the Low Countries, flying thence for religion's sake, in one ruinous town called Surd [Swords]; an truly sir, it would have down any man good to have seen how diligently they wrought, how they re-edified the quite spoiled old catell of the same town and repayred almost all the same and how godlie and claenaly, they, their wifes and children lived. They made diaper and tickets for beddes, and other stuffes for man's use; and as excellent leather of deer skynnes, goat and sheep fells, as is made in Southwarke' (Smiles 1889).

Although the insertion of a red-brick oven in the corner of the Knights and Squires building is often ascribed to the Dutch settlers, the archaeological evidence for the sixteenth-century activity within Swords Castle comes from the north-east corner of the site. A kiln was located here, close to burning activity that overlay a flagged floor and a large assemblage of bread wheat grains recovered from a burnt deposit within what had formerly been the north mural tower. The date ranges returned for all three areas were similar, encompassing the period from 1419 to 1636. The kiln consisted of a lime-rendered bowl, a flue and the fire-pit, expanding out towards the southern baulk of the excavation trench. The area exposed

Pl. 7.17—Kiln, Trench 7, after excavation.

suggested a keyhole kiln, although it may have been of dumb-bell design. Comparatively little cereal was recovered from the kiln, which suggested either that it had been cleaned out or that it was used primarily for other activities. Charcoal analysis indicates that oak predominated in the kiln. Owing to its density and its longevity in burning, oak was used for activities that required extremely high temperatures, such as metalworking or lime production. During experimental firings of grain-drying kilns temperatures never exceeded 65°C (Monk and Kelleher 2005, 97–100), while the temperature required for the making of lime was closer to 900°C. There was, however, no evidence within the kiln of heat-affected stone or burnt clay such as occurred at comparable kilns (keyhole-shaped, in the 1460–1660 date range and with little grain recovered) in County Wexford (Tierney and Johnston 2009). In any case, this sheltered corner was a focus for sixteenth-century activity, whether that consisted of drying grain for storage nearby or making lime to undertake repairs to the castle.

Few features and a relatively small collection of artefacts could be assigned specifically to the post-medieval period, and most were in the kiln area. Part of a knife, a lace-tag and a belt decoration dating from the late sixteenth/seventeenth century were found here, along with a silver sixpence from the reign of Elizabeth I. A total of 26 nails, representing seven different types, were recovered from Trench 7. Retrieved from five different features, all of which also contained artefacts dating from the sixteenth and seventeenth centuries, these may relate to structures in this area in post-medieval times. In particular, a collection of Type IV nails may provide evidence of timber flooring. Most of the evidence for seventeenth-century smoking at the castle was also concentrated in Trench 7, with some examples of clay pipe fragments suggesting a post-1650 date.

The pottery and animal bone of this period were more widely spread across the site, with a mix of imported wares dating from the seventeenth century. These were mostly utilitarian wares, including jugs, jars, cups and bowls typical of the period, although sherds of an olive jar of Seville coarseware conjure up a more cosmopolitan image. The presence of vessels dating from the decades on either side of 1700 may indicate settlement within Swords Castle at this time, although it could also relate to the spreading of manure sourced from the town of Swords. The animal bone evidence indicates that, while cattle continued to be slaughtered and dismembered within the precinct of the castle, there was less on-site consumption. The higher proportions of vertebrae, skull fragments, isolated teeth and peripheral elements, indicative of primary butchery waste, may mean that joints were being prepared for distribution. Pigs were also being slaughtered, although the age range suggests that they continued to be reared within the grounds of the manor during the post-medieval period (McCarthy, this volume).

The historical evidence for the seventeenth and eighteenth centuries at Swords Castle is scant, as is the archaeological evidence. It may be that the cultivation of the interior that is prominent throughout the nineteenth century commenced in the eighteenth century. Much of the material recovered from that period is portable and personal rather than indicative of settlement or activity. A single buckle (E4619:1:1037) could be dated to this period: this was a large shoe-buckle with openwork design, typical of the latter half of the eighteenth century. Of perhaps similar date was a holder for the key of a pocket watch with raised beaded decoration. Two halfpenny coins may represent stray losses at the site. The earlier of the two, from Trench 5, was from the reign of George II, although its level of preservation meant that it could not be dated more closely than to the period 1727–60. The second coin (E4619:6:4) was not official coinage but had been produced by the Hibernian Mining Company in 1794 to compensate for a dearth of small-denomination coinage in the later eighteenth century; such coins were widely used at this time. The evidence for smoking was confined to a single complete bowl and a small number of bowl fragments.

The archaeological evidence for the Dunne family is the doorway from the bakery that breached the wall in the north-east corner of the site and the rough path that led from it. Here, too, was found the lead seal from a flour bag imported from Paris in 1903, continuing the tradition of high-quality bread at Swords Castle. Traces of cultivation furrows were evident across the site, and the deep and disturbed topsoil layer was a product of the garden and orchard activity of the nineteenth and twentieth centuries. A number of artefacts were recovered from this topsoil layer, although it is difficult to distinguish between artefacts initially disposed of at the castle and those introduced from outside, which should probably be regarded as relating to activity in the wider vicinity of the site rather than in the castle precinct itself. Artefacts from the modern era associated with personal attire were primarily associated with nineteenth-century men's clothing. These included eight bone buttons, twelve shell shirt buttons and a decorated copper-alloy strap-adjuster from a pair of braces. The bulk of the clay pipe assemblage recovered during excavations at Swords Castle was dated to the nineteenth century and appears to be associated with the use of the site as a garden and orchard. Pottery was typical of the nineteenth and twentieth centuries, with fragments of plates, cups and jars of stoneware, earthenwares, transfer-printed wares and delftware. It is likely that these arrived at the site within refuse material intended for manure. Other objects, such as a lead pencil-sharpener, toy cap-gun, clay bubble pipes and marbles, may have been the stray losses of children in the castle or, more likely, from the town's refuse. A partial toothbrush and a nit-comb reflect the personal hygiene of the local inhabitants.

Restoration works began here in the 1990s. The curtain walls, the Constable's Tower and the Chapel were reconstructed as part of a FÁS scheme which provided training in masonry and carpentry for local people. This was evidenced in Trench 3, where a spread of mortar and lime mix was recorded just below the sod.

CONCLUSIONS

Over three seasons of archaeological excavation within the precinct of Swords Castle, long-standing questions have been answered, but results have also given rise to more questions. The presence of a significant pre-Norman enclosed burial-ground has been confirmed. With burials dating from the late tenth century to the early thirteenth century, the identification of a 4m-wide enclosure ditch and settlement evidence from pits and post-holes, this was perhaps the site of the early church of St Brigit or a previously unknown cemetery settlement. New questions centre on the preponderance of female and juvenile burials and just how long the burial-ground remained in use after the construction of the castle began.

Excavation has revealed hitherto-unknown structures within the castle grounds and produced evidence for the sequence of construction of the extant buildings. Granted, not all questions have been answered. The conundrum of the tile floors of the same date within two buildings of different construction has yet to be solved but the evidence points to the Chapel being of later construction. Assumptions made on the basis of historical documentation such as the inquisition of 1326 have been refuted by the archaeological evidence, although it is perhaps telling that the active historical records of the fourteenth and mid-fifteenth/sixteenth centuries coincide with active periods in the archaeological record.

The application of scientific methodologies has provided mixed results. Geophysical survey did not identify the large enclosure ditch or the subsurface walls that survive but did record the large pits in Trench 3 and modern drain and later insertions. Radiocarbon dating of seed and bone samples have, on the other hand, provided consistent date ranges for activities across the site. The environmental and artefactual records have given us an insight into the diet, economy and lives of those within the castle and the adjacent town, which were planned as a whole. From the stores of grain and the importation of wine, the story of Swords Castle is one of administration and commerce, punctuated by visits from the archbishop, and reflects a wealthy household given to displays of status. Overall, the medieval finds appear to relate to the more secular activities at the castle and may have a greater association with the constable and his household than with the archbishop himself. The artefacts recovered at Swords Castle represent the deposition of personal items, both during its occupation and its later, more communal use.

The excavations at Swords Castle, using a model of community volunteers and professional archaeologists, have provided a glimpse of the occupational tasks, leisure activities and personal habits of the people who lived, worked and died at Swords Castle for over 1,000 years. That the people who have uncovered this information for future generations are from Swords, Fingal and beyond reflects the contribution of local knowledge, skills, ideas and perspectives that have enriched the experience for all.

PART III: MATERIAL CULTURE

8

Osteoarchaeological report on human remains

Dr Linda G. Lynch, MA, MIAI

INTRODUCTION

This report details the osteoarchaeological analysis of fourteen human burials (thirteen of which were excavated) and a small quantity of disarticulated human skeletal remains that were recovered over the course of three seasons of archaeological excavations at Swords Castle. Accelerated mass spectrometry (AMS) dates from three of the *in situ* burials returned results spanning the period from the late tenth to the late twelfth century, which tally with dates previously received from disarticulated human remains. The burials confirm that there was an extensive early medieval burial-ground at the site of Swords Castle before its construction *c.* 1200. The analysis of the skeletons was limited by the low sample number and the very poor preservation of the bones, but a significant amount of information could still be teased from the remains. Very meticulous excavations ensured the recovery of unusual ossifications/calcifications with two burials, as well as smaller bones of the hands and feet, which greatly assisted in the assessment of the disarticulated human remains.

METHODS

In situ human burials (fourteen in total) were only uncovered during the third season of excavation at Swords Castle in 2017. Disarticulated human remains (3,524 fragments) were recovered in all three seasons, but in significantly greater quantities in 2017.

Pl. 8.1—General view of burials, from north, showing modern shallow depth (note baulk in background).

The normal methods of skeletal assessment of the individuals from Swords Castle were somewhat hindered by the very poor levels of preservation, particularly in terms of truncation and fragmentation. The ages at death of the adult individuals were determined, when possible, on the morphology of both the auricular surface of the ilium (Lovejoy *et al.* 1985) and the pubic symphysis (Brook and Suchey 1990). Rates of fusion of secondary epiphyses may be considered in relation to younger adults (Schaefer *et al.* 2009; Scheuer and Black 2000). Archaeological adult skeletons cannot be aged very accurately and are assigned into broad age categories: 'young adult' (18–25 years), 'middle adult' (26–44 years) and 'old adult' (45+ years).

The sex of the adults was determined on the basis of morphological traits in the pelvis and skull (Buikstra and Ubelaker 1994) and on metrical analysis (Bass 1995), when possible (again, poor preservation was a major factor). In some instances, general robusticity, or lack thereof, was taken as an indicator of possible sex. Generally, females tend to be slender and smaller, with marked particular traits in the pelvis for the birthing process, while males tend to be larger and more robust.

The methods used in the determination of the age at death of juvenile individuals are more accurate and specific than those used in relation to adults, and are assessed on the basis of the known rates of growth and development of parts of the skeleton (Schaefer *et al.* 2009; Scheuer and Black 2000). The most reliable method is to assess the calcification and eruption of teeth (Moorrees *et al.* 1963a; 1963b; Smith 1991). The lengths of the long bones may also be used to determine the age at death (Maresh 1970; Scheuer and Black 2000), although long bone growth may be highly influenced by nutritional factors. Juveniles may be grouped together under the broader age ranges of 'infant' (<1 year), 'juvenile1' (1–6 years), 'juvenile2'

(7–12 years) and 'adolescent' (13–17 years). The methods utilised to determine the age at death of each individual (in the case of Swords just one individual) are provided below. It is not possible to accurately determine the sex of juvenile individuals, as the sex-specific morphological bone manifestations do not develop clearly until the onset of puberty.

The statures of the adults may be estimated following the standards recommended by the British Association for Biological Anthropology and Osteoarchaeology or BABAO (Brothwell and Zakrzewski 2004). In the case of the adults from Swords Castle, owing to poor preservation it was only possible to determine the stature of a single adult (SK14, possible female, adult).

In addition to the fourteen skeletons, quantities of disarticulated human remains were recovered. Most of the disarticulated human remains recovered from Irish excavations tend to be the result of later disturbances of graves, through additional grave-digging or developments in burial-grounds, whereby bones simply become truncated from burials, mixed and redeposited across a site. Such is the case with the disarticulated remains from Swords Castle. There is no deliberate action in the deposition of the bones: they have simply been churned and scattered across the site over the years. The interior of Swords Castle was in use as an orchard from the eighteenth through to the twentieth century, and this would certainly have contributed to the disturbance of earlier burials.

ANALYSIS

Analysis of *in situ* burials

In total, the remains of fourteen *in situ* burials were identified in Trench 9. One burial (SK15), however, was not excavated but was instead left *in situ*; fragments from the broken cranium were taken for AMS dating. It was only possible to determine that the latter burial was of an adult individual.

Demography

Of the thirteen excavated burials, all but one were adult individuals; the exception was SK04, which comprised the remains of an individual aged approximately 6–8 years at the time of death. A summary of the age at death and sex of the twelve adults is provided in Table 8.1.

Table 8.1—Summary of age at death and sex of adult burials excavated in 2017 (SK15 has been excluded, as it was not technically excavated).

	Young adult (18–25 yrs)	Middle adult (26–44 yrs)	Old adult (45+ yrs)	Adult (age at death undetermined)
Female	—	SK06, SK08	SK01, SK05	SK1, SK12, SK14
Male	—	—	—	SK02, SK09
Unsexed	—	—	—	SK03, SK07, SK11

Poor preservation ensured that it was only possible to determine the age at death of four of the twelve adults, or just 33.3%. All four were female and were aged over 26 years at the time of death. No young adults were identified (it is noted, however, that SK15—unexcavated and therefore excluded here—may be a younger adult on the basis that the cranial sutures were open at the time of death, but there is no other corroborating evidence for this). In terms of the determination of sex, the results were a little better: it was possible to determine the sex of 75% (nine of the twelve). The overwhelming majority of those individuals (seven, or 77.8%) were female.

Stature

It was possible to determine the stature of a single adult. The stature of SK14 (possible female, adult) was estimated as 166.3cm. This female was AMS-dated to AD 995–1053 (cal. 2σ). The average stature of three of the females excavated from the Gatehouse of Swords Castle in 2014 was 153.9cm (Tobin 2015), while the average female stature at Mount Gamble in Swords was 158cm (O'Donovan and Geber 2010, 233). Other early medieval female averages include 157cm for eighteen females from Solar, Co. Antrim (Hurl *et al.* 2002, 72), and 155.6cm for nine females from Ratoath, Co. Meath (Fibiger 2010, 120). This suggests that the female from the present assemblage was taller than her average contemporary.

Dental remains

Dental remains were recovered with three of the adults: SK03 (?sex, adult), SK09 (possible female, adult) and SK11 (?sex, adult). In the case of the latter two, just two teeth and one tooth were recovered respectively, while six teeth were recovered from SK03. Dental remains, comprising both deciduous and permanent teeth, were also recovered with SK04 (6–8 years). All individuals, including the juvenile, had evidence of calculus deposits. This is a common finding in archaeological skeletons. Deposits of calculus or calcified plaque may be reduced through good dental hygiene, and they may also be inadvertently removed through the consumption of grittier foods. The aetiology is multi-causal but its formation is aided by alkaline in the mouth and a high-protein diet (Hillson 1996, 255–7; Lieverse 1999). Carious lesions were identified in the dentitions of all three adults. These lesions are cavities in the enamel of a tooth and are typically caused by the consumption of sugars and refined carbohydrates (Hillson 1986, 293; Mays 1998, 148; Woodward and Walker 1994). The frequency of the disease has increased over time owing to the increased consumption of refined foods from the post-medieval period onwards. Periodontal or gum disease was identified in the surviving alveolar bone of SK03 (no alveolar bone survived in the other two skeletons with dental remains). The disease was identified through the abnormal resorption of the alveolar bone of the jaw, exposing the roots of the teeth. In terms of attrition, the evidence was overwhelmingly limited by the low number of dental remains available for analysis; the rates were moderate in SK03 and SK09. Finally, one of the teeth of SK11 had an indented line in the enamel (Pl. 8.3). More extreme expressions of this condition were evident in the dentition of the juvenile SK04 (6–8 years), where numerous teeth, both deciduous and permanent, exhibited lines and pitting. These defects, known as enamel hypoplastic defects, manifest as a depressed line or series of lines or pits on the surface of the enamel. The defects occur in childhood (when the teeth are developing) when, as a result of a physiological stress, the enamel of the tooth stops developing. If an individual recovers, the enamel will begin to grow again. As teeth generally develop at a known rate, it is possible to estimate the time of occurrence of the stress/es (Hillson 1986; Mays 1998). In the adult, SK11 (?sex, adult), the lesion indicated a period of stress when s/he was approximately 11–

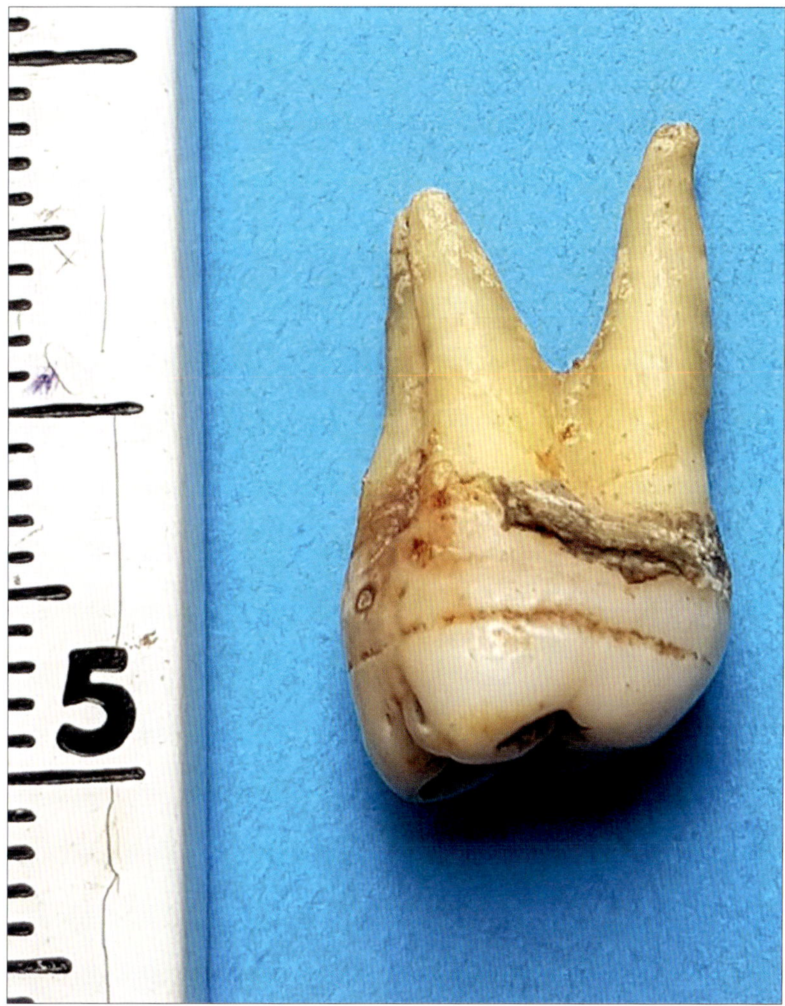

Pl. 8.3—Upper left third molar of SK11 (?sex, adult), showing calculus deposits and linear impression of enamel hypoplastic defect.

12 years old. In the juvenile, SK04 (6–8 years), the multiple and significant manifestations of enamel hypoplastic defects indicate multiple periods of stress in early infanthood (0–9 months) and early childhood (4–4.5 years).

Skeletal pathological lesions

In terms of skeletal pathological lesions, degenerative joint disease (DJD) was the most prevalent; it was recorded in ten out of twelve adult individuals, the exceptions being SK10 (female, adult) and SK12 (female, adult). The prevalence (83.3%) is certainly not unusual for archaeological samples and reflects the normal physicality of life in the past. The onset of the disease is closely linked with aging, as it appears to occur primarily as a result of repeated 'wear and tear' through degeneration of the articular cartilage (Ortner and Putschar 1981, 419–20). The degeneration may be accelerated by occupational activities and may also be brought on by trauma. The evidence of DJD in skeletal remains manifests through porosity (pitting) of the joint surface and/or additional bone growths or osteophytes, typically around the margins. In more advanced cases eburnation or polishing of the bone can occur, as the bones of the joint rub off each other. The presence of eburnation is pathognomonic of osteoarthritis (Rogers and Waldron 1995).

Given the low numbers of individuals involved, it is not possible to analyse the samples statistically in terms of patterns in prevalence rates. It appears, however, that the spine was commonly affected; this is a common finding, as the spine is consistently under pressure in humans through the upward gait, as well as through normal work practices. It then appears that the joints of the elbow and wrist, hips and knees were commonly affected, followed by those of the hands and ankles. The poor preservation has significantly hindered any viable interpretation of the results. The bias in the presence of female adults over male adults (which may or may not be real) may also have influenced the results significantly. In reality, the skeletons of just two males were observable, compared with seven females. The severity, in general, was relatively mild, though there were exceptions; moderate DJD was recorded in the right knee of SK01 (female, adult), while severe expressions, including eburnation, were present in the spine of SK11 (?sex, adult).

In addition, one individual, SK14 (possible female, adult), had distinct lesions in the spine known as Schmorl's nodes. Mild lesions were present in some of the mid- to lower thoracic and in the upper lumbar vertebrae. A severe Schmorl's node is present in the inferior of T12. These distinct lesions typically manifest as small depressions on the superior and/or inferior bodies of the thoracic and lumbar vertebrae in particular. The defects typically occur in youth (in 'softer' bone) as a result of the rupturing of the nucleus pulpous (the pulpous gelatinous core of the intervertebral disk), which can then burst into the adjacent vertebral body as a result of pressure (Mann and Murphy 1990, 52; Ortner and Putschar 1981, 323). This pressure can be caused either by a fall or by straining the spine by, for example, lifting heavy objects incorrectly. In T12 of SK14, the large defect had, rather unusually, burst through into the vertebral canal. The impact of this is unknown.

Evidence of trauma was identified in two individuals. SK01 (female, 45+ years) had a well-healed fracture to the right third proximal hand phalanx, i.e. at the midpoint of the middle finger of the right hand. In addition, another female, SK05 (45+ years), had a fracture to one of the vertebrae of the lower spine. The remains of this individual were poorly preserved, particularly the spine, but a fragment of the right arch of the fifth lumbar vertebra survived and the morphology indicates that it was separated from the rest of the arch at the pars interarticularis (Pl. 8.4.). This is a distinct and well-known spinal fracture, spondylolysis, whose occurrence may be linked to an abnormal weakness in the vertebra at this particular point. It results in the separation of elements of a vertebra: typically the vertebral body, the pedicles, and the transverse and superior articular processes are separated from the laminae, spinous process and inferior articular processes (Aufderheide and Rodríguez-Martín 1998, 63). Although congenital weakness may be 'an important factor in the expression of this abnormality' (Ortner 2003, 147–8), repeated stresses appear to be the major factor involved. The typical age of onset is between ten and fifteen years; the condition is more common in males than in females and has a modern prevalence in Europe of 5–6% (Bergmann *et al.* 2002; Fibiger and Knüsel 2005; Waldron 2009, 153). The condition can be asymptomatic, i.e. it may be largely undetected in the living individual, unless it develops into the more extreme condition of spondylolisthesis.

Two adult individuals exhibited lesions that may be linked with infectious disease. SK07 (?sex, adult) had thickened remodelled deposits of fibre bone in the right femur (Pl. 8.5) and the tibiae. SK09 (possible male, adult) had active, or partly active, fibre bone on a left (medial end) and a right rib (midshaft), as well as active deposits on the anterior aspects of the scapulae. A quantity of disarticulated human bones with periosteal lesions were recovered directly in association with SK09 and may originate from that individual. Fibre bone typically develops in response to an inflammatory process, which may often be linked with infections. The lesions as seen in the Swords individuals are typically referred to as periosteal deposits. This occurs when the periosteum, the fibrous layer directly overlying the normal bone surface, becomes infected. The process of inflammation, with the accumulation of pus and infected matter, forces the periosteum to rise, and a new layer of bone may form underneath. When the lesions

Pl. 8.4—Spondylolysis of right side of fifth lumbar of SK05 (female, possibly 45+ years).

are active, the layer of bone may be grey in colour and may be striated or disorganised. With time the new layer of bone can heal and be remodelled into lamellar bone (the normal surface of the bone). The occurrence of these deposits in multiple locations on the skeleton of an individual, such as is the case with the Swords adults, may be indicative of a systemic infection (Larsen 1997, 83). The tibiae are often the most common location for the lesions (*ibid.*, 85; Roberts and Manchester 1995, 129–30). Periosteal lesions on the ribs (on the internal surface in terms of the body) may be linked with tuberculosis (Roberts *et al.* 1994), although they may be associated with any pulmonary infection (Mays *et al.* 2002). It is not possible to determine the cause of the lesions in the two Swords adults, but they had clearly suffered from some infectious process prior to death. While the lesions were not active in one individual, the opposite was true for the other, although some of the lesions in the latter were partially remodelled. It would be wrong to suggest, however, that the cause of death was an infectious disease, as there is no actual skeletal evidence to corroborate this.

Unusual biological objects (in addition to the actual skeletal remains) were recovered with two individuals, SK01 and SK11. In the case of SK01 (female, 45+ years), numerous small, isolated concretions or biological stones/calculi were recovered with the vertebrae, the right ribs, the right pelvis and the sacrum (Pls 8.6 and 8.7). The surfaces of all were smooth and

Pl. 8.5—Periosteal bone on right femur of SK07 (?sex, adult).

were the same colour as the preserved bone of the individual, having a pale brown hue. The descriptions of each are detailed in the catalogue. While some comprise single, relatively smooth nodules, others appear as conglomerates of a number of smaller nodules. Post-mortem breaks in at least two of the nodules reveal that the interiors are filled with a white chalky substance (Pl. 8.7). They range in size from 5.86mm x 5.88mm x 4.29mm to at least 15.73mm x 13.69mm, with the smallest weighing just 0.1g and the largest *c.* 2g. The distribution of the concretions was particularly concentrated in the pelvic region, with a number of smaller nodules recovered with the vertebrae and right ribs. How accurate this distribution is remains debatable; the concretions were not commented on during excavation and appear to have been inadvertently recovered. It may be assumed, however, that most, if not all, of the stones originated from the abdominal area.

Calcifications can occur as a result of a wide variety of pathological processes and have been linked with vascular, infectious, inflammatory, metabolic and neoplastic conditions (Binder *et al.* 2016, 24). These objects are typically classified as organic concretions and calcifications of pathological lesions in soft tissue. Soft tissue calcifications may be dystrophic or metastatic, with the former being dramatically more common (*ibid.*). The aforementioned stone-like appearance of these particular calcifications found with SK01 is immediately suggestive of the concretions ('stones' or calculi) that may occur in the biliary (gallstones) and urinary (kidney and bladder stones) systems of the body, all of which result from the precipitation of salts and minerals (Binder *et al.* 2016; Waldron 2009, 233–5), but they also bear a similarity to hydatid cysts. The latter result from an infection with the dog tapeworm *Echinococcus granulosus* and can be recovered from archaeological human skeletons. These, however, survive as shell-like structures (Waldron 2009, 111–13), quite unlike the concretions recovered with SK14. In reality, the aforementioned inclusions with SK01 are likely to relate to biological calculi.

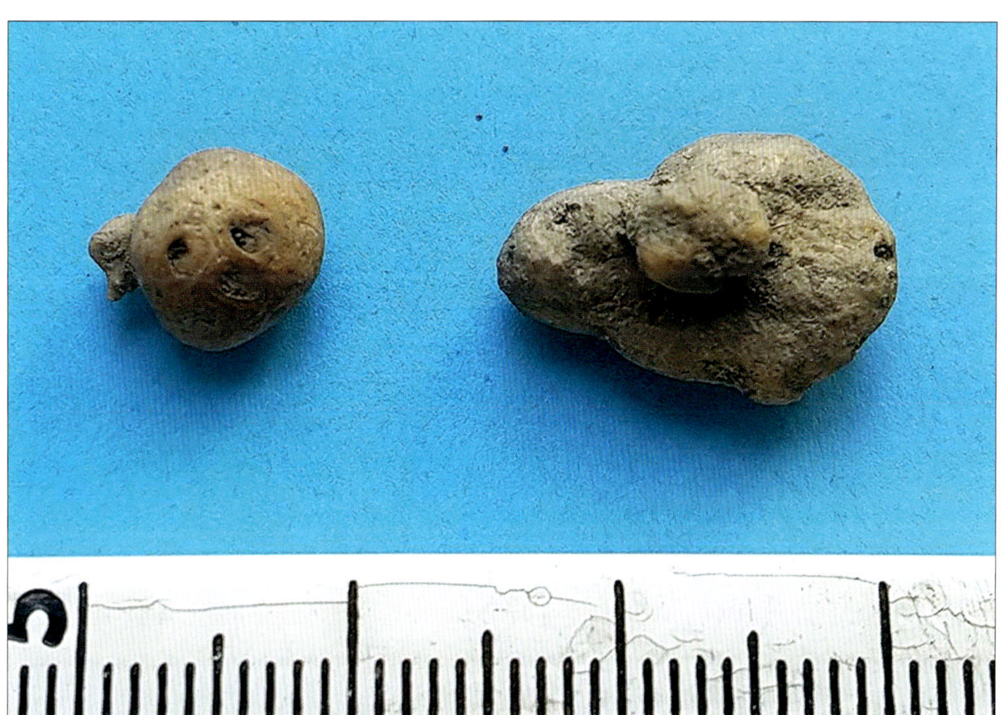

Pl. 8.6—Concretions recovered with sacrum of SK01 (female, possibly 45+ years).

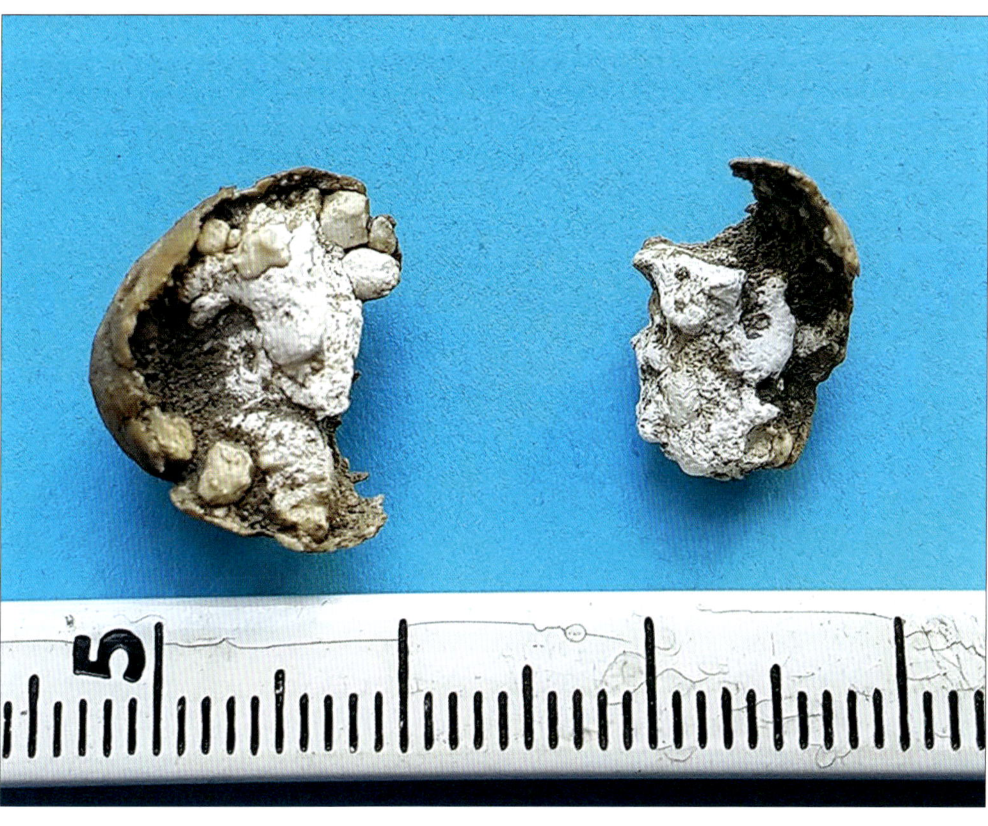

Pl. 8.7—Concretion recovered with pelvis of SK01 (female, possibly 45+ years), revealing chalky interior.

Gallstones (Waldron 2009, 233; Aufderheide and Rodríguez-Martín 1998, 272) are very common, particularly in older individuals such as SK14, and may be asymptomatic until they actually cause a blockage. Occurring in either the gall-bladder itself or the bile ducts, these stones, being yellow to black in colour, may be composed of either cholesterol or pigment, essentially hardened digestive fluids. The interiors of the latter are typically either dark or banded, while the interiors of the former also have a radiating structure. The calculi found with SK14 do not appear to resemble the typical manifestations of gallstones. Moreover, the fact that the stones found with SK01 were recovered from skeletal elements of the lower abdomen may also suggest that they are not gallstones, although, as mentioned above, the actual original location of the stones is unknown. The composition of urinary stones varies depending on time and place, but they occur essentially as a result of supersaturation of the urine's solutes. In terms of size, they may range from very tiny to very large, with one removed from a Sir Walter Ogilvie in 1808 weighing 1.36kg (Waldron 2009, 234). Kidney stones tend to form mainly from calcium oxalate or calcium phosphate. These may become very large or may be expelled into the ureter when no more than 2–3mm in diameter. It is these smaller stones that can cause particular issues, as they can lead to blockages (Aufderheide and Rodríguez-Martín 1998, 284). Bladder stones, while they can occur in adults, are more common in children, particularly boys, and can grow to very large sizes. They are commonly comprised of calcium oxalate, but uric acid may also be a frequent element. Interestingly, bladder stones are also more commonly associated with poverty and a vegetarian diet (*ibid.*, 285; Gładykowska-Rzeczycka and Nowakowski 2014). When urinary stones cause blockages, the results can be notoriously painful and can lead to blood in the urine (haematuria, as a result of haemorrhaging), infections and urinary retention (Aufderheide and Rodríguez-Martín 1998, 284–5; Waldron 2009, 234–5). If the stones were problematic, the only solution in the past was to hope to pass them naturally or to undergo a dangerous invasive operation. At this point, based solely on morphological analysis, the stones are likely to be urinary in origin, but this may only be conclusively confirmed with further tests such as X-ray spectrometry and scanning electron microscopy (SEM), amongst others.

The calcifications recovered with SK11 (?sex, adult) were very different. A large and a small calcified nodule, both highly irregular in form and apparently dense in composition, were recovered with the vertebrae and right ribs respectively (Pl. 8.8). The precise location of these in relation to the *in situ* skeleton is not known (specifically, perhaps, in relation to the spine, it would be useful to know whether the large fragment was in the abdominal area or the thoracic area). The larger calcification measured 35.44mm x 32.4mm x 21.99mm thick and weighed 7.6g, while the smaller fragment measured 13.2mm x 9.04mm x 8.06mm thick and weighed 0.5g. There is no indication that the objects were ever attached to actual bone, although the fragments may have originally been joined together. The surfaces are highly irregular, comprising quite smooth nodules in some locations and an ossified fibre-like morphology in others. These are not like the organic concretions, such as urinary and biliary stones, described above, but comprise actual soft tissue calcification. As mentioned, these may be dystrophic or metastatic, with the former being dramatically more common (Binder *et al.* 2016, 25). Metastatic calcifications may relate to hypo/hyperparathyroidism, renal osteodystrophia and hypervitaminosis D, while dystrophic calcifications may relate to trauma, tumours (e.g. in uterus, lymph nodes, pancreas, thyroid), osteonecrosis, anterosclerosis, tuberculosis and parasitic cysts (*ibid.*).

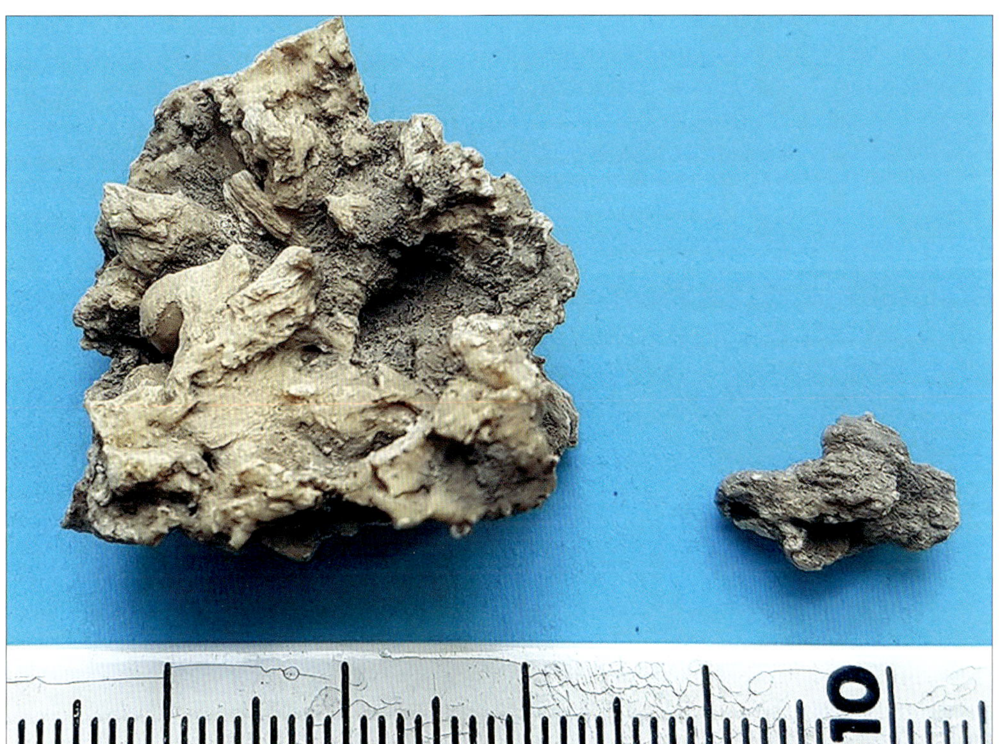

Pl. 8.8—Calcifications recovered with vertebra (left of image) and right ribs (right of image) of SK11 (?sex, adult).

Unfortunately, neither the age at death nor the sex of SK11 could be determined (which could have assisted in diagnosis), and the actual location of these calcifications within the body is unknown. As mentioned, the larger fragment was recovered with the entire vertebral column, but the fact that the smaller fragment was recovered with the right ribs suggests a possible thoracic origin for the calcifications. In fact, they bear a resemblance to ossified pleural plaques, which form within the narrow pleural cavity surrounding the lungs. Ossified pleura can be associated with tuberculosis but can occur owing to other conditions, such as Diffuse Idiopathic Skeletal Hyperostosis (Roberts and Buikstra 2003, 107, 149). Ossified pleura tend to be relatively flat, however, while the calcifications with SK11 are bulkier in volume. More irregular-shaped calcified nodules can also form in the lungs owing to tuberculosis. The only other skeletal pathological lesions observed in this individual were in the form of joint disease, and there were certainly no other skeletal indicators of tuberculosis, but this in itself does not necessarily mean that this individual did not suffer earlier in his/her life.

In tuberculosis, the typical route of infection in humans is through the inhalation of droplets containing *Mycobacterium tuberculosis*, exhaled by infected individuals. Only a small number of individuals actually become infected and only about half will develop active disease. As with most skeletal pathological lesions, only a small percentage (*c.* 2%) of individuals will subsequently go on to develop actual skeletal lesions. During the early stage (primary pulmonary tuberculosis), the immune system fights back and essentially encloses the bacilli (the Ghon focus), which results in latency; this can occur in up to 90% of individuals who become infected. The actual enclosing element, a granuloma, can calcify, ultimately perhaps remaining latent for years or sometimes breaking down and reactivating (Aufderheide and Rodríguez-Martín 1998, 119–20; Ortner and Putschar 1981, 227;

Waldron 2009, 91; Wilbur *et al.* 2008, 965). It is possible that this may be what was recovered with SK11, rather than ossified pleura. Until further tests are performed on these calcifications, however, their origin remains unconfirmed.

ANALYSIS OF DISARTICULATED HUMAN REMAINS

The disarticulated remains were recovered from almost all trenches excavated at Swords Castle, with the exception of Trench 7. Table 8.2 lists the numbers of fragments recovered from each trench.

Table 8.2—Number of fragments of disarticulated human remains by trench.

Trench no.	No. of fragments	% of total*
1	1	0.03
2	18	0.51
3	8	0.23
4	1	0.03
5	1	0.03
6	33	0.94
7	0	0
8	6	0.17
9	3,413	96.85
10	43	1.22
Total	3,524	100.01

*Although percentages in this report are typically rounded to one decimal point, two decimal points are used here to illustrate the quantity when only one fragment was recovered.

Minimum number of individuals (MNI)

All of the disarticulated skeletal remains from the three seasons were considered together in order to establish an overall MNI. The evidence, combining age at death, sex and/or duplication of elements, indicates an MNI of eight individuals: four juveniles (<18 years) and four adults (18+ years). Variations in age at death apparent in various bones and/or teeth in particular, as opposed to duplication of elements, indicate the remains of at least one infant (<1 year), one young juvenile (1–6 years), one older juvenile (7–12 years) and one possible adolescent (12–17 years). Numerous instances indicate the remains of at least four adults, primarily on the basis of the duplication of elements.

Dental remains

In total, the remains of up to 30 teeth were recovered in the disarticulated material. One (ID1310) from Trench 9 and another from Trench 10 (ID1272) comprised single, unidentified tooth roots, while five unidentified tooth roots, also recovered from Trench 9, were grouped together under ID1167. All but one of the teeth was permanent; ID1057 was an upper right deciduous canine. Most of the permanent teeth were probably from adult individuals, the exception being an upper right third molar (ID1037), recovered in Trench 6, which was probably from an adolescent, and an upper left permanent canine (ID1205), recovered in Trench 9, which was probably from an older juvenile.

A number of disarticulated teeth exhibited excessive attrition; the roots mentioned above were all in that condition owing to excessive wear during life. Slight to moderate deposits of calculus were present on at least sixteen teeth, while carious lesions were identified on at least five teeth. A single tooth from the entire disarticulated assemblage from all three seasons exhibited enamel hypoplastic defects, with pitting visible on the enamel of a lower right deciduous canine (ID1057). This tooth was initially indicated as possibly originating from SK04 (6–8 years), but a lower right deciduous canine was recovered with that burial and therefore the disarticulated tooth is not from SK04. The enamel on a single tooth (ID1007, a lower left third molar from Trench 2) was chipped, probably post-mortem.

Pathological skeletal lesions

A number of pathological lesions were observed on the disarticulated skeletal remains, almost exclusively on adult remains. Most, such as the evidence of degenerative joint disease (DJD) below, were also observed in the remains of the *in situ* burials. The exception was evidence of porosity on a number of cranial fragments, all adult in origin. ID1008 from Trench 1, ID1001 from Trench 2 and ID1219 from Trench 8 all exhibited healed porous lesions on the ectocranial (external) surfaces. This is indicative of a condition known as porotic hyperostosis. The lesions can occur when the middle layer of the bone (diplöe) expands and there is a corresponding thinning of the outer surface of the bone, which can result in the diagnostic appearance of small holes (foramina) on the external surface of the bone (Mays 1998, 142). Typically the lesions occur in the occipital and parietal bones, but can appear on the frontal (such as ID1219). Older studies generally linked the lesions with iron deficiency anaemia, but many studies recognise them as general indicators of physiological stress: when a body is under stress from an invading organism (such as an infection), the system increases its output of iron to counteract the stress. This pathological process may therefore actually be a sign of a healthy defence system (Roberts and Manchester 1995, 166–7; Stuart-Macadam 1991, 105). More recently, the lesions have been specifically linked with a diet deficient in vitamin B_{12}, which may be derived from foods of animal origin (Walker *et al.* 2009). In any case, it is taken as being an indicator of general physiological stress.

Joint disease was a common finding, particularly in the bones from Trench 9, although this is most likely linked with the sheer quantity of bone recovered from that trench. From the latter, DJD was identified in elements of the hip (ID1132, 1107), the spine (ID1097, 1130, 1134, 1243), the knee (ID1222, 1283), the ankle (ID1213) and the foot (ID1081). DJD was also evident in two cervical vertebrae (ID1010, 1012) from Trench 3. In general, the lesions were slight to moderate, although eburnation, indicative of cartilage destruction and subsequent polishing of the joint surfaces as bone rubbed against bone, was present on a right hip joint (ID1107).

The latter bone also had significant periosteal lesions. In fact, evidence of inflammation/infection was observed on a number of bone fragments in Trench 9 and was particularly associated with SK09 (possible male, adult), who had active fibre bone in the scapulae and left and right ribs. The affected disarticulated bones included active fibre bone on two fibular fragments (ID1111 and ID1117) and significant periosteal lesions on the aforementioned right femoral shaft (ID1107, which also had osteoarthritis with eburnation) and on a right tibia (ID1108), all associated with SK09. Incidentally, the *in situ* remains of SK09 only comprised the upper part of the skeleton, and it is entirely possible that the disarticulated bones with periosteal lesions found directly in association with that individual may originate from SK09. In addition, active circumferential fibre bone was present on another fibula fragment (ID1320). Partially remodelled periostitis was present on the internal surface of a juvenile rib (ID1015, from Trench 3), which may suggest some form of pulmonary infection.

Just a single example of trauma was found in the disarticulated assemblage: a healed fracture was present on the plantar aspect of the proximal end of a proximal foot phalanx (ID1324).

Finally, although not a pathological lesion, a fragment of an adult frontal bone from the cranium, ID1219 from Trench 8, showed evidence of the retention of a metopic suture. This suture, which divides the frontal bone of the forehead of an infant into two halves, typically closes in the first year of life, although fusion can continue as far as the seventh year (Nikolova and Toneva 2012; Nikolova *et al.* 2019; Scheuer and Black 2000, 107). Metopism (retention of the suture) may present in anywhere between 0.8% and 15% of a population and has no known side-effects, although it has been recorded as a concomitant finding in numerous disorders (Nikolova *et al.* 2019). In archaeological studies it has been studied as a non-metric variant with possible genetic links (Şarbak *et al.* 2017).

DISCUSSION

All fourteen burials and 96.9% of all the individual fragments of disarticulated bone recovered at Swords Castle during the *Swords Castle: Digging History* project were from a single trench, Trench 9. This trench was located immediately to the north of the area where *in situ* burials were identified by Tom Fanning in the 1970s. The recent findings clearly confirm previous evidence that burials in Swords Castle—or at least in the area of what became Swords Castle—were confined to the south-west of the site and did not extend significantly to the north or east sides of the site. This is corroborated by the distribution of the disarticulated human skeletal remains.

In terms of the dating of the current burials, three of the thirteen were sampled and returned dates ranging from the late tenth to the late twelfth century—all pre-dating the construction of Swords Castle *c.* 1200 by the first Anglo-Norman archbishop of Dublin, John Comyn (Baker 2018, 9). This was confirmed by the two samples of disarticulated human remains from the first two seasons' work, which produced similar dates. Based on the current evidence, there is nothing to suggest that any burials in the most recently examined areas post-dated the construction of the castle. Four of the burials excavated from the area of the Gatehouse in 2014 were subject to AMS dating and returned dates from relatively early in the eleventh century through to the late thirteenth century (Tobin 2015). One of those burials returned a date potentially post-dating the construction of the castle: Sk. 5 (in that catalogue) was dated to AD 1190–1281 (*ibid.*, 1). In reality, the remains of this late adolescent/adult were recovered *under* the west wall of the Gatehouse, indicating that burials had perhaps just ceased at the site prior to the building of the castle. Fanning, however, surmised after his 1971 excavations that at least some of those burials post-dated the occupation of the castle (Baker *et al.* 2005, 55). Based on the evidence established to date, this premise appears highly unlikely and may only be really tested if any of the skeletons that Fanning identified are rediscovered (C. Baker, pers. comm.). The burial activity at the site does largely appear to pre-date the castle. The fact that burial may only have ceased just prior to the construction of the castle raises the question of how deliberately chosen was the siting of the castle. Was this a very definite attempt by the newly established Anglo-Normans to make their mark by literally building a castle over a significantly sized, presumably Irish, burial-ground?

How does the current assemblage compare with that from the Gatehouse (Tobin 2015), as both appear to be of a similar date and were subject to modern osteoarchaeological analysis? The Gatehouse report, while recognising the limitations imposed by the small sample size, suggested a possible bias in that sample towards children (excluding infants and older children) and older females. Interestingly, some comparable data emerged from the burials excavated in 2017. It must be stressed again, however, that the sample number is small (just thirteen actual individuals) and is certainly compromised by issues of significant truncation and poor preservation: 30.8% were classed as poorly preserved, while the remaining 69.2% were classed as very poorly preserved. In terms of ages at death of the adults, it was unfortunately only possible to assess four of the thirteen adult individuals. The assessment of sex, however, was more fruitful: seven of the nine adults whose sex could be determined were female (77.8%). This agrees somewhat with the findings from the 2014 excavations. It also raises the question of whether this apparent bias was entirely by chance and that another part of this burial-ground contained many of the male individuals, or whether there was indeed some form of separate burial practised at this site prior to the building of the castle.

The information regarding juveniles (those aged less than eighteen years at the time of death) was also interesting. Just a single burial of a juvenile was unearthed in the 2017 excavations, that of an individual aged between six and eight years at the time of death. When the disarticulated material is considered, the remains of four juveniles were identified out of a total MNI of eight. It is impossible to determine whether this is more representative of the real burial population. The age profile is interesting, however, as one infant (<1 year), one young juvenile (1–6 years), one older juvenile (7–12 years) and one adolescent (13–17 years) were identified, representing the whole span of juvenile ages. This suggests that the apparent potential biases in burial patterns (such as a lack of infants in the Gatehouse excavations and, indeed, in the current excavations) may be entirely random, although the aforementioned infant is represented by a single bone (ID1275). This very limited evidence, in a disarticulated assemblage of 3,524 fragments of bone from the *Swords Castle: Digging History* project, tallies with the fact that no infant burials were identified in the same project, nor in the 2014 Gatehouse excavations. Unfortunately, Fanning's report only refers to 'children' in the burials uncovered in 1971. Based on the current data, it is possible that infants in particular (here defined as anyone less than one year old at the time of death) were excluded from burial in at least this area of the early medieval cemetery.

As regards the health status of the mostly recently excavated individuals, the results are interesting, if somewhat limited. There was a range of commonly observed pathological lesions; unfortunately, the inherent biases of sample size and incompleteness prevent any coherent assessment of prevalence rates. The most commonly observed disease was degenerative joint disease, with the spine in particular being affected; in total, 83.3% of individuals exhibited some degree of joint disease. The observed traumas were minor: a healed broken finger and a stress fracture in the spine. There was also some evidence of infectious disease, with two individuals probably affected by a systemic infection (although there is no proof that this was the cause of death in either case). All of these are commonly observed, in some form, in many archaeological skeletal samples. The only variant observed in the disarticulated assemblage was evidence of metabolic disease (in the form of porotic hyperostosis); again, this can be common in such skeletal assemblages. All of these pathological lesions, in some variation, were also observed by Tobin (2015) in the individuals excavated from the Gatehouse area. Given the biases, it is difficult to surmise anything definitive in terms of health and, to a certain degree, the evidence is somewhat contradictory. The female adults buried in the area of the Gatehouse were smaller than their contemporaries. In comparison, while it was only possible to estimate the stature of a single female from the present assemblage, she was considerably taller than the aforementioned females and, indeed, than most of her peers. This may suggest that she had better nutrition as a child, with fewer physiological stresses, suggestive of a possible higher status, but realistically this would be making too many assumptions.

The dentitions of the skeletons excavated in 2017 were, unfortunately, very poorly represented. They exhibited the commonly observed deposits of calcified plaque, carious lesions and periodontal disease, amongst others. Perhaps most noteworthy, many teeth, particularly in the disarticulated assemblage, exhibited excessive attrition, sometimes to such a degree that only roots remained. This is reflective of the coarse dietary intake of the early medieval period.

Essentially, the dental and skeletal pathological lesions that were observed in the skeletal remains recovered during the *Swords Castle: Digging History* project are commonly observed in most skeletal assemblages, and certain traits, such as the dental attrition and the general lack of evidence of infection (*not* actually denoting that there was a lack of infection in the population but rather a lack of evidence *on* the skeletal remains), are consistent with the date of the skeletons. As mentioned numerous times, the low number of individuals and the very poor levels of preservation hinder some in-depth assessment. Perhaps the most important factors regarding these individuals, apart from the possible discrepancies in terms of demographic profile, were the biological objects recovered with SK01 (female, 45+ years) and SK11 (?sex, adult). The former had numerous probable urinary tract stones, while the latter appears to have had some pulmonary calcifications, which may be associated with tuberculosis. Further, more detailed, laboratory assessments would be required to confirm these diagnoses, but the presence of these features clearly illustrates the hazards of life in the past. The probable urinary stones had the potential to be debilitatingly painful and may have caused further physiological problems. The calcified structures recovered with SK11 may relate to a pulmonary issue, possibly in the past and not actually active at death, and, although significant, do not indicate cause of death. The recovery of these important pathological features is also a testament to the care taken by the team both on site and in post-excavation work. This is also attested by the fact that the MNI of the disarticulated adult remains in TR9 was finally determined from elements of the feet and hands—typically the elements that are least represented in a skeletal assemblage, being small and more easily missed.

In terms of burial practices, all the individuals were buried supine and extended, aligned west/east with the head to the west, in what may be considered the 'traditional' mode of Christian burial. A pillow stone was recorded with one burial, SK09 (possible male, adult), and is not an unusual find for burials of this date. In most cases the lower arm bones were crossed slightly over the abdominal areas. The exceptions appeared to be at least SK10 (female, adult) and SK11 (possible female, adult), whose arms were placed parallel to the body. The significance, if any, of this variation is unknown. In most cases it was difficult to assess the actual outline of the hand bones in particular, but the on-site photographs appear to suggest that the hand phalanges (finger bones) of SK02 (male, adult) were extended (Pl. 8.9), perhaps indicating that this individual was buried either before rigor mortis set in or after it had dissipated. Rigor mortis begins approximately two to four hours after death. After 24 hours the body will be so rigid that it may be capable of supporting its own weight. This rigidity will disappear approximately 48 hours after death (Clark *et al.* 1997, 152). This all depends on a wide variety of factors, however, and unfortunately it is not possible to determine how soon after death this individual may have been buried, although it does appear that the fingers were flexible. Where observable, the legs appeared to be placed relatively close together, such as in SK01 (female, possibly 45+ years), which suggests that the bodies were bound or wrapped prior to burial; there was no evidence of coffins, again a common finding in early medieval Irish cemeteries. More variation was evident in the contemporary burials in the area of the Gatehouse, including some significant evidence of deviancy in the form of at least a prone burial (see Tsaliki 2008). Certainly, the latter may be considered to be other than what might be expected of the respectable Christian burial, but its location within what appears to be a relatively average burial-ground should not denote that many others here

Pl. 8.9—Extended finger bones of SK02 (male, adult).

were also 'deviant'. Such burials have been recorded in association with other apparently 'normal' burials in early medieval cemeteries in Ireland (e.g. at Faughart Lower, Co. Louth; see Buckley and Conway 2010), which indicates that physical separation may not have been a requirement for deviant burials; the body position was punishment enough.

The plan of the burials indicates the density—and, indeed, the order—of burial exposed in Trench 9 (Fig. 8.1). SK1, SK5 and SK03 appear to form at least one approximate row, suggesting ordered burial. Others, however, intercut older burials, as mentioned earlier in relation to disarticulated material. For example, SK06 (possible female, 40–44 years) was truncated by SK11 (?sex, adult), and SK14 (possible female, adult) was truncated by SK09 (possible male, adult) (see below also). This suggests that any grave-markers that existed may have been quite transitory. Regarding the truncation, an interesting analogy exists between the burials excavated in 2014 at the Gatehouse and the current assemblage. In the former study, it was noted that in one burial concentration some of the disarticulated long bones of a disinterred juvenile burial (Sk. 7 in that catalogue) had been placed parallel to the limbs of the later adult burial (Sk. 8 in that catalogue), which was, incidentally, the aforementioned prone burial. A similar trait was noted in the 2017 burials in relation to SK09 (possible male, adult), whose burial truncated a previous interment, SK14 (possible female, adult). A significant quantity of disarticulated bones of the lower limb, possibly from SK14 but also possibly from SK09, were rearranged along the left and right sides of SK09, with long bones aligned with the long axis of the burial. This may, in reality, have had next to no significance in terms of burial practice and may simply have been a trait of the individual/s digging the grave.

CONCLUSIONS

Although the actual osteological data from the burials uncovered during the 2017 excavations are somewhat limited, they still provide some crucial information regarding the history of Swords. The remains of at least fourteen burials were uncovered, as well as the disarticulated remains of possibly eight individuals. The dating of three of the burials, as well as disarticulated samples, confirms that there was likely a quite extensive burial-ground at the site of Swords Castle prior to its construction *c.* 1200. There are tantalising indications of variations in who was buried where, with a possible emphasis on adult females, and a lack of infants in particular. Overall, the burials, including the observed skeletal and dental pathological indicators, are largely what might be expected from an early medieval cemetery, although two burials had rather rare biological inclusions which clearly indicate the trials of life without modern medicine. The very normality of the burial-ground may initially appear to contradict the clear evidence of at least one significant deviant burial in a previous excavation in the area; realistically, it confirms the great diversity of burial practices in this period. Based on the current evidence, it appears that burial ceased at the site once the building of the castle began. The significance of this, if any, needs further research.

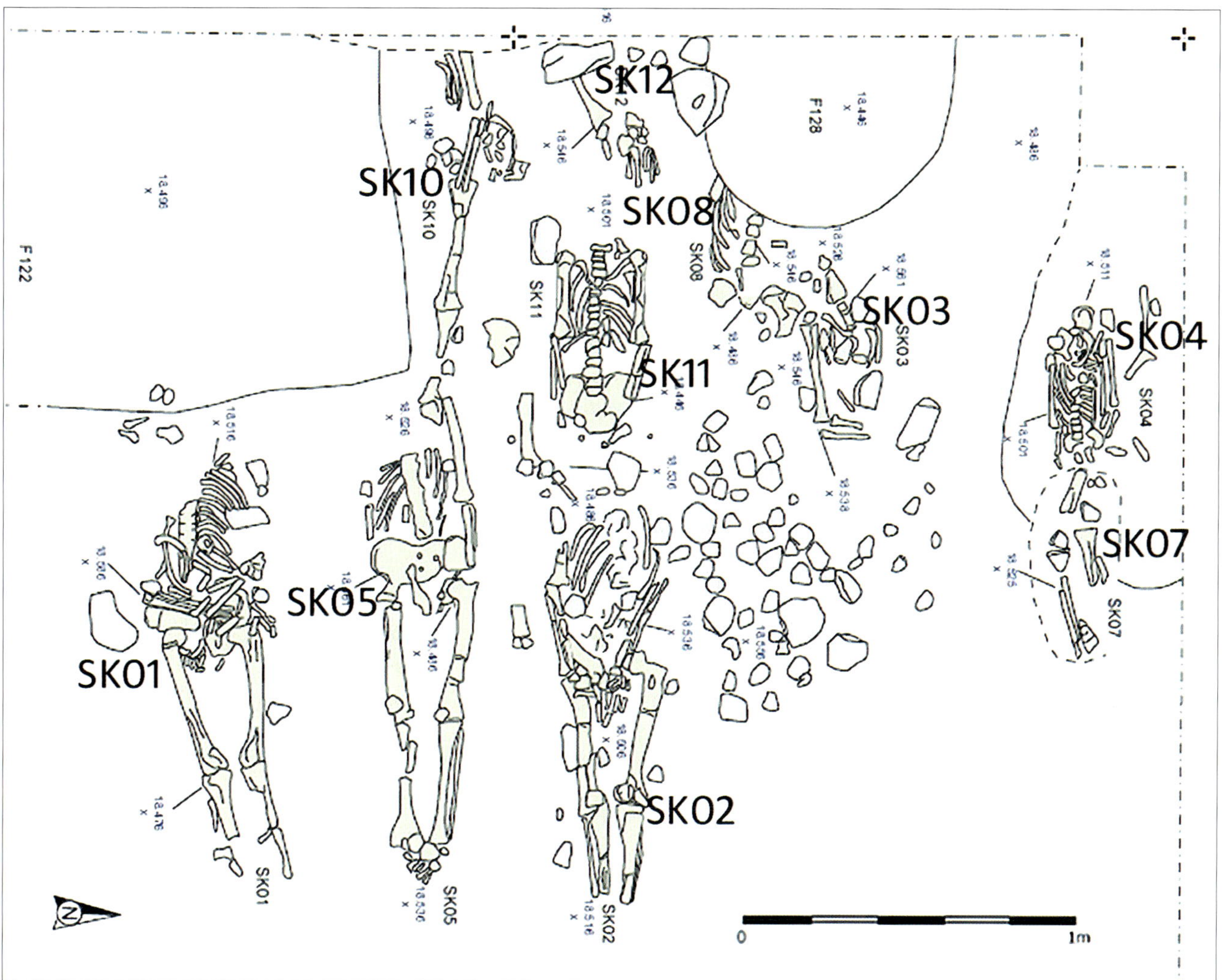

Fig. 8.1—Plan of some burials in Trench 9; north to right (courtesy of C. Baker).

CATALOGUE OF *IN SITU* HUMAN SKELETAL REMAINS

A summary of the *in situ* skeletons from Swords Castle is provided in Table 8.3 (overleaf).

Table 8.3—Summary of the osteoarchaeological analysis of in situ *skeletons.*

Burial	Age	Sex	Stature (cm)	Dental remains	Skeletal pathology
SK01	Poss. 45+ yrs	Female	—	—	Joint disease—mild DJD in elbows, left wrist, hands, left hip, knees; moderate DJD in right knee. Trauma—well-healed fracture of right third proximal hand phalanx. Other—small calcified nodules recovered with right pelvis, vertebrae, right ribs, sacrum: possible urinary stones.
SK02	Adult	Male	—	—	Joint disease—mild DJD in elbows, wrists, knees.
SK03	Adult	?	—	Six permanent teeth, minimal alveolar bone. Calculus—6/6, slight to moderate. Caries—1/6, moderate. Periodontal disease—moderate to severe. Attrition—level 5.	Joint disease—mild spinal DJD.
SK04	6–8 yrs	—	—	Sixteen deciduous teeth and four erupted, two erupting, and sixteen unerupted permanent teeth. Calculus—7/16 deciduous, slight. Enamel hypoplastic defects—pitting and lines on 7/16 deciduous and seventeen observable permanent, stress 0–9 mths and 4–4.5 yrs.	-
SK05	Poss. 45+ yrs	Female	—	—	Joint disease—mild DJD in hips, spine, left knee, left ankle. Trauma—spondylolysis, L5. Non-metric—sternal foramen.
SK06	40–44 yrs	Poss. female	—	—	Joint disease—mild DJD in wrists, right hand, left hip, knees, right ankle. Other—enthesopathies in patellae, femora, right calcaneus.

Skeleton	Age	Sex	Stature	Dental	Pathology
SK07	Adult	?	—	—	Joint disease—mild DJD in left knee. Non-specific infection—active, and some partially remodelled thickened fibre bone on right femur and tibiae.
SK08	35–39 yrs	Poss. female	—	—	Joint disease—mild DJD in left hip.
SK09	Adult	Poss. male	—	Two permanent teeth, no alveolar bone. Calculus—1/2, slight. Caries – 1/2, small. Attrition—level 6.	Joint disease—mild DJD in right elbow, wrists, spine. Non-specific infection—active fibre bone on anterior scapulae and one left and one right rib.
SK10	Adult	Female	—	—	—
SK11	Adult	—	—	One permanent tooth, no alveolar bone. Calculus—1/1, slight to moderate. Caries—1/1, small. Enamel hypoplastic defects—line on one indicating stress c. 11–12 yrs.	Joint disease—mild DJD on two unsided hand phalanges, eburnation in spine. Other—calcified nodules, possibly representing pulmonary calcifications, recovered with vertebrae and right ribs.
SK12	Adult	Female	—	—	—
SK14	Adult	Poss. female	166.3cm	—	Joint disease—mild DJD in right elbow and wrist, and spine. Slight Schmorl's nodes in thoracic and lumbar vertebrae, severe in inferior T12.
SK15	Adult	?	—	—	—

9

Medieval and post-medieval pottery

Clare McCutcheon MA, MIAI

INTRODUCTION

In total, 1,172 sherds of pottery from three seasons of excavation were presented for study. Following identification and some reassembly within and between contexts, this was reduced to 1,118 sherds, of which 936 (82.8%) are medieval in date.

METHODOLOGY

The identification of the sherds has been entered on a database as per the requirements of the National Museum of Ireland. The material has been identified visually and the detailed information is presented in Tables 9.1 and 9.2. These show the number of sherds in each fabric type, the minimum number of vessels (MNV) present and the minimum number of vessels represented by the sherds (MVR). The form of the vessels represented is also shown, with the known date range of the material. Sherd links were established between the following contexts: 21+31; 70+80+87; 74+80+81; 74+77+87; 80+86; 81+87; 106+142. The pottery listed in the database is summarised in Table 9.3, with the quantity of pottery after reassembly.

MEDIEVAL POTTERY

Leinster Cooking Ware

This micaceous, hand-built ware 'is the single most widespread medieval pottery type in Leinster' (Ó Floinn 1988, 340). It has been found in varying quantities on both urban and rural sites from Dungarvan to Dublin and further north. The fabric contains large plates of mica, quartz grits and other inclusions such as decomposed feldspar (*ibid.*, 327), and the vessels are unglazed. While similar clay can be found in Dublin-type cooking ware and other locally made unglazed wares of the period, the method of construction and firing leaves the Leinster Cooking Ware vessels with an easily recognisable sand-pitted base. The vessels represented are cooking jars, the standard medieval form with everted rim, ovoid body and sand-gritted base.

Dublin-type wares

The designation of a fabric with the suffix '-type' is recommended pottery practice to indicate

Pl. 9.1—Medieval pottery diagnostic sherds (photo: John Sunderland).

Fabric	Sherds	MNV	MVR	Form	Date
Ham Green B	1	—	1	Jug	L12th–M13th
Leinster Cooking Ware	80	—	3	Cooking jars	L12th–M14th
Dublin-type cooking ware	49	—	1	Cooking jar	L12th–13th
Dublin-type coarseware	37	—	3	Jugs	L12th–E13th
Dublin-type ware	435	3	6	4 jugs, 2 storage jars, pedestal bowl?	13th
Dublin-type fineware	327	1	4	Jugs	L13th–E14th
Saintonge green-glazed	7	—	2	Jugs	13th–M14th
Total medieval	**936**	**4**	**20**		

Table 9.1—Medieval pottery, Swords Castle (E4619), Seasons 1–3.

Pl. 9.2—Medieval pottery body sherds (photo: John Sunderland).

that a ware has been consistently found in a particular area where evidence for a production centre or kiln has not yet been discovered (Blake and Davey 1983, 39–40). The general term 'London-type', for example, has been adopted to describe wares that share general traditions and clay sources (Pearce *et al.* 1985, 2). A fuller discussion of the names of the Dublin-type wares has been detailed elsewhere (McCutcheon 2000, 120–3; 2006) and only a general outline is included in this report. The relative dating of the Dublin-type wares has been developed as a result of consistent recovery in the stratigraphic levels of the Dublin excavations, and the absolute dating is developing through the association of imported wares and the dating information from coins and dendrochronology.

Dublin-type cooking ware
The most distinctive difference between the cooking ware and the largely contemporary Leinster Cooking Ware is the method of construction of the base. Dublin-type cooking ware bases are smooth rather than sand-gritted and the fabric tends to be less coarse.

Dublin-type coarseware

One strap handle (96:15) is decorated with slashes on either side of a central deep stabbing, while the second (7:1) is similar in style but with more closely overlapping outer slashes and a central line of slashes. A third small fragment (1:95) appears to have two outer lines of slashes with a central continuous line. A further reassembled piece (23:2+18+19) appears to be a decorated tubular spout from a jug, with a second sherd (23:17) with a part of the rim still extant. The decoration consists of lines of small square rouletting and reflects the earlier type of Ham Green Ware.

Dublin-type ware

The majority of the fragments are small, detached body sherds. An unusual thick, rim-like sherd (131:98), found in Season 3, is most likely the base of a large footed bowl. A rim/handle (131:97) is decorated with pinched applied clay around the rim and four deep slashes at the top of the strap handle.

Dublin-type fineware

The majority of the pottery from Season 3 was the later Dublin-type fineware. This is the lower-fired, clean clay that is typical of the later thirteenth to mid-fourteenth century. These also tend to be plainer jugs with little in the way of decoration, although five body sherds out of some 140 are decorated with horizontal incised lines. Three sherds have applied ladder strips, and three have applied pinched clay below the neck. One undecorated rim/handle from Season 3 is almost complete (106:77+142:5; 106:76; 131:100), while a second handle fragment has a single central incised line (131:62). An unusual item is an undecorated glazed body sherd (109:29), modified for secondary use as a gaming counter. These are occasionally

Pl. 9.3—Saintonge mottled green-glazed (photo: John Sunderland).

found in seventeenth- and eighteenth-century pottery such as tin-glazed earthenware and creamware.

Saintonge mottled green-glazed
The term 'Saintonge' has been used as something of a catch-all in Irish ceramic studies. It is becoming increasingly apparent, however, that a number of production centres in the wider Bordeaux area shared similar clay and forms, thus making it difficult to distinguish on the basis of chemical analysis. It may be that certain vessels will be recognised by their individual decorative motifs as coming from a particular area. The principal production of the Saintonge to be found in Ireland are tall standard jugs with mottled green glaze, minimal decoration, flat splayed bases, strap handles and applied spouts. As with the majority of the French wares, the clay is off-white, micaceous and containing quartz and haematite. The application of a lead glaze containing copper filings leads to the mottled effect that constitutes the primary decoration. While the height and width of the jug varied at times, the size of the bases and rims is very standard.

LATE MEDIEVAL AND POST-MEDIEVAL POTTERY

Frechen
Grey stonewares with a mottled brown surface were made in the towns of Cologne and Frechen from the sixteenth century (Hurst *et al.* 1986, 208). Potters originally from Frechen moved to Cologne in about 1500 but were moved out in the mid-sixteenth century on account of the pollution from the kilns (*ibid.*).

Westerwald
This pottery was made in the Westerwald area, east of the Rhine, at a number of production sites following the influx of potters from Raeren in the 1590s. The ware was traded in the seventeenth and eighteenth centuries to the Americas, Africa and the Far East. The industry continues to the present day (*ibid.*, 221). The fabric is grey stoneware with an overall blue-grey salt glaze, the colour resulting from the cobalt used for decoration. A single sherd (625) is decorated with incised lines enclosing a dark cobalt blue decoration.

Seville coarseware
Olive jars were produced in the Seville area from the Roman period through to the nineteenth century (Jennings 1981, 77) and were widely distributed to northern Europe and America in the seventeenth century (Hurst *et al.* 1986, 66). The fabric is coarse, pink-buff in colour with a light-coloured exterior, resulting from 'the reaction of salt and calcium carbonate during firing' (Gerrard *et al.* 1995, 281). The jars were sometimes green-glazed on the interior. A large sherd (109:47) with the typical cream exterior was recovered in Season 3.

North Devon wares
The production of these wares was centred on the towns of Bideford and Barnstaple in North Devon, with a large-scale export trade to Ireland in the seventeenth century, peaking in the early 1680s (Grant 1983, 109). Considerable quantities were exported to Ireland to service the

Table 9.2—Late medieval/post-medieval pottery, Swords Castle (E4619), Seasons 1–3.

Fabric	Sherds	MNV	MVR	Form	Date
Frechen	11	—	1	Jug	L16th–17th
Westerwald	1	—	1	Jug?	17th
Seville coarseware	2	—	1	Olive jar	17th
North Devon gravel-free	3	—	1	Bowl	17th
North Devon gravel-tempered	21	—	1	Jar	17th
Bristol/Staffordshire slipware	1	—	1	Cup	18th
Mottled/treacle ware	2	—	1	Tankard	18th
Porcelain	1	—	1	Plate	18th
Black-glazed ware	17	—	1	Bowl	L17th–19th
Glazed red earthenware (GRE)	30	—	2	Bowls	L17th–19th
GRE: slip-decorated	5	—	2	Plates	18th–19th
Unglazed red	51	—	3	Flowerpots	18th–19th
Pearlware	1	—	1	Jug?	L18th–20th
Transfer-printed ware	1	—	1	Plate?	19th
Ironstone	2	—	1	Jug?	19th
Brown-glazed earthenware	1	—	1	Teapot?	L19th–E20th
Stoneware	15	—	>2	Bottles	19th–20th
Unidentified	17	—	>1		
Total post-medieval	**182**		**>20**		

provisions trade to the North American colonies. The same basic fabric and glazes are used but the addition of gravel temper and slip and sgraffito patterns enhances a wide variety of vessels.

North Devon gravel-free
This is the basic fabric, clean pink- and grey-firing clay, with a clear lead glaze that appears green/brown on firing. Vessels are generally jugs, bowls, chamber-pots, lids etc.

North Devon gravel-tempered
The basic fabric is strengthened with a fine, water-rolled quartz gravel to assist in opening out the thicker bodies to allow for complete and consistent drying. Larger vessels for the kitchen and dairy were made in this fabric, but the lead glaze reacts in the same way as the North Devon gravel-free wares. These tripod pots were made in imitation of metal pots but

with a rod handle projecting at *c.* 45° from the rim, probably to assist in steadying the pot on the fire.

Bristol/Staffordshire slipware
This ware was made in both the Bristol and Staffordshire areas in the late seventeenth and eighteenth centuries (Jennings 1981, 104). While Bristol's close connections with Ireland might lead to the assumption that the slipwares came from there, the overwhelming majority of later seventeenth- and eighteenth-century pottery was imported from Staffordshire. In addition, no close study has been carried out in Ireland to differentiate between the Bristol and Staffordshire slipwares—hence the somewhat cumbersome name—although a further indication of Staffordshire over Bristol is the consistent presence in the assemblages of press-moulded plates, not currently thought to have been made in Bristol (*ibid.*). The basic white firing clay is decorated with red slip, combed or feathered to provide a trailed pattern. The clear lead glaze then produces highly decorative tablewares in yellow and brown. Most of the vessels were decorated with feathering, although occasional sherds were also decorated with blobs of contrasting clay.

Mottled/treacle ware
The fabric of these Staffordshire wares varied from fine buff to orange/red, with the vessels covered in a rich dark brown slip (*ibid.*). Tankards are the most typical vessel form recovered in excavations in Ireland. One of the two sherds recovered at Swords Castle is the base (1:503) of one of these tankards, roughly finished with sand in the outer glaze stuck to the lower base and with a very thick layer (max. 15mm) of glaze and red clay build-up on the inside.

Black-glazed ware
Black-glazed wares are most commonly found in Dublin and the east coast, originating from Lancashire and north Wales, i.e. the so-called Buckley wares. Both black-glazed and glazed red earthenwares (below) are the successors of the North Devon gravel-tempered wares—large vessels used for the dairy, kitchen and toilet. Some tablewares, such as cups and jugs, were also made in these wares, as were roof tiles. In contrast, the industrial production of tablewares in Staffordshire supplanted the corresponding seventeenth-century North Devon sgraffito wares. Black glazing results from the addition of iron to lead glaze on the red earthenware fabrics. The fabric is often highly fired to an almost stoneware purple, although other varieties have a white marbled appearance.

Glazed red earthenware
The fabric is generally sandy earthenware, usually oxidised to buff to light orange through to brown. The clear lead glaze takes its colour from the fabric, with variations owing to firing conditions (Jennings 1981, 157). These are also known as brownwares and were made widely in England and Ireland in the later seventeenth and eighteenth centuries (Dunlevy 1988a, 24–5).

Anglo-Netherlands slipware
This is a term used to describe sherds previously thought to be Metropolitan slipwares, imported from the London area. There was such a variety of well-made redwares with slip decoration produced in the later seventeenth century, however, that the broader term of Anglo-Netherlands

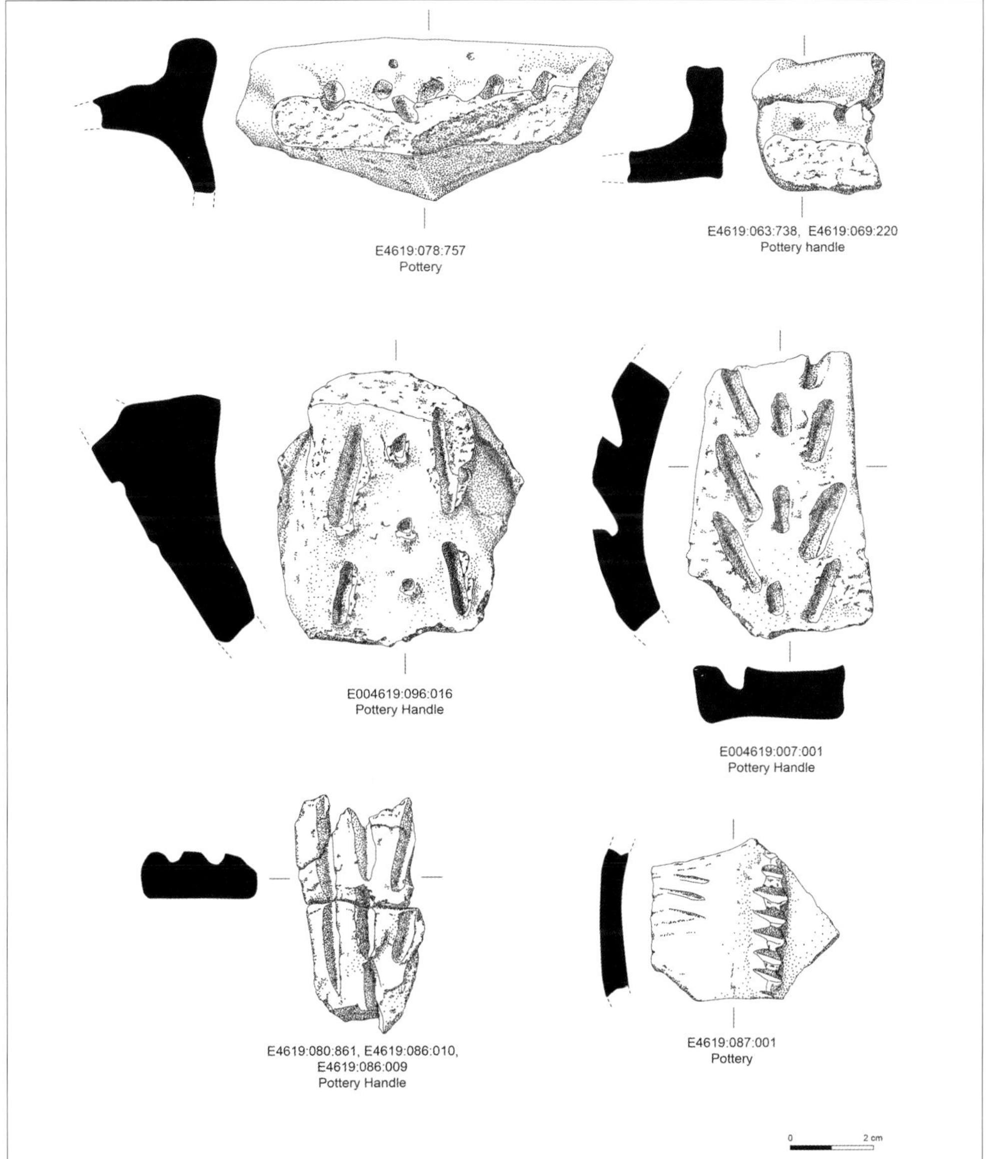

Fig. 9.1—Medieval pottery (drawing: Sara Nylund).

slipware has been advised (Walter Davey, pers. comm.). The ware is generally dark red earthenware with a considerable quantity of cream slip on the rim and base of the plate. This is unlike the treatment of the later glazed red earthenware slip-decorated plates, where the clay is generally lighter and the slip decoration is confined to the rim.

Stoneware

The term is used here to cover all English stonewares, made of a clay and fusible stone which can be fired to partial vitrification, not then requiring a glaze to make it impervious to liquids (Savage and Newman 2000, 275). Stoneware was first introduced into England in the late seventeenth century and was often termed 'Cologne ware' (*ibid.*). The surface tends to have a more matt glaze than the mottled tiger ware from Frechen (above).

145

Table 9.3—Pottery by context, Swords Castle, Seasons 1–3 (E4619).

Trench	Context	Context description	Pottery
1	1		Leinster Cooking Ware x7; Dublin-type cooking ware x2; Dublin-type coarseware x1; Dublin-type x3; Dublin-type fineware x14; Frechen x1; North Devon gravel-free x1; Bristol/Staffordshire slipware x1; black-glazed ware x2; glazed red earthenware x4; GRE slip-decorated x1; unglazed red earthenware x11; pearlware x1; stoneware x8; unidentified x3
1	3	Stony layer	Leinster Cooking Ware x2; Dublin-type coarseware x1; Dublin-type ware x3; Frechen x1; glazed red earthenware x1; stoneware x1; unidentified x1
1	4		Dublin-type fineware x1; North Devon gravel-tempered x1
1	8		Dublin-type coarseware x6; unidentified x2
1	7		Dublin-type x5; Dublin-type fineware x3; Saintonge green-glazed x1; unidentified x1
1	14		Dublin-type x15
1	15		Dublin-type coarseware x1
1	23		Dublin-type coarseware x8
1	37		Leinster Cooking Ware x13; Dublin-type fineware x4
1	40		Dublin-type x1
1	43		Leinster Cooking Ware x6
2	1		Dublin-type x9; North Devon gravel-tempered x4; GRE slip-decorated x2; stoneware x1
2	3		Dublin-type x9; Dublin-type fineware x1
2	5		Dublin-type fineware x1
3	1		Ham Green B x1; Leinster Cooking Ware x13; Dublin-type cooking ware x1; Dublin-type coarseware x4; Dublin-type x38; Dublin-type fineware x17; Saintonge unglazed ware x1; North Devon gravel-tempered x4; Anglo-Netherlands slipware x1; glazed red earthenware x2; unglazed red earthenware x1; unidentified x4
3	18		Dublin-type coarseware x1; Dublin-type x9; Dublin-type fineware x3
3	20	Around stones at east of F21	Dublin-type x5; Saintonge green-glazed x1; unidentified x1
3	21	Stony surface under F22	Leinster Cooking Ware x1; Dublin-type coarseware x3; Dublin-type x7
3	22	Black silty material over F21	Dublin-type x2; Dublin-type fineware x1
3	28		Dublin-type coarseware x1; Saintonge green-glazed x1
3	31		Leinster Cooking Ware x2; Dublin-type coarseware x7; Dublin-type x1
4	1		Leinster Cooking Ware x1; Dublin-type cooking ware x1; Dublin-type x12; Dublin-type fineware x23; Saintonge green-glazed x1; Frechen x3; North Devon gravel-free x1; North Devon gravel-tempered x4; black-glazed ware x1; glazed red earthenware x9; GRE slip-decorated x1; unglazed red earthenware x17; stoneware x6; unidentified x1
4	65		Leinster Cooking Ware x2; Dublin-type cooking ware x4; Dublin-type x17; Dublin-type fineware x21; Frechen x3; North Devon gravel-tempered x1; unglazed red earthenware x1
4	69		Leinster Cooking Ware x1; Dublin-type x2
4	70		Dublin-type x10; Dublin-type fineware x1; glazed red earthenware x1; unglazed red earthenware x1
4	71		Leinster Cooking Ware x3; Dublin-type x5; Dublin-type fineware x3
4	73		Dublin-type coarseware x1
4	74		Dublin-type x27; Dublin-type fineware x1
4	76		Dublin-type fineware x3; glazed red earthenware x1; unidentified x1
4	77		Leinster Cooking Ware x6; Dublin-type x6; Dublin-type fineware x17
4	79		Leinster Cooking Ware x1; Dublin-type fineware x1
4	80		Leinster Cooking Ware x3; Dublin-type x27; Dublin-type fineware x2
4	81		Dublin-type x2; Dublin-type fineware x4
4	84		Leinster Cooking Ware x2; Dublin-type x38; Dublin-type fineware x4; Saintonge green-glazed x1

Table 9.3—Pottery by context, Swords Castle, Seasons 1–3 (E4619) (cont.).

Trench	Context	Context description	Pottery
4	86		Dublin-type cooking ware x2; Dublin-type coarseware x1; Dublin-type x12
4	87		Dublin-type x12; Dublin-type fineware x2
4	99		Dublin-type cooking ware x1; Dublin-type x5
5	1		Dublin-type x9; Dublin-type fineware x4; glazed red earthenware x1; unglazed red earthenware x2; stoneware x1
5	64		Dublin-type cooking ware x3; Dublin-type x17; Dublin-type fineware x1; Westerwald x1; North Devon gravel-tempered x1; glazed red earthenware x1; unglazed red earthenware x1
	66		Dublin-type x2; Dublin-type fineware x1
5	67		Dublin-type x1
5	68		Leinster Cooking Ware x1; Dublin-type cooking ware x2; Dublin-type x10; brown-glazed earthenware x1
5	78		Dublin-type x2; Saintonge green-glazed x1
5	83		Dublin-type x1; Dublin-type fineware x4
5	85		Dublin-type cooking ware x1; Dublin-type x10
5	96		Dublin-type cooking ware x2; Dublin-type coarseware x2; Dublin-type x9; Dublin-type fineware x1
5	97		Dublin-type cooking ware x1; Dublin-type x1
6	1		Leinster Cooking Ware x1; Dublin-type cooking ware x2; Dublin-type ware x3; Dublin-type fineware x1; Frechen x1; black-glazed ware x2; glazed red earthenware x3; unglazed red earthenware x1; unidentified x1
6	63		Dublin-type x18; Dublin-type fineware x3; Seville coarseware x1; North Devon gravel-tempered x1; unglazed red earthenware x3
6	72		Dublin-type x2; Dublin-type fineware x1
6	75		Dublin-type x2
6	90		Dublin-type x2
6	93		Saintonge unglazed x1
7	1		Dublin-type ware x3; Dublin-type fineware x2; North Devon gravel-free x1; mottled ware x1; porcelain x1; black-glazed ware x1; glazed red earthenware x3; unglazed red earthenware x5; stoneware x2
8	1		Leinster Cooking Ware x2; Dublin-type ware x2; Dublin-type fineware 3; Saintonge green-glazed x1; glazed red earthenware x1; unglazed red earthenware x1
9	1		Leinster Cooking Ware x1; Dublin-type ware x3; North Devon gravel-tempered x1
8	101		Baked clay x1
8	106	Sherd link F142	Dublin-type ware x12; Dublin-type fineware x28; North Devon gravel-tempered x1; black-glazed ware x2; glazed red earthenware x3
8	107		Dublin-type ware x4; Dublin-type fineware x1
7	109		Dublin-type cooking ware x1; Dublin-type ware x4; Dublin-type fineware x4; Seville coarseware x1; North Devon gravel-tempered x2; black-glazed earthenware x7; unglazed red earthenware x2
7	110		Dublin-type fineware x1
7	111		Leinster Cooking Ware x1
8	112		Dublin-type ware x5; transfer-printed ware x1
7	114		Dublin-type ware x2; Dublin-type fineware x1
7	115		Dublin-type ware x2; Frechen x1
7	117		Leinster Cooking Ware x1; Dublin-type ware x1; Dublin-type fineware x1
8	118		Dublin-type ware x7; Dublin-type fineware x21
10	119		Leinster Cooking Ware x2; Dublin-type ware x5; Dublin-type fineware x1; Frechen x1; stoneware x2
9	122		Leinster Cooking Ware x1; Dublin-type cooking ware x1; Dublin-type ware x1
7	124		Leinster Cooking Ware x2; Dublin-type fineware x1; black-glazed ware x1; glazed red earthenware x1

Table 9.3—Pottery by context, Swords Castle, Seasons 1–3 (E4619) (cont.).

Trench	Context	Context description	Pottery
7	126		Leinster Cooking Ware x1
9	127		Leinster Cooking Ware x1; unglazed red earthenware x1
8	129		Leinster Cooking Ware x1; Dublin-type ware x3; Dublin-type fineware x20
8	131		Leinster Cooking Ware x1; Dublin-type ware x15; Dublin-type fineware x45; ironstone x1
8	142	Sherd link F106	Dublin-type ware x1; Dublin-type fineware x23
7	144		Dublin-type ware x1
7	146		Dublin-type ware x2; Dublin-type fineware x1; Saintonge green-glazed x1; unglazed red earthenware x1
10	151		Dublin-type ware x1
8	152		Dublin-type cooking ware x8; Dublin-type ware x1; Dublin-type fineware x10; ironstone x1
9	153		Dublin-type ware x2
7	158		Dublin-type ware x1
8	159		Dublin-type cooking ware x16
7	162		Dublin-type ware x1
9	166		Dublin-type ware x1
?	1		Leinster Cooking Ware x2; Dublin-type fineware x2 (109201095); GRE slip-decorated x1; unglazed red earthenware x1 (1103–1104)

Clay building materials

Joanna Wren

INTRODUCTION

The assemblage of clay building material consists of 936 sherds, 732 of which were complete enough to classify. The majority of these (59%) were medieval, including a substantial proportion (48%) from line-impressed floor tiles, derived from one *in situ* floor. The rest of the assemblage was comprised of post-medieval roof and floor tiles, pantiles and brick.

MEDIEVAL TILES

Three medieval fabrics were recorded in this assemblage. Two of these have been identified previously and occur frequently on sites in Dublin (Wren 2006, 182). The first fabric, Dublin Tile Two (DT2), was used exclusively in the manufacture of ridge tiles, but the second, Dublin Tile Three (DT3), was also used to make floor tiles. Thin-section analysis of both fabrics has indicated that they were produced using locally sourced clays (McCorry 1997), and the tiles were probably made somewhere in the city. The third fabric was also used for making floor tiles. Floor tile wasters in this fabric (E4619:1:190, E4619:77:790) were recovered during the 2017 season at the site, indicating that these tiles were made on site using locally sourced clays. The fabric has been named Swords Castle Tile One (SCT1). The tiles were grouped according to fabric. Because the size of the sherds varied widely, they were weighed as the most accurate way of assessing quantity. They were dated using a combination of typology, contextual information and comparative material from other sites.

The forms of medieval tiling found at Swords were introduced into Ireland by the Anglo-Normans in the thirteenth century. Initially craftsmen were brought from Britain to work on specific projects, but an Irish tiling industry quickly developed, using versions of the forms that they introduced (Wren 2010, 142). The clays used to make these tiles indicate that they were made in Ireland, either on site as part of a building project or in a commercial kiln nearby.

DT2 (ridge tiles)

There were 82 sherds of ridge tile made in this fabric, five of which had the remains of stabbed cresting (E4619:1:185, E4619:1:186, E4619:75:7, E4619:118:7, E4619:119:23). Three of the crests (E4619:1:185, E4619:118:7, E4619:119:23) were high and flat-topped, and these

Pl. 10.1—DT2 ridge tile (E4619:1:185) (photo: John Sunderland).

tiles and five others (E4619:1:483, E4619:1:185, E4619:3:50, E4619:64:580, E4619:72:5) were decorated with incised curving lines. Four sherds were decorated with applied strips, three slashed (E4619:3:47, 48, 51) and one thumbed (E4619:1:28). Another ridge tile made in DT2 fabric was recovered from a rubble deposit at the Gatehouse during excavations by IAC in 2014.

Ridge tiles adorned with high, flat-topped crests and decorated with incised curving lines are common on sites in Dublin and they also occur as far north as Drogheda (Wren 1987, 56). Tiles decorated with slashed strips, however, are usually found on sites in south Leinster and Munster, with a few occasional examples known from Dublin (Wren 2006, 184). During the thirteenth and early fourteenth centuries this form of decoration was used exclusively with cockscomb cresting, but by the later fourteenth century it was also used on flat-topped crested tiles (Wren 2007, 229).

The fashion for crested ridge tiles was introduced into Ireland as part of the Anglo-Norman building campaigns of the thirteenth century (Wren 2006, 180). Roof tiles in general were not simply decorative but also had an important functional role in fireproofing a building. The ever-present threat of fire in medieval towns eventually led to the banning of thatch and other organic roofing materials (Wood 1965, 292; Gilbert 1885, 292–3), which were replaced by roof tiles over time. The ridge tiles' functionality meant that they were more widely used than floor tiles and they occur in religious, secular and urban contexts. In England they have even been found at deserted medieval villages (Rahtz 1969, 124). Small amounts of tile in DT2 fabric (9%) were found in medieval deposits. Two sherds in particular were found in the remains of the bedding for the line-impressed floor in Trench 10. The others were incidental deposits, in a burial horizon in Trench 9, in rubble in Trench 4 and on metalled surfaces in Trenches 5 and 6. Another group of sherds (16%) came from late sixteenth-century deposits associated with the kiln in Trench 7, and the rest (76%) were found in post-medieval rubble and topsoil.

Pl. 10.2—DT3 ridge tiles (photo: John Sunderland).

DT3 (ridge tiles)

The assemblage also included 26 sherds from ridge tiles made in DT3 fabric. Three of them (E4619:106:43, E4619:65:773, E4619:63:568) were adorned with low, flat-topped cresting, while a fourth (E4619:65:688) was decorated with an incised curving line. The crests on one sherd (E4619:106:43) were knife-cut and stabbed to aid firing. On the other tiles (E4619:65:773, E4619:63:568) each crest was moulded in advance and then applied individually to the tile's ridge. One of these (E4619:65:773) was actually a complete low, flat-topped crest.

These tiles are a late fourteenth-century development of earlier DT2 flat-topped forms. As firing techniques improved over time, ridge tile crests became lower, simpler and more stylised. The same curved line decoration continued but it too was more standardised. Tiles made in DT3 fabric, with low, flat-topped cresting, occur on a number of sites in Dublin city, and the same form of cresting was in use at the Augustinian priory at Kells, Co. Kilkenny (Wren 2006, 191). A large proportion of the DT3 sherds (49%) were found with other building debris such as slate, mortar and cut stone. Three of them were deposited in the vicinity of the Great Hall (F106, F118, F131), north of the wall (F123) in Trench 8, and another ten came from rubble deposits in Trench 4. The rest of the DT3 sherds (51%) came from post-medieval layers.

POST-MEDIEVAL RED EARTHENWARES (PANTILES, RIDGE TILES, ROOF TILES)

This category is a generic term used to cover a number of different forms of post-medieval tile made in varieties of red earthenware fabric.

Pantiles

There were 41 pantile sherds, made in the kind of sandy red earthenware fabric which is typical of this form of tile. Pantiles are a post-medieval development of earlier curved roof

Table 10.1—Chart of floor tile motifs.

Excavation no.	Fabric no.	Description	Motif no. (Eames and Fanning 1988)	Sites where examples found previously
E4619:3:44	SCT1	Four-tile lion's face within cusped spotted circular band	T59	Swords Castle
E4619:151:45				Jerpoint Abbey
E4619:151:46				
E4619:151:47				
E4619:151:48				
E4619:3:46	SCT1	Lion rampant sinister in quatrefoil	L4	Dublin: Dublin Castle, Kilmainham, St Audoen's Church, St Kevin's Church, St Nicholas's Church, St Patrick's Cathedral. Ship Street.
E4619:3.46				
E4619:1:1216				Lusk church, Swords Castle, Kildare Cathedral.
E4619:119:115				Kilkenny: Dominican priory, St Canice's Cathedral, St Francis's Priory, St John's Priory.
E4619:120:2				Jerpoint Abbey, Kells Priory, Drogheda Dominican Priory, Mellifont Abbey, Monasterboice church, Trim Castle, Clonmines Priory, Dunbrody Abbey.
E4619:120:9				Waterford: Deanery Yard, John Street, St Peter's Church, Blackfriars
E4619:151:12				
E4619:151:13				
E4619:151:14				
E4619:151:15				
E4619:151:16				
E4619:151:17				
E4619:151:2	SCT1		L10	Dublin: Christchurch Cathedral, St Audoen's Church, St Patrick's Cathedral.
E4619:151:3				Lusk church, Swords Castle, Jerpoint Abbey, Kells Priory, Mellifont Abbey, Dunbrody Abbey.
E4619:151:4				Waterford: St Peter's Church
E4619:151:5				

E4619:151:7		springing from a central quatrefoil in a quatrefoil frame		Drogheda: Bessexwell Lane, St Peter's Church, Shop Street.
E4619:151:8				Slane church
E4619:151:9				
E4619:151:10				
E4619:151:11				
E4619:151:42				
E4619:151:43				
E4619:151:44				
E4619:63:566	SCT1	Nine-tile vine leaf (Eames 224)	L27	Dublin: Christchurch Place, St Patrick's Cathedral, Wood Quay.
				Kildare Cathedral
E4619:18:29	SCT1	Fleur-de-lis set diagonally	L33	Swords Castle
E4619:151:18	SCT1	4-foil in a clockwise scroll	L46	Dublin: Christchurch Cathedral, College Street, Dublin Castle, St Audoen's Church, St Patrick's Cathedral, St Begnet's Church.
E4619:151:19				Lusk Church, Swords Castle, Great Connell Priory, Mellifont Abbey.
E4619:151:20				Waterford: Deanery Yard
E4619:151:21 & 22				
E4619:151:23				
E4619:151:24				
E4619:151:26				
E4619:151:27				
E4619:151:28, 29, 30				
E4619:151:31				
E4619:151:32 & 33				
E4619:151:34				
E4619:151:35, 36				
E4619:151:37				
E4619:151:38				
E4619:151:39				
E4619:151:40				
E4619:151:41				

tiles. They are usually found in association with gravel-tempered ridge tiles in contexts dating from the seventeenth and eighteenth centuries. It is possible that they were used together, with the pantiles covering the body of the roof and the gravel-tempered tiles used along the ridge (Wren 2007, 232). Complete pantiles are subrectangular in shape, with an S-shaped profile and nibs attached inside their upper edges. The nibs were used to attach the tiles, by hooking them over the timber roof laths, and they were then further secured by back-pointing with mortar from inside the building (Moorhouse 1988, 36). The pantiles found at Swords Castle were all amongst mixed post-medieval and modern deposits. Pantiles were common throughout Ireland and comparative evidence would suggest that they were mainly used in the seventeenth and eighteenth centuries.

Roof tiles

Another five sherds of post-medieval roof tile made in red earthenware fabrics were recovered from the topsoil. These sherds were largely undiagnostic, but their red earthenware fabric suggests that they date from sometime in the post-medieval or modern period.

SCT1 (floor tiles)

There were 403 sherds of floor tile made in this hard, rough fabric, which had oxidised to grey or brick orange and which contained frequent inclusions of an unidentified white matter, possibly calcite (<1mm), moderate amounts of angular grey material (*c.* 1mm) and sparse amounts of a soft orange substance, possibly grog.

Decorative motifs identified on 57 of the sherds included examples of nine line-impressed motifs and one two-colour motif (see chart). Nearly all of these tiles (88%) were found in medieval levels. Most of them (86%) came from deposits associated with the *in situ* floor in the Archbishop's Apartments. There were also some sherds found in layers near the wall (F123) in Trench 8, on metalled surfaces in Trench 6 and in rubble deposits in Trench 4. Two complete tiles, decorated with quatrefoils with anticlockwise scrolls (L47), were found outside the area of the *in situ* floor, set in a deposit of yellow clay in Pit A at the north mural tower. Another three sherds came from late sixteenth-century deposits associated with the demolition of the kiln (F143), and the rest were found in post-medieval and modern layers.

Post-medieval–modern floor tile

A single sherd from a plain, unglazed, red earthenware floor tile was found amongst the topsoil. Plain undecorated floor tiles in this kind of fabric are found throughout Ireland and could date from any time between the late seventeenth century and the end of the nineteenth century.

BRICK

Swords Castle Brick One

There were 23 sherds of brick made in this rough, coarse fabric which was oxidised to brick orange. It contained frequent unidentified inclusions, including some angular white matter and rounded reddish pebbles. This fabric has not been found previously and therefore a source of manufacture for the bricks cannot be determined. Building materials were often manufactured on site, however (Eames and Fanning 1988, 12), especially when working on a building the size of Swords Castle. For the purposes of this report, therefore, it is named Swords Castle Brick One (SCB1). The bricks were all found in modern deposits. The fact that they were very narrow (45–55cm), mostly crude and handmade suggests that they date from the seventeenth century. Thicknesses of 1¾–2⅝ inches (44–66mm) were recorded for Irish bricks before 1660 (Lynch *et al.* 2009, 15).

Swords Castle Brick Two
There were thirteen sherds of brick made in this rough but well-fired red earthenware. The bricks in this fabric were thick and were probably handmade, factors which combine to suggest a date in the eighteenth century for their manufacture (*ibid.*). By this period, while bricks continued to be made on site, they were also manufactured on an industrial scale throughout Ireland and even occasionally imported from England (*ibid.*, 9). In the absence of any other evidence, a source of manufacture cannot be determined for these bricks, and for the purposes of this report the fabric is named Swords Castle Brick Two (SCB2).

DISCUSSION

The tiles from this excavation form part of a much larger assemblage recovered from the castle during the course of previous excavations (Fanning 1975, 64–73; O'Sullivan 2001; Wren, forthcoming). The most significant feature of this assemblage is that it includes line-impressed floor tiles associated with the *in situ* medieval floor, the most complete example of a line-impressed floor in Ireland, which also included a panel of two-colour tiles. The vast majority of the sherds in SCT1 fabric in this assemblage (82%) were derived from this floor.

Pl. 10.3—Fanning's in situ *tile pavement (courtesy of the National Monuments Service).*

Pl. 10.4—L10 vine-scroll motif, Season 3 (photo: John Sunderland).

Fig. 10.1—Eames and Fanning L4 (E4619:151: 12), Season 3, Swords Castle (drawing: Sara Nylund).

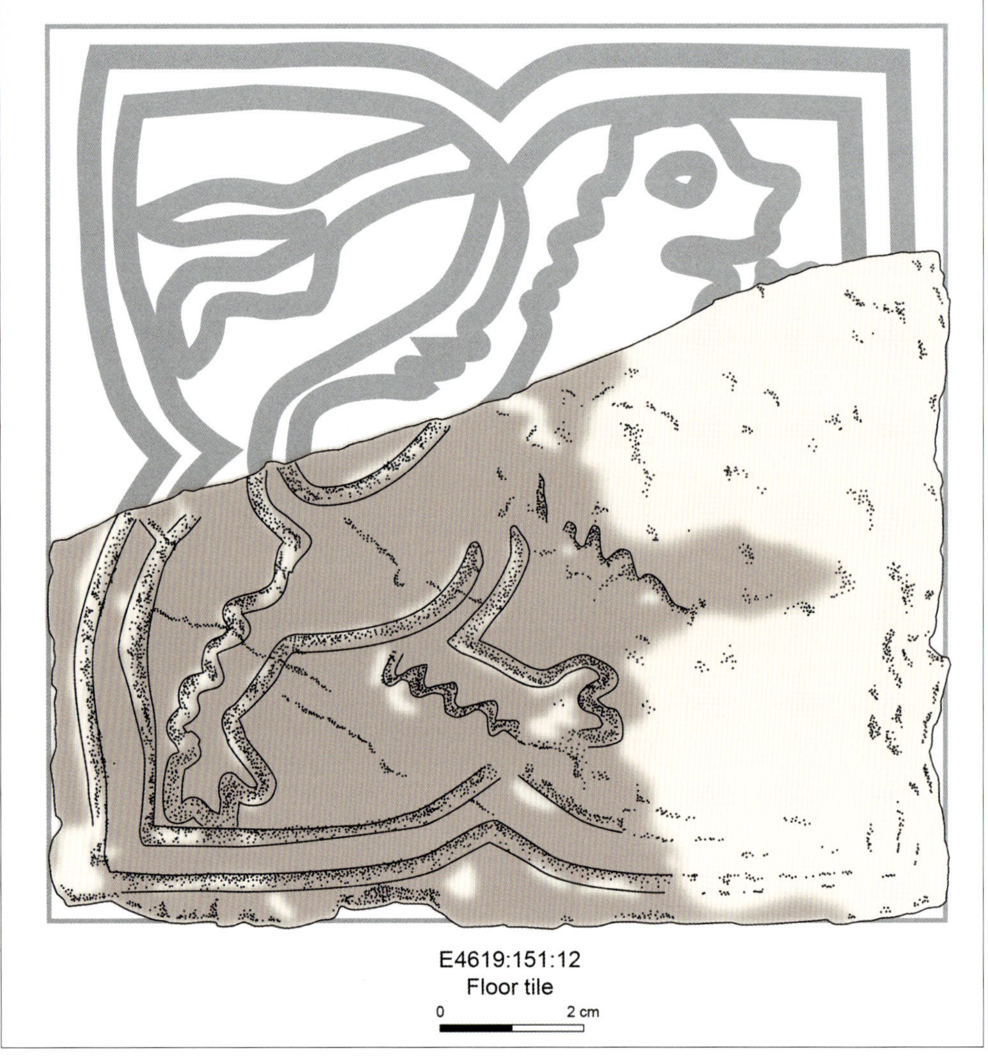

Fanning uncovered the *in situ* floor within a building 'in the south-east angle of the curtain wall', which he suggested might be the Archbishop's Apartments—the 'chamber for the Archbishop' referred to in the inquisition of 1326 (Fanning 1975, 48). This interpretation is still a valid explanation for the use of this structure (R. Stalley, pers. comm.).

The tiled floor, which measured 6m by 3.5m, was uncovered at ground-floor level of the Archbishop's Apartments. Its layout implied an east–west orientation for the chamber, as three of the surviving panels were aligned in that direction. A fourth panel on the eastern side of the room was set at right angles to the others. There was a gap between this panel and the eastern wall, which Fanning suggested as the possible location of a wooden or stone dais at the eastern end of the floor. Fanning also proposed that the southern chamber housed the archbishop's bedchamber and his adjacent private oratory with its tiled floor, the two separated from each other by a wooden screen. The adjacent room to the north-west he interpreted as an antechamber for receiving guests or supplicants. He derived the details of this arrangement from comparative material from Anglo-Saxon sites (Fanning 1975, 64).

The floor panels each consisted of recurring examples of either a single-tile repeated setting or one four-tile setting. They were surrounded by border tiles with a vine-scroll motif (L10) (*ibid.*, 62–3). As well as the vine-scroll, Fanning recorded four other decorative motifs in the floor: the two-colour four-tile lion's face within cusped spotted circular band (T59), the lion rampant sinister in quatrefoil (L4), the quatrefoil in a clockwise scroll (L46) and the four-leaves in the quatrefoil (L14) (Eames and Fanning 1988, 119). This assemblage includes examples of all five of these motifs. On one of the east/west-facing panels the tiles were decorated with the lion rampant in sinister quatrefoil. The tiles within the panel were set on the diagonal, and a mix of glaze and slip had been used to create alternating colours for effect. Half of the tiles were covered in a dark green lead glaze, and these were placed alongside tiles with a white slip covered by a bright green glaze. The lion rampant motif was the most popular in medieval Ireland and examples are known from Dublin, Meath, Louth, Kildare, Kilkenny and Wexford (*ibid., 41*).

The panel adjacent to this was comprised of a two-colour four-tile setting of a lion's face within a cusped spotted circular band (T59). On this tile the band enclosing the lion's face is a quarter-circle and there is a small floral motif outside it. When four of these tiles were placed together on a floor they would have formed part of a recurring pattern, with four lions' faces enclosed by a circle, alternating with four floral motifs within a lozenge. The third east/west-facing panel was made up of tiles decorated with a quatrefoil in a clockwise scroll (L46). When these tiles were set side by side in a floor it would have given the impression of a carpet of four-petalled flowers encircled by intertwining stems. A variant of this motif, where the image was reversed (L47), was also found amongst the tiles in this assemblage (Eames and Fanning 1988, 89). Examples of this second motif usually occur on the same sites as the first.

The fourth panel was at right angles to the rest and was located at the eastern end of the floor in front of Fanning's 'dais' area. The floor here had subsided somewhat, and the tiles sloped sharply downwards towards the eastern wall. The panel consisted of a single-tile repeating pattern of four-leaves in a quatrefoil (L14). As with the previous motif, the quatrefoil is in the centre of foliage, which appears to be some form of pinnate leaves.

One of the aims of the 2017 season of excavation was to see what remained of Fanning's *in situ* floor. It was known that the more complete tiles had been removed from the pavement

Pl. 10.5—Eames and Fanning's L46 and L47, Season 3, Swords Castle (photo: John Sunderland).

Pl. 10.6—Eames and Fanning's L14, Season 3, Swords Castle (photo: John Sunderland).

and deposited in the National Museum. The remaining tiles were covered in plastic sheeting topped by a layer of topsoil and chippings. What survived on site was some of the floor's mortar bedding and some fragmentary *in situ* tiles beside the southern wall of the building.

This area of tiling is depicted on Fanning's ground-plan of the building but not in his illustration of the floor. It consists of broken sherds of tile and half-tile showing two motifs, the lion rampant (L4) and the quatrefoil in the clockwise scroll (L46). These motifs were laid in a disjointed pattern, unlike the panels in the rest of the floor. It is likely that this area of the floor had become worn over time and that these tiles were taken from elsewhere to patch it. This may be why Fanning did not include them in his depiction or amongst the

Fig. 10.2—Eames and Fanning's L14 (E4619:151:42) (drawing: Sara Nylund).

pieces he sent to the NMI. As well as the more complete tiles, a significant proportion of the tiles made in SCT1 fabric (48%) survived as small chippings. Most of these were found within the Archbishop's Apartments. At the time of his excavation, Fanning (1975, 63) observed that the tiles in the pavement were in poor condition, and the sherds of tile that he left *in situ* were very friable (C. Baker, pers. comm.). The chippings presumably derived from material which had eroded from the floor over time.

Fanning recorded that a large number of tiles, 'upwards of 500 sherds' (1975, 58), were recovered at the east end of the adjacent building, interpreted as the Chapel. This second group of tiles included examples of twelve different decorative motifs, four of which (T59, L4, L10, L46) were also found in the *in situ* floor. The other eight motifs included two from line-impressed mosaic settings (LM3, LM4), three from four-tile patterns (L75, L82), two from nine-tile patterns (L22, L27), one single-tile motif (L33) and one zigzag border tile (L13) (Eames and Fanning 1988, 86–91). This assemblage includes examples of two of the new motifs, the single-tile fleur-de-lis set diagonally (L33) and an oak-leaf motif from a nine-tile pattern (L27). Fanning believed that this building was the castle chapel and that the tiles formed part of a floor located at its eastern end, within the sanctuary. The most significant piece of evidence to support this idea is the number of sherds involved, which is significantly

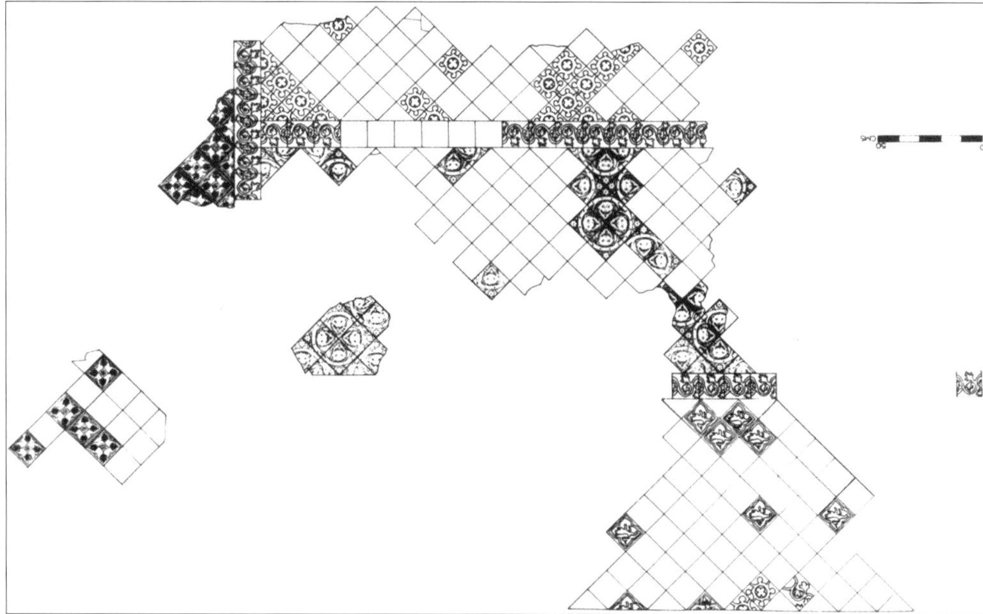

Fig. 10.3—Fanning's plan of the medieval pavement (after Fanning 1975).

larger than the combined total of medieval floor tiles uncovered during the excavations in the rest of the site, including those from the *in situ* floor. Fanning also says that these tiles were 'scattered throughout the shallow deposits overlying the boulder clay'. This pattern is more indicative of erosion or the dismantling of an adjacent floor rather than of the dumping of a single deposit of debris from a floor elsewhere in the castle. This material also included six extra forms of tile and decorative motif beyond those found in the *in situ* floor in the Archbishop's Apartments, including examples of a completely different form of decoration— the line-impressed mosaic. The evidence suggests that the four surviving decorative panels uncovered by Fanning (1975, 62) in the Archbishop's Apartments represent the full extent of that floor. The mortar bedding was confined to the immediate area of the *in situ* tiles and the northern edge of the floor was defined by a row of half-tiles, deliberately cut to create a straight edge. The material found in the chapel is indicative of a much more elaborate floor, contemporary with the one found *in situ* in the Archbishop's Apartments.

The presence of a kiln waster in this fabric (E4619:10:151) indicates that the tiles were manufactured on site using locally sourced clays. This was a common practice on larger medieval sites (Blair and Ramsay 1991, 291). It is likely that the tile-makers would have travelled to Swords for a specific job, bringing their decorative stamps with them and then setting up a workshop using locally sourced clays and a temporary kiln. If the floor tiles in SCT1 fabric were made at Swords, then they were probably products of this kind of kiln rather than a commercial tilery in operation over a long period of time. The decorative motifs used on the tiles suggest an early to mid-fourteenth-century date for the floors. The line-impressed mosaic tiles in particular can be securely dated to this period by comparison with material from British sites (Eames and Keen 1972, 60; Stopford 2005, 186). A similar date is likely for the two-colour tiles from the oratory floor, as this form of decoration was largely obsolete in Ireland after *c.* 1330 (Eames and Fanning 1988, 32).

There are indications of a similar date for the other floor tiles. Six of the motifs (L4, L10,

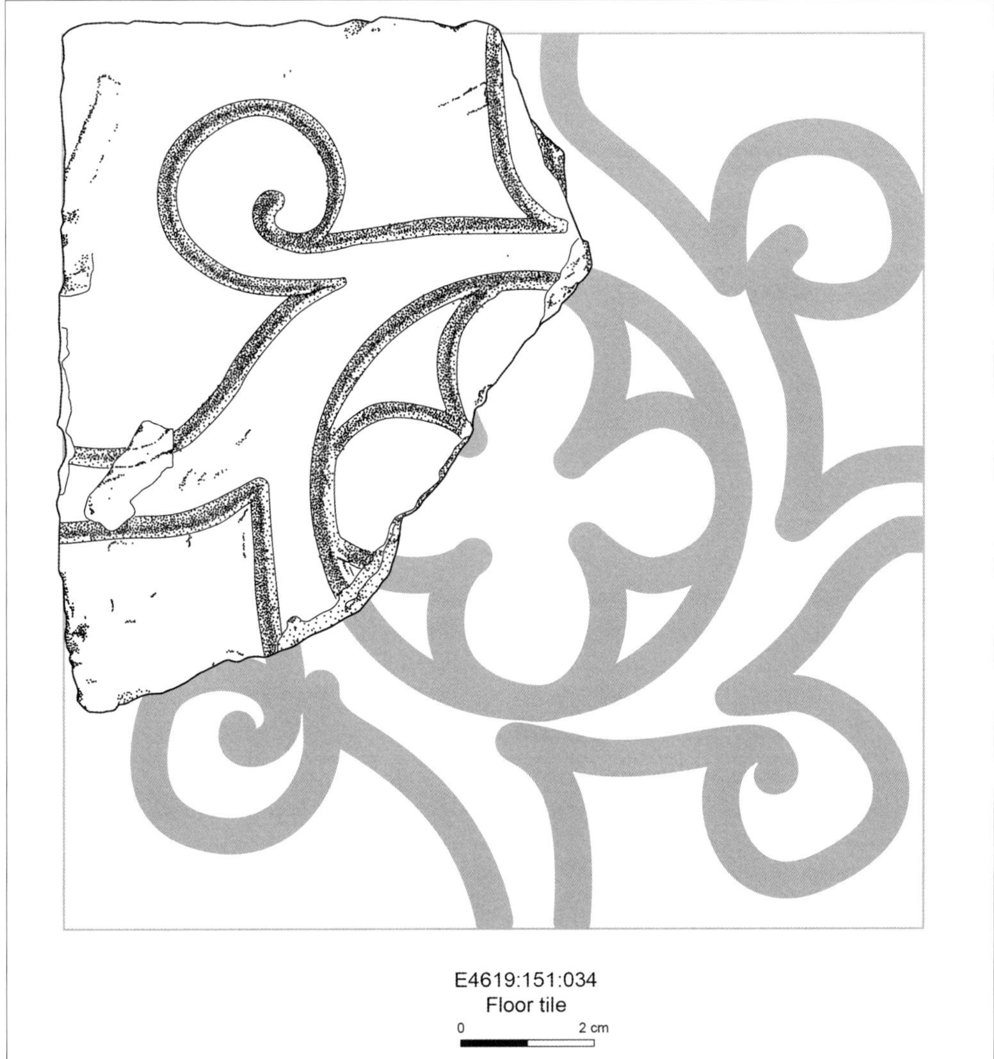

Fig. 10.4—Eames and Fanning's L46 motif (E4619:151:34).

L27, L33, L46, L47) belong to a group of designs which also occur in Chester (*ibid.*, 34). Close links between the Irish line-impressed floor tiles and those in Cheshire suggest that some of the same tilers may have worked in both areas. This kind of connection with the English industry normally occurs when a tile form is first introduced into the country (Wren 2006, 193). The tile evidence strongly suggests that there were two contemporary floors, one in the Archbishop's Apartments and the other in the Chapel. There are, however, some issues regarding the construction sequence for these two buildings, primarily that the latter post-dates the former. One explanation for this could be that the construction of the Chapel formed part of a building project which also included the refurbishment of the other building, perhaps so that it could be used as the Archbishop's Apartments.

This idea is dependent on both buildings being in use at the same time. When the Chapel was built, the south-west corner of the Archbishop's Apartments was removed to allow for the insertion of its east wall. If this breach were repaired, however, this in itself would not discount contemporaneous use of the two buildings. This idea is reinforced by the fact that the insertion of this wall does not appear to have damaged the *in situ* floor, making it more likely that the floor was laid after the Chapel was built. There is also evidence of rebuilding in the surviving south wall of the Archbishop's Apartments (Fingal County Council 2014, 56). If this was in response to the insertion of the Chapel wall, it is feasible that the two buildings were in use simultaneously.

If this is the case, the building now called the Archbishop's Apartments may originally have had a different function. It was built over a backfilled ditch which contained Saintonge pottery, giving a *terminus post quem* of the mid-thirteenth century for its construction. In the early–mid-fourteenth century a floor of decorated tiles was laid in a room at the southern end of the building. At the same time a similar floor was apparently laid at the east end of the Chapel. This time-frame is consistent with the date of 1310 given for the *denier tournois* coin found in one of the post-piles for the Chapel's north wall. A building project such as the construction of a chapel and the laying of two floors would have been elaborate, particularly if it involved converting an older building into the Archbishop's Apartments. This interpretation of the two buildings, however, is partially reliant on the floor tiles. In Ireland, *in situ* floors of medieval tile are currently confined to religious structures and thus they normally indicate an ecclesiastical function for the building. They usually occur within the church itself (Eames and Fanning 1988, 26, 68; Campbell 2007, 248; Walsh 2000, 196–7), with occasional evidence for tiling in adjoining structures like the chapter house at Dunbrody Abbey (Stalley 1987, 211).

In Britain, however, while tiled flooring is still largely prevalent in religious settings, it is also found in secular contexts. Many of the secular British floors are found on royal sites, like Clarendon Palace or Windsor Castle (Eames 1992, 37; Betts and Cromwell 2011, 1), although tiled floors also occur in high-status private residences like Stokesay Castle and Northolt Manor house (Lancaster 1975, 341; Munby 1993, 25), and even in some merchants' houses (Schofield 2013, 7; Steane 1985, 202; Eames 1992, 65). In ecclesiastical contexts, Britain has examples of *in situ* tiled floors in chapter houses (Eames 1992, 40; Henderson 1974, 40), refectories (Eames 1992, 51) and halls (Di Folco 1985, 293; https://historicengland.org.uk), but also in private chapels or oratories like that suggested for Swords. Some of these oratories are also found within private chambers, such as the early fourteenth-century chapel in Prior Crauden's house at Ely Cathedral (Pugh 2002, 79), which was completely floored with rare elaborate mosaic tiles (Eames 1992, 33).

The building that housed Fanning's Archbishop's Apartments at Swords was of two storeys, with the second storey supported on a timber floor and the area below divided into two rooms. Fanning believed that the southern room housed the archbishop's bedchamber and adjacent oratory. The idea of an oratory in this area is reinforced by the fact that the tiled floor was orientated roughly east–west, as is normal for a chapel. The size of the area it covered, 6m by 3.5m, was also consistent for a private prayer-room of its type. Fanning (1975, 64) proposed that it was partitioned from the rest of the bedchamber by means of a timber screen. The room to the north was seen as a public chamber for receiving guests and supplicants. In the wider context, it is unusual to find this kind of bedchamber and oratory on the ground floor of a building. In Britain these rooms are normally found in the upper storey, with the exception of a few notable examples like the Archbishop's Palace at Lincoln (Steane 1985, 19), and two-storey chapels are also prevalent in Europe (Fernie 2000, 244).

These buildings, however, were sophisticated, with their first-storey apartments supported on substantial vaulted undercrofts. The Archbishop's Apartments at Swords was a much simpler building, with an upper storey supported by a simple wooden floor on timber joists (Fingal County Council 2014, 56). It makes more sense in this context to locate the oratory on the ground floor.

It has also been proposed that the reason for a tiled floor at this level is that this room was in fact the castle chapel, while the other, larger building was the hall. Comparisons were made with double chapels at British sites like St Ethelreda's in Ely, London. The suggestion was that the tiled area represented a sanctuary, with the ordinary congregation in the room to the north and the more important members of the household in a gallery above (Fingal County Council 2014, C5). The problem with these interpretations is that the building housing the Archbishop's Apartments is aligned roughly north–south, which would be highly unusual for a chapel (R. Stalley, pers. comm.). With the exception of a few examples from very congested urban areas, medieval churches faced east (Hoare and Sweet 2000, 169). An east–west orientation is indicated for Fanning's oratory by the layout of the floor.

The simplest interpretation of this structure is that it was built as a chapel. This is consistent with its east–west orientation, the presence of the statue niche and the likelihood of a tiled floor at its eastern end, the location of the sacristy. If the floor is original to the building, it suggests a construction date sometime in the early fourteenth century, at the same time as the *in situ* floor was laid in the Archbishop's Apartments. It is possible that the chapel's size owed more to the status of the residence than to necessity. Archbishops' palaces hosted significant ceremonial activities; in London, for example, ordinations took place in some of the larger palaces (Philpotts 1999, 51). Although Swords was a small residence when Archbishop de Bicknor came to hold court in 1310 (Reeners 2014, 40), he would have brought his full household from Dublin (*ibid.*, 47). Even though there was a functioning parish church in Swords, it is still possible that their needs may have been better met by a purpose-built chapel at the castle.

There is also the question of whether there would have been a necessity for a private prayer-room so close to the castle chapel (R. Stalley, pers. comm.). It is not uncommon to find both chapels and private oratories at archbishops' residences. Numerous examples exist throughout Britain and in continental Europe (Fernie 2000, 55). Most of these sites, however, are far larger than Swords Castle, and the chapels were sometimes built during different phases of their usage (Pugh 2002, 77–82; RCAHMW 2000, 50). In medieval Ireland, while tiled floors do occur in adjacent locations like chapter houses and accommodation for vicars choral, they are predominantly found within the body of the church. Taking this together with the orientation of the *in situ* floor at Swords Castle and the size of room it implies, Fanning's idea of a private oratory is still completely valid. The idea, then, that a tiled floor was laid in the larger building at the same time does suggest a deliberate plan and design, perhaps indicative of buildings with a similar function like a chapel and an oratory.

The ridge tiles in the oratory were found with bedding mortar and roof slates, and they probably derived from a slate roof with the crested tiles along the ridge. This form of roofing was very common at medieval Irish sites (Wren 2010, 142; 2007, 225). The Swords Castle inquisition of 1326 uses the word 'shingled' to describe the roofing on both the chapel and the archbishop's chamber. Technically, the word 'shingle' refers to wooden roof tiles, but it was also used to describe stone slates (Wren 1987, 82), and this was probably the case at Swords.

The collapsed roofing, sealing the floor (Fanning 1975, 75), included ridge tiles made in DT2 fabric. The tileworks that manufactured these tiles was in business from the thirteenth to the early fourteenth century, and the crest forms and decoration which adorn the Swords Castle tiles were popular during this period (Wren 2006, 184). The roof of the Archbishop's Apartments could not have stayed up while the Chapel was being built and therefore these tiles must have been erected late in the date range for this fabric, sometime in the early fourteenth century. Tiles can stay on a roof for up to 150 years, so the roof could have collapsed at any time during this period.

Unlike the floor tiles, the ridge tiles were probably made in Dublin and transported to Swords. Research points to the presence of a ceramic industry outside Dublin's West Gate (McCutcheon 2006, 21), and kiln wasters, probably in DT2 fabric, were found during recent excavations in this area, close to St James's Gate (Giacometti and McGlade 2015, 52). It is likely that a kiln was located somewhere nearby. The tiles made in DT3 fabric were basically later refinements of those in DT2. They date from the later fourteenth and fifteenth centuries. All three fabrics used clays derived from the same local source and were probably also brought to Swords as products of the same industry as the earlier ridge tiles.

Research has established that medieval craftsmen commonly travelled up to 40 miles to work on a building project (Jope 1961, 194), and they could journey much farther. The evidence indicates that those who made the floor tiles at Swords were part of a group which travelled between jobs in Britain and Ireland (Eames and Fanning 1988, 34–5). Given that Swords Castle was less than ten miles from Dublin, it is quite feasible that the tilers sourced their roof tiles from commercial tileries in the city. A Malvernian ridge tile found during the Gatehouse excavations may derive from the period in the late sixteenth century when the castle was home to Dutch Calvinist refugees who 're-edified' it 'and repaired almost all the same'. There are some indications of repair work at the castle during this period (Fanning 1975, 57).

The other post-medieval tiles and brick range in date from the late seventeenth century to the nineteenth century. They indicate later activity at the site. The small pieces of roof tile are too worn to be diagnostic, and the modern floor tile may be derived from flooring like that recorded by Fanning (1975, 60) north of the Chapel. Of most significance in this period are the seventeenth-century bricks, the gravel-tempered ridge tiles and the pantiles. The bricks from the site were all handmade and most of them were very thin (44–45mm), which suggests that they were made sometime in the seventeenth century. Thicknesses of 1¾–2⅝ inches (44–66mm) were recorded for Irish bricks before 1660 (Lynch *et al.* 2009, 15). Pantiles are usually found in association with gravel-tempered ridge tiles in contexts dating from the seventeenth and eighteenth centuries. They were probably employed together, with the pantiles covering the body of the roof and the gravel-tempered tiles used along the ridge (Wren 2007, 232).

11

Metal finds

Siobhán G. Duffy, BSc., MA

INTRODUCTION

A total of 671 metal objects were recovered from three seasons (2015–17) of excavations at Swords Castle, Co. Dublin. These ranged from objects associated with personal dress to items relating to craftworking and fittings from larger items and structures. Ferrous artefacts were the most numerous, some 631 in total (including a sizeable collection of nails). In addition to this, there were seven items of lead, 32 objects composed of copper alloys (e.g. brass and bronze) and one of silver alloy. Metal finds were recovered from all ten trenches excavated, although not in even quantities. Most notably, Trench 3 accounted for over a quarter of all metal finds recovered, while a further 22% were recovered from Trench 4. Such concentrations appear to be specific to activity within a trench, however, rather than to a sector of the overall site: the 147 metal artefacts recovered from Trench 4 contrasted markedly with the adjacent Trench 1 from Season 1, where just 23 metal finds were recovered. The metal artefacts recovered are described in this report under the following categories, where identification was possible.

- Personal attire (28)
- Trade and industry (11)
- Domestic items (7)
- Structural and furniture fittings (474)
- Horse equipment (49)
- Miscellanea (102)

Measurements were taken from the artefacts themselves, as far as possible. In the case of unconserved finds, this was not always possible, owing to encrustation or noticeable deformation of the object as a result of corrosion. In such cases measurements were taken from X-ray plates, although this limited the range of measurements that could be taken. All radiographic imaging and conservation of artefacts were carried out by Susannah Kelly.

PERSONAL ATTIRE

Buttons

Archaeological and historical sources indicate that buttons were used on clothing from at least medieval times (White 2005, 50). Nonetheless, they are not considered to have been in common usage until the post-medieval era, from which time they diversified in form and use (*ibid.*). In the eighteenth and nineteenth centuries, industrial production of metal (usually copper-alloy) buttons flourished, particularly in Birmingham, England (*ibid.*, 50–1). The most common type of button identified (six out of the eight) comprised a single-piece disc with a looped shank at the back for attachment (South's Types 7 and 18; Noël Hume 1969, 90). One two-piece button was identified (E4619:1:1040); this comprised a separate convex front crimped over the edge of a slightly convex back, with a metal loop for attachment (South's Type 27; Noël Hume 1969, 90). The eighth button (E4619:1:1243) was a sew-through button, with four eyes to allow for attachment to a garment, probably used for an inner rather than an outer garment.

Two buttons (E4619:1:1039 and E4619:112:1) carried the stamped inscription 'TREBLE GILT' on their backs. Gilding of buttns became common in the late eighteenth century, and by the early nineteenth century men's coat buttons almost always had a gilt finish (White 2005, 65). Laws ensured that a minimum weight of gold was required for a button to be considered gilt (*The Buttonmonger* 2011), and the 'Treble' on the back of the Swords examples serves to proclaim that three times the minimum was used. A second button (E4619:106:2) with a surviving gilt finish was recovered, although this lacked an accompanying 'gilt' stamp on the back. It was, however, the only button with a surviving decoration on the front, the design of which is typical of buttons from the early to mid-nineteenth century (www.buttoncountry.com/; thepragmaticcostumer.wordpress.com/). A similar date range is the most likely for all the buttons carrying looped shanks (Noël Hume 1969, 91; White 2005, 51–2). The sizes of these buttons suggest that they represent buttons from coats and waistcoats.

E4619:1:308
Copper alloy with tinned surface. Disc-like head. Flat front with silver-grey colouring and possible faint remnants of design. Stamped inscription on back: 'EXTRA PLATED'. 'Omega' shank; complete copper-alloy loop; only a small portion of tinning survives on back. Plating worn away at edges on front. South's Type 18; nineteenth century. Diam. 18.8mm. Th. 0.9mm. Diam. of loop. 4.1mm.

E4619:1:1039
Copper alloy. Small, flat button with oval shank, also of copper alloy. No surviving design on front; inscription on back, encircling shank: 'TRE[BLE] GILT'. South's Type 18; nineteenth century. Diam. 15.7mm. Th. (max.) 06.4mm. Shank 5.2mm x 5.1mm.

E4619:1:1040
Copper alloy. Composite button, comprising domed front crimped over slightly convex rear, with circular shank. No design or lettering evident. South's Type 27; nineteenth century. Diam. 15.7mm. Th. (max.) 06.4mm. Shank 5.2mm x 5.1mm.

E4619:1:1041
Copper alloy. Small, flat button; shank missing; plain front; plumes and stars design on rear above shank; inscription below shank: 'BEST QUALITY'. South's Type 18; nineteenth century. Diam. 14mm. Th. 1mm.

E4619:1:1243
Circular sew-through button; inner concave circle with four stitching holes. Partly illegible inscription on flat, outer band at front: 'EXCELS[IO]R'. Similar to South's Type 32; late nineteenth–early twentieth century. Diam. 14.1mm. Th. (at rim) 1.2mm.

E4619:106:2
Flat button; looped shank on back with low foot and casting spur. Gilded with decorated front: four raised bands with leaf motif, interspersed with fine cross-hatching, all encircled by raised band with closely spaced, recessed cross-hatching. South's Type 7; early/mid-nineteenth century. Diam. 25.3mm. Th. 1.1mm. Diam. of shank 6.8mm.

E4619:109:3
Slightly domed button with plain front; omega-type shank on back. Partly legible stamped inscription on back: 'STRONG'. Similar to South's Type 28 or 18; nineteenth–early twentieth century. Diam. 14.4mm. Th. 0.9mm. Diam. of shank 5mm x 4mm.

E4619:112:1
Flat disc button with oval loop shank. Gilt surface surviving on back; no visible decoration on front. Stamped inscription on back: 'TREBLE GILT; STANDARD COLOUR'. South's Type 18; nineteenth century. Diam. 23.4mm. Th. 1.5mm. Diam. of shank *c.* 8.2mm.

Buckles and strap loop
Four buckle frames, a strap loop and a total of five loose buckle pins were recovered. Buckles were widely used in the past to fasten belts, straps, stocks, shoes and harnesses, and it is not always possible to distinguish those used in personal attire from those associated with horse equipment (Egan and Pritchard 1991, 50). This is especially true in the case of loose pins, as the shape and style of the buckle remain unknown.

E4619:1:202
Iron. Incomplete pin from buckle. Small, elongate trapezoidal bar; plano-convex in cross-section. L. 22.7mm. W. 9.5mm. Th. 4mm.

E4619:1:1037
Copper alloy. Incomplete frame of large, oval shoe buckle. Pin terminal on one side, comprising extension from outer edge of frame, covered by looped knot design on upper side; notably arched frame, to fit over foot; openwork with raised bead and knop decoration; 1750–1800. L. 43.6mm. Th. 1.8mm. H. of terminal 4.7mm. Diam. of pinhole 1.5mm.

E4619:1:1066
Copper alloy. Complete single-loop trapezoidal buckle frame. Pin missing. Narrow, slightly offset, strap-end, with wider segment off-centre. Expanded front of buckle forms wide, peaked terminal, flanked by curved knops at either side of frame; slight depression on inside to facilitate pin. Fourteenth–fifteenth century. L. 45.6mm. W. 34.5mm. Th. 3.4mm.

E4619:1:1067

Iron. Incomplete single-loop rectangular buckle frame; rectangular cross-section. Accretion of iron on one side probably represents remnant of iron pin. Utilitarian in style. L. 29.8mm x 29.3mm. Th. (max.) 5.8mm.

E4619:20:18

Iron. Complete pin from buckle with intact loop. Small area of copper staining suggests originally within copper-alloy frame. L. 18mm. Max. W. 5mm. Th. 3mm. Diam. of loop 6.7mm.

E4619:21:40

Iron. Incomplete buckle pin. Loop broken off at base. Elongate trapezoidal form; rectangular in cross-section. L. 33.3mm. W. 8.6mm. Th. 5mm.

E4619:63:10

Iron buckle pin. Small tapering shank, with evidence of thickening at wider end and rounded blunt tip at narrow end. Rectangular cross-section. X-ray suggests wider end may represent broken attachment loop. L. 27mm. W. 4.6–7.3mm. Th. 2.3–5.6mm.

E4619:80:1

Iron. Spur buckle. Elongate, sub-oval form. Pin has fused to frame with corrosion. Short neck and ring-loop below the pin, for attachment to spur frame. Separate semicircular flat plate fused to front of buckle may represent a fragment of a mount or other strap attachment. L. 48.3mm. W. 38.7mm. W. (neck) 9mm. W. (pin) 4.1mm.

E4619:106:1

Copper alloy. Large buckle pin with incomplete loop. Short shank tapers to blunt point; rectangular cross-section, with rounded corners on shank. Two transverse bands in relief at interface of shank and loop, on upper face only. No other decoration visible. Probably from circular buckle, *c.* 1250–1450. L. 43.4mm. L. of shank only 30.1mm. Diam. (shank, max.) 4.4mm x 3.7mm. W. (at loop) 3.3mm. Th. (at loop) 3.1mm.

Pins

Stick-pins were used as clothes-fasteners and are considered to date from the tenth to thirteenth centuries, although later examples have been recorded outside Dublin (Hayden 2011, 327–9). They are derived from the ringed pins or thistle brooches of the Hiberno-Norse period. O Rahilly (1998) identified a chronological typology of stick-pins recovered from excavations in Dublin. The example from Swords Castle accords with O Rahilly's Type 13B, characterised by an upright, rounded, spatulate head (*ibid.*, 30). Pins of this type date from the late twelfth–mid-thirteenth centuries, putting them quite late in the stick-pin chronology. A parallel for the Swords Castle pin was recorded from Trim Castle, Co. Meath, and considered to be of early fourteenth-century date (Hayden 2011, 327).

E4619:21:41

Copper alloy. Complete stick-pin with rounded spatulate head (O Rahilly's Class 13B).

Collared neck with unequal pointed projections. Circular cross-section to shank, which expands in mid-length. Dot-and-circle design, off-centre, on both faces of head. Four vertical rows of stabbed horizontal lines extend down upper part of shaft from collar for 11.5mm; each row is terminated by an incised 'V'. Late twelfth–fourteenth century. L. 73.2mm. Diam. (max.) of shank 2.6mm. Head: W. 5.5mm, Th. 1.4mm.

E4619:1:303
Copper alloy. Fragment of lower end of shank of pin/needle. L. 7.8mm. Diam. 0.8mm.

E4619:63:51
Copper alloy. Incomplete brooch pin, with tapering circular cross-section; curved at wider end towards attachment point for brooch; broken at both ends; no decoration identifiable. L. 45.3mm. Diam. 2.1–3.2mm.

E4619:93:3
Copper alloy. Long length of wire-pulled pin with circular cross-section, bent into acute angle in lower shank. Thinning to point at one end, broken at thicker end. L. (if straightened) 115mm. Diam. 0.9mm.

Lace-tag
A slender, tapering copper-alloy tube (E4619:144:2) was identified as a lace-tag or aglet. Lace-tags covered the ends of leather or silk laces in medieval and post-medieval times: the earliest lace-tags recovered in London were of mid-thirteenth-century date, although elsewhere they are more usually found to be of late medieval and post-medieval date. In the example from Swords, the edges of the tube fold inwards to the centre, thus gripping the lace without the need for rivets; this is consistent with a design form identified as mid-sixteenth- to seventeenth-century in date (Cox 1996, 56). Its narrow diameter suggests an association with finer fabric, and it is of a size with lace-tags associated elsewhere with silk braids (Egan 2005, 53).

E4619:144:2
Narrow, tapering, sub-cylindrical tube, edges along seam turned inwards. Closed over at narrower end. No decoration or distinguishing marks. Mid-sixteenth–seventeenth century. L. 41.1mm. Diam. (wider end) 3mm x 2.8mm, (narrower end) 2.2mm x 1.9mm.

Mount
A small, rectangular, copper-alloy mount was recovered from a later medieval occupation layer. It is uncertain whether this would have adorned an item of clothing or a horse harness, although its small size and fragility may suggest the former. By post-medieval times the use of mounts to decorate clothing had declined, although they are known to have still been used on belts at this time (Egan 2005, 39).

E4619:126:11
Incomplete subrectangular fragment of copper alloy, with wide, curving, tag-like shank at back. Slight raised border on front face; no other visible surviving decoration owing to poor

preservation. L. 13mm. W. 9.3mm. Shank: L. 5.1mm; W. 6mm at base.

Chain

Five links from a chain were recovered from Trench 3. These are of an unknown alloy, although the silver-grey colour suggests a high lead or tin content (S. Kelly, pers. comm.). The links are simple ovals, with each link soldered at mid-length to form a loop. The lightness of the links suggests that the chain would not have borne any great weight and is likely to have been for personal use. An alloy of base, rather than precious, metal argues against jewellery, although it may have been associated with a personal item such as a purse, watch or spectacles. The precise nature of its use, however, remains unknown.

E4619:18:45

Copper alloy. Fragment of chain, comprising five oval, straight links (in two sections of two and three joined links). Two links partially opened mid-length, at solder. One other with small break at narrow end. Subcircular cross-section, flattened at narrow ends; silver-coloured. Link: L. 13.1mm; W. 3.5–4.8mm; Diam. 1.3mm max.

Strap adjustor and strap-end

A decorated, tinned copper-alloy fitting (E4619:1:307) was identified as the moveable part of a strap adjustor. Such adjustors are most associated with men's braces, and the size of the Swords Castle example suggests that this may have been its origin. Braces were first developed in the early nineteenth century, as trousers changed in style (albertthurston.com). The style and decoration of the present example suggest a late nineteenth- or early twentieth-century date. A poorly preserved iron forked object (E4619:3:58) may represent a spacer from a strap-end. Composite strap-ends, consisting of a forked spacer between two solid metal plates, are associated with the thirteenth and fourteenth centuries (Egan and Pritchard 1991, 145).

E4619:1:307

Copper alloy with tinned surface. L-shaped polygonal fitting with two sections. Envelope-shaped upper section with band of swirling decoration along chevron edge. Lower section with round-toothed long edge. Originally held within frame by short, rectangular projections. Fitting from adjustor for braces. Late nineteenth/early twentieth century. L. 34.9mm. W. upper section 6.6–11.6mm. W. lower section 3.6–4.8mm. Th. 0.5mm. Projections: L. 1.8; W. 1.6mm.

E4619:3:58

Iron. Elongate object with expanded rounded terminal at one end. Forked at other end, with one straight arm and shorter (broken) arm curving slightly away from main body before extending roughly parallel to longer arm. Cross-section plano-convex or double convex. Possible spacer from strap-end. L. 46.3mm. W. 8.6mm. Th. 3mm.

Watch key

An incomplete copper-alloy key from a pocket watch (E4619:70) was recovered from a modern feature. Pocket watches were wound using external keys until at least the mid-nineteenth century, when keyless watches were introduced and gained popularity (Boettcher

Pl. 11.1—Coins and tokens from Swords Castle (photo: John Sunderland).

2016, www.vintagewatchstraps.com). The key recovered at Swords is of unknown date but is similar to watch keys from the nineteenth century.

E4619:70:4
Copper alloy. Key for pocket watch, comprising central ring with beaded design; swivel fob attachment at one end and hollow attachment for key at opposite side; key-bit missing. Eighteenth–nineteenth century. L. 23.4mm. Diam. of central ring 15mm. W. 2.2mm. L. of fob attachment 6.3mm, with narrower 2.7mm for loop.

TRADE AND INDUSTRY

Coins and tokens

Six coins were recovered that range in date from the sixteenth to the eighteenth century and probably represent accidental losses at various times in the site's later history. The earliest coin identified (E4619:126:1) was a silver sixpence from the reign of Elizabeth I, dating from 1569 (Fig. 11.1). Falling between the listed diameters for a groat (fourpence) and a sixpence, its denomination was ascertained by the presence of the Tudor Rose on the obverse: this emblem did not appear on groats (Savage 2015, 12). The crown mint mark, just discernible above the monarch's head, indicates that the coin was issued from the London mint and for circulation in England rather than Ireland, as coins issued for Ireland carried a harp as mint mark (Symonds 1917, 107). This easy distinction was perhaps necessary, as officially circulated coins in Ireland continued to be of less value than their English counterparts. Nonetheless, the more valuable English coinage appears to have been used alongside the Irish coins during Elizabeth's reign and would probably have been a necessity for anyone trading with, or travelling to and from, England (Seaby 1970, 57; Maginn 2011, 72).

The earliest identifiable copper-alloy coin (E4619:1:305) was a halfpenny from the reign of James II, bearing the date 1686 (Fig. 11.2). James II ascended the throne in 1685 following

Fig. 11.1—Coin of Elizabeth I, 1569 (E4619:126:1) (drawing: Sara Nylund).

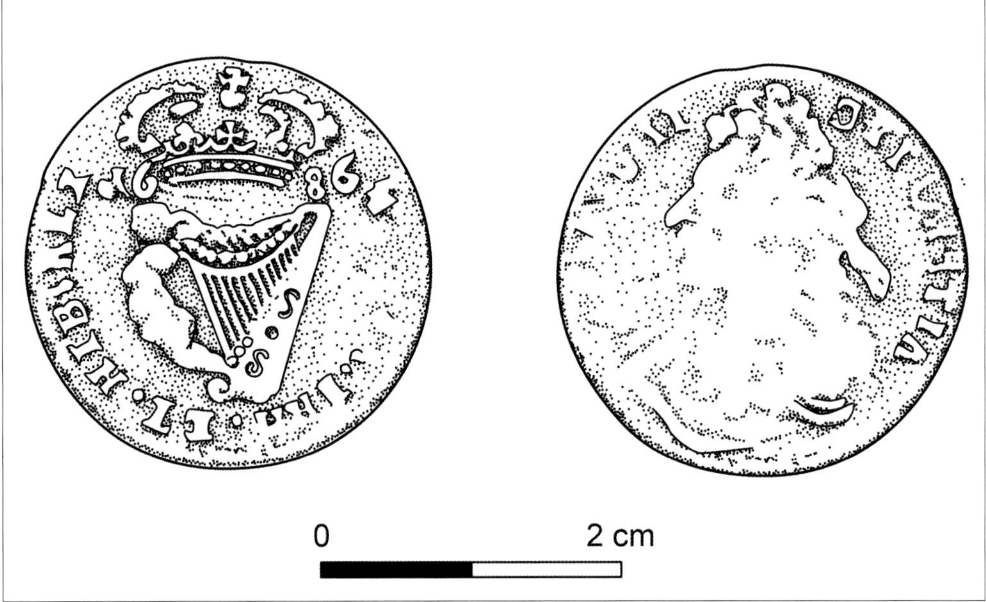

Fig. 11.2—Coin of James II (E4619:1:305) (drawing: Sara Nylund).

the death of his brother, Charles II. Coins were first minted in his name that same year, and official minting continued until his abdication in 1688 (Stafford-Langan, irishcoinage.com).

A very worn coin (E4619:109:2) was identified as a farthing from the reign of William III. Coins with William as sole monarch were minted between 1692 and 1702, following the death of Queen Mary (Seaby 1970, 79). On the reverse of the coin the seated figure of Britannia could be distinguished, although little of the legend was discernible. Although the date was not legible beyond '16__', its position within the legend rather than below the Britannia figure narrows its range to 1698–9. Outside of these years, farthings of William

III carried the date below the Britannia figure (www.britishfarthings.com). The obverse of the coin has been defaced by a countermarked 'SS' over the head of the monarch. Countermarks on coins appear to have been a widespread phenomenon, especially from the nineteenth century onwards. Slogans, initials and messages were stamped on coins, as a means of protest, advertising or creating a personal token (Jones 2010, numistories.com/; Scott 1974). The style of the countermark on the Swords example suggests that it is of a much later date than the coin, most probably nineteenth-century. As the coin would have been long out of circulation at that point, it would have had no use as a form of either protest or advertising. It is more likely, therefore, to have been a way of personalising the coin, for use either as a token or as a memento.

A commercial token was recovered (E4619:6:4) bearing the logo of the Hibernian Mining Company (HMC) on the obverse, along with the legend 'Camac Kyan and Camac' and its denomination, 'Halfpenny'. The HMC was an Irish-owned company operating copper mines at Ballymurtagh, near Avoca, Co. Wicklow (Smith 1998, miningmemorabilia.co.uk). Its founders were brothers John and Turner Camac and John Howard Kyan (Hargaden 2015, countywicklowheritage.org). The later eighteenth century saw a severe shortage of coins of smaller denominations, as the minting of these had been halted at the Royal Mint in 1775. To counter the problems this posed for businesses, the principal copper-mining companies in County Wicklow, the Associated Irish Mine Company (AIMC) and the HMC, both issued coinage in the 1790s. In the absence of official small coinage, these tokens formed the basis for day-to-day trading towards the end of the eighteenth century, while variations in design meant that they quickly became popular as collectors' items. They were issued in large numbers until 1795, when production was stopped; shortly after this the royal mint once again produced small coins (*ibid.*).

The reverse of token E4619:6:4 shows the date of issue as 1794. The main design on it is the seated figure of Hibernia with one arm resting on an Irish harp, a common emblem on HMC tokens. To the fore of Hibernia, a small beehive structure bellowing smoke is depicted, and this seems to be particular to tokens issued in 1794. The structure appears to be a smelting house and is probably a reference to the company's smelting works in Arklow: unlike their main rivals, the AIMC, who shipped ore to Swansea for smelting, the HMC could smelt their ore locally (Fraser 1801). On the edge of the coin the partial inscription 'Payable in [Dublin] o[r] at Ballymurtagh' is visible. Such inscriptions were usual on these tokens, signifying that the company could and would exchange them for official coinage; it was this, along with the quality of the coins, that distinguished them from the numerous counterfeit coins that were in circulation.

E4619:1:304
Copper alloy. Possible token. Badly degraded, no detail evident. Unidentifiable. Size suggests farthing token. D. 16.4mm. Th. 1mm. Wt <1g.

E4619:1:305
Copper-alloy halfpenny. Obverse: monarch's head, facing left; legend, partial only: '___ II DEI GRATIA'. Reverse: harp surmounted by crown; date '1686' flanking crown; legend, partial only: 'M__. FRA. ET. HIB. REX'. D. 26–26.5mm. Th. 1.5mm. Wt *c.* 7g.

E4619:1:1038
Copper-alloy halfpenny. Clipped at one side; badly worn. Obverse: faint bust of monarch—younger image of George II. Reverse: worn smooth. Date: 1727–60. Wt 8g. Diam. 28.2mm. Th. 1.7mm.

E4619:6:4
Copper-alloy halfpenny. Obverse: company logo 'HMCo'; legend reads 'CAMAC KYAN AND CAMAC' 'HALFPENNY'. Reverse: Hibernia seated, arm resting on harp, and facing small, domed smelting house issuing smoke; date: '1794'. Faint inscription on edge: 'PAYABLE IN _____ O_ AT BALLYMURTAGH'. Token of the Hibernian Mining Co. D. 28.5mm. Th. 1.8mm. Wt *c.* 10g.

E4619:109:2
Copper-alloy farthing. Very worn. Right-facing monarch's bust on obverse, with partly legible legend: 'GIVLIVMVS TERTIVS'. Monarch's bust counter-stamped with letters 'SS' at later time. On reverse, faint outline of Britannia with partly legible legend '[BRITAN] NIA 16[9]_'; date following legend. D. 22.6mm. Th. 1.5mm. Wt *c.* 3g.

E4619:126:12
Silver alloy. Hammered sixpence. Obverse: faint outline of monarch's head facing left, with Tudor rose at back. Partly legible legend following crown privy mark: 'ELIZABETH D.G. [ANG:FR ET] HI REGIN[A]'. Reverse: long cross; quartered shield of arms, bearing three lions in top right and bottom left quadrants, three worn fleurs-de-lys in lower right; top left worn smooth. Date of 1569 over shield; partly legible legend: '[POSVI] [D] EV. AD IVTORE M. MEV'. Fill 1 of F126. D. 24.5mm x 23.9mm. Th. 0.4mm. Wt *c.* 3g.

Lead seal
A circular lead seal (E4619:109:1) was recovered from an earlier topsoil layer. Seals made from lead were used to close up cloth bundles and other goods from medieval times up to the twentieth century. As they usually contain inscriptions referring to the origin and nature of the goods involved, they can be an important means of examining trade in the past. The seal had stamped inscriptions on both faces. Although only partly legible, these were sufficient to identify the seal as a flour-bag seal from the Grands Moulins de Corbeil mill in Paris, and it carried the date of March 1903. The mill at Corbeil was owned by the Darblay family and was one of the largest mills in France in the early 1900s (Elton 2011, www.bagseals.org). The presence of the seal at Swords Castle almost certainly relates to the adjacent bakery, owned by Patrick Dunne in the early 1900s. The Dunnes at this time appear to have been using imported French flour, which may have been considered superior to the more local produce.

E4619:109:1
Lead. Subcircular bag seal with remnant of string/textile within apertures; stamped inscription on both faces, partly legible: '1903; GRAND[S] MOU[LINS] DE COR[BEIL]'; 'MARS; ______ [SUP]ERI[O]RES'. Date: March 1903. D. 21.4mm. Th. 4.6mm.

Spindle-whorl

A circular lead weight with a central perforation (E4619:1:316) probably functioned as a spindle-whorl. Whorls were circular weights, generally of stone or lead, which attached to one end of a spindle stick through a central hole. Different weights of whorl were required for spinning different thicknesses of yarn, as the weight affects the speed at which the spindle spins. From about the fourteenth century the spinning-wheel supplanted the spindle and distaff as the principal means of spinning yarn (Walton 1991, 325.). Spindle-whorls of similar type, size and weight to the Swords Castle example were recovered from fourteenth-century levels in London (Egan 1998, 261) and Perth (Ford 1987, 130).

E4619:1:316

Lead. Roughly circular plano-subconvex weight with central circular perforation. Rough-finished exterior, particularly on convex surface; smooth surface on sides of perforation. Wt 33g. Diam. 25.1mm. Th. 9mm. Diam. of perforation 8.4mm.

Tweezers

A pair of iron tweezers (E4619:28:4) were larger and more robust than would be expected of personal tweezers and may have been associated with craftworking. The interpretation of similar tweezers from thirteenth- and fourteenth-century levels in York and London as tools used in the cloth-making industry seems plausible. The process known as burling, traditionally undertaken by women, involved the use of very sharp, pointed tweezers to pluck foreign matter and knots from woven wool prior to fulling (trowbridgemuseum.co.uk; clothtrade.co.uk).

E4619:28:4

Iron. Tweezers, broken at head where arms join. Arms are flattened, widening gradually away from the head. At their widest point the arms then step in at an angle to form narrow points. Arms are rectangular in cross-section; the points are plano-convex. Date: medieval. L. 153.6mm. W. of arm 13mm (max.). Th. of arm 2.8mm. L. of point 24.9mm.

Punch

A large iron, nail-like object (E4619:18:20) may have functioned as a smith's punch. There is no true head, but repeated hammering appears to have created an irregular rounded end, with expansion of the shank on two sides. Such 'burred' heads were noted as characteristic of punches from medieval levels at York (Ottaway and Rogers 2002, 2720).

E4619:18:20

Iron. Long straight shank with rectangular cross-section, turning to oval close to top end. Slightly blunt at tip. No true head; burred, oval, expanded end, owing to repeated hammering. L. 85.9mm. Max. W. of shank 5mm x 4.7mm. Top: 8mm x 5.7mm.

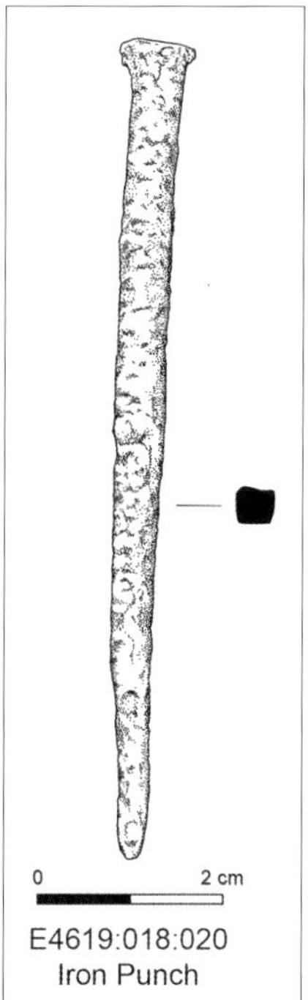

Fig. 11.3—Iron punch (E4619:18:20) (drawing: Sara Nylund).

Fig. 11.4—Possible woodworker's auger or gouge (E4619:76:4) (drawing: Sara Nylund).

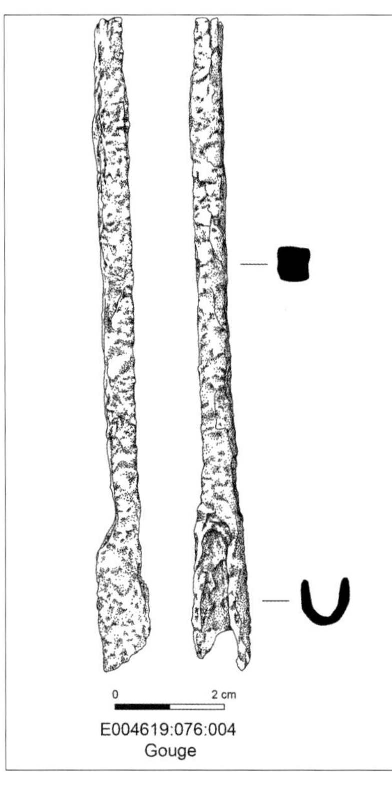

Gouge

An iron tool with a long tang (E4619:76:4) appears to be a woodworker's auger or gouge. The head is shouldered and forms a cylindrical bit with a relatively straight edge. In this it bears a greater resemblance to a turner's gouge than to an auger. The long tang indicates a relatively long wooden handle for the size of the tool, typical of a turner's gouge, as the long handle would enable the turner to hold the gouge under his arm for greater stability and control while working at a lathe (Moxon 1703, 183). A similar style of gouge was recovered from unstratified levels at Lagore, referred to as 'hand gouges' by Hencken (1950, 109).

E4619:76:7

Iron. Gouge/tool consisting of long tang with rectangular cross-section, flattening and widening to form shouldered, deep, semi-oval scooped tool. L. 115.6mm. L. of head 22.8mm. W. of tang 6.3mm x 5mm. W. of head 10mm. Th. of head 09.6mm.

DOMESTIC ITEMS

Knives

Two incomplete knives (E4619:106:71 and E4619:124:2) were recovered. Both had scale tangs, where a wide tang extends the length and width of the handle, to which it is attached by rivets. Scale tang knives are thought to have been developed in the thirteenth century, although whittle tangs remained more common up to the fifteenth century (Cowgill 1987, 25; Ottaway and Rogers 2002, 2751). It was not possible to assign a date to either of the two knives recovered, although the absence of a visible bolster between blade and tang suggests that they are likely to be sixteenth-century or earlier in date (Goodall 2005, 399). A small iron tanged object (E4619:98:1) may represent a fragment of a whittle tang blade. This showed evidence of being surface-treated with a copper-alloy metal, comprising a narrow band extending around the lower part of the possible blade and, to a lesser extent, extending onto the tang itself (S. Kelly, pers. comm.). Whittle tang knives with inlaid copper-alloy design or bands of copper alloy around the base of the blade (referred to as hilt bands or hilt plates) are known from medieval and post-medieval levels in London and York (Cowgill 1987, 25–7; Ottaway and Rogers 2002, 2759). The band of copper alloy identified on E4619:98:1 may represent the remnants of such a hilt band, although no parallel could be found for similar surface treatment on the tang itself.

E4619:106:71

Iron. Incomplete knife with scale tang. Blade bent to almost right angle *c.* one third of the length from tang. Straight-backed blade and tang; blade runs parallel to tang at first, then tapers to meet back, forming tip; blade expands at obtuse angle from tang; tang widens slightly towards end (end broken off); single rivet hole in surviving portion of tang; no bolster or shoulder plate evident. Blade: L. (if straight) *c.* 111mm; W. (max.) 18.4mm; Th. (at back) 3.2mm. Tang: L. (surviving) 40.2mm; W. (max.) 11.4mm; Th. 4mm. Diam. of rivet hole 2.4mm.

E4619:124:2

Iron. Incomplete knife with scale tang. Straight-backed blade and tang; blade expands nearly at right angle from tang, then tapers steadily on cutting side towards tip; tang narrows slightly towards end; single rivet hole near blade—tang thins in this area and rivet may have held a shoulder plate in place. Blade: L. (surviving) 52.5mm; W. (max.) 16.6mm; Th. (at back) 2.4mm. Tang: L. (surviving) 36.1mm; W. (max.) 9.2mm; Th. 2.4mm. Diam. of rivet hole 1.5mm.

E4619:98:1

Iron. Fragment of small tanged object, possibly a blade. Rectangular cross-section; raised copper-alloy band across wider part; tang coated in copper alloy. L. 3.34cm; L. of tang. 1.57cm. W. max. 0.86cm; W. of tang 0.46cm. Th. 0.33cm; Th. of band 0.6cm.

Candle-holder

An L-shaped socketed iron candle-holder (E4619:118:18), forged from a single piece of iron, was recovered. Socketed candle-holders are typical of medieval times, formed either from a single piece of iron or with the socket soldered to a separate shank. Shanks could be either straight or L-shaped and would originally have been held in small, portable wooden bases. It has been suggested that socketed candle-holders were used for tallow candles, while the superior wax candles were held on iron prickets (Egan 1998, 134). Both socketed and pricket candle-holders were in use over a long period of time, although Egan noted a general increase in the diameter of sockets over time. The example from Swords Castle has a relatively small diameter (12–13mm), and candle-holders of similar size are known from fourteenth-century levels in London (*ibid.*, 142).

E4619:118:18

Iron. Socketed candle-holder; L-shaped, tapering shank with rectangular cross-section; flattened and folded to form socket on outside of angle; socket open at top and base; flanges overlap slightly. Thirteenth–fourteenth century. Shank: L. horizontal 43.7mm; L. vertical 28.3mm; W. 10.5mm (at top); Th. 7mm. Socket: H. 28mm; Diam. (int.) 13.1mm x 12.3mm.

Candle-snuffer

A badly corroded iron object (E4619:106:28), consisting of a flat, tapering bar with a semicircular expansion on one side, has been tentatively identified as part of a scissors-style candle-snuffer. Candle-snuffers of this type are known from the sixteenth century (Egan 2005, 83) and continue in use up to the present day.

E4619:106:28
Iron. Elongate, flat object, tapering towards one end. Straight lower edge, expanding to form semicircle on upper edge. No further detail on X-ray owing to poor preservation. L. 51.1mm. H. 22.2mm. Th. 4mm.

Handles
An incomplete iron handle with a curved profile was recovered (E4619:77:16). Although one terminus was intact, the level of corrosion meant that it was not possible to identify whether the handle was fixed or a drop-handle. In size and overall form it resembles handles recovered from medieval levels in York (Ottaway and Rogers 2002, 2845) and London (Egan 1998, 87), identified as drop-handles from caskets or chests. It is likely that the Swords example performed a similar function, although the possibility that it was a fixed handle from a vessel lid should also be considered. A large iron drop-handle (E4619:107:1) was also recovered. This had a circular cross-section, and its size and robust form suggest that it would have been used on a heavy vessel, such as an iron crock.

E4619:77:16
Iron. Curving handle with rectangular cross-section. One terminus broken; form of other terminus uncertain owing to corrosion, but appears to widen and flatten. Not identifiable on X-ray. L. 92.5mm. H. 31mm. W. 8mm. Th. 5mm.

E4619:107:1
Iron. Large drop-handle. Circular cross-section, widening and flattening at one end to form attachment loop. Broken at other end. U-shaped and twisted back on itself towards surviving end. Heavily corroded and encrusted in places. L. (if straight) 347mm. Diam. 9.5mm. Loop: Diam. 22mm; Th. 2.6mm. Diam. of hole 9.7mm.

STRUCTURAL AND FURNITURE FITTINGS

Nails
A total of 435 nails (excluding horseshoe nails) were recovered, of which 338 were from below topsoil levels. The greatest collections by far came from Trenches 3 and 4, with 112 and 111 nails recorded respectively. The next closest to these was Trench 8, with 71 nails recorded. Some 272 nails were considered complete enough to sort by type, and twelve categories of nails were identified (Types I–XII below). Of these, Type I was by far the most common nail recovered (142 in total; 112 from below topsoil levels). This corresponds with Ford and Walsh's (1987, 138–9) Type A nail and probably represents the ordinary carpentry nail that would have been used for most woodworking purposes. All three nails recovered from Trench 2 were of Type I, as were all but one of the six nails identified to type from Trench 1: these probably represent timber structural remains in these areas. The other trenches had much more mixed assemblages of nails, especially Trenches 3 and 4, which had nine and eight different nail types respectively.

Most nails show signs of use, with evidence of clenching of the tips on many, but a small number may never have been used. In particular, one nail from Trench 3 (E4619:1:264) lacks

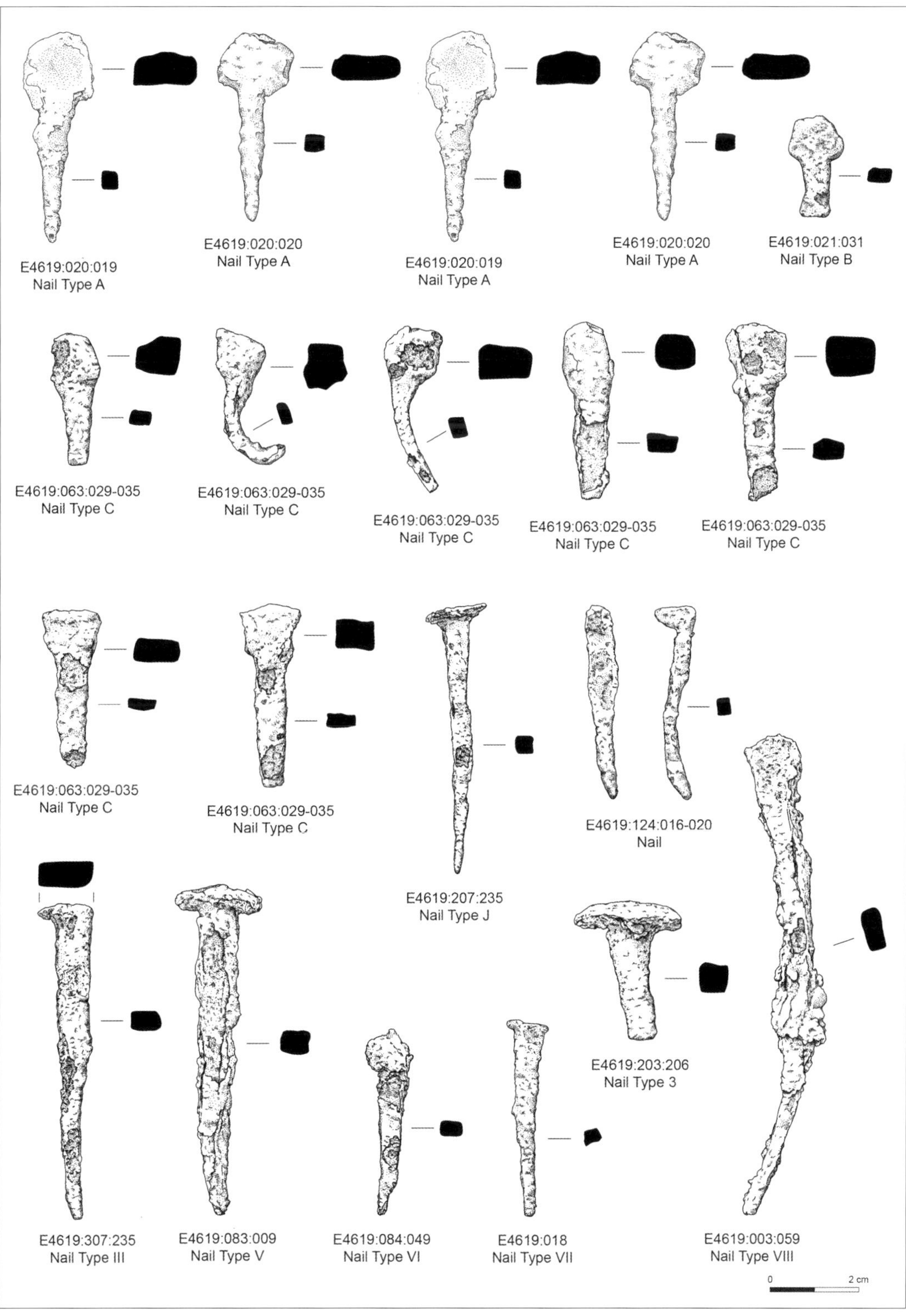

Fig. 11.5—Nail types (drawing: Sara Nylund).

179

a head but displays a narrowing of the upper end of the shank to take a head (similar to a short tang), suggesting that it was unfinished and had never been used. Some of the other nails without heads may have been similar but the level of preservation meant that this could not be confirmed. These may represent faulty nails included in a carpenter's store or may indicate that nails were made at the site. The presence of other evidence of smithing at the site, in the form of iron slag and the horseshoe and associated nails, strengthens the latter supposition.

One of the nails recovered from Trench 4 (E4619:74:3) presents another scenario. This consisted of two Type I nails, the shanks of which appear to have been deliberately twisted around each other to form a single nail similar in size to Type III nails. Indeed, it was recovered from the same feature as a small group of Type III nails. This suggests the use of readily available nails to replace another, unavailable type of nail, perhaps during repair work, and may indicate that more specialised nails were not produced or present at the castle at that time.

Type I

Wrought-iron nail with square or rectangular cross-sectioned shank, and a flat, oval or subrectangular head. The shank is joined to the centre of the head, although this is not entirely uniform. In some cases the top of the shank almost protrudes from the head, as a result of pressure from hammering. Although all Type I nails share these characteristics, there is a wide variety of shank length, breadth-to-width ratio and head size within this type. This is probably due in part to the handmade nature of the nails, along with a lack of specialisation in their use. Some 142 nails were identified as Type I or possible Type I. It is probable that many of the uncategorised nails were also of Type I but were too fragmentary or poorly preserved to be identified. Type I nails were widespread on the site and were found in all trenches except Trench 10.

Type II

Wrought-iron nail with square to rectangular cross-sectioned shank and a convex, oval head. The shank is joined to the centre of the head. Type II nails are identified with Ford and Walsh's (1987, 138–9) Type B nails. Type II nails were represented by 36 specimens from six different trenches. These were probably also used for various woodworking purposes, although the convex head means that they were designed to be visible in the finished product; they may have been used in visible joinery and fittings rather than in the underlying structure.

Type III

Wrought-iron nail characterised by a very robust near-square cross-sectioned shank and a large oval or subrectangular head, usually convex (although one, E4619:21:18, has a flat head). Type III may be considered as a sub-type of Type II, but the robust square shank sets them apart. They closely resemble the nail used in the clench bolt E4619:21:30, and it is likely that this type represents nails for this or a similar purpose. A total of twenty Type III nails were identified: six of these were recovered from Trench 4 (including that made from two smaller nails) and five from Trench 8. Both of these trenches were associated with structural remains.

Type IV

Wrought-iron nail with rectangular cross-sectioned shank and a flat head that extends beyond the shank on one side, giving the nail an overall L-shape. This corresponds to Ford and Walsh's Type E. Type IV nails were represented by eighteen nails. The greatest concentration was from Trench 7, which yielded eight of the total and five from a single feature (F124). Type IV nails are similar to modern floor brads and may have had a similar use.

Type V

Wrought-iron nail with a rectangular cross-sectioned shank and a narrow oval head that only extends beyond the shank on two sides. This corresponds to Ford and Walsh's Type F, T-shaped nails. Seven Type V nails were identified, five of which were complete.

Type VI

Wrought-iron nail with a rectangular cross-sectioned shank surmounted by a flat, bilobed head. The head is little wider than the shank on two sides, while the shank itself has a breadth/width ratio of nearly 2:1. This type was classified as Type G by Ford and Walsh. Twenty nails of Type VI were identified: seven of these were recovered from Trench 4, with four from a single feature, F84. A further four nails were recovered from Trench 8.

Type VII

Wrought-iron nail with a rectangular cross-sectioned shank. The head is blocky, almost cuboid, and the shank joins it close to one edge. The almost L-shape of these nails resembles Type IV, although it is unlikely that they would have been used in floorboards, as the head would protrude above the floor. Type VII is represented by just three nails, two of which were recovered from F18 in Trench 3. The third was retrieved from topsoil in Trench 8.

Type VIII

This is represented by a single nail, from Trench 1 (E4619:3:59). It is characterised by a very long, flat, rectangular cross-sectioned shank. The head is almost cuboid and extends beyond the width of the shank on one side only.

Type IX

This type of nail has a circular or oval cross-sectioned shank and a flat, circular head. Three examples were identified, two from topsoil in Trench 3 (E4619:1:243 and E4619:1:244). The third was recovered from F120 in Trench 10, the tile surface previously excavated by Fanning.

Type X

Nails with a rectangular cross-sectioned shank which expands on all sides to form a flat, rectangular head. This is somewhat similar to Ford and Walsh's Type H but with a shorter shank. It may also be a variant of horseshoe nail Type C, although the proportions of the shanks make this less likely. Type X was represented by eleven specimens.

Type XI

Nails with a short, narrow shank of rectangular cross-section, and a relatively small, slightly domed head. The size of Type XI nails is approaching that of a tack, and these may have been associated with fittings rather than structural woodwork. Four Type XI nails were identified, all from consolidation layers beneath the topsoil: three of these were recovered from Trench 4, while the fourth came from Trench 5.

Type XII
Nails characterised by a heavy, robust shank and a small, flat head. Shanks have a rectangular cross-section, while heads are rectangular or subrectangular in shape. A total of seven Type XII nails were identified, five of which were recovered from Trench 6.

Clench bolt
Clench bolts, used to join overlapping planks of timber together, consist of two separate elements: a nail and a metal plate, or rove, with a central hole. The nail is driven through both planks, the rove is attached on the inner side, and the tip of the nail is hammered down or clenched (Ottaway 1992, cited in Zori 2007, 33). This holds the nail in place and gives extra strength to the timber joint. In medieval times, clench bolts were used in the construction of boats, structures and doors. A complete clench bolt (E4619:21:30) was recovered from a stone surface (F21) and was probably used in a door at the castle. A partial clench bolt (E4619:74:2) was recovered from a rubble layer and may have been a component in a substantial door. A rectangular rove (E4619:63:44) from a consolidation layer in Trench 6 was also identified from its radiograph image. The nail element of the clench bolt bears a marked similarity to Type III nails, and these may represent unused nails intended for clench bolts, or nails used in structural fittings in conjunction with such bolts. It was noted that Type III nails were also recovered from features containing clench bolts, as was the improvised Type III (E4619:74:3), and these may have been used alongside the bolts or in similar substantial timber fittings.

E4619:21:30
Iron. Complete clench bolt with rectangular rove. Cross-section of shank uncertain owing to corrosion; head of nail irregularly oval and slightly convex. L. 38.4mm. Head W. 21.3. Shank Th. 5mm. Rove L. 23.8mm.

E4619:63:44
Iron. Identified from X-ray as square/lozenge-shaped rove. Heavy corrosion and encrustations completely obscure form. Dimensions from X-ray: L. 22mm; W. 22mm; Diam. of hole 10mm x 8.5mm.

E4619:74:2
Iron. Lozenge-shaped rove with end of nail attached. Heavily corroded. Dimensions approximate owing to corrosion products. Rove: W. 37mm x 33.4mm; Th. 9.6mm. Nail: L. 28.5mm.

Tacks
A total of twelve tacks or studs, all of iron, were recovered during the three seasons of excavations. These are characterised by having much shorter or smaller shanks than nails and

would have been unsuited to general woodworking. In addition, the three Type XI nails may in fact represent larger-sized tacks rather than true nails. Within the collection of tacks a number of different styles were obvious, and these probably served varying functions. Two in particular (E4619:18:21 and E4619:65:15) consist of a very short shank surmounted by a large, diamond-shaped or oval convex head and may have had a decorative function in either wood or leather. In contrast, a tack recovered from Trench 3 (E4619:31:13) is almost like a pin in appearance, but with a flat head and square cross-section. This may have been used in very fine woodworking or leatherworking, but is unlikely to have been a visible component of the finished item.

Wall hook

A small, complete wall hook was recovered from Trench 6 (E4619:63:2). The shank is bent through 90° at its narrower end, for hammering into a wall, while a stepped base separating the hook itself from the shank would also have facilitated its attachment to a wall. Similarly formed wall hooks were recovered from twelfth/thirteenth- and fifteenth-century levels in York and from late fourteenth-century levels at Trim Castle (Ottaway and Rogers 2002, 2835; Sweetman 1978, 178, 181).

E4619:63:2
Iron. Small wall hook comprising tapering shank, stepped at base, with hook extending to one side. Narrower end of shank bent into L-shape for driving into wall/structure. Shank: L. 46.4mm (57.5mm if straight); W. 9.7mm max.; Th. 6.3mm. Hook: L. 13.8mm (25mm if straight); Th. 4.7mm.

Lead came

A small length of lead window came (E4619:63:54) was recovered from Trench 6. Lead was used in paned windows from early medieval times: initially this was largely confined to ecclesiastical structures, extending to domestic structures during the medieval period (Egan 1998, 51). Nonetheless, window cames are relatively uncommon in the archaeological record, as the ease with which lead could be melted and reused meant that it was generally recycled (Scully 1997b, 485). The fragment recovered at Swords Castle appears to be of the typical 'H' cross-section, but the level of distortion in shape meant that the width of the central channel could not be ascertained.

E4619:63:54
Lead. Short fragment of window came, twisted into sinuous shape. 'H' cross-section. L. 40.8mm. W. 5.3mm. Th. 4.9mm.

Mounts

Metal mounts made from iron or copper alloy, or occasionally from precious metals, were commonly used to decorate wooden and leather items throughout the medieval period. While most furniture during this time was solidly functional and static, items such as chests, caskets and vessels were more personal and valued and accompanied their owners from location to location. As a result, they were more likely to be personalised and decorated. In particular, elongate mounts, or strip mounts, of iron or copper alloy were attached to chests, caskets, books and wooden vessels, although distinguishing which specific item they decorated is not always possible (Ottaway and Rogers 2002, 2848; Brenan 1998, 65).

Wooden drinking vessels, known as mazers, were prized personal possessions in medieval times and were often decorated with metal. In Waterford, a number of wooden mazers that survived had a band below the rim, suggesting that they were originally decorated with an applied metal band (Hurley and McCutcheon 1997, 564). These bands, often made of precious metal, would have been of greater value than the bowl itself and may have been removed prior to disposal of the bowls. The mount (E4619:1:302) probably represents part of a decorative strip from the rim or stem of a mazer, although the possibility of its being a decorative element from a book cannot be discounted. The metal had been tinned (S. Kelly, pers. comm.) to produce a silvered colour, giving somewhat the appearance of a more precious metal. Nonetheless, the use of base metal rather than precious suggests that it did not originate in the household of the archbishop but would have belonged instead to others who worked and lived at the castle.

Fragments of iron mounts recovered over the three excavation seasons were probably more functional than decorative in purpose. A small, triangular iron fragment (E4619:20:9) may represent a mount from a larger wooden chest or coffer. Another (E4619:63:49) resembles examples recovered from fourteenth- and fifteenth-century examples from London (Brenan 1998, 78), and may once have formed part of a fleur-de-lys shape or the end of a strap hinge from a chest or coffer. Three fragments of curved iron bands (E4619:111:4, E4619:111:5 and E4619:6) with rivet hole may all be related. The size and morphology of these suggest that they may have formed iron bands or hoops around a small wooden cask or bucket, such as that found in York (Ottaway and Rogers 2002, 2807–8).

E4619:1:302
Tinned copper alloy. Fragment of rectangular strip of thin metal with openwork design. Central, complete quatrefoil, with partial adjoining quatrefoils extending to broken edges; vertical pairs of circles lie midway between each quatrefoil. A rectangular projection, extending from the edge of the strip immediately above the central quatrefoil, appears to be broken. The other edge is marked by semicircular indentations below the quatrefoil and adjacent circle. Max. L. 19.9mm. Strip W. 9.9mm. L. of projection 4.2mm. H. of projection 1.4mm. H. of quatrefoil 5.3mm. Diam. of circles 1.3mm. Th. of strip 0.5mm.

E4619:1:309
Copper alloy. Elongate, sinuous strip with rectangular cross-section. Curved through *c.* 90º close to one end (may not be original). Expanded circular terminal with perforation on shorter arm. On longer arm, strip expands to form triangular projection, close to second perforation. From this, strip thins gradually, curving slightly to rounded terminal. A slight bend mid-length appears to be damage rather than original design. L. 6.9mm. W. 3.8–4.5mm. Th. 1.3mm. Diam. of terminal 10mm. W. at projection 8.9mm.

E4619:20:9
Iron. Triangular fragment of iron. Shortest edge is turned downwards at a *c.* 70º angle for *c.* 7mm. Semicircular notch along longest edge may represent partial rivet hole. Dimensions: 33.6mm x 23.4mm x 22mm.

E4619:63:49
Iron. Lozenge-shaped terminus of mount—possible fragment of fleur-de-lys design. No rivet hole; possibly broken at attachment point. L. 66.2mm. W. max. 37.7mm. Th. 1.6mm.

E4619:65:31
Copper alloy. Terminal of flat mount with rivet hole; polygonal end to mount, broken other side of rivet hole. No decoration evident. L. 1.17cm. W. 1.19cm. T. 0.99cm. Diam. of rivet hole 0.26cm.

E4619:111:4
Iron. Curving band, rectangular and flattened. X-ray shows rivet holes for attachment to object/vessel. Size suggests probably from bucket/cask. Probably from same object as 111:5 and 111:6. Curvature suggests vessel of diameter *c.* 22.5cm. L. 116mm. W. 31mm. Th. 3mm. Diam. of rivet hole 5.5mm.

E4619:111:5
Iron. Curving band, rectangular and flattened. X-ray shows rivet holes for attachment to object/vessel. Size suggests probably from bucket/cask. Probably from same object as 111:4 and 111:6. L. 58.6mm. W. 33.7mm. Th. 5.2mm.

E4619:111:6
Iron. Curving band, rectangular and flattened. X-ray shows rivet holes for attachment to object/vessel. Size suggests probably from bucket/cask. Probably from same object as 111:4 and 111:5. L. 79.5mm. W. 32.5mm. Th. 6mm. Diam. of rivet holes 3.8mm and 5mm.

Strap hinge
A large iron strap hinge was recovered (E4619:64:13). Although heavily corroded, the hinge element was evident in radiography, as were two rivet holes—one on each 'strap' element. The hinge was broken close to the identified rivet holes, and thus its overall length and form are unknown. Strap hinges were widely used on wooden fixtures such as shutters and doors, and on chests, while they also formed parts of locking mechanisms in conjunction with hasps (Brenan 1998, 75–7; Egan 1998, 48–9).

E4619:64:13
Iron. Large strap hinge. Comprises elongate, flat rectangular section, widening slightly towards one end. Hinge in mid-section, identified from X-ray and consistent with expansion in this section. Rivet hole evident near wider end; possible second rivet hole visible close to opposite end. Poorly preserved. L. 146.5mm. W. 46mm. Th. 2.4mm. Diam. of rivet hole *c.* 5.5mm.

Fittings
Four iron objects recovered from Trench 7 and a fifth from Trench 9 (E4619:1:1076) may represent fragments from larger fittings. These consisted of shanks or bars with rectangular cross-sections, but were morphologically inconsistent with large nails. A high degree of corrosion meant that it was not possible to identify their original complete form or function more clearly.

E4619:1:1076

Iron. Heavy shank of object with almost square cross-section; tapering towards one end, with oblique bevelling at other end. L. 56.1mm. W. 9.3mm. Th. 9.1mm.

E4619:1:1234

Iron. Robust rectangular shank/arm, with tongue-shaped 'head' extending beyond shank in one plane only. Overall size and shape make it unlikely to be a nail. X-ray shows a slight rise at back of head where joined to shank. L. 51mm. Shank 8.4mm x 7.8mm. Head: L. 16.1mm; W. max. 12mm; W. min. 5.6mm; Th. 4.7mm.

E4619:109:9

Iron. Incomplete fitting. Elongate square–rectangular bar; squared off at surviving end; flattening from mid-length; broken at possible attachment point. L. 91.3mm. W. 9.9mm x 9.9mm and 10.5mm x 7mm.

E4619:114:6

Iron. Robust shank of fitting with rectangular cross-section. Tapering to blunt tip at one end. L. 75mm. W. 9.4mm x 7.8mm.

E4619:112:2

Iron. Flat, pear-shaped attachment/fitting. Circular part with wide aperture widens to oval part with a small rivet hole at either end (these last visible only on X-ray). Modern. Oval area: D. 53mm x 26.3mm; Th. 4.5mm; Diam. of rivet holes 4mm. Circular area: D. 30.4mm; Th. 2.8mm; Diam. of aperture 11.6mm.

HORSE EQUIPMENT

Horseshoes

There is no consensus on when the shoeing of horses with iron was introduced, but it is generally accepted that it was common practice by the eleventh century. The purpose of the horseshoe is to protect the hoof from excessive wear and subsequent lameness. Studies of horseshoes from excavations in London have identified a progressive development in the form of both shoes and nails throughout the medieval period (Clark 1995, 76–9), and therefore they can be regarded as a useful datable artefact on medieval sites. This is especially true when one considers that horseshoes have a relatively short lifespan and would be discarded upon replacement. A partial horseshoe recovered from Trench 3 at Swords Castle (E4619:28:5) comprises the forepart of the shoe, with characteristics consistent with Clark's Type 2B horseshoe (*ibid.*, 86). This form of horseshoe was in use in London from *c.* 1150 to 1350 and was the predominant form of shoe used in the period *c.* 1150–1225 (*ibid.*, 92).

A second fragment of horseshoe (E4619:18:19) consisted only of the end of one heel. This was notably narrow and from a much heavier shoe than E4619:28:5. Unfortunately, it was not possible to assign a type or date to this fragment with any degree of certainty, although some resemblance in form was noted to an early sixteenth-century shoe from London (Egan 2005, 180). The absence of a fullered groove for the nail holes may also suggest a pre-seventeenth-century date. An incomplete branch of a third horseshoe with a narrow web (E4619:121:1) was very corroded, with four rectangular holes visible close to a straight outer edge suggesting a seventeenth-century or later date (Clark 1995, 82; Egan 2005, 179).

E4619:18:19
Iron. Terminus of left branch of horseshoe. Very narrow terminus; no calkin obvious, although thickened relative to branch. Broken at first nail hole: hole does not appear countersunk, original shape uncertain. No evidence of fullering. Straight-sided branch, with no obvious curvature to shoe. Width tapers from outer to inner edge at hole. Wt 28g. L. 52.5mm. W. 8–21.7mm. Th. 4.5–6.4mm.

E4619:28:5
Iron. Incomplete horseshoe. Clark's Type 2B, comprising the forepart of a wide-arched shoe with wavy edges. Nail holes are subrectangular and countersunk: three holes on left branch, two on right, with shoe broken at third hole on left and after second hole on right. Holes not consistent in size or spacing. Greatly worn at toe. Max. W. 107.4mm. Max. W. of web 23.9mm. Max. Th. 6.3mm.

E4619:121:1
Incomplete branch of horseshoe. Very heavily encrusted—detail only from X-ray, on which four rectangular holes are visible. Two holes at front closer together; holes appear regular in size. X-ray suggests fullered groove present around nail-holes. L. 115mm. Web W. 23.6mm. Th. 3.2. Holes (from X-ray) 5.5mm x 3.6mm.

Horseshoe nails
A total of 46 horseshoe nails were recovered at Swords Castle, of which 33 were retrieved from Trench 3 and the remaining thirteen from Trenches 4, 6, 7 and 8. As horseshoes changed in form over time, so did the associated nails. Five distinct types were identified, closely paralleling nails recovered in London (Clark 1995, 86–92), Perth (Ford and Walsh 1987, 137) and Trim Castle (Hayden 2011, 351). Types A, C and E were recovered from stratified features across the five trenches, while Types A, B, C and D were found among 21 nails recovered from the topsoil layer (F1) in Trench 3.

Type A was represented by ten nails, all from stratified levels, although identification of two nails (E4619:80:12 and E4619:101:2) was less certain owing to the degree of corrosion present. These were typified by a 'fiddle-key' head, of which there were two variants: a rounded D-shaped head and a more angular, trapezoidal head, both of equal thickness to the shank. Both variations were present in equal numbers. They are consistent with Ford and Walsh's Type J1 and the 'fiddle-key' nails of Clark associated with Type 2 horseshoes, dating from *c.* 1050–*c.* 1350 (Clark 1995, 92).

Type B was represented by twelve nails, cruciform in profile, with the head being both wider and thicker than the shank and characterised by the presence of expanded ears or lobes. These are identified with Ford and Walsh's (1987, 137) Type J2 nails and associated with Type 3 horseshoes by Clark (1995, 87), which date from *c.* 1175–1375 and were commonest in the period 1270–1350 (*ibid.*, 92).

Type C was represented by 21 nails of which the head expanded gradually on all sides to form a flat, square or rectangular top, with the head having a triangular profile. These are

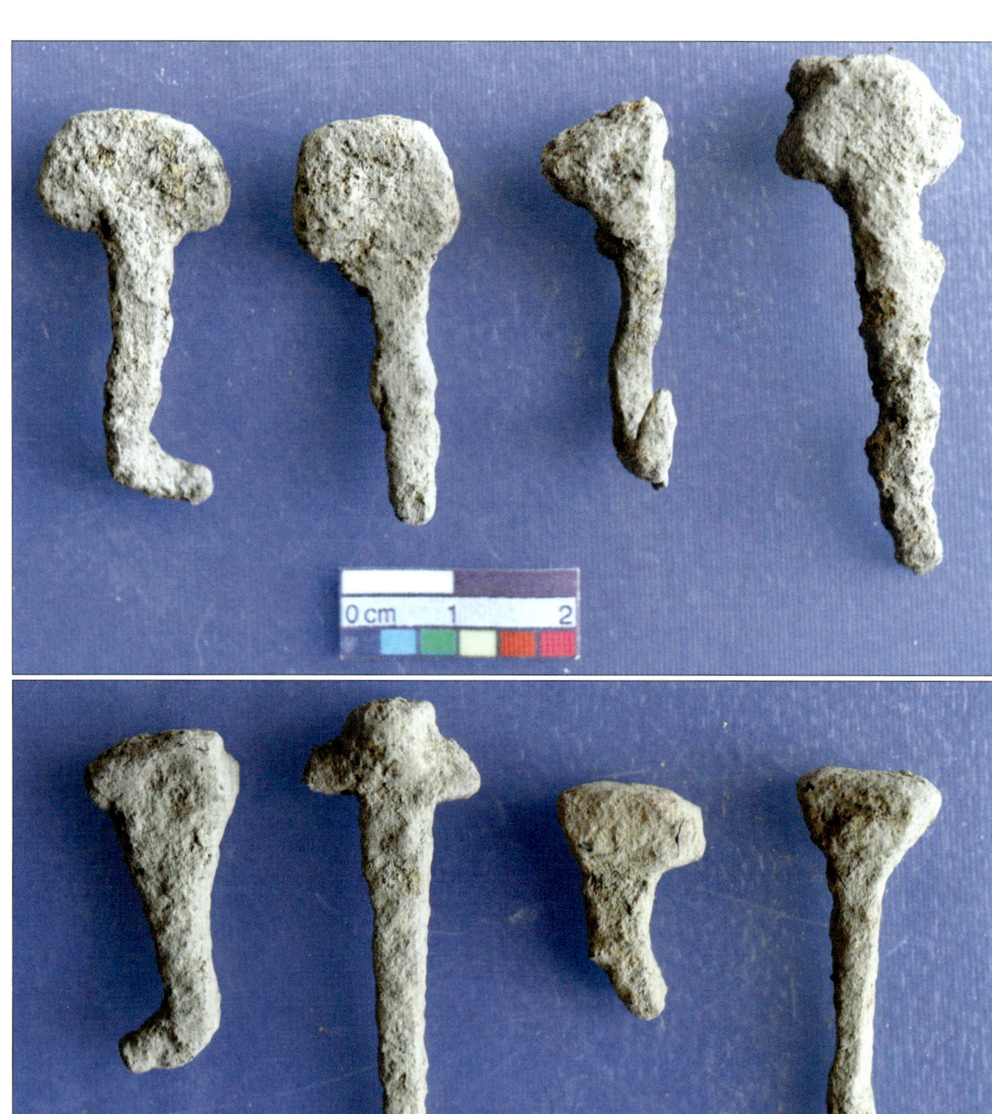

Pl. 11.2—Horseshoe nail types A and B from F21, and Types B, D and C from F1 (photo: Siobhán Duffy).

identified with Hayden's (2011, 351) Type C and Ford and Walsh's Type J3, dating from the sixteenth century in Perth (Ford and Walsh 1987, 137). They are also similar to nails found *in situ* in sixteenth-century horseshoes in London (Egan 2005, 180).

Type D is represented by a single nail (E4619:1:270) from the topsoil in Trench 3. This has a cuboid head, both wider and thicker than the shank, and closely resembles Hayden's Type B. No close parallels were noted in the London publications, although it may be a variant of the rectangular-headed nails associated with Clark's Type 4 horseshoes, dating from the later medieval period (Clark 1995, 89–92).

Type E is also represented by a single nail (E4619:109:84). This was characterised by a relatively short shank, which expanded to form a flat-topped head. This differed from Type C in the head narrowing towards the top, giving a polygonal rather than triangular profile. Nonetheless, it may be a variant of Type C. The straight shank suggests that this nail had never been used.

Many of the nails were worn: this was particularly noticeable in Type B nails, many of which showed a very uneven wear pattern. The degree of wear, along with the absence of tips on many examples, suggests that the nails were removed for replacement. When shoeing, the tip of the nail comes through the hoof wall and is then hammered back into the wall to secure it, a practice known as clenching (Clark 1995, 82). In order to remove the nails, it would generally be necessary to clip off the tip, although this practice does not seem to have been universally employed (*ibid.*, 84). The presence of clipped nails and unclipped clenched nails at Swords Castle suggests that shoeing was taking place at the site. It is noted, however, that complete nails with clenching may have worked loose from the hoof and been lost. A small number of nails (E4619:1:272, E4619:1:279, E4619:18:44) show evidence of spiral clenching, where the tip of the nail is curled tightly back on itself rather than into the hoof (Clark 1995, 87). Clark equates this with the lobed nails and suggests that it is a fourteenth-century practice (*ibid.*). Only one of the three spirally clenched nails from Swords Castle was the lobed Type B (E4619:1:279), however, the others being of Type C and A.

A small number of nails from Trench 3 with complete tips show no evidence of clenching and thus can be considered to have never been used (E4619:20:19, E4619:20:20, E4619:1:268, E4619:1:269). This may not, however, indicate their manufacture at the site, as they may equally have been brought onto the site as spares and subsequently lost. Nonetheless, the range and number of nails present indicate that a smith or farrier worked within the precinct of Swords Castle during the medieval period.

Harness fitting

An iron fitting (E4619:111:3), comprising a D-shaped ring with a subtriangular extension from its straight side, may represent a harness fitting. The corrosion present masks much of the surface, however, making it difficult to be certain of its completeness or function.

E4619:111:3
Iron. D-shaped ring, the curved segment with circular cross-section, the straight segment with rectangular cross-section. A subtriangular arm projects outwards from the straight part, widening along its length, and with rectangular cross-section. Ring: 43.7mm x 30.9mm; Diam. curved 6.5mm; W. straight 9.3mm x 7.6mm. Arm: L. 29.6mm; W. 14.7mm x 8.6mm.

MISCELLANEA

Sharpener

An incomplete pencil-sharpener, made of lead, was recovered from topsoil (E4619:1:1043). It was conical in shape and would originally have had a suspension loop at the apex, now broken off. Pencil-sharpeners of this type developed in the nineteenth century, and sharpeners identical to the Swords example are dated to 1883 (www.ebay.ie/).

E4619:1:1043
Lead alloy and iron. Conical pencil-sharpener; iron blade still present in slit along one side; broken at top—scrollwork would have extended up to form suspension loop; oval cartouche on one side with 'SO' lettering in relief. Date: *c.* 1870–1900. H. 2.62mm. Diam. (base) 1.24mm.

Toy gun
A cast-iron toy gun was recovered from topsoil (E4619:1:795). Although the level of corrosion meant that no external details or features were visible, the X-ray image showed the gun to be intact, with the exception of side panels on the handle. In particular, the presence of a spring mechanism connecting the trigger to the hammer, thus allowing paper caps to be set off, identified the item as a cap gun. Toy cap guns developed in the US in the mid-nineteenth century, as armament companies looked for new marketing outlets following the end of the Civil War. These early cap guns were similar in style to the Civil War pistols from which they were derived, although often embellished with additional designs. During the early twentieth century, styles of cap guns changed to resemble the Western revolver (Scott 2010, 135). The gun from Swords Castle falls into the former category and is clearly a pistol in design. This overall shape and the lack of a trigger guard are consistent with late nineteenth-century cap guns.

E4619:1:795
Iron. Cast-iron toy cap gun in form of pistol. Heavily corroded, but trigger, barrel, handle and hammer still identifiable. Mechanism clearly visible in X-ray. Spring connecting trigger to hammer hidden in handle. Handle may have had a cover of organic material, since decomposed. Date: late nineteenth/early twentieth century. L. 115.3mm. Barrel L. 63.6mm. Diam. at muzzle 10.6mm x 9.4mm. Handle: L. 53.8mm; W. 19.7mm; Th. 8.1mm.

Attachment/pendant weight
A small, iron, skittle-shaped object was recovered from Trench 4 (E4619:76:8). It appears to have a circular attachment loop surmounting an oval body, although corrosion obscures any detail. This probably represents an attachment from a larger object, or a pendant weight. It is also similar in shape to a small staple hasp, although no evidence for the former presence of a staple could be identified on the X-ray image, making such identification unlikely.

E4619:76:8
Iron. Pendant-like object. Circular loop at one end; drop-shaped body widens in centre. Lack of detail owing to corrosion. Possible hasp or pendant weight. L. 50mm. Diam. of loop end 11.3mm. Max. W. of body 11mm. Th. 6.1mm.

Fitting/hinged object
One of the more enigmatic artefacts recovered is an iron fitting from F22 in Trench 3 (E4619:22:4). This consists of a central, solid, rectangular plate, with a small rectangular

Pl. 11.3—Iron fitting E4619:22:4 (photo: Siobhán Duffy).

protrusion on the centre of the rear surface. Two narrow, rectangular bars of iron are soldered to the upper rear surface, with the effect of forming a large 'M'. One of these arms turns outwards, away from the main body, and has an expanded rounded terminal pierced with a central hole. The second arm is thinned from the front to form a slightly expanded flat terminus. The metal is visibly folded back on itself to give a straight edge to this terminus, indicating that the fitting is complete.

Only one parallel could be found in published sources; unfortunately, this was an unstratified find from the British Museum's Portable Antiquities Scheme (finds.org.uk, Id. no. KENT-DC0C81) and thus there was no contextual information available. The object has only a single point of attachment: this is the pierced terminus of one arm. A pin or rivet through the hole would have held the fitting in place while allowing it to swivel around this point. The location of this attachment point at the lower end of the fitting, rather than at mid-height, indicates that the fitting would have been upright and surmounting a horizontal, flat surface. It was noted that the lower edge of the central plate rises slightly towards the attachment arm, lending credence to the idea of its sitting on a flat surface: this rise would prevent the edge catching on such a surface when swivelled around the attachment. A similar rise is noticeable on the copper-alloy version (finds.org.uk, Id. no. KENT-DC0C81), indicating that this is deliberate rather than the result of wear or damage to the Swords Castle find.

At the front of the fitting, the central plate and arms create a flush surface, while at the rear only the small protrusion extends to be level with the arms. This suggests that the object was backed against a vertical surface, with the protrusion providing the necessary stability for the plate to hold the fitting steady. It is unknown, however, whether this was required for when the fitting was at rest or in use. Overall, this portrays an upright fitting, surmounting a horizontal surface, held permanently in place on one side (by a pin or rivet) and temporarily in place on the other side by a raised slot. It could then be released from one side and swung outwards by a simple, slight compression of the arms. Any further interpretation of its purpose, however, would be pure speculation at this point. It can only be noted that it would have related to activities carried out at Swords Castle during its medieval occupation.

E4619:22:4

Iron. Fitting with central subrectangular plate of thin sheet metal, with a small subrectangular protrusion from the centre of rear surface. Two lengths of wrought iron with rectangular cross-section soldered to the rear surface near the top. These extend a short distance beyond the plate before curving outward and down (in a U-shape). They then extend parallel to either side of the plate to the opposite end. At this point one turns outward, away from the plate, and expands to a subcircular terminus perforated by a circular hole. The other 'arm' expands laterally and thins from the front, being folded to the back to create a straight lower edge. Medieval. Plate: L. 40mm; H. 33.4–35mm; Th. 1.9mm. Projection: L. 8.2mm; W. 4.6mm; H. 3.4mm. Arms: W. 6.9mm; Th. 3.5mm. Diam. of perforation 4–4.4mm.

Disc

Thin, circular copper-alloy disc with tinned surface (E4619:1:306); beaten appearance; plain surface. Diam. 31.1mm. Th. 0.5mm.

Lead strip

Three small, elongate fragments of lead were recovered, one each from Trenches 3, 6 and 8 (E4619:20:25, E4619:63:1 and E4619:106:24 respectively). Owing to its malleable nature and low melting-point, lead had many uses and was easily recycled in medieval and post-medieval times (Scully 1997b, 485). The fragments recovered at Swords Castle may represent waste fragments or fragments broken off larger strips.

Wire

Eight fragments of thin iron wire were recovered from Trench 1 (E4619:4:4), Trench 6 (E4619:1:1025, E4619:1:1026, E4619:63:7, E4619:63:8, E4619:63:42) and Trench 8 (E4619:112:3, E4619:112:4). Of these, two fragments (E4619:63:8 and E4619:112:3) form a loop, while the second fragment from Trench 8 (E4619:112:4) is also curving and may have formed a similar loop. The function of these is unknown, and they may have served as means of attachment for larger objects. The remaining fragments vary in length and appear to be from longer pieces of wire of unknown age and function.

Tube

A short length of narrow iron tubing or pipe (E4619:109:11) was recovered from an earlier topsoil level in Trench 7. This was too incomplete and poorly preserved for further identification as to its original function. L. 79.9mm (combined). Diam. 10.4mm x 10.6mm; int. Diam. 6.5mm x 5.5mm.

Iron vessel

Two small fragments from the rim of an iron vessel were recovered from Trench 6 (E4619:63:5 and E4619:63:6). Their similarity in thickness and morphology suggests that they are probably from a single vessel. Only a small part of the vessel below the rim survives on either: where it does, it suggests a thin-walled vessel of unknown size and shape. A much heavier, curving fragment of iron recovered from Trench 4 (E4619:65:1) may also have originated as part of a vessel, as either a rim or a hoop. One edge had broken at a rivet hole, suggesting that it had formerly been attached to another material, such as wood. Extrapolation of the curve of the fragment suggests an original diameter of *c.* 100.5mm (4in.).

E4619:63:5

Iron. Fragment of curving rim of small iron vessel or object, with fragment of thin iron plate extending from one side. Possibly associated with E4619:63:6. L. 49.6mm. W. (rim) 4.4mm. Th. (rim) 2.4mm. Th. (body) 1.5mm.

E4619:63:6

Iron. Small fragment of rim of small iron vessel or object, with fragment of thin iron plate extending from one side. Possibly associated with E4619:63:5. L. 23mm. W. (rim) 3.9mm. Th. (rim) 2.4mm. Th. (body) 1.3mm.

E4619:65:1

Iron. Curving, heavy, rectangular plate fragment with complete end/rim at one edge; half a rivet hole remains at one broken edge. If circumference completed, diameter would measure *c.* 100.5mm (*c.* 4in.). Possible fragment from vessel hoop or mount. L. 68mm at extant end/rim, 72.5mm max. Max.W. 59mm. Th. 3.5mm. Diam. of rivet hole 9.4mm.

Tanged object

A small iron object (E4619:7:12) recovered from F7 in Trench 1 may represent the tang of a small blade or other object. Heavily encrusted with products of corrosion and foreign matter. Examination of a radiograph image suggested a long, narrow shank or tang, widening and flattening at one end. L. 35.6mm. Max. W. 8.4mm. Tang: L. 28.1mm; Th. 5mm (from X-ray).

Unidentified

A total of 74 iron artefacts consisted of fragments from unidentified larger objects or were so heavily corroded and encrusted with iron oxide and matter from the surrounding soil that their original form could not be identified. Some of these latter are probably fragments of nails, while others are small fragments from larger unknown iron objects.

CONCLUSIONS

The varied assemblage of metal finds recovered over the three seasons represents life and activity in and around Swords Castle from at least the twelfth century to the twentieth century. The largest collection of datable artefacts was associated with the medieval occupation of the castle, relating to both the physical elements of the buildings and the daily life of the occupants. Personal items recovered suggest a wealthy if not extravagant household, although how representative this is of the overall site is unknown. The collection of artefacts recovered from Trench 3 is indicative of the presence of a smith within the precinct, while further evidence for the use of horses by the inhabitants of Swords Castle was found across the site.

Evidence for post-medieval life at Swords Castle is scarcer within the assemblage and primarily confined to features within Trench 7. While this indicates some activity at the site in the later sixteenth and seventeenth centuries, there were no activity-specific collections of finds relating to this period. Artefacts relating to the period from 1800 onwards were varied, mixed and dispersed across the site. With the exception of those from Trench 7, these were largely recovered from the garden soil layer and are likely to relate to life within the town of Swords rather than at the castle itself. Here, too, however, personal items suggested a degree of wealth, while other items reflect literacy and the presence of children. The artefacts recovered in Trench 7 may be more localised in origin, the presence of a flour-bag seal suggesting a strong connection with the adjoining bakery. These more recent finds within the assemblage serve to emphasise the deep-rooted links between castle and town that have existed up to the present day.

12

Non-metal finds

Siobhán G. Duffy, BSc., MA

INTRODUCTION

This report deals with objects made of bone, antler, stone, shell and glass, which include items associated with personal attire, labour and leisure activities. These are first categorised according to their parent material and then by purpose or individual type. Of the 37 artefacts recorded, nineteen were of bone or antler, one of shell, ten of stone (excluding flint finds), three of glass, three of fired clay and one textile fragment.

BONE AND ANTLER ARTEFACTS

A total of nineteen artefacts made from skeletal materials were recovered. These included combs, buttons, a bead, a toothbrush, a die, a tuning-peg, a handle or needle-case and a fragment of worked bone.

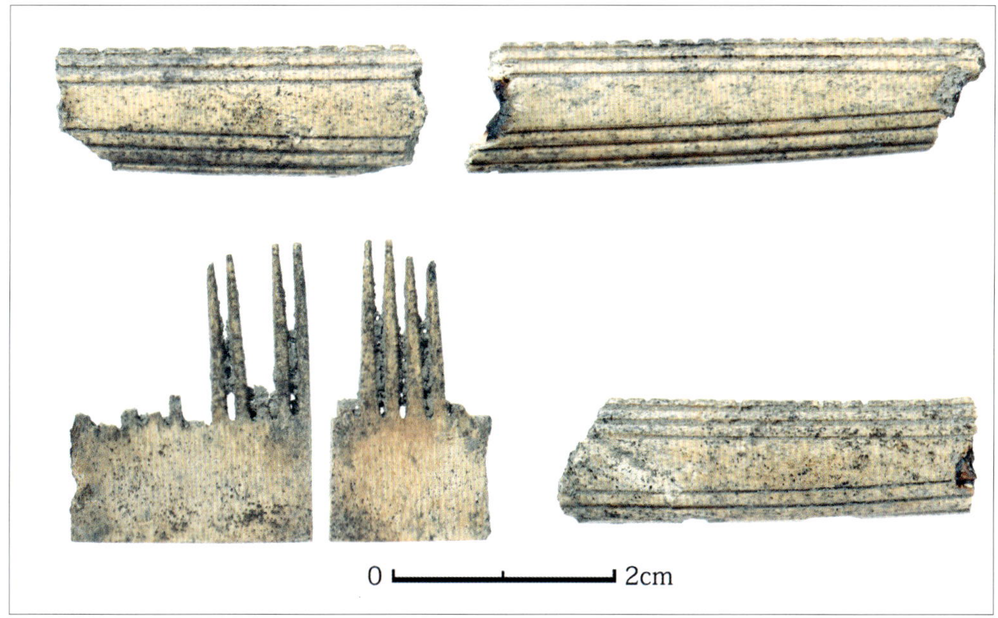

Pl. 12.1—Medieval antler comb (E4619:72:15) (photo: John Sunderland).

Combs

Five fragments from a single antler comb (E4619:72:15) were recovered from between two stone surfaces in Trench 6 at Swords Castle. Combs have long been an essential toiletry and personal item, with the earliest being cut from a single piece of wood or bone (Dunlevy 1988b, 349). Antler was the preferred material for such combs, as it was less likely to break from the stresses produced by the action of combing tangled hair (MacGregor 1989, 108). The overall morphology of the comb suggests that it belongs to Dunlevy's Class G, although the teeth are coarser and longer than is usual for this class and closer to combs of Class F (Dunlevy 1988b). Combs with similar mixed classification points were identified in Waterford (Hurley 1997a, 654), where twenty of the 81 combs recovered showed hybrid class G/F characteristics.

E4619:72:15

Antler. Partial single-sided composite comb, in five fragments. One complete and one partial tooth-plate; three fragments of side-plate, with location of rivets present on two fragments. Longest fragment of side-plate broken at rivet point at both ends; second-longest fragment broken at rivet point at one end and close to rivet point at other end; shallow side-plates with C-shaped cross-section; decorated by three parallel incised lines close to top edge, and repeated close to lower end of side-plates; saw-tooth marks extend into lower edge of side-plates. Five–six teeth per 10mm, with uneven lengths (owing to wear); wear leading to 'beading' visible on surviving teeth. Dunleavy Type G. Ninth–thirteenth century. Complete tooth-plate: L. 21.4mm; Th. 2.7mm; depth 26.7mm. Teeth: L. 15.4mm. Side-plate (longest fragment): L. 46.3mm; W. 10.6–11.6mm; Th. 3.2mm.

E4619:121:8

Incomplete machine-made double-sided comb; curved side; finely toothed at both ends. Probable modern mass-produced nit-comb. Nineteenth/twentieth century. L. 2.16cm. W. 3.75cm. L. tooth 1.19cm. Th. 0.17cm.

Buttons

Archaeological and historical sources indicate that buttons were used on clothing from at least medieval times, although it was only in the post-medieval era that they became a common clothing accessory and diversified in form (White 2005, 50). Eleven bone buttons in total were recovered at Swords Castle, all from topsoil levels. Six of the buttons were very similar in style, being medium-sized saucer-shaped buttons, with four subcircular perforations through which they could be attached by thread to fabric. In form these are not unlike many of the buttons available today.

A variant on this type of button (E4619:1:1184) but with five perforations rather than four (E4619:1:1184) and a single button with two perforations were recovered. The remaining three buttons consisted of a flat disc with a central perforation. These correspond to South's Type 15, occurring in the mid-eighteenth and mid-nineteenth centuries (Noël Hume 1969, 90–1).

E4619:1:310

Lathe-turned polished bone button. Concave upper surface with groove separating outer rounded rim and inner circle with four perforations. Back is plain, with irregularity in curve. Nineteenth century. Diam. 18mm. Th. 2.2mm. Diam. of perforations 1.7mm.

E4619:1:311

Broken bone button. Concave upper surface with groove separating outer rounded rim and inner circle with perforations. One complete and two half-perforations remain. Back is plain. Nineteenth century. Diam. 19mm. T. 2.6mm. Diam. of perforations 2.5mm.

E4619:1:312

Lathe-turned bone button. Shallow, dished upper surface with raised rounded rim and four unequal perforations. Perforations bevelled on upper surface. Plain convex back. Nineteenth century. Diam. 17.7mm. T. 2.3mm. Diam. of perforations 1.6–1.9mm.

E4619:1:313

Lathe-turned flat bone disc with central perforation. Ridge around circumference of edge. Slight pressure damage to one face. Eighteenth/nineteenth century. Diam. 11.6mm. T. 1.6mm. Diam. of perforation 1.6mm.

E4619:1:1046

Lathe-turned flat bone disc with central perforation. Ridge around circumference edge. Tool marks from some shaping and filing on one face. Eighteenth–nineteenth century. Diam. 17.9mm. Th. 1.6mm. Diam. of perforation 2.6mm.

E4619:1:1047

Lathe-turned polished bone button. Concave upper surface with raised, rounded rim and four perforations. Perforations bevelled at upper surface. Plain convex back, with guidelines from centre to mark position of holes. Nineteenth century. Diam. 19mm. Th. 2.5mm. Diam. of perforations 2.3–2.7mm.

E4619:1:1183

Polished bone button. Concave upper surface with groove separating outer rounded, raised rim and inner circle with four perforations. Plain convex back. Damage at one edge. Nineteenth century. Diam. 19.3mm. Th. 2.9mm. Diam. of perforations 2.6mm.

E4619:1:1184

Lathe-turned polished bone button. Raised outer rim; flat inner upper surface with five perforations, placed unequally. Flat back with parallel tool markings. Nineteenth century. Diam. 19.8mm. Th. 3.5mm. Diam. of perforations 1.9–2.1mm.

E4619:1:1185

Polished bone button. Concave upper surface with rounded outer circle and raised inner circle with four perforations. Groove around perimeter edge of rim. Plain convex back. Nineteenth century. Diam. 19mm. Th. 2.7mm. Diam. of perforations 2.4mm.

E4619:1:1186

Simple bone button; slightly convex on both sides with rounded rim. Badly degraded on one face. Two circular perforations. Uneven thickness around edge. Appears to be cut as a roundel from bone and hand-finished rather than lathe-turned. Eighteenth–nineteenth century.

Diam. 14mm. Th. 2.9mm. Diam. of perforations 3.1mm.

E4619:1:1199
Lathe-turned flat bone disc with central perforation. Ridge around circumference edge. Slight damage to one face. Eighteenth–nineteenth century. Diam. 10.3mm. Th. 1.6mm. Diam. of perforations 2mm.

Bead
Bone beads are known from medieval and post-medieval excavations in Ireland and Britain (Hurley 1997b, 260; 2004, 464). The bead (E4619:1:314) recovered from topsoil levels in Trench 3 at Swords Castle is more unusual, being oval in shape and decorated with two parallel lines around the middle. It compares well, however, in both size and shape to oval beads recovered from a late fifteenth/sixteenth-century rosary-bead-manufacturing site at Saint-Denis, Paris (MacGregor 1989, 118). The more elongate beads (such as the example from Swords Castle) may have functioned as spacers or 'gauds' on a rosary, between groups of the more numerous elliptical beads (Laning 2007–9, http://paternoster-row.medievalscotland.org/gauds). Two bone beads of similar shape and style to the Swords example were recovered with infant burials in an eighteenth- to early twentieth-century *cillín* in County Meath (Whitty and Gill 2004), lending further credence to an association between such beads and rosaries or prayer-beads.

E4619:1:314
Elongate, oval bone bead, tapering towards both ends. Parallel incised lines around circumference at widest point. Central perforation, wider at one end, from which it was probably drilled. Eighteenth/nineteenth century. L. 13.1mm. Diam. 4–7.7mm. Diam. of perforation 2.4–3mm.

Toothbrush
A partial toothbrush was recovered from the backfilled spoil associated with Fanning's excavation in Trench 10. The manufacture of bone brushes is known from the seventeenth century onwards and was an established industry by the later nineteenth century (MacGregor 1985, 183).

E4619:119:2
Elongate form with rounded tip and polished finish; broken off at neck. Three parallel rows of ten bristle holes, with an additional single hole at curve of tip. Three parallel linear slits on the reverse side correspond to the rows of bristle holes. Slight green staining around holes and slits indicates bristles held by copper-alloy wire; small fragment of wire visible within one slit. From long bone of large mammal. Eighteenth–twentieth century. L. 5.56cm (head), 7.04cm (max.). W. 1.4cm (max., head), 0.7cm (handle). Th. 0.56cm.

Die
A small bone die was recovered from the topsoil in Trench 6. This was cut from a single piece of bone and is irregularly cuboid in shape, with evenly spaced 'dot-in-circle' roundels denoting values. The values on opposite faces add up to seven: this is known as the 'standard

arrangement', found on dice since Roman times. During the medieval period, however, an alternative arrangement was widely used, whereby opposite faces carried consecutive values (i.e. 1/2, 3/4, 5/6) (MacGregor 1985, 131–2). Recorded medieval dice in Ireland almost all have this second arrangement, leading to the belief that this was by far the predominant arrangement at that time. Nonetheless, medieval dice with the standard arrangement are known from England (Egan 1998, 290; Ottaway and Rogers 2002, 2949) and from Trim (Hayden 2011, 370). This last was recovered from late thirteenth- to early fourteenth-century levels and provides perhaps the closest parallel for the Swords die in size and appearance, although the values are less evenly placed on the Trim die. The use of 'dot-in-circle' values appears to be characteristic of medieval dice both in England and Ireland, with simple roundels appearing on later dice. This suggests a potential medieval date for the die recovered from Swords, although owing to its unstratified provenance this cannot be stated with certainty.

E4619:1:1045
Irregularly cuboid bone die made from single piece of bone; dot-in-circle numerals in standard arrangement; damage to one roundel on the 'six' face. Medieval/post-medieval. L. 8mm x 7.6mm x 8.1mm.

Tuning-peg
Bone tuning-pegs for stringed musical instruments were first used in the twelfth century and continued in use into post-medieval times. These consist of solid cylinders of bone, carved from the long bones of large mammals such as cattle. The string would have passed through a perforation close to one end, and the tension was adjusted by turning the peg from the opposite end, or 'head', which was usually squared or spatulate in shape; while a spatulate head could be turned by hand, turning a squared or polygonal head required a key (MacGregor 1985, 147–8). An incomplete tuning-peg was recovered from a pit in Trench 3 at Swords Castle, broken jaggedly at the widest point of the shaft. The complete peg is unlikely to have measured much more than 60mm in length. Studies of tuning-pegs from other sites in Ireland have indicated that larger pegs (*c.* 100mm in length) are likely to be harp pegs, while smaller pegs (*c.* 60–65mm in length) were probably from smaller instruments, e.g. lyres, fiddles or lutes (Hurley 1997a, 666; 1997b, 270; 2003, 332).

E4619:31:15
Bone tuning-peg, carved from long bone of large mammal; broken at widest point. Circular cross-section; tapers to end, with perforation 4.6mm from edge. Change in shape evident at break, with apparent shoulder. Tool marks evident on complete end. Polished surface; no evidence of wear around perforation. Medieval. L. 45.5mm. Diam. 5.7–7.5mm. Diam. of perforation 1.9mm.

Needle-case/bone tube
A fragment of a small, polished bone tube was recovered from a medieval surface in Trench 4. Similar tubes recovered from other sites were identified as either handles, needle-cases or bobbins and were frequently decorated (Hayden 2011, 370; Hurley 1997a, 676–8; 1997b, 257–8).

E4619:86:22
Short length of highly polished bone; hollow in centre; jaggedly broken but with small portion of cut edge at one end. Polishing marks visible on surface. Cylindrical, but widens slightly in centre. Possible needle-case. Medieval. L. 37.8mm. Diam. (max.). 9.5mm. Diam. of interior 5mm.

Possible scoop
A fragment of scapula (shoulder-blade) from a large mammal has been filed or planed down to form a flat surface on one side. The other side appears unworked in any manner. The small size of the fragment means that identifying its purpose is difficult. It may be waste material from craftworking, although MacGregor (1985, 179–80) notes that scapulae required little modification other than the removal of the dorsal spine to form useful scoops for grain or flour. The fragment from Swords Castle may represent a scapula being put to such use, with the dorsal surface being smoothed flat while the ventral surface, left in its natural state, formed a shallow scoop.

E4619:43:12
Fragment of scapula from cow-sized mammal, modified on one face to form flattened, smoothed surface; unaltered on other face. Broken on all sides. Manufacturing waste or simple scoop. L. 35.8mm. W. 30.2mm. Th. 2.2mm.

SHELL ARTEFACTS

Button
A single small button made from shell was recovered from topsoil in Trench 5. Buttons manufactured from shell or nacre (mother-of-pearl) were used from the early nineteenth century and continued in use into the twentieth century. The button from Swords Castle corresponds with Type 22 in South's typology (Noël Hume 1969, 90–1). The small size of this button suggests that it would have been used on lighter cloth and would not have taken much strain. It may have been used on a collar or cuff.

E4619:1:1048
Circular shell button with concave upper surface; four perforations for attachment. Nineteenth–twentieth century. Diam. 8.8mm. Th. 1.9mm. Diam. of perforations 1.2mm.

STONE ARTEFACTS

A total of eleven non-flint small stone finds were recovered from all three seasons of excavation. These included inscribed stones, a hone, a gaming piece, three stone pencils, two architectural fragments and a stone implement. Geological identifications were carried out by Dr Julian Menuge of UCD School of Earth Sciences, with additional identification of E4619:13:1 by Dr Stephen Mandal, CRDS.

Pl. 12.2—Musical notation, interpreted by Siobhán Duffy.

Inscribed stone

One of the most intriguing finds from the excavations was uncovered in Trench 8. This consisted of two narrow lengths of slate with a series of parallel lines incised along the length of the smoother surface of both. Although the fragments were recovered from separate but adjoining layers, they were found to fit together, forming a single slate that had broken vertically into two unequal parts. Arranged as two sets of five, the lines were identified as staves, with musical notation identified on the lower stave of the larger fragment. The break separating the two slate fragments clearly occurred after the staves had been incised into its surface. It is uncertain, however, whether this happened before, during or after the notes were drawn. Nor could it be ascertained why the notation is confined to the lower staves. Two possible scenarios can be considered:

- The main break in the slate occurred prior to the inscription of the notes, leaving the top staves too short for the intended notation. This may explain why no notes continue onto the smaller fragment.
- Alternatively, the notes may have been sketched in first using a pointed slate fragment. It would then have made sense to incise the lower notes first, to avoid their being accidentally erased while the upper notes were being incised. In this case the slate is likely to have broken during the process of writing the notes, leaving the notation unfinished.

The lines of the staves were drawn freehand, becoming noticeably less regular in their spacing towards the right-hand side of the slate. The notes themselves are well formed, suggesting a confidence and ability in the writer. This does not appear, then, to be the work of a novice, but rather of someone well versed in the reading and writing of music.

Both lines and notes were formed with the use of a sharply pointed implement. Two faint incised triangles are set apart from the staves, at the left-hand side of the slate. These may represent practice etchings, suggesting that the tool used was not intended for that purpose and was appropriated for the task in hand as a matter of convenience. Slate has been used as a medium for writing since medieval times (Bliss 1965–6, 44). The uneven finish of the slate suggests, however, that it, too, was used because it was close to hand rather than being acquired specifically for the task. This apparently *ad hoc* collection of materials would be consistent with the notation's being both written and discarded at the castle, perhaps within a short time-frame. Certainly, there are references to work being carried out at the castle in the fifteenth century and slate fragments may have been readily available there as a result. Reused roof slates with both written words and musical notation incised into their surfaces were recovered at Smarmore, Co. Louth, in 1959 and were dated to the fifteenth century (Bliss 1965–6).

Examination of the slate under well-lit conditions and by Reflectance Transformation Imaging or RTI (this latter undertaken by Gary Devlin of the Discovery Programme) allowed for complete transcription of the etched marks. In total, the notation comprised some 30 musical notes and symbols, formed by incised rectangles, triangles and vertical lines, and was entirely confined to the larger slate fragment. The notes are consistent with mensural notation, associated with the development of polyphonic music in the later medieval period (Apel 1953). The style of the notation suggests a fifteenth-century date (Anne Buckley, pers. comm.). This was confirmed by David Fallows, a musicologist specialising in fifteenth-century music studies, who identified the style of the line and major prolation as having been composed in the 1420s or thereabouts. It remains unknown whether the notation relates to a known piece of music or an original composition. It is, however, considered to be secular rather than liturgical in nature (*ibid.*).

E4619:106:74
Fragment of roof slate. On the smoother surface two sets of five-line staves are inscribed, the lower of which contains inscribed musical notation formed by lines, rectangles and triangles. Fifteenth century. Originally joined to E4619:112:19. L. 239mm. W. 106mm. Th. 6.8mm.

E4619:112:19
Fragment of roof slate. On the smoother surface two sets of five-line staves are inscribed. No notation was identified on either stave. Fifteenth century. Originally joined to E4619:106:74. L. 133mm. W. 105.6mm. Th. 4mm.

E4619:106:96
Oblong fragment of larger stone, broken on three sides with a curving edge to the fourth. Incised marks criss-cross the upper face—these appear deliberate rather than a product of use. The extant portion was insufficient to decipher these marks. L. 147.5mm. W. 50.5mm. Th. 18.7mm.

Gaming counter
Small discs composed of stone, ceramic or bone recovered from early medieval to post-medieval levels on excavations in Ireland and Britain are generally identified as gaming counters (Ottaway and Rogers 2002, 2949; McCutcheon 1997, 409). A small disc made from dolomitised limestone was recovered from topsoil levels and is likely to have been a

gaming counter. It is similar in size to such counters found during excavations in Waterford (McCutcheon 1997, 409), although these were primarily made from slate. Limestone and dolomitised limestone counters are known from medieval levels at York, although sandstone was more commonly used there (Gaunt 2002). It is likely that such counters were made from stone convenient to the area, such as waste material from buildings or other stone implements.

The use of such counters probably originated in Norse times, as did many of the table games played throughout the medieval period; indeed, Ottaway and Rogers (2002, 2951) suggest the possibility of stone counters from medieval levels in York being residual from earlier times. A group of slate counters were recovered from a seventeenth-century tomb in Waterford, however, indicating that the use of stone counters extended into the post-medieval period (McCutcheon 1997, 406).

E4619:1:315
Dolomitised limestone. Subcircular disc. Smooth, rounded edge for *c.* one third of its circumference, irregular on remaining edge. One surface is flat and smooth, the other slightly stepped. Diam. (max.) 30.5mm. Th. 8.2mm.

Hone

A common find on medieval and post-medieval excavations, hones or whetstones come in a range of shapes and sizes but are typically elongate and small enough to be portable and easily used by hand. Likewise, although different rocks are used in their manufacture, the parent material generally contains harder inclusions within a softer matrix, providing a gritty surface to facilitate their use as sharpening tools (McCutcheon 1997, 410; de Neergaard 1987, 53).

The hone recovered from Trench 3 at Swords Castle is made from sandstone, an ideal and commonly used rock. Of a large number of whetstones recovered from excavations in Waterford, some 64% were composed of sandstone. The continued use of hones across time and their simplistic form make dating any isolated example difficult. Only six examples from Waterford were of similar shape to that from Swords Castle, however, being wider at the centre and tapering towards both ends, and these were all recovered from twelfth–thirteenth-century levels (McCutcheon 1997, 410–17). The Swords hone is likely to have been used to sharpen knives or larger blades, although no wear patterns or striations from use were visible; its surface was uniformly smooth apart from one damaged corner. Its large size and the lack of a perforation for suspension suggest that it is unlikely to have been a personal item, and it may have belonged to a workshop.

E4619:21:43
Sandstone. Oblong, tapering to both ends; damaged close to one end; smooth surfaces with no visible wear marks. L. 187.5mm. W. (max.) 28.8mm x 27.9mm.

Slate pencils

Three elongate, roughly cylindrical stone objects recovered from topsoil levels were identified as slate pencils. These were used for writing on slate tablets from at least the eighteenth century, although they are perhaps most commonly associated with use in schools in the nineteenth century (Samford 2008, https://www.jefpat.org/CuratorsChoiceArchive/2008CuratorsChoice/Sep2008-WritingSlate.html). It is uncertain when the widespread use of slate pencils began, although in the United States it is considered to have been in the 1840s (www.officemuseum.com/), continuing into the early twentieth century. In England their widespread use in schools from the early nineteenth century has been attributed to the noted educator Joseph Lancaster (Samford 2008). Slate pencils have been recovered from nineteenth-century levels on excavations in York (Hunter-Mann 2008, 29–30) and Galway (McCartan 2004, 534–5). The examples from Swords Castle represent broken fragments of pencil and may represent evidence of some form of schooling in the Swords vicinity in the nineteenth century.

E4619:1:1049
Multi-faceted fragment of slate pencil, flattening towards one end. No point present. L. 29.6mm. W. 5.9mm. Th. 4.5mm.

E4619:1:1050
Fragment of slate pencil; blunt point at one side. Subcircular cross-section, becoming faceted away from point. File marks visible along one facet. Heavily marked constriction close to point may represent attempt to sharpen point. L. 35.4mm. Diam. 5mm.

E4619:1:1051
Small fragment of slate pencil with point at one end; subcircular cross-section. L. 16.8mm. Diam. 4.8mm.

Architectural fragments
Two small fragments of stone, both recovered from Trench 3, appear to have been parts of elements of buildings rather than tools or other objects. The first of these is a small, subrectangular fragment with two smooth edges forming a rounded corner, suggesting that the fragment represents a corner broken off a larger item such as a stone flag or tile, or possibly a very shallow step, of limestone mud (E4619:21:44). Concretions visible on the uneven surface and the external edges may represent a binding element such as mortar, although they may also be post-depositional in origin. Limestone mud (calp) forms the bedrock for much of Dublin and this fragment may have had a local origin (J. Menuge, pers. comm.).

The second fragment is definitely not local to the area: this is a small sliver of white marble (E4619:18:46). The height is likely too great to have come from a marble tile, and it may have broken off a fitting such as a fireplace or surround. The fragment recovered is not unlike Italian Carrara marble (J. Menuge, pers. comm.), highly valued for centuries and much sought after for use in statues and buildings (www.webmineralshop.com/). It is tempting, then, to form an association between the fragment and Newbridge House, home to the Cobbe family who owned Swords Castle throughout the nineteenth century. Without further physical evidence, however, such association must remain in the realm of speculation.

E4619:21:44
Limestone mud. Subrectangular fragment of blue-grey limestone with white patina at edges. Smooth, finished edge on two sides, with rounded corner forming slightly obtuse (*c.* 100º) angle; irregularly broken on other two sides. Flattened, smooth upper surface; lower surface flattened but rough. Possible evidence of mortar on lower surface and finished edges, for

attachment to other substance. Possible step or stone flag/tile. H. 21.3mm. L. (max.) 39.1mm. W. (max.) 34.7mm.

E4619:18:46
Marble. Irregular wedge-shaped sliver of white marble. Finished, polished upper surface; finished unpolished lower surface. Irregularly broken elsewhere. Architectural fragment, e.g. surround/fireplace. H. 22.4mm. L. (max.) 30.8mm. W. (max.) 9.6mm.

Stone implement
An unusual stone implement was recovered from Trench 2. The stone itself is of considerable weight and dark grey in colour, but is almost completely covered with a heavy grey to yellowish-grey reticulated patina. This is consistent with its identification as a clay ironstone nodule (S. Mandal, pers. comm.). Such nodules occur in sedimentary rocks such as mudstone and shale, and it probably originated in the north Dublin region. Subrectangular in shape and rather bulbous, it is blunt at both ends but sharp along the longer edges. These sharper edges are likely to have occurred naturally during the formation or fracturing of the nodule (S. Mandal, pers. comm.), but the stone has evidently been deliberately shaped at the blunter ends. One end appears shaped for hafting or to provide a handhold: indeed, using this end as a grip, the stone fits comfortably in a hand, and it provides the only practical means of holding it for any utilitarian purpose. The opposite end (considered the front or working end) is blunt, rounded and shows evidence of wear from use. The wear at the front end extends onto the patina, suggesting that it represents a secondary use of the implement as a rubbing stone. Some wear or burnishing at the grip end is also evident over the patina,

Pl. 12.3—Stone implement E4619:13:1 (photo: Siobhán Duffy).

possibly from being held at this end during the secondary phase of use. No evidence of wear or chipping is visible along the sharpened sides, with the exception of some apparent modern damage.

It was not possible to determine the original use of the stone, although it was noted that if the sharper edges were unnecessary or inconvenient to its use it would have taken little effort to blunt them (S. Mandal, pers. comm.). It is likely that the stone was discarded after the first phase of use, following which the patina would have re-established itself over a period of time. At some point it was rediscovered, during which time a small amount of damage occurred to the working end (evident from loss of patina at this point), and it was used as a rubbing stone before being discarded for a second time within the castle precinct. The original date and use of this implement remain unknown.

E4619:13:1
Clay ironstone nodule. Subrectangular shape, slightly waisted at mid-length; elliptical in cross-section. Butt-trimmed at more bulbous end; sharp-edged along long edges; rounded, blunt edge opposite to butt end—evidence of secondary wear at this edge. Almost the entire surface is covered with a heavy, rough, reticulate patina; this obscures or has obliterated any primary working or wear patterns. L. (max.) 102mm. W. (max.) 80.2mm. Th. (max.) 33.8mm.

ARTEFACTS OF GLASS

Bead
A small, doughnut-shaped glass bead was recovered from a heat-affected layer in Trench 8. It appeared corroded and pitted on the surface, almost black in colour and with a lack of vitrification. The original use of this bead is uncertain, as it may have been associated with jewellery or a rosary. Glass beads are also known from medieval levels in London (Egan and Pritchard 1991, 316) and Waterford (Bourke 1997, 386–9).

Pl. 12.4—Glass bead E4619:129:35 (photo: Siobhán Duffy).

E4619:129:35
Doughnut-shaped bead; appears almost black in colour, with a greenish cast. This may be due to degradation or may represent a high lead/copper content. Diam. 8mm x 7.7mm. Th. 3.3mm. Diam. of perforation 3.5mm x 2.8mm.

Pinhead
An irregularly hemispherical bead-like glass object was also

recovered from Trench 8, from a layer immediately above that which contained the glass bead. A perforation extended only partly into the object from one side, identifying it as a pinhead. It was almost black in colour and with a matte appearance. Wire-drawn copper-alloy pins were used in association with items of clothing during medieval and post-medieval times. Although pins are more commonly found with copper-alloy heads, the use of glass pinheads is known from medieval levels at York and Kilkenny (Ottaway and Rogers 2002, 2915; Duffy 2011a), the latter of similar size to the example from Swords Castle.

E4619:131:41
Irregular, domed head of pin; hole in concave side extends into but does not penetrate through dome. Appears badly degraded, and almost black in appearance. Diam. 8.6mm x 6.8mm. H. 5mm. Diam. of perforation *c.* 1.5mm.

Bottle
A single small fragment of bottle glass, recovered from below topsoil levels in Trench 6, was examined. This appears to be bottle glass, of an olive-green colour. The surface is almost entirely covered by a heavy brown patina, suggestive of a pre-nineteenth-century origin for the glass. Glass fragments of similar colour and patina recovered in Dublin were dated to the seventeenth century (Rajic, n.d., 66).

E4619:63:56
Fragment of olive-green bottle glass with heavy patina. Possibly seventeenth–eighteenth century. L. 21.5mm. W. 16mm. Th. 4.2mm.

CERAMIC SMALL FINDS

Marbles
Two complete ceramic marbles (E4619:1:1187 and E4619:1:1188) were recovered from Trench 7, both from the topsoil. Marbles made from salt-glazed stoneware, or stone, were manufactured on a small scale in Europe from the seventeenth century (Samford, n.d., https://www.jefpat.org/diagnostic/SmallFinds/Marbles/index-marbles.html; Horning 2004, 460). Throughout the nineteenth century, wide-scale commercial manufacture of ceramic marbles increased, especially in Germany, and continued up until World War I (Samford, n.d.). At this time, too, marbles began to be manufactured in other materials, notably unglazed fired earthenware, porcelain and glass. Ceramic marbles of similar dimensions have been recovered from nineteenth-century levels on excavations in Kilkenny and Galway (Duffy 2011b; Horning 2004), and the examples from Swords Castle are almost certainly of this date. The larger of the two marbles (E4619:1:1188) is irregularly spherical and may pre-date the introduction of machine-shaped marbles in 1859 (Samford, n.d.).

E4619:1:1187
Spherical unglazed marble or bottle-stopper. Green-brown paste. Smooth, burnished appearance. Diam. 12.3mm.

E4619:1:1188
Irregularly spherical marble. Pink-orange and grey colour; small fragments of glaze (of pink-orange colour) present in recessed points on uneven surface. Diam. 20.5mm.

E4619:111:10
Partial unglazed marble or bottle-stopper. Grey-white paste with inclusions. Diam. 15.8mm.

TEXTILE

A small fragment of woven textile was recovered from the unstratified layer F119 in Trench 10. This survived primarily as an accretion on and within a ferrous base. The best-surviving segment was visible as a closely woven textile (approx. twenty threads per cm) *c.* 1cm² in size. Around the edges of this, frayed threads and fibres were identifiable, along with remnants of stitching on the lower surface of the ferrous object.

E4619:119:1
Imprint and fibres of woven textile within matrix of iron and aggregated materials. Overall L. 29.9mm x W. 20.6mm. Woven L. 13.2mm x 9.7mm.

Pl. 12.5—Textile fragment E4619:119:1 (photo: Siobhán Duffy).

13
Clay pipes

Siobhán G. Duffy, BSc., MA

INTRODUCTION

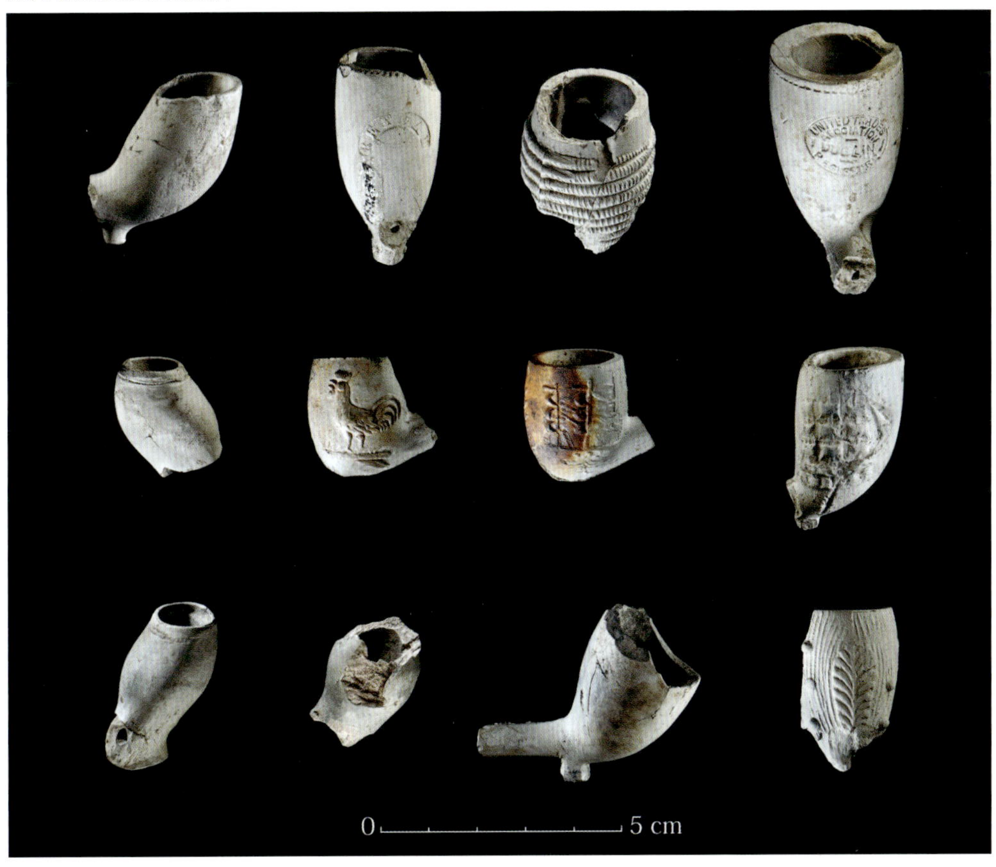

Pl. 13.1—Clay pipes (photo: John Sunderland).

A total of 127 bowl fragments from clay pipes were recovered. While the assemblage included ten complete bowls, the overall fragmentation rate was high: bowl fragments representing less than a quarter of a bowl comprised some 61% (77 fragments) of the total. Fragments were recorded from all ten excavated trenches, with the majority (109 bowl fragments) recovered from an extensive topsoil layer (F1). The bowls date from the seventeenth to the nineteenth or early twentieth century. A total of 55 stem fragments were identified as decorated, and a total of 31 mouthpieces analysed. Dating of pre-nineteenth-century bowls follows the typologies of Oswald (1975) and Ayto (1987).

SEVENTEENTH-CENTURY BOWLS

One complete and three partial bowls were identified as of seventeenth-century date (E4619:65:637–E4619:1:352, E4619:1:1236, E4619:111:9). All were recovered from topsoil levels in the north-eastern portion of the castle precinct. These bowls were characteristically small, with a globular shape, constricted rim and a wide, flat heel. Where the rim was present (on all but E4619:1:1236), some form of milling was evident, although this was not consistent around the circumference. Two of the bowls (E4619:65:637 and E4619:1:352) retain a flat heel, although only a portion survives on the latter. No portion of stem survives on any of the bowls, nor could any maker's mark be identified. In size and shape they are consistent with Oswald's Type 4G or 5G and Ayto's Types 2 and 3, and probably date from the early or mid-seventeenth century. Unlike the general typologies, however, the rim of E4619:65:637 is cut parallel to the heel: this is probably a regional variation and has been recorded on mid-seventeenth-century examples of southern English origin (Higgins, n.d.; Atkinson and Oswald 1969; Oswald 1975). In addition to these bowls, a partial flat heel attached to a stem fragment (E4619:124:5) indicates a seventeenth-century date for the pipe.

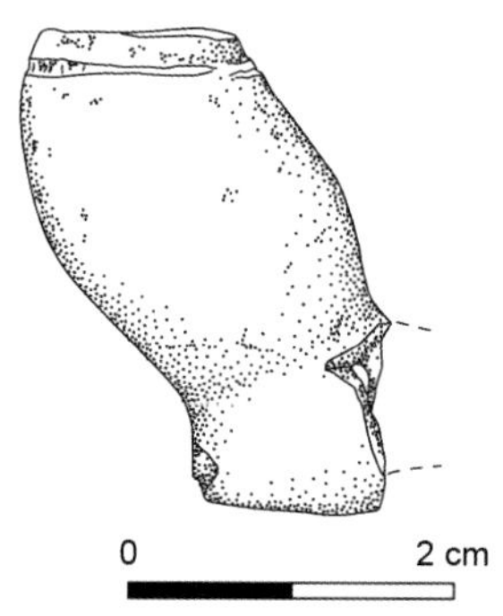

E4619:065:637
Clay Pipe Bowl

Fig. 13.1—Seventeenth-century clay pipe bowl (drawing: Sara Nylund).

EIGHTEENTH-CENTURY BOWLS

A complete bowl (E4619:3:64) corresponds to Oswald's Type 20G, dating from 1690–1730. It has a plain, slightly globular bowl and lacks any trace of milling around the rim. The rim itself is almost parallel to the stem, a change in style associated with new manufacturing techniques introduced into England around 1700 (Ayto 1987, 6). Two other partial bowls are probably of a similar date. The first of these (E4619:1:362) consists of the lower rear of a bowl and is of similar style to late seventeenth/early eighteenth-century pipes. The second (E4619:1:330) comprises the rear of a long, fairly straight, thin-walled bowl set at an angle to the stem and with a shallow, flat, oval spur. No distinguishing marks were visible on the spur or bowl, but it is very similar to Irish-made examples from Galway, which were dated to the start of the eighteenth century (Norton 2004, 436).

A fourth probable eighteenth-century pipe (E4619:1:355) is represented by a single bowl fragment. This is from a straight-sided bowl with a very thin-walled rim and an incised double line around the rim. The outer surface, blackened from use, is very highly polished with vertical paring visible, while faint horizontal striations are visible on the inner surface, suggesting that it may be of Dutch origin (Oswald 1975, 17, 115; Noël Hume 1969, 307). Clay pipes produced in Holland, and in the city of Gouda in particular, were highly regarded and were imported into Ireland from the seventeenth to the late nineteenth century (Norton 2004, 431).

In addition, four small fragments (E4619:1:360, E4619:1:358, E4619:64:622, E4619:64:623) are from thin-walled bowls and are of probable eighteenth-century date. One of these (E4619:1:360) has milling around the rim, while another (E4619:1:358) forms part of the front of a more upright bowl, similar to Oswald's Type 12G.

NINETEENTH-CENTURY BOWLS

By far the largest datable group of bowl fragments, however, are of nineteenth- or early twentieth-century date. Fragment thickness and size indicate that these are predominantly from large, upright, thick-walled bowls. These are probably Irish-made and closely resemble Ayto's Type 14 (Ayto 1987). A total of 44 fragments, representing 39 bowls and including four complete bowls, display some form of stamp or decoration, providing further evidence as to their origin and date. This usually takes the form of a stamped logo or name on the rear of the bowl, applied at the end of the manufacturing process, or a moulded decoration where the decoration is integral to the pipe-mould.

Makers' and traders' marks

There are eighteen examples with makers' or traders' stamps on the bowls, representing both Irish and foreign origins for the pipe assemblage. Of these, eight relate to pipe-makers or traders operating out of Dublin in the nineteenth century. Francis Street, in particular, was a well-known centre for clay pipe production in the city (Norton 2013, 32), and three pipe fragments could be identified as having their origins there. Families such as the Cunninghams (E4619:1:348 and E4619:1:546) and the O'Connors (E4619:1:555) were well-established pipe-making families, sometimes with different family members based at separate locations on Francis Street. The pipes identified at Swords Castle are typical of the mid- or later nineteenth century, from the workshops of Thomas Cunningham, John or James Cunningham and Joseph or P. O'Connor (*ibid.*, 35).

In other cases, stamps on pipe bowls represent retailers rather than manufacturers. This appears to be the case for five fragments recovered at Swords Castle, representing three pipes. One bowl fragment (E4619:1:340) carries the brand of the Downey Brothers of 8 Brunswick Street, Dublin. While Norton (2013, 35) lists James Downey as a pipe-maker active between 1855 and 1881, he is listed as either a 'tobacco and cigar manufacturer' or a tobacconist in Dublin directories of that era (Shaw 1988 [1850]; *Thom's Irish Almanac and Official Directory for the year 1862*), suggesting that he may have been a retailer rather than a maker of pipes. Likewise, J. Phelan of North King Street (E4619:1:336, E4619:1:343 and E4619:1:346) and R. Sullivan of Werburgh Street (E4619:1:551) are identified as tobacconists in the trade directories of the mid-nineteenth century (*Thom's Irish Almanac* …, 1862; Pettigrew and Oulton's *Dublin Almanac & General Register of Ireland*, 1844; *Thom's Irish Almanac* …, 1845; Pettigrew and Oulton's *Dublin Almanac* …, 1847; Shaw 1988 [1850]; *Thom's Irish Almanac* …, 1860). The second of these relates to Richard Sullivan, who, the directories indicate, ran a tobacconist's shop at 25 Werburgh Street between 1845 and 1860, while his widow continued the business for a further year (Pettigrew and Oulton's *Dublin Almanac* …, 1844 and 1847; *Thom's Irish Almanac* …, 1845, 1860 and 1861; Shaw 1988 [1850]). This provides quite a narrow date range for the pipe in question, as it must have been sold between 1845 and 1861. How widespread the practice of pipes carrying the stamp of retailers rather than makers was is uncertain, but such cases do caution against automatically ascribing any such marks to the manufacturer of a pipe.

Dutch influence

A complete bowl (E4619:1:794) and seven other fragments recovered over the three seasons bear a stamped 'Crowned L' mark on the rear of the bowl. This is a mark commonly found on pipes recovered from Irish excavations, and was the most commonly repeated design in the Swords Castle assemblage. The 'Crowned L' originated as a maker's mark in the Dutch pipe-making centre of Gouda in the seventeenth century. Little is known of its very early history, but from 1730 it was owned by the de Licht family of pipe merchants (Duco 2004). It is suggested, however, that this was in fact a means of allowing their pipe-making relative Franz Verzijl to secure a second mark for lesser-quality pipes, something not permitted at that time under guild rules (*ibid.*).

From the mid-eighteenth century, changes in guild rules meant that pipe-makers could own a second mark, and the 'Crowned L' mark became associated with the Verzijl name. It continued to be used as a secondary mark for the rest of the eighteenth century and throughout the nineteenth century, first by the Verzijl family and later by the Stromman & Van der Want dynasty (*ibid.*). This meant that it was used for a lower grade of pipes, largely destined for export; such pipes were rarely made by the owner's workshop but were outsourced to smaller workshops, and secondary marks appear on a variety of pipe shapes and styles (*ibid.*). The situation of the 'Crowned L' mark in Ireland is even more confusing: the high esteem in which pipes from Gouda were held and the familiarity with the 'Crowned L' mark led to its being copied as a mark on Irish-made pipes in the later nineteenth century (Norton 1997, 183; 2004, 445). Further to this, 'Irish-style' pipes bearing the mark on the rear of the bowl appear to have been produced in Gouda in the later nineteenth century, to cater for what was probably a lucrative market (Duco 2004; Lane 1995, 105). It is difficult, then, to be certain of the origin of fragmented bowls bearing this mark.

Nevertheless, the complete bowl (E4619:1:794) from Swords Castle is of Dutch style, finely made, with a burnished surface and milling at the rim—all characteristic of Dutch manufacture. It is likely, then, that this example at least originated in Gouda, during the Van der Want use of the mark in the later nineteenth century (at this time the maker's name would often have been carried on the stem).

Four of the fragments (E4619:1:320, E4619:1:322, E4619:1:1153 and E4619:1:545) are also from finely made, thinner-walled bowls with small, well-formed marks, suggesting a probable origin in Gouda in the nineteenth century. The other three fragments (E4619:1:332, E4619:1:333 and E4619:65:702), by contrast, bear larger, less-distinct marks on straight-sided, thick-walled bowls, and are far more likely to have been manufactured in Ireland in the later nineteenth century.

In addition, a complete large, upright bowl (E4619:1:317) probably falls into this latter group. It bears a large, somewhat indistinct oval stamp, with a crown over what appears to be 'N' standing on a horizontal pipe, and may represent a personalised variation on the more usual Gouda style.

A fragment of a bowl (E4619:1:573) bore a second maker's mark associated with Gouda. Although damaged and indistinct, this could just be identified as a milkmaid within a circular stamp. The style and size of the mark suggests that the die used was probably designed for marking spurs rather than the sides of bowls and was well worn. Like the 'Crowned L', the milkmaid mark had a long history in Gouda, and throughout the nineteenth century it was one of a number of marks owned by the members of the Prince family of pipe-makers (www.claypipes.nl/; www.goudapipes.nl/). The example found at Swords probably represents a nineteenth-century Dutch import, produced under the auspices of the Prince company.

Political and other marks

A small fragment from a bowl bears the incused wording 'NEVIS: _UTTY' (E4619:1:565); this would originally have read 'Ben Nevis: Cutty', and was stamped on short-stemmed late nineteenth-century pipes of Irish and Scottish manufacture (Hammond 1986, 27), with the maker's name usually marked on the stem. 'Cutty' pipes were favoured by manual workers, as the stem was short enough to enable the pipe to be held between the teeth while continuing to work (Coleman 2015, www.dawnmist.org/; www.cafg.net/).

In the nineteenth century, marks on pipe bowls were also used to advertise organisations and ideals, and some examples of this were identified in the Swords Castle assemblage. Two complete bowls (E4619:1:540 and E4619:1:1148) bear an oval stamp with the slogan 'UNITED TRADES ASOCIATION [*sic*]: DUBLIN:REGISTRD'. This association existed from 1863 to *c.* 1877 and was a precursor to the trade union movement (www.irishlabourhistorysociety.com/). It is likely that pipes bearing their logo were handed out at meetings or given to prospective members. Three other pipe fragments (E4619:1:338, E4619:1:566 and E4619:114:1) also bear the stamp of DUTA, albeit with a different design. Both E4619:1:338 and E4619:114:1 display the name of the Dublin United Trades Association around a pair of clasped hands and the word 'Trademark'. The third example (E4619:1:566) bears identical lettering, although only partially present, and probably bore the same design. A third variant on the DUTA logo was recovered at Swords Castle during excavations in 1971 (Fanning 1975, 69).

Patriotic slogans and designs associated with Irish nationalism were increasingly popular in the nineteenth century. A small number of bowl fragments appear to fall into this category, most notably an almost complete bowl (E4619:1:361). This is a finely made, smaller bowl, made in the 'Dutch style'. It bears the stamp 'REPEAL' on the rear of the bowl and a shamrock in relief on either side of the spur, indicating a date of 1830–50, the era of O'Connell's movement to repeal the Act of Union. An identical pipe bowl is known from excavations at Quay Street, Galway (Norton 2004, 437–8), while examples found in Waterford also appear to be of the same make (Lane 1997, 373).

In addition, a fragment (E4619:1:552) was recovered bearing part of an incused logo of which 'HOME' is visible, forming an arc around a more floral central design or wording. This is probably a 'Home Rule' pipe, common in the later nineteenth century in a variety of designs (e.g. Norton 2004, 438; Lane 1995, 103). On a small fragment (E4619:1:580) the letter 'P' is followed by what appears to be the lower leg of 'A' and may have once spelt 'Parnell', although this cannot be certain. An equally small fragment of bowl bears the lettering 'ELL' on the side and may also have borne Parnell's name. Pipes bearing Parnell's name were widespread in the 1870s to 1890s (Norton 1997, 183). Three other fragments bear shamrocks, either on the bowl (E4619:1:567 and E4619:1:584) or on the side of the spur (E4619:1:579), and these were probably associated with patriotic designs or slogans.

The lower part of a thick-walled bowl (E4619:65:700), typical of the late nineteenth or early twentieth century, retains a small portion of a crudely stamped logo on the rear of the bowl. Although barely legible, this reads '_OTH', or possibly '_OOTH'; the original form of the full stamp is unknown, and no parallels were found at the time of writing.

Moulded decoration

Throughout the nineteenth century a growing trend for the use of decorated moulds in the manufacturing process led to a wide variety of elaborately designed pipes (Oswald 1975,

110; Ayto 1987, 6–10). Despite the popularity of such designs, only thirteen examples of bowls with moulded decorations were identified in the present assemblage. Three fragments (E004619:1:349, E004619:1:350 and E4619:1:351) refit to form an almost complete bowl elaborately designed to appear as a coiled rope. A second bowl, represented by two fragments (E004619:1:321 and E004619:1:323), has a moulded ridged petal and leaf design covering the bowl, which itself is moulded into the shape of a tulip.

Two fragments (E4619:1:559 and E4619:1:560) have a moulded design comprising acorns in relief; both are thin-walled, without any evidence of milling, and are so alike that they are probably parts of a single bowl. Acorns and oak leaves were a common design on pipes in the later nineteenth century (Coleman 2015, www.dawnmist.org/; Ayto 1987, 28).

Five other separate fragments have evidence of moulded designs. On one (E4619:1:354) a talon extends up from the base, and the bowl would have appeared as a claw holding an egg. Variations of this motif were popular in the later nineteenth century (Ayto 1987, 10–11), and late nineteenth-century examples are also known from Dublin (Norton 1997, 184) and Galway (Norton 2004, 447). A small, very abraded fragment (E4619:1:328) bears what appears to be the tips of two fingers and may represent a hand design on the side of the bowl, as is known from Patrick Street, Dublin (Norton 1997, 184). A fragment (E4619:108:5) is covered with a 'rustic' design representing knotted wood with a leaf motif along the front seam; designs of this type typically date from the later nineteenth century (Coleman 2015, www.dawnmist.org/). Another much-abraded bowl fragment (E4619:1:355) has the letters 'Port' in Irish script on the side: this would probably have spelt out a place-name. The fifth fragment (E4619:119:3) has a moulded raised keel along the mid-line and may have formed part of a larger design.

Only two examples of bowls with moulded designs were complete, with a similarity in their design if not in their overall manufacture. The first of these is a small, well-made spurred bowl of nineteenth-century date (E4619:1:569), with a maritime decoration in moulded relief. On one side is a fully rigged three-masted ship depicted on water, while on the other side is the stylised figure of a sailor with a characteristic bow-legged stance and carrying a long pole over one shoulder. Maritime themes were a typical design on bowls in the nineteenth century (Coleman 2015, www.dawnmist.org/; Ayto 1987, 6).

The second example (E4619:1:568) is a complete miniature rounded bowl, also with a moulded maritime design. Here, too, one side carries a three-masted ship in full sail, but in this case the opposite side has an anchor, while a foliate design runs along the mould line. A partial bowl recovered (E4619:1:331) is of similar size and design, but in this case the moulded design comprises a cockerel on the side and a leaf design along the front seam. Along with maritime themes, animal and plant motifs were common on pipes of the Victorian era. The small size and design of both of these pipes has led to their identification as bubble pipes. The use of clay pipes to blow bubbles for children in the later nineteenth and early twentieth centuries is known from contemporary sources (www.artistsandart.org/). While regular clay pipes were used for this, miniature pipes were also made especially for the purpose, particularly in England and Germany, and were even included with bags of sweets (Coleman 2015, www.dawnmist.org; Ayto 1987, 10). Both examples from Swords Castle display an orange-brown discoloration on the front of the bowl, suggestive of heat damage or close proximity to iron oxide, and they were probably discarded in a similar manner.

STEMS

Stem bore diameter

Studies in America indicate a correlation between the diameter of the stem bore-hole and the age of the clay pipe. In general, the larger the diameter, the older the pipe; this provides a general date range for stems, although more precise dates were found to be consistent only for the period 1680–1760 (Noël Hume 1969, 298–300). The bore diameters of 325 stem fragments from Seasons 2 and 3 at Swords Castle were measured and compared. Where bore-holes were not symmetrical, the smaller diameter was measured; where a mouthpiece existed, only the broken end was measured. The results ranged from 1.6mm to 3.5mm in both seasons, with 211 stems (65%) having bore diameters of 1.6–2.1mm (corresponding to $^4/_{64}$in. and $^5/_{64}$in.).

Measurements taken on a sample of 31 stems from the 2015 season of excavations indicated a wide variety of bore diameters in nineteenth-century pipes; only diameters greater than 3mm were considered datable and likely to be seventeenth-century in origin (after Noël Hume 1969, 298). The range of measurements recorded from the 2016 and 2017 assemblages was consistent with the findings from 2015, with bore diameters of otherwise identifiable nineteenth-century stems ranging from 1.7mm to 2.5mm.

A total of 27 stem fragments recorded bore diameters of 3mm or more ($^8/_{64}$in. and $^9/_{64}$in.), identifying them as seventeenth-century in date. Over 44% of these (twelve) were recovered from topsoil. A single seventeenth-century stem fragment (E4619:117:3) was recovered from a post-medieval topsoil, F117, and thus may be more contemporary with its surrounds.

Nineteen out of the 27 stems (almost 70%) considered to be of seventeenth-century date originated in the north-eastern part of the site, as did all the identified seventeenth-century

Pl. 13.2—Stem fragments from F109, showing the variety of stem and bore diameters recovered. The stem on the right has a bore diameter of 3.1mm ($^8/_{64}$in.), suggesting a seventeenth-century date.

bowls. Bore diameters as narrow as $^5/_{64}$in. (*c.* 1.8–2.1mm) are also known from seventeenth-century pipes (Noël Hume 1969, 298), however, and it is unknown how many of the narrower-bore pipes recovered from more disturbed levels at Swords Castle may also have an earlier date. Indeed, a stem identified as seventeenth-century from the presence of a partial heel (E4619:124:5) had a bore diameter of just 2.5mm ($^7/_{64}$in.), while a second stem fragment from the same feature is likely to be contemporary, although with a bore diameter of 2.8mm ($^7/_{64}$in.). Similar diameters are found in pipes from 1650 onwards (*ibid.*, 298).

Mouthpieces

Mouthpieces were present on 31 stem fragments. Of these, fourteen were of the 'nippled' variety typical of later pipes. A variation on this was present on one stem (E4619:110:10), where the mouthpiece was wider than the stem, as with the nippled type, but flattened at the end. A further ten mouthpieces were formed by a straight, horizontal or slightly angled cut at the end of the pipe. In these cases, the end of the stem was finished to the same degree as the stem itself. It was noted that the nippled mouthpieces were associated with the larger, oval or lozenge-shaped stems of the late nineteenth and early twentieth centuries, while straight-ended mouthpieces were found on stems of various widths and shapes. Interestingly, six stems appeared to have secondary mouthpieces: instances where the pipe continued to be smoked following the loss of the end of the stem, resulting in a rounding or smoothing of the otherwise unfinished stem-end. In some cases this may have been deliberate, as a shorter stem could be held between the teeth, leaving the hands free for work (Ayto 1987, 10). Three examples (E4619:1:607, E4619:1:735 and E4619:1:1108) have notable bite marks on either side of the stem close to such a secondary mouthpiece. In two of these (E4619:1:735 and E4619:1:1108) the opposite end of the stem is broken just as it widens to form the bowl. Thus the complete final (shortened) length of the pipe stem is present: at 5.8cm and 4.44cm long respectively, this makes for a very short pipe indeed.

Decorated stems

The most common form of decoration identified on stems was a repeating roller-stamped design, identified on 29 fragments. This was achieved by rolling the stem on a die or stamp, so that the design formed a band wrapping itself around the stem. This could be carried out either perpendicular to the stem or spiralling along the stem. Such designs occur on pipes from the eighteenth and nineteenth centuries (Norton 2004, 442–6; Higgins 2009, 43; Oswald 1975, 32–3), and in general it was not possible to assign a date to individual designs. It was noted, however, that the most commonly recurring design—that of a ring of pearls, bounded by scalloped lines—is known from Dutch pipes of the eighteenth century (Higgins, n.d., 22). The range of time over which such designs were used is not known, however. Other designs identified consisted of scalloped lines, circles and lines, diamonds and dots, and broken diagonal lines.

In addition, three stem fragments bore a roller-stamped design incorporating the maker's name and place of production. One of these bore the name ':PRINCE', preceded by what appears to be a C (E4619:1:739). A second stem bore the words 'IN:GOUDA' (E4619:1:743), while the third contained the lettering 'C:PRINCE' at the top of a wide band and 'IN:GOUDA' at the bottom (E4619:1:753). The design on all three stems is nearly identical, with a wide band of up to four rows of incused squares below 'Prince' and above

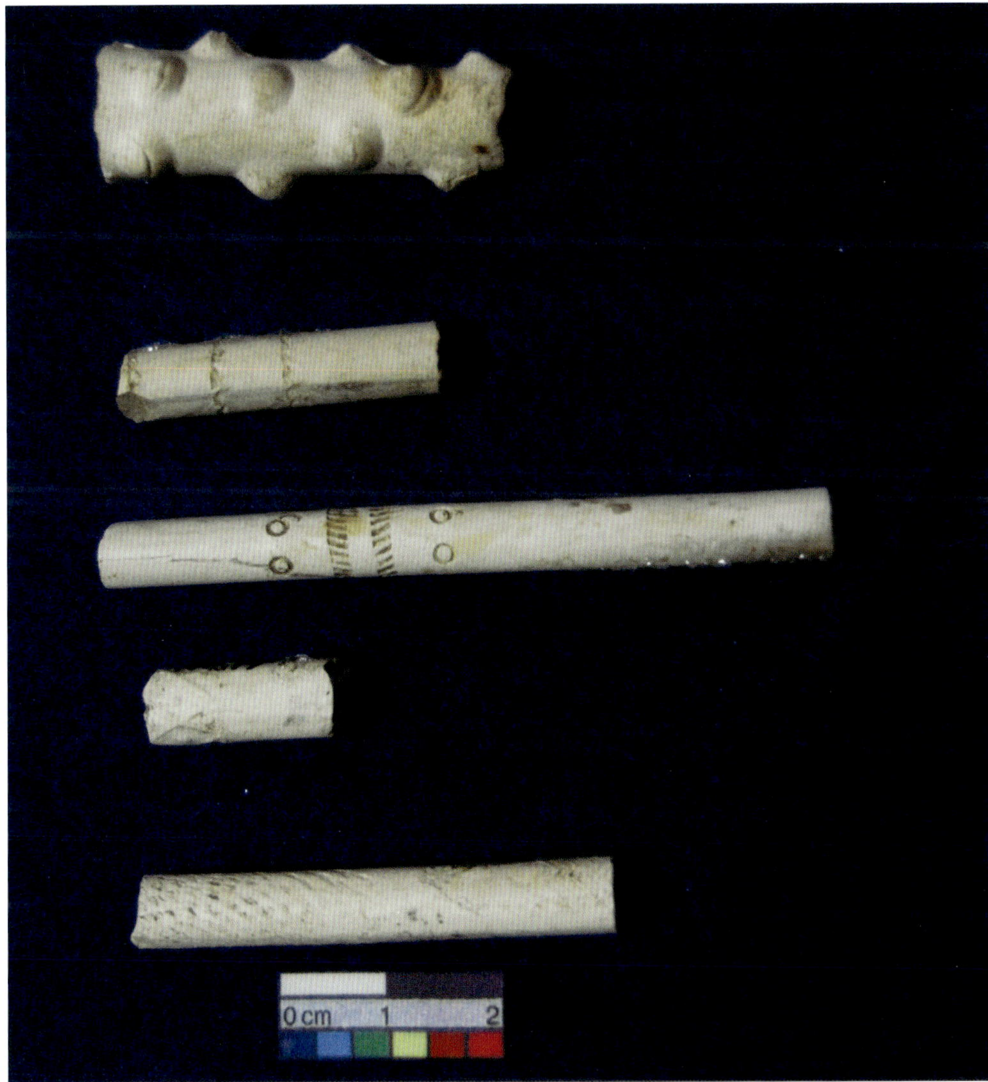

Pl. 13.3—Decorated stems (photo: Siobhán Duffy).

'In Gouda', suggesting that they are of a similar date and origin. Cornelis Prince appears on lists of Gouda pipe-makers and was active between 1797 and 1833, from which time the company transferred to Gerrit and then Jan Prince (www.goudapipes.nl/). It is likely that 'C. Prince' refers to Cornelis, giving a very late eighteenth- or early nineteenth-century date for the stems recovered.

Only four stem fragments showed examples of moulded decoration, and in three of these only the spur was decorated. The decoration on the fourth (E4619:1:367) took the form of thorns covering the surface of the stem: this was a popular theme on nineteenth-century pipes and the thorns would have continued onto the bowl (Ayto 1987, 11).

Of the other three, one (E4619:593) is a finely made example with a shamrock in relief overlying a ribbed background, and probably formed part of a patriotic design on the bowl. A second has a spur in the shape of an acorn (E4619:1:594), and the third a flattened leaf shape instead of a spur (E4619:1:611). The fragment with the acorn design was recovered

Pl. 13.4—Stem fragments bearing makers' stamps of (a) Cunningham's of Dublin (E4619:1:747), (b) McDowell's of Dublin (E4619:64:745) and (c) Hanley's of Waterford (E4619:1:742) (photo: Siobhán Duffy).

from the same trench as the acorn-decorated bowl fragments and may well have derived from the same pipe. A total of fourteen stem fragments had incused lettering stamped along the length of the stem. This form of stamping the maker's name and location on the stem rather than the bowl was increasingly common in the nineteenth century, especially where a different logo or design occupied the bowl.

Unsurprisingly, Dublin pipe-makers featured prominently in the Swords Castle examples. Six fragments represented three well-known manufacturers, all based at Francis Street, Dublin: the Cunningham (E4619:1:587 and E4619:1:747), McDowell (E4619:1:589 and E4619:64:745) and Devlin (E4619:1:364, E4619:1:588 and E4619:1:738) families. Francis Street was the principal hub of clay pipe-making in nineteenth-century Dublin, with some sixteen different families operating from there over the course of the century (Norton 2013, 35). Of these, the Cunninghams were one of the longest-standing, with successive generations producing pipes from at least the early nineteenth century until the mid-1870s (*ibid.*). Similarly, four members of the McDowell family are recorded as pipe manufacturers on Francis Street between the 1850s and 1935 (*ibid.*), one of the few to survive into the twentieth century. The third family, the Devlins, outlasted them, however: Patrick Devlin was the last pipe-maker to operate in Dublin, and was based at Francis Street from *c.* 1878 to 1941 (Norton 1986, 29; Norton 2013, 31).

A small fragment from a large, oval stem (E4619:1:365) has '_blin' stamped on one side, suggesting that it, too, had been manufactured in Dublin. The stamp on the opposite site has been eroded away but would probably have given the maker's name in the same way as the Devlin stem.

Only one fragment (E4619:1:742) bore the name of a non-Dublin-based Irish manufacturer: this had 'WATERFORD' on one side of the stem and the barely legible 'HANLEY & CO' on the other. Hanley & Co. made clay pipes at John's Lane, Waterford, for nearly a century and are considered to have been the last clay pipe-makers in Ireland (in operation until the 1950s) (Lane 1997, 373; Norton 2013, 33–5). Stems carrying the Hanley & Co. name have also been recovered in Cork (Lane 1995, 103), Waterford (Lane 1997, 373) and Kilkenny (Giacometti and Rico 2010).

A small fragment with the lettering 'DER_' stamped on one side (E4619:1:590) may have originated in Derry but was too incomplete to identify with any certainty. Another was even more difficult to decipher (E4619:1:591), with only an 'I' legible. A fragment (E4619:1:733) has the end of a cartouche with the letters '_GH', or possibly '_AGH'. The style of the cartouche and lettering bears a close resemblance to a known, later nineteenth-century design carrying a harp on the bowl and the wording 'Erin Go Bragh' on the stem (Basford 2012, 349), and may have carried a similar patriotic slogan.

The final three stems may also have carried patriotic slogans rather than references to their manufacturer. A fragment (E4619:1:745) bears a partial inscription, with 'HILL' on one side and 'VINE_' on the other. This suggests that the original wording may have been 'Vinegar Hill' on both sides, commemorating the 1798 uprising in Wexford. Similarly, a large oval stem (E4619:1:382) has the partial inscription 'VINE_' and '_PHY', suggesting 'Vinegar Hill / Murphy', a reference to Fr Murphy of 1798 fame. Both stems are of late nineteenth- or early twentieth-century style and may have been made around 1898 to commemorate the centenary.

One undecorated stem is also worthy of mention (E4619:1:691). This is a curving portion of pipe stem with a normal bore-hole at one end (with a bore diameter of 2.7mm) which widens considerably towards the other end to give an internal diameter of 6.1mm. In contrast, the stem itself widens towards the end with the smaller bore, as if to form a bowl. The most likely explanation for this is that it represents part of a stub-stemmed pipe: these had a short stem into which a replaceable stem of wood or reed would be inserted (www.pijpenkabinet.nl/; Humphrey 1969, 23). As a result, they were considered to have a longer lifespan and often had highly decorative bowls. Stub-stemmed pipes developed during the nineteenth century and were popular in the United States in the mid-nineteenth century, with both decorated and undecorated examples known (Coleman, www.dawnmist.org/; Humphrey 1969, 23–5). No parallels from Irish sites were found in published sources.

CONCLUSION

The clay pipe assemblage recovered during excavations at Swords Castle appears to be predominantly nineteenth-century in date. This is perhaps unsurprising, as the bulk of the assemblage was recovered from a very deep topsoil layer associated with the use of the site as a garden and orchard throughout the nineteenth century. Moreover, with only a few exceptions, pipe fragments recovered from below topsoil levels were retrieved from layers and features which were of a mixed or disturbed nature or deemed nineteenth-century in date.

PART IV:
ECONOMY AND ENVIRONMENT

14

Animal bone

Margaret McCarthy, MA, MIAI

INTRODUCTION

The excavation of Swords Castle resulted in the recovery of over 17,000 fragments of animal, bird and fish bone, retrieved both by hand collection in the investigated trenches and through sieving a series of sediment samples. Most of the stratified assemblage, over 10,000 fragments, came from medieval layers and deposits spanning a broad period of occupation from the early twelfth to the sixteenth century. The medieval assemblage was found primarily in dump deposits and accumulation layers, although some cut features, including waste pits, wall foundation trenches and a kiln, also contained bone. Earlier, pre-Anglo-Norman activity was limited, and the post-medieval use of the site was largely confined to gardening and farming activities, resulting in small samples of animal bone being recovered from ploughsoils that accumulated across the precinct of the castle. Relatively large samples of unstratified bone were retrieved from the topsoil and from modern features in the upper horizons; these were identified for potential interesting features but they are not further considered in the assessment. In total, 15,239 bones came from features that could be assigned to a specific period of occupation and these provide the basis for the analysis of the faunal assemblage.

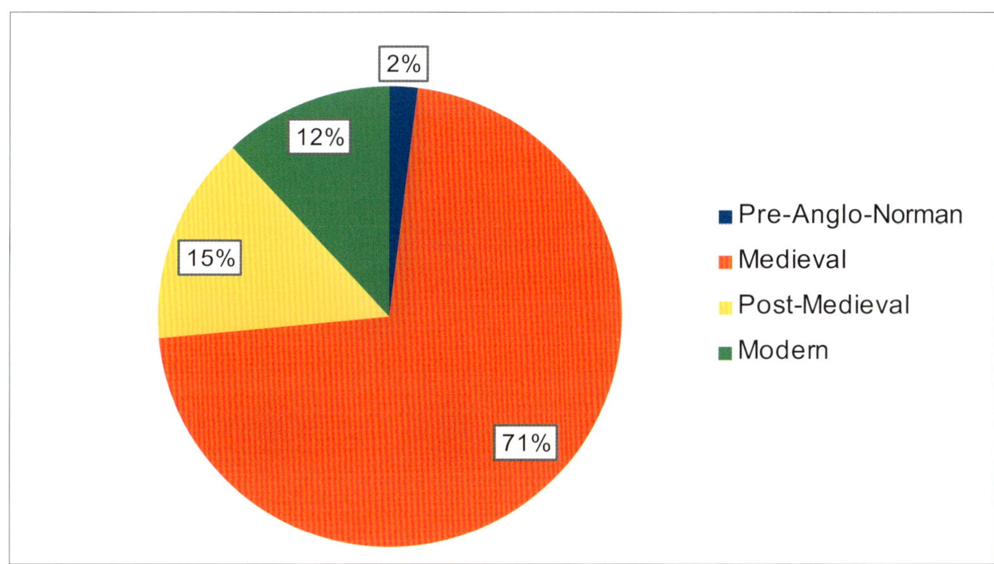

Fig. 14.1—Chronological distribution of animal bones.

METHODS

All material recovered from dated contexts was assessed and the bones were identified using the writer's reference collection and the more extensive collections of birds and fish in the Natural History Museum, Dublin. Data were recorded onto an Excel database, which includes categories for butchery, ageing and sexing, as well as species and element identification. Bones not identified to species were categorised according to the relative size of the animal, i.e. large mammal and medium mammal remains. The material recorded as 'large mammal', for instance, is likely to belong to cattle but was too small to eliminate the possibility of horse and red deer, although just two horse bones were recovered and there was no evidence for the consumption of venison at the site. Similarly, specimens that in all probability were sheep but which may have also originated from goat, pig or large dog were recorded as 'medium mammal'. Where possible, sheep were distinguished from goats using guidelines recommended by Boessneck (1969) and Prummel and Frisch (1986). There were no specific identifications of goat, and those postcranial bones that allow for discrimination between the two species were identified to sheep. All ovicaprid specimens are therefore classified as 'sheep' in the text, as the majority of the bones bore anatomical criteria distinguishing them to that species. Determination of the age at slaughter was established using epiphyseal fusion data and the eruption and wear of mandibular cheek teeth. The state of fusion of articular ends of suitable bones was calculated using Silver's (1971) data. The sample of mandibles that provided ageing evidence was small and consequently the results cannot be said to be conclusive. Age determination by the eruption and wear of teeth followed the criteria outlined by Silver (1971) and Grant (1975b). The relative proportion of the different species was assessed using the total number of identified specimens (NISP) and the minimum number of individuals (MNI) represented. All specimens were also examined for taphonomic alterations such as burning, butchery and gnawing by carnivores. Measurements followed the criteria of Von den Driesch (1976). Methods for the identification and analysis of birds and fish followed those of Wheeler and Jones (1989), Serjeantson (2009) and Yalden and Albarella (2009). Palaeopathological descriptions relied on those used by Waldron (2009). Information on the distribution and habitat preferences of wild birds was obtained from D'Arcy (1981) and Dempsey and O'Clery (1993), and of fish from Wheeler (1978).

CONDITION AND RECOVERY

Overall, the vertebrate remains are reasonably well preserved given the circumstances of most of the finds, scattered in a relatively unspecialised manner across the castle grounds and into open areas that were later used for horticultural purposes. The lateral dispersal of bone can also be attributed to the continued use of the castle during the post-medieval period for farming and gardening, including the planting of extensive orchards. The potential for reworking and redeposition of bone is therefore considerable, and the very high fragmentation rate might imply that food waste was left exposed on the living surface in high-traffic areas where it would have been subject to damage and breakage. Canid and rodent gnawing is not present in significant amounts, however, and only a small number of bones show evidence of reworked or residual material. The indications are therefore that food waste was buried fairly rapidly following deposition and not disturbed too much at a later date. There are occasional calcined and scorched bones, but these rarely account for more than 3% of the remains from any one feature. The proportion of loose teeth is frequently used by faunal analysts to gauge the degree of fragmentation and at Swords Castle the proportion is very high (23%), which is attributed more to butchering and food-processing activities and to the rigorous on-site retrieval programme, which ensured the recovery of a representative collection of animal, bird and fish bones.

ANALYSIS

The bones were recovered over three seasons of excavation and from ten trenches that were strategically placed to investigate anomalies identified in the geophysical survey. In total, over 17,000 bone fragments were recovered, comprising 15,913 mammal bones, 863 bird bones and 691 fish bones. Of these, 11,107 specimens were too small and fragmented to enable identification of the species and these were classified according to the two main size groupings described above. This left 6,360 fragments that could be identified with certainty to species level. The very high proportion of unidentifiable bone (63%) is attributed to very careful hand excavation, along with on-site sieving and wet-sieving of selected soil samples in the laboratory. Birds and fish make up the remaining portion of the assemblage, and many of the fish bones in particular were recovered from the soil samples. The total assemblage has been divided into four main chronological groups identified by the excavation director, and the results for each phase are discussed below. For the post-medieval period, where there is little evidence for actual occupation of the castle, the small quantities of material recovered could be residual from the earlier medieval period but there is no definitive evidence of this.

In examining the bone assemblage, the aim was to outline the economy of the site in each of the different phases of occupation. The bones were studied in individual chronological groups in the expectation of distinguishing differences in diet and animal husbandry practices, and also to highlight any changes or anomalies in the status of the settlement throughout the span of its occupation. This was achieved by the identification of every possible bone to species level and by the analysis of their relative frequencies and identifiable traits such as age, sex and butchering techniques. Further analysis then attempted to look at the different types of information that the bones could yield, and assess their value for the interpretation of the site and the economy of the early medieval community that used this enclosure for over six centuries. The bones of the animals present were examined for traces of butchery as well as for evidence of disease.

MAMMAL BONES

Pre-Anglo-Norman
An early phase of pre-Anglo-Norman activity (tenth/eleventh century) was identified during investigations in Trenches 1–6 and in Trench 9. The faunal sample is well preserved but limited in size, with a combined total of just 366 bones being recovered from a timber building and a ditch, as well as from a series of waste pits. The individual samples are described below.

Timber building

The foundation trench (F101) for a timber building was cut into the natural subsoil in Trench 4, and radiocarbon analysis of bone from this feature advanced a date of AD 936–1013. Only eleven bones were recovered from the fill. Cattle and pig are both represented; the cattle bones include a fragment of a first neck vertebra (atlas) and a complete first phalanx from an individual over at least one and a half years of age at slaughter. Pig was identified from fragments of radius, ulna and vertebra, and the remainder of the sample consists of five small fragments of long bone from a large-sized animal and one fragment from a medium-sized animal.

Ditch F85

Organic material from the basal fill of a deep ditch (F85) in Trench 5 yielded a radiocarbon date of AD 975–1037, indicating that it represents a possible enclosure ditch associated with the pre-Anglo-Norman phase of activity. Faunal remains contained in the ditch were sparse, with just 40 bones recovered. Overall, the vertebrate remains are well preserved and the fragmentation rate is moderate, indicating that they represent a primary deposit of food waste into the ditch. The identified sample consists mostly of cattle, with at least two individuals being represented by the nine bones: a cow older than four and a half years of age at death and a younger animal, probably around two years old. The range of body parts includes vertebrae, metatarsals, phalanges and femora, suggestive of local slaughter and processing of cattle carcasses. Six sheep bones were identified, all representing prime meat-bearing joints, including radius, vertebrae, tibia and femur. The few pig bones were identified as an ulna, a pelvis, an incisor and a complete first phalanx from an individual less than a year old at slaughter. The pre-Anglo-Norman occupants of the site also kept poultry, as evidenced by the recovery of a lower leg bone (tibio-tarsus) of a young chick.

Pits F95 (fill F93), F92 (upper fill F88), F97 and F19

The vertebrate assemblage from a pit, F92, that truncated pit F95 amounted to 107 bones, and the usual complement of domestic animals are present. Sheep/goat remains are marginally more frequent numerically than cattle and at least two individuals are represented: a young lamb that died around two–four weeks after birth, and an individual between two and four years of age at slaughter. The two pig bones found in the pit represent two individuals: a piglet around two months old at slaughter and an adult individual. Cattle are also present, the ten bones coming from an individual that was slaughtered for its meat at less than two years of age. There was a single chicken bone, and the one feature that stands out is the recovery of the only hare bone identified at the site. Another pre-Anglo-Norman pit (F97) was partially excavated and this resulted in the recovery of just five animal bones: a proximal fused cow radius, an unfused pig metacarpus, two large mammal long bone fragments and a rib fragment from a medium-sized mammal. Pit F19 provided a date of AD 937–1019 and contained 24 bones, the bulk of which are indeterminate. Just three fragments can be taken to species level: two fragments of a cow femur, one of which is affected by canid gnawing, and a small piece of a sheep maxilla.

Layer F163

This layer in Trench 9 was cut by a burial (SK15) which returned a date of AD 994–1059. A total of 51 animal bones were recovered, and over 35% of the fragments show the somewhat eroded surfaces that are often characteristic of disposal in exposed living surfaces. Identified species include cattle, sheep and pig, each represented by fewer than ten bones. Cattle dominate the identified sample of just thirteen bones and, despite the small sample size, there are sufficient peripheral and primary meat-bearing elements present to indicate local slaughter and dismemberment of this individual. The cattle pelvis has cut-marks typically associated with dismemberment. Three sheep bones represent a single individual that was slaughtered after it had reached two and a half years of age, and the few pig bones represent an individual that was less than two years old when selected for the table.

Medieval period

The majority of the vertebrate remains were dated to the medieval period. A total sample of 12,292 bones was collected. Radiocarbon evidence indicates that the material began to accumulate in the early twelfth century and continued over the thirteenth and fourteenth centuries, with an apparent upsurge in activity in the fifteenth and sixteenth centuries. The animal bones were mostly found scattered in a somewhat unspecialised manner within surface accumulation layers and dump deposits (87%), as well as in the fills of rubbish pits, a foundation trench for a wall (F14), a kiln (F143) and a deposit (F153) associated with the East Tower (Fig. 14.2). In general, the bones are highly fragmented and the proportion of identified fragments is consequently low. Many of the bones from the fill of the wall trench (F14) have a somewhat battered and eroded appearance and seem to represent redeposited bone from elsewhere on the site. Traces of dog, cat and rodent gnawing are present on some specimens but the evidence is not extensive. The remains were recorded by the different context groupings identified by the excavation director and the results are presented below under these headings.

Layers and deposits
In total, 11,249 bones were recovered from a variety of layers and deposits scattered across the ten excavation trenches, representing episodic dumping during the medieval occupation

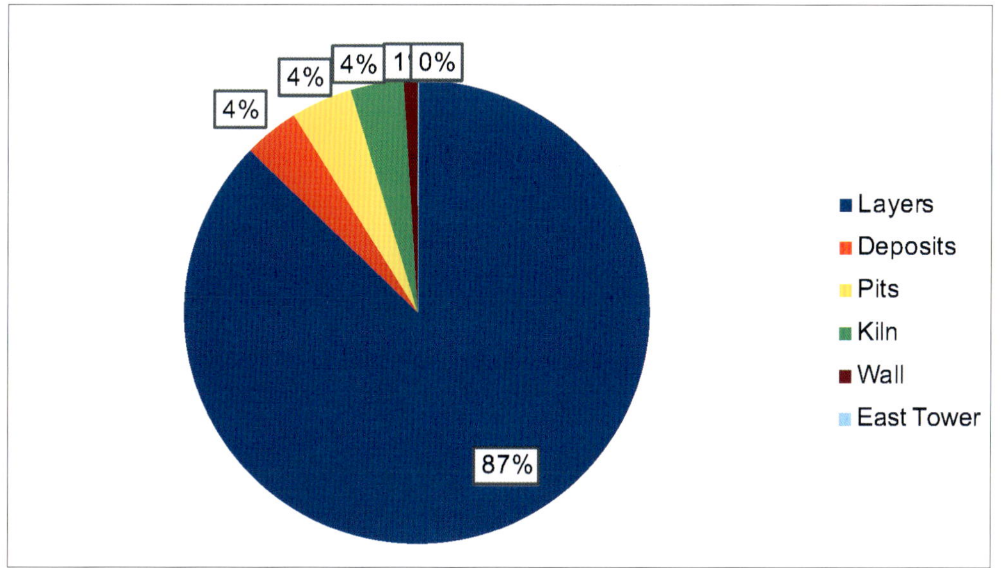

Fig. 14.2—Distribution of animal bones across feature groupings: medieval period.

of the castle. The material spans a broad date range, with some layers (F8) producing early dates of the twelfth century while others (F124–F126) are fifteenth- and sixteenth-century in date. Preservation of the vertebrate material is mainly good, although some of the larger fragments have eroded surfaces. Some small calcined fragments are also present. Fresh breakage and dog gnawing was observed in the main bone-producing layers but in general few bones are affected. Of the major domesticates, cattle and sheep remains predominate, followed by considerably smaller quantities of pig. Cattle bones account for 43% of the diagnostic fraction (NISP), sheep for 33% and pig for 15%. In terms of the minimum number of individuals present, sheep (23 individuals) are slightly more frequently represented; at least 26 cattle are present, while pig rank third in importance with just eight individuals being represented. The bones are variously chopped and broken and belong to animals that ranged in age from a young calf to animals that were killed specifically for their meat at 2.5–4 years of age, and a few older individuals kept for milk production and perhaps ploughing. The proximal joint surface of a first phalanx from an adult bovid shows splaying, grooving and polishing (eburnation) associated with stress on the lower limbs, and it is possible that this particular animal was used for ploughing.

The remains represent a combination of primary butchery and food waste, as most portions of the beef and mutton carcass have been identified; bones from joints of high meat value (upper limb bones/pelvis/scapula) are slightly more numerous than those considered to represent waste from primary carcass dismemberment. Skeletal element representation suggests that, for cattle, a mixture of primary butchery and domestic refuse is present in the deposits, with roughly equivalent numbers of non-meat and meat-bearing elements. There are, however, sufficient quantities of peripheral non-meat-bearing bones to indicate that livestock were brought to the castle on the hoof, where slaughtering and butchery were carried out in the vicinity of the buildings. Epiphyseal fusion data indicate that the average age of slaughter of cattle and sheep fell slightly between three and four years, though the presence of bones from a cow less than one year old, two lambs *c.* three months old and at least two piglets indicates that young animals were also slaughtered for their meat on occasion. The recovery of late-fusing elements, albeit in lesser numbers, indicates that older animals were also consumed, and the value of live beasts to the economy in terms of dairy and traction should not be overlooked. The dentition-based cull patterns for cattle and sheep/goat also suggest slaughter at a stage when the animals had reached their optimum size for meat production. The cattle mandibles possess Grant (1975b) numerical values of 22–30, and five have completed their tooth eruption sequence as the fourth permanent premolar is in wear. Three mandibles have numerical values of 9–14 with the first molar in an early stage of wear, possibly belonging to an animal about a year old. The range of skeletal elements for sheep suggests that there is a slightly larger component of table waste than primary butchery waste, with vertebrae, pelves, tibiae and scapulae being the most commonly occurring elements. Sheep were over two and a half years old at slaughter, although there was also evidence for the occasional consumption of lamb, with a single individual less than four months old being represented. The only clear evidence for goat was a couple of horn cores which had been chopped horizontally roughly two thirds of the way down their length, presumably to utilise either the horn or the core or both. Mandibular ageing data for sheep are quite scarce but five have fully erupted cheek toothrows and belong to adult animals probably around four years of age.

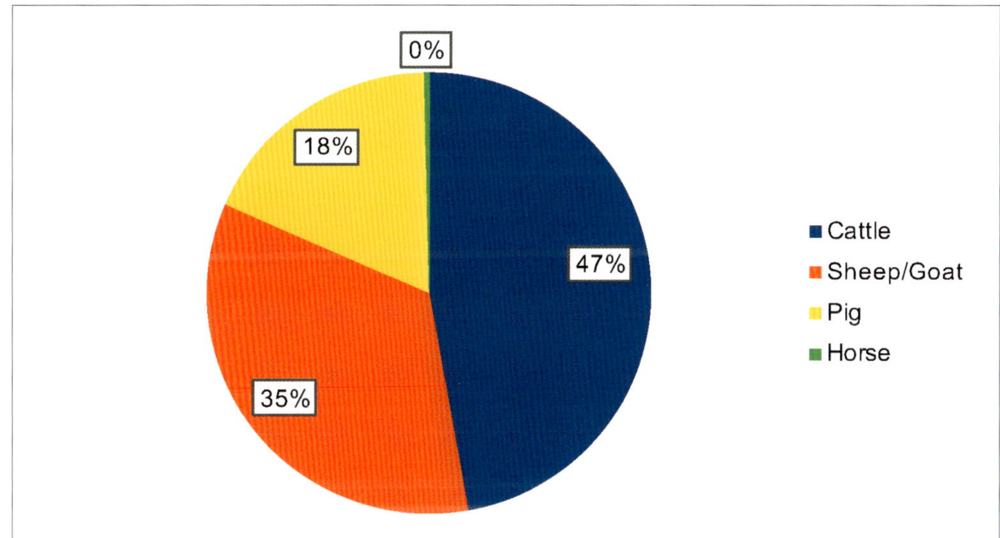

Fig. 14.3—Proportions of main livestock species: medieval period.

Pig is the least frequently occurring of the three main species, as is the case in many other medieval urban and rural assemblages. The remains account for just 15% of the identified mammalian sample and at least eight individuals were recognised, including one newborn piglet and an individual that was less than two months old at death. There is also evidence for a few adult boars, and the limited number of bones belonging to mature individuals probably represent breeding stock. While the sample is dominated by isolated teeth and metapodials, there are sufficient quantities of other elements present to suggest local slaughter and consumption of pigs within the grounds of the castle. Skeletal element analysis indicates that all parts of the carcass are present, including bones from the hind and forelimbs, the axial skeleton (ribs and vertebrae) and loose deciduous and permanent teeth. As with other assemblages, most of the bones belong to immature animals but the paucity of quantifiable data makes detailed ageing or metrical analysis impossible. Mandibular wear patterns show that seven mandibles had reached the stage where the second molar had come into wear, indicating that most mortalities were in the second and third year. There is evidence that suckling pig was occasionally consumed and this, combined with the recovery of a boar's tusk, indicates that pigs were reared within the precinct of the castle.

Butchery marks are typical of those noted on other medieval sites, and the bones are variously split and broken as a result of dismemberment and division into suitable joints for cooking. A layer (F80) overlying metalling in Trench 4 was particularly rich in chopped and split animal bones relating to primary butchery, food-processing and kitchen preparation. Cut-marks are more frequently observed on cattle bones, owing to their greater size, and are consistent with initial dismemberment and further reduction of the carcass into more manageable joints of beef. Marks associated with the separation of the girdle bones from the main trunk of the body are commonly found on the distal humerus, proximal tibia and femur, and proximal radius. Disarticulation marks are also found on several distal scapulae and pelves, while chopping and knife marks on distal metapodials relate to the removal of the hide. Cut-marks associated with meat-stripping are found on some vertebrae and a high proportion of the limb bones are split open, inferring that marrow extraction was significant.

Most of the cattle vertebrae were split longitudinally during the division of the carcass into right and left sides, a type of butchery typical of medieval assemblages. Various chop-marks and knife marks on cattle and pig mandibles seem to have resulted from the consumption of cheek meat and tongue and the extraction of marrow from the horizontal ramus. The smaller size of sheep and pig carcasses resulted in fewer butchery marks being observed; knife cuts are observed on the major limb bones associated with dismemberment, while finer marks on the scapula relate to the stripping of meat from these bones. A pig skull was split medially prior to the removal of the brain.

All other mammalian species are only nominally represented and include horse, dog and rabbit. A small proportion of horse is present, scattered widely across layers, deposits, pits and the kiln (F143). A stone surface (F86) produced one of just four horse bones identified, along with a worn molar from an adult individual. A proximal metatarsus from layer (F77) displays chop-marks on the shaft just below the articulation, made during the dismemberment of the carcass for consumption either by humans or dogs or to facilitate the disposal of the animal.

Non-edible domestic species are represented by at least two dogs and a cat. Seven dog bones were found scattered across a relatively limited number of layers. Two dog bones from layer F74 are identified as an axis and a metapodial from an adult individual similar in size to a modern Labrador. Other dog bones were found scattered across other deposits/layers, all from medium-sized (collie/Labrador) individuals. The proximal portion of a radius from an adult individual came from a layer (F13) in Trench 2, and four dog bones, representing at least two individuals, were found in Trench 3. An astragalus from a small adult sheepdog was found in layer F18, and three bones (ulna, radius and femur) from a larger, Alsatian-sized individual were present in layer F21. The six cat bones also came from Trench 3 and were found in layers F20 and F21. They belong to a single adult individual, kept no doubt to control vermin in and around the manor and its associated outbuildings.

The wild mammal component consists of 129 rabbit bones and a single rat bone. At least nine rabbits were estimated, accounting for 8% of the identified mammalian sample. The bones were found scattered in various layers in Trench 1 and Trench 3, being particularly abundant in the fish-bone-rich layer F43 in Trench 1. Adult individuals are mostly represented but the presence of two limb bones from younger animals indicates that rabbits were kept and bred within the grounds of the castle, which was common practice during the medieval period. The recovery of a rat bone in layer F18 in Trench 3 confirms that rodents, as might be expected, frequented those areas of the castle used for domestic waste disposal.

Pits

In general, the density of bones in the pits was lower than in the surface layers that accumulated across the site. The faunal material is well preserved and would seem to have been found in primary contexts. Five pits (F28, F30, F31, F33 and F81) produced a total sample of 295 bones. Deposition of the bones into the pits spanned a wide date range, with pit F31 returning a radiocarbon date of 1021–1186 and pit F30 a considerably later date of 1419–1512. The bulk of the recovered bone came from pit F31. Pit F33 contained just ten fragments of bone, which indicates that its primary function cannot have been for the disposal of meat waste. Of these, just one bone was diagnostic to species and was identified as a phalanx from a juvenile pig. Analysis of botanical material from pits F31 and F33 demonstrated intensive activity associated with the processing and storage of grain, as well as perhaps the eventual disposal of cereal foodstuffs into these pits. Most of the recovered bone from the earliest pit (F31) is calcined from being in contact with intense heat for a considerable period of time, suggesting that these bones originated from the castle kitchen and may represent the rakings of fires used to roast meat on spits. Mammal species present include the usual range of domestic livestock as well as horse, cat, dog and rabbit. Pit F30 excavated in Pit A produced a late medieval date of the fifteenth/sixteenth century and is most noteworthy for containing eight cat bones, representing two individuals, including a juvenile. A waste pit (F81) in Trench 4 contained medieval pottery, nails and marine molluscs as well as a moderate collection of butchered animal bone. The bones are from an adult individual between two and a half and four years of age at death. In addition to the main livestock animals, chicken bones representing both wing and leg elements are present.

As might be expected, cattle remains predominate, the other two livestock animals (sheep and pig) providing the bulk of the rest of the assemblage. Cattle are dominant both numerically and in terms of minimum numbers of individuals present but the identified samples from the pits are too small for this to be significant. Ageing evidence indicates the presence of two adult individuals. Cattle are represented by a range of skeletal parts and, while non-meat-bearing elements such as metapodials, phalanges and isolated teeth are prevalent, a sufficient component of meat-bearing elements such as pelves, tibiae, femora and scapulae are also present to indicate that this is a mixed collection of primary butchery waste and meals from tables. From pit F81, 48 well-preserved bones were examined, with the remains of cattle, sheep and pig identified. The eight cattle bones include both meat-bearing elements (radius, femur, pelvis and vertebra) as well as peripheral bones representative of primary butchery waste, including tarsal/carpal bones and phalanges.

Sheep are second in importance numerically, comprising twelve bones representing the remains of two individuals between two and a half and three years of age at death. Skeletal element representation shows that a mixture of primary butchery and domestic refuse was present in the pits, with roughly equivalent numbers of meat-bearing and non-meat-bearing bones. For pigs, isolated teeth are prevalent. With the exception of a single piglet radius, the remainder of the pig bones come from individuals that were slaughtered between one and two years of age.

Many of the cattle and sheep bones show evidence for butchery, and the types and frequencies of cut-marks are similar to those described for the larger assemblage from the general accumulation layers. The major limb bones of cattle are chopped through the articulations and across the shaft, and two skull fragments have fine knife marks on the occipital condyle where the head was separated from the body. Vertebrae of all three livestock species are variously cut and chopped, and knife marks are present on a few pelves and scapulae fragments where meat had been stripped from these bones. Splitting on a few long bones indicates that marrow was extracted, as a secondary process perhaps during cooking; the presence of a few knife marks on the distal articulations of metapodials and on some of the phalanges relate to skinning.

Kiln F143
A date of AD 1451–1528 was obtained from one of the fills (F146) of this kiln excavated in Trench 7. From the various backfill deposits of the kiln, some 204 (46%) could be identified

from a total assemblage of 447 animal bones. The usual range of cattle, sheep, pig, horse and dog is present in the domestic assemblage, while rabbit makes up the wild component, although it is possible that this individual was bred within the precinct of the castle.

Wall F14

This wall was exposed in Trench 1, where it was shown to form a boundary between distinct areas of activity, with thin fish-bone-rich layers to the north and burnt material to the south. Identified vertebrate remains in the fill of the wall trench amount to 121 fragments, with a further 81 assigned to broader size categories. Preservation of the bone was mainly poor and the fragments were probably not found in a primary context. Sheep make up the largest proportion (nine specimens) of the identified material and the elements consist of bones from the meat-bearing regions of the carcass. There are four cattle bones, including three vertebrae and a skull fragment. A young pig (< one year) is represented by fragments of a fibula and an ulna. Limited ageing data indicate that cattle and sheep were over four years old at slaughter, and butchery evidence consists of the longitudinal splitting of cattle vertebrae. Rabbit is the only wild species and is represented by humerus, ulna, phalanx and tooth. A relatively large sample of bird bones were found, which are reported on separately below.

East Tower

Only four fragments of bone were recovered from a deposit (F153) associated with the East Tower. Two were identified as fragments of a cow scapula and a sheep pelvis, and the other two as pieces of bone from a large-sized animal.

Table 14.1—Cattle ageing data.

	Approx. age at fusion	UF	F
Scapula D	10 months		37
Humerus D		4	51
Radius P	18 months	1	34
Ph. 1 & Ph. 2		15	119
Metapodial D	2–2.5 years	9	19
Tibia D		9	32
Femur P	3.5 years	28	28
Calcaneum		5	10
Humerus P		5	5
Radius D		10	10
Ulna P	3.5–4 years	2	3
Femur D		1	4
Tibia P		9	8

Table 14.2—Sheep ageing data.

	Approx. age at fusion	UF	F
Scapula D		1	21
Humerus D		2	51
Radius P	10 months	4	25
Ph. 1		14	29
Metapodial D	1.5–2 years	4	6
Tibia D		9	39
Ulna P		5	6
Femur P	2.5–3 years	23	7
Calcaneum		15	8
Radius D		28	8
Humerus P		11	2
Femur D	3–3.5 years	14	12
Tibia P		13	2

Table 14.3—Pig ageing data.

	Approx. age at fusion	UF	F
Scapula—glenoid		1	19
Humerus D	1 yr		5
Radius P		3	24
Phalanx 1		14	9
Tibia D		20	3
Metapodial	2–2.5 years	55	6
Calcaneum		3	
Phalanx 2		9	8
Humerus P		3	
Radius D		5	2
Ulna P	2.5–3.5 years	10	
Femur P		4	
Femur D		2	
Tibia P		12	

.

Post-medieval period

By this time Swords Castle had fallen into disrepair and the grounds were being used for farming and for the planting of extensive orchards. The excavation of accumulation layers and deposits in the upper horizons of the investigated areas collectively produced a moderate assemblage of 3,555 vertebrate remains, although, in contrast to the medieval period, few deposits produced substantial quantities of material. Most bones (84%) were found in a limited range of layers and deposits, and a combined total of 411 bones were contained in four waste pits (F4, F6/38, F69 and F76). In view of the circumstances of the finds, faunal material is reasonably well preserved, although some bones are battered, eroded and damaged from being exposed on the surface for a while before being sealed. Fresh breakage and gnawing, almost certainly by dogs, were observed on a few bones, while other fragments were scorched and damaged from proximity to heat during cooking.

Consolidation layer F3

This layer was encountered in Trenches 1 and 2 and appeared to have been deliberately introduced in the earlier post-medieval period to create a level surface prior to horticultural activity. The total recovered sample amounts to 1,124 bones, but the majority (76%) of these can only be classified into the large mammal and medium mammal categories. The on-site sieving programme resulted in the recovery of many small fragments of bone, most of which were not diagnostic to species level. The identified sample of 280 bones consists almost entirely of domestic livestock, with cattle (36%) and sheep (37%) being almost equally represented. In terms of the minimum number of individuals present, sheep (7) are almost twice as frequent as cattle (4). A wide range of cattle skeletal parts are represented, including non-meat-bearing elements such as metapodials, phalanges and isolated teeth, as well as meat-bearing elements including pelvis, scapulae and upper limb bones. Skeletal element representation for sheep shows a similar mix of bones, with vertebrae, femora, radii and tibiae (meat-bearing bones) and mandibles and metapodials (non-meat-bearing bones) being most frequent. Although not particularly numerous in terms of recovered fragments, at least three pigs are represented, with the remains chiefly being composed of upper limb bones and metapodials. Ageing data are generally scarce but a dominance of unfused late-fusing limb bones indicates that livestock supplied to the castle were slaughtered at around three to four years of age. Most sheep femora and tibiae are unfused proximally, representing individuals less than three to three a half years of age at slaughter. At least one lamb less than six months old is present and two piglets were identified. The cattle bones are also mostly from individuals that were around four years of age at slaughter and there is no evidence for the consumption of veal. Cut- and chop-marks were noted on all the major cattle limb bones; these were made during the disarticulation of the scapula from the humerus and the femur from the pelvis and during the removal of meat from the blades of the girdle bones. Many of the upper limb bones of cattle and sheep show chop-marks associated with further carcass division, and there is evidence for the medial division of the vertebral column into right and left sides. The only other species present in the consolidation layer was rabbit. At least two adult individuals were identified, and it is possible that these animals were kept in warrens within the grounds of the manor as a source of additional food. Fine knife marks associated with removing the pelt were observed on one limb bone.

Layers and deposits
A total of 2,120 bones were recovered from various accumulation layers and deposits, with the bulk of these (44%) being extracted from an extensive layer (F65) in Trench 4. Relatively large samples of bone were also recovered from layer F117 in Trench 7 and from a consolidation layer (F63) in Trench 6. Fragmentation rates are high and there is a relatively high proportion of isolated teeth, indicating that the bones were exposed on the living surface for some time before being sealed. A similar range of species to those identified for the medieval period was recorded, with all the common domesticates being present, along with a small number of chicken and geese. A few bones of marine fish species, identified primarily as gadid (cod family) species, were also present in the sample. In terms of the total number of identified specimens, there are overall suggested proportions of 45% cattle, 29% sheep and 11% pig (Fig. 14.4). The remains of cattle make up the largest proportion of the identified material and at least eighteen individuals are represented. As is usual, the proportion of sheep and pig increases slightly when an assessment of minimum number of individuals present is calculated. MNI figures for sheep, for instance, show that they represent 38% of the domestic component, and the frequency of pig also increases from 11% (NISP) to 25%. The range of skeletal elements for cattle suggests a larger component of primary butchery waste than was noted for the earlier periods, suggesting that, while cattle continued to be slaughtered and dismembered within the precinct of the castle, a certain amount of prepared joints were subsequently distributed around the town, thereby reducing the quantity of meat-bearing bones in the assemblage. There are higher proportions of vertebrae, skull fragments, isolated teeth and peripheral elements, indicative of primary butchery waste. Cattle bones are extensively butchered, including split long bones, chopped skulls and mandibles and heavily butchered pelvis fragments. Evidence of longitudinally chopped vertebrae is common, these being typically noted in medieval and post-medieval assemblages, indicating the splitting of carcasses into sides. A wide range of sheep elements were also identified, including skull fragments, vertebrae, peripheral limb bones, major upper and lower limb bones and isolated teeth. At least ten individuals are represented, all over two and a half years of age at slaughter and perhaps older. While pigs are the least frequently occurring species in terms of frequency of skeletal elements, an assessment of the minimum number of individuals present indicates that at least eight individuals are present: two were slaughtered at around one year old, when they would have attained their maximum size for meat production, two died or were slaughtered at around two months old and the remainder were over two years of age at slaughter. The indications are that pigs continued to be reared within the grounds of the manor during the post-medieval period.

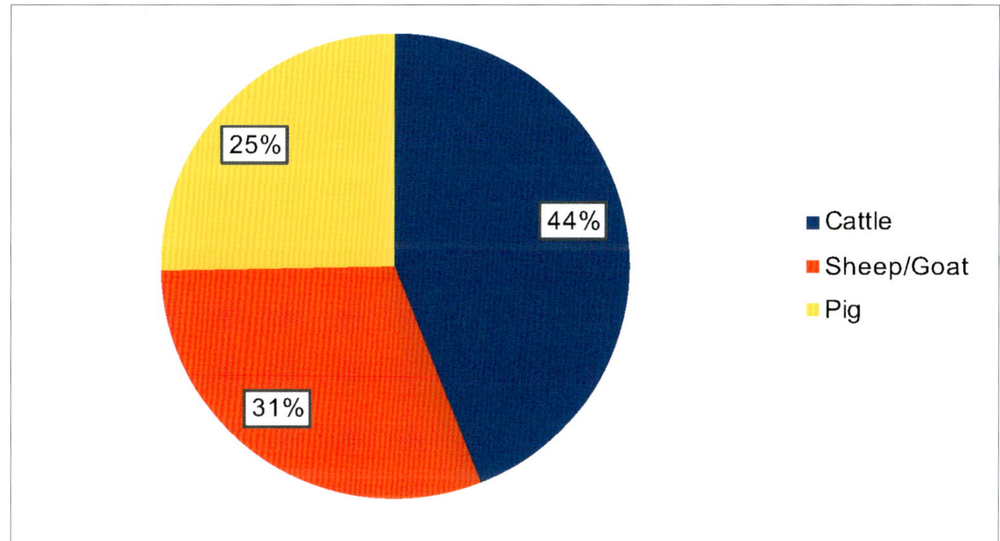

Fig. 14.4—Proportions of main livestock species: post-medieval period.

There is no great variety of other taxa in the post-medieval accumulation layers. Dog, with seventeen fragments, is the most frequent. Fourteen of these were recovered from layer F65 and two from layer F64. Identified bones include vertebrae, an axis, a calcaneus, an astragalus, an isolated tooth, three metapodial and four rib fragments, all from two adult collie-sized dogs, kept within the grounds of the castle as useful ratters and guard dogs. The proportion of rabbit bones is notably smaller than for the preceding medieval period, suggesting that there was no management of this species during the post-medieval period. Rabbits may well have been captured in the wild at this stage. The extensive accumulation layer F65 is notable for producing the only rat (*Rattus rattus*) bone from the site, a femur from a young rat being recognised.

Pits

A total of 411 animal bones were recovered from four pits (F4, F6/F38, F69 and F76), of which 75% were recovered from pit F69. The remaining three pits contained limited quantities of bone but it is considered that they were all excavated to contain food waste. In Trench 1, two pits (F6/F38 and F4) truncated the consolidation layer F3. In general, vertebrate remains from the pits show good preservation, with little evidence of post-depositional disturbance. The sample recovered from waste pit F69 amounts to 310 bones; pig remains appear to be numerous, although the figure is artificially inflated owing to the recovery of a partial skeleton. This individual, aged between one and two and a half years, suffered from a severe degenerative joint disease, manifested as gross pathological abnormalities in the form of pitting and lipping on some of the vertebrae and on the lower limb bones as severe additional bone growth (exostoses). The animal seems to have lived, no doubt very uncomfortably, for some time with the disease and, as most of the bones are complete and lacking butchery marks, it is clear that the meat was not processed once the animal was slaughtered and its body discarded in the pit. The fourteen cattle bones include fragments of tibia, femur, scapula, mandible, phalanges and vertebrae and represent a single adult individual. A few butchered bones are present. At least two sheep are estimated from the sample of 25 bones, including an adult over three and a half years of age at slaughter and a small lamb, probably around a month old when it died.

A large pit (F6/F38) excavated at the north side of the trench contained a vertebrate assemblage of 107 bones, of which 33 were taken to species level. The usual range of domestic animals is represented, with cattle remains predominating. Sheep are the next most abundant species. A mixture of meat waste is present. Of the major domesticates, cattle and sheep are almost equally represented by fewer than twenty bones each. While most parts of the skeleton are present, isolated teeth, vertebrae, pelvis and scapulae are the most frequent. Although the ageing sample is small, some of the cattle and sheep long bones have unfused epiphyses and come from animals around two and a half years of age at slaughter. Evidence of butchery is not extensive, confined to a couple of chop-marks on the cattle vertebrae. Just two pig bones were found in this pit, a skull fragment and a metacarpus from an individual over a year old at slaughter. The unidentified component includes large mammal (assumed to be cattle) and medium mammal (probably sheep) remains.

Animal bones were found in very small numbers in pit F4 in Trench 1, with just ten fragments recorded, two of which were identified as cattle scapula fragments. One of these displays modern saw marks and may be intrusive from a later phase of activity. Pit F76, which extended into the western baulk of the trench, yielded 25 animal bones; cattle, sheep, pig and chicken are all represented by fewer than five bones each, and the remains come from both meat-bearing areas of the body and peripheral regions associated more with primary butchery.

Modern activity

Work on the upper horizons in all excavated areas revealed a topsoil layer (F1) sealing numerous modern features and disturbed layers which contained faunal remains. Animal bones were found in a variety of cut features, including pits, gullies, drains and furrows associated with the use of the castle precinct for recent agricultural and horticultural activities. In addition, small samples of bone were retrieved from deposits associated with a wall (F110) and a path (F111) that were shown by excavation to have formed part of the nineteenth-century bakery. These are clearly not ideal contexts for assessing diet and economy, as there is the possibility that much of the bone is reworked and residual from the two earlier phases of medieval and post-medieval occupation. The combined total of animal bones from the topsoil layer was 2,959 fragments, representing 17% of the recovered assemblage. A high proportion (27%) of bone was also found in disturbed layers, in particular layers F106 and F118, and the samples from these deposits include numerous bones with modern butchery marks. In common with the two earlier phases of activity, the samples are very fragmented and the percentage of bones that can only be classified into large and medium mammal groupings is high (68%).

The bones were scanned for interesting finds and assessed in terms of overall species frequency and skeletal element representation but are not further considered in the discussion. A range of species are present, dominated, as might be expected, by the major livestock animals. Cattle and sheep are the dominant species, accounting for 44% and 40% respectively of the identified livestock remains. Pigs are the least well represented of the main livestock animals, accounting for just 13% of the identified specimens. A pit (F83) in the south-east corner of Trench 5 contained a mixture of modern and medieval finds, and the 72 recovered animal bones consist entirely of domestic livestock remains, including adult individuals as well as a piglet and a lamb. A cultivation furrow (F67) contained 23 animal bones, most of which cannot be identified to species. Cattle are the only identified species and a modern saw mark on a rib fragment confirms the recent origin of this bone sample. A total of 295 animal bones were recovered from a modern trench or gully (F70) extending the width of Trench 4; most of these are eroded and abraded and some show traces of gnawing. Cattle and sheep are the most frequent animals, followed by almost equal numbers of pigs and rabbits, along with relatively numerous fish and bird bones. Other species include dog and rabbit, along with the remains of chicken, geese and duck.

In general, faunal material from the last phase of activity at Swords Castle is modern in date and merits little comment aside from establishing the expected dominance of cattle, sheep and pigs, along with rabbits, dogs, horses, domestic fowl, geese and possibly duck, as well as fish resources. What is interesting is that all parts of the skeleton are represented, suggesting local slaughter and dismemberment of these animals during the most recent phase of agricultural activity in the castle grounds.

Palaeopathology

The bones were carefully examined for skeletal abnormalities but it would seem that the majority of the assemblage represents healthy animals, as just three examples of palaeopathological lesions were recorded. It should be pointed out, however, that only a few diseases commonly affect bone, most commonly injuries associated with trauma and stress. The three anomalies from Swords Castle are characteristic of degenerative joint disease, perhaps as a result of trauma and stress. The partial remains of a pig recovered from a post-medieval pit (F69) were affected by some form of degenerative joint disease, which included a grossly distorted tibia as well as severe lipping around the thoracic vertebrae and pitting of the centrum. This may be associated with advanced age and possible arthritis. A cow first phalanx from one of the medieval layers (F77) was splayed asymmetrically and exhibited bony growths and slight eburnation (polishing) of the joint surface caused by cartilage destruction between articulating bones, which results in joint surfaces abrading each other. Ploughing and the pulling of heavy carts can cause excessive stress and strain to the lower leg joints, and the example from Swords Castle presumably represents an elderly ox that was used for traction and ploughing before being slaughtered in the latter stage of its working life.

BIRD BONES

A total avian assemblage of 863 bones was recovered, most of which came from normal trench recovery and were widely scattered in small numbers across the site in a variety of different features. The majority of bones are medieval in date; this period alone contributed 734 fragments to the total sample. Considerably smaller quantities of bones were found in the pre-Anglo-Norman deposits, the post-medieval layers and the excavated modern features. The sieved deposits produced some bird bones but the majority of these were too fragmentary to allow positive identification to be made. A few of the smaller passerine bones recovered from the fills of a medieval pit (F43) would not have been retrieved in the absence of sieving.

Some of the bones have been gnawed and one has puncture marks resembling those caused by cat teeth. The list of identified species in Table 14.4 illustrates well the role played by avifauna in the diet of the medieval occupants of the manor. Domestic fowl (*Gallus* sp.) was the most common bird species, contributing 351 bones to a total identifiable sample of 863 fragments. Many of the 242 unidentified fragments are also likely to be of fowl on the basis of their size and morphological features. The majority of the fowl were mature at the time of slaughter, bones being classified as adult or juvenile specimens on the degree of porosity and fusion of the long bones. A total of 39 bones were classified as juvenile and these represented young chickens killed solely for their meat. Three newborn chicken bones were recovered from the fish-bone-rich layer (F43) in Trench 1. Those bones that could be sexed indicated a mix of male and female domestic fowl. A few mature males representing cockerels with spurs were recorded. Birds were also kept in the castle to provide eggs, as evidenced by the presence of medullary bone on five femora. In terms of skeletal representation, large and robust limb bones were the most common while fragile elements such as the skull were underrepresented, as were small peripheral elements such as carpals, tarsals and phalanges. Few fowl bones bore traces of butchery but this is not unusual, as most bird species can be prepared and eaten without leaving any butchery evidence. Two tibio-tarsal bones displayed fine cut-marks on the distal articulation which are associated with the removal of the lower limbs before preparation for cooking.

Table 14.4—Identified bird species.

Domestic birds

Domestic fowl	*Gallus* sp.
Domestic goose	*Anser* sp.
Domestic duck/mallard	*Anas* sp./*Anas platyrhynchos*

Wild ducks

Teal	*Anas crecca*
Widgeon	*Anas penelope*

Waders

Plover	*Pluvialis squatarola*
Woodcock	*Scolopax rusticola*
Snipe	*Gallinago gallinago*
Curlew	*Numenius arquatus*
Greenshank	*Tringa nebularia*
Bar-tailed godwit	*Limosa lapponica*

Gamebirds

Partridge	*Perdix perdix*

Rails and crakes

Water rail	*Rallus aquaticus*

Corncrake	*Crex crex*
Herons	
Grey heron	*Ardea cinera*
Swans	
Mute swan	*Cygnus olor*
Crows/rooks	
Rook/crow	*Corvus frugilegus/Corvus corone*
Jackdaw	*Corvus monedula*
Jay	*Garrulus glandarius*
Starlings	
Starling	*Sturnus vulgaris*
Doves	
Rock dove	*Columba livia*
Passerines	Passiformes sp.

After fowl, domestic goose (*Anser* sp.) bones are the most frequent of the bird remains at 134 fragments. Although not quite as numerous as the fowl, the quantity of meat produced would have been considerably larger, given the size of these birds. Differentiation between domestic goose and its wild ancestor, greylag goose (*Anser anser*), is difficult to determine from archaeological material, as the morphology of the bones is very similar. The occurrence of eleven porous limb bones suggests, however, that the goose remains represent domestic birds that were bred within the grounds of the castle. Geese would have provided valuable commodities such as down and eggs, quills for pens and bones for working, as well as being a rich and abundant source of meat.

Less common are the remains of duck. The problems of distinguishing domestic duck from mallard are similar to those in the case of domestic goose and greylag goose, as the difference in size between the domestic strain and its wild ancestor (*Anas platyrhynchos*) was very small until recent times. Just ten duck bones were recovered, including two bills from a medieval pit (F43) and a medieval layer (F3). The absence of young duck bones, combined with the small sample, suggests that the bones probably originated from wild mallards living in the vicinity of the manor, perhaps even in ornamental ponds within the grounds. Single finds of two small species of wild duck were identified, including teal (*Anas crecca*) from a medieval pit (F43) and widgeon (*Anas penelope*) from a disturbed layer (F106). The teal is Ireland's smallest duck and frequents water marshes, lakeshores, estuaries and sometimes coastal bays. The slightly larger widgeon is an abundant winter visitor to Ireland and can be found on open water, both coastal and lakeshore. Both species make good eating birds and were presumably captured in nearby wetland areas for the table.

A wide variety of other wild birds, both edible and presumed inedible, were identified and can be divided into different species groups, including waders, gamebirds, rails and crakes, swans, herons, doves, corvids, starlings and small perching birds (Table 14.4). The five species of wader include plover, woodcock, snipe, curlew, greenshank and bar-tailed godwit. Of these, woodcock was the most frequent species, represented by 28 bones scattered across nine features, with the largest individual sample coming from a medieval layer (F43). Woodcock bones were also found in a disturbed layer (F119) and in the topsoil layer (F1). This bird is a well-distributed resident in woodlands, scrubland and marshy areas and was presumably captured to be eaten. The remains of snipe are also relatively frequent (23 examples) and were found scattered across eight features, with the largest quantities being found in pit F43 and layer F3. Snipe is one of Ireland's best-known wading birds and is usually found in marshes and bogs, and occasionally in open mud-flats. Curlew, a widespread resident wader, is found throughout Ireland and is a heavy winter immigrant. The species is represented by five bones: one from the topsoil layer (F1), three from medieval features (F39, F74 and F144) and one from a post-medieval layer (F117). The other two wading species identified, greenshank and bar-tailed godwit, are represented by just a few bones from two medieval layers (F74 and F77). Greenshank is a regular winter visitor from northern Europe and is only found in small numbers during the summer months. Bar-tailed godwit is an abundant winter visitor and is mostly coastal, found on mud-flats and estuaries. It is presumed that all the identified wading species were exploited for their food and captured on hunting and fowling expeditions to nearby areas of marshland and mud-flats.

The only gamebird identified was partridge, represented by two humeri found in an insecure context in upper topsoil layer F1. This species was formerly very widespread in Ireland but is now found only very locally in remote marginal grassland areas. The two species of rails and crakes include water rail, which is a common resident found in dense reed beds and marshes. A coracoid bone identified as water rail was found in a disturbed layer (F118). Two corncrake bones were identified: a humerus found in disturbed layer F119 and a tibiotarsus in a medieval layer (F129). Corncrakes were formerly very widespread in Ireland but modern farming methods led to its demise in many areas of the country and its distinctive call is rarely heard today. It would have been a relatively common bird in north Leinster during the medieval period, found mostly in grassy fields and agricultural areas, and occasionally in sand-dunes and coastal islands.

Other bird species identified which may have been kept in the grounds of the manor include dove, swan and heron. A total of nine dove bones were found in three excavated features: the topsoil layer (F1), a disturbed layer (F106) and a sixteenth-century layer (F125). The bones make a good match with rock dove (*Columba livia*), the wild ancestor of domestic pigeon. Ecclesiastical sites always had dovecotes and these birds would have been kept not only as a readily abundant source of food but also for the provision of rich manure for arable land. Heron and swan were also present in the assemblage. The proximal half of a tarso-metatarsus from an adult heron was found in a medieval layer (F39). Six swan bones were identified; two phalanges were found in post-medieval layer F3 and a portion of a humerus in medieval layer F74. An additional three phalanges were recovered from disturbed layers (F112 and F118). Commensal species present include three species of crow: rook, jay and jackdaw. All are common and widespread and would have lived in and around the grounds of the manor, scavenging on discarded food remains. The bones were found scattered mostly across medieval layers, and the smaller jay was found in the fill of medieval pit F43.

There was no evidence for the presence of raptors, which might have been expected given the high social rank of the occupants of the manor. It is likely that falconry was practised, however, as the skeletal remains of a sparrowhawk were found during previous test excavation near the Archbishop's Apartments (C. Baker, pers. comm.). The ownership and display of birds of prey were paramount in terms of prestige and wealth during the medieval period and there was a recognised hierarchy of species, with the peregrine falcon at the top and goshawk and sparrowhawk closer to the bottom (Creighton 2009).

FISH BONES

A relatively large number of fish bones were recovered from various layers and deposits across the site. They almost certainly represent general domestic refuse and demonstrate the range of fish supplied to the castle. The total assemblage amounted to 827 bones, of which 446 were identifiable to species. Many, in particular the remains of smaller fish species such as herring, were recovered from sieved soil samples, but fish bones, in particular the larger skull bones, were also collected by hand. In general, preservation was poor and the remains were mostly flaky, fragile and incomplete. The densest concentration of fish bones was in the medieval layers and dump deposits, but layer F43 in Trench 1 merits special mention in that it contained the largest quantity of fish bones, including clumps of fin rays, spines and scales associated with the preparation of fish prior to cooking. An area of fish-gutting activity to the north of the medieval wall F14 was dated to AD 1298–1373. Over half of the fish bones represented small skull fragments, fin rays and branchiostegals which were not identified to species. The fish fauna represented are all marine species and the identified component consisted mainly of large marine Gadidae, the cod family. Of these, cod (*Gadus morhua*) dominated with 125 bones, hake (*Merluccius merluccius*) was second with 28, haddock (*Melanogrammus aeglefinus*) third with eighteen, ling (*Molva molva*) fourth with ten and pollack (*Pollachius pollachius*) last with seven. The dominance of cod is typical of medieval and post-medieval assemblages and these fish were widely consumed across Europe as fresh and as dried and salted fish (stockfish). There were many fragments (171) that were too fragmented or non-diagnostic for species determination but are likely to be of the gadid family. A smaller member of the gadid family, whiting (*Merlangius merlangus*), was also recorded. Anatomical distribution was uneven and clearly biased in favour of the more resilient skull elements. The best-represented head bones were articular, quadrate, cleithrum and vomer, and vertebrae were also very numerous. Haddock was represented almost entirely by the hyperosted cleithra, which are often the only elements recovered for this fish. Butchery marks were noted on four bones; a cod cleithrum was chopped through during beheading, and three vertebrae with lateral cuts indicated the filleting of fish. The cod and ling remains represented large fish (>1m), indicating sophisticated fisheries that exploited deep-water marine species.

Remains of other taxa were infrequent but of a wide range; they include conger eel (*Conger* sp.), possible red sea bream (*Pagellus bogareveo*), gurnard (*Aspitrigla* sp.), plaice/flounder (*Pleuronectes platessa/Platichthys flesus*) and herring (*Clupea harengus*). Gurnard was identified from its distinctive opercular bones and spines. The smaller taxa such as gurnards and breams are more likely to have been captured in the summer months and are also more likely to have been eaten fresh. Conger eel was found in a number of deposits and is a relatively common fish species in medieval urban assemblages.

DISCUSSION

Animal bone is the most common organic material from the excavations at Swords Castle and it was found spread across all areas of the site. There was continuous activity on site between the tenth and nineteenth centuries, and the animal bone collections represent episodes of domestic refuse dumping over almost nine centuries. The bones accumulated mostly in successive layers of organic soil and dump deposits in and around the manor buildings. Faunal material was also found in more localised deposits, in pits, in a medieval kiln, in wall foundations and in general occupation surfaces. The use of the castle grounds in the eighteenth and nineteenth centuries for horticultural activity and as an orchard appears to have resulted in extensive disturbance and reworking of the earlier faunal assemblages. The results from the four main chronological periods represented cannot profitably be broken down to reveal changes in diet and animal husbandry, as the material was mostly recovered from extensive layers that accumulated during the medieval period, which spanned a considerable period of time from the early thirteenth century to the sixteenth century. Little can be said about the sample that was dated to the pre-Anglo-Norman phase of activity, as the quantities involved are considerably smaller than for any other period. The amount of bone from post-medieval features also suffers from smallness of size and therefore possible changes in stock improvement and animal husbandry practices between the two periods could not be meaningfully investigated. Overall, the species present do not differ radically between periods and, as might be expected, the major domesticates are the most common taxa, with cattle dominating all phases. The pattern of cut-marks and the general method of bone disposal show that the bulk of the remains come from food waste. Small changes can be seen between the medieval and post-medieval phases in terms of species representation, in particular the apparent fall in the proportion of rabbit in the post-medieval period. The domestic species represented are those which would be expected on almost any site of the periods in question, and the only species not represented which might have been expected in a high-status episcopal manor is deer. It is clear that, for all periods represented, meat supply to the manor was mostly provided by cattle and sheep, and the presence of butchery marks on a high proportion of the bones indicates that the material derives from primary slaughter and butchery to food preparation and consumption. In interpreting the results, it is taken into account that the faunal remains are mostly from the medieval period, when the site was an episcopal manor possessing large tracts of agricultural land as part of its demesne. It is this land that would have provided the bulk of the meat resources for the manor kitchen. There is no suggestion of any organised outside meat provisioning, and the presence of all body parts suggests the procurement of animals on the hoof and their slaughter within the precinct of the manor. Skeletal element representation shows an almost equal presence of household/kitchen refuse and butchery waste, with a lower proportion of meat-bearing elements in the post-medieval period being attributed to the possible redistribution of meat joints around the town. Cattle are generally the most frequently represented animals throughout the samples, followed by a relatively high proportion of sheep and considerably smaller amounts of pig. Calculation of minimum numbers of individuals show that sheep were of considerable importance in the local economy and, while beef would always have constituted the greater part of the meat diet, mutton and lamb were also significant food items. Sheep were also a valuable source of wool for the thriving medieval woollen industry. Pigs are relatively scarce throughout, although there is evidence that these animals were reared in the castle and that suckling pig was occasionally consumed. The relatively small proportion of pig bones is an indicator that meat production was by no means the only aim of local animal husbandry practices at this time. Both quantification techniques clearly indicate the importance of sheep, suggesting that during the medieval period the local husbandry system shifted its emphasis towards the rearing of these animals in response to an increasing European demand for wool.

The range of other mammalian taxa is extremely limited. Horse, dog and cat are present and, while not in any great quantity, in sufficient numbers to demonstrate that these animals were kept within the grounds of the manor during the medieval period. There is no evidence for horse or cat in the post-medieval deposits. In common with contemporary urban sites (McCarthy 2003a), horse bones are generally rare and all are from older individuals who probably gave many years of service before death. The low proportion of horse supports the notion that their meat was not regularly consumed. A few individuals were probably kept in and around the manor grounds and, to judge by their size, were small, ideal for riding and pack animals. A wide range of dogs are represented for the two main periods of occupation and the sizes vary from small through medium to large, the latter certainly suitable for hunting purposes, despite there being no evidence for deer in the assemblage. The wild bird fauna does show a wide range of wading species, however, which would seem to have been exploited for the table, and some of the medium-sized dogs, similar to modern springer spaniels and beagles, may have been used in the capture of wild birds. Dogs may also have been used for catching rabbits in the warrens. The largest dog is comparable in size to a modern Alsatian, which would have made a very effective guard dog as well as being a status symbol around the grounds to be admired by guests. Not all dogs may have been regarded as functional animals by the élite classes, and a small terrier-sized individual probably represents a genuine pet that was kept indoors by the occupants of the manor house.

The wild component consists entirely of rabbits, and the age profiles of the animals suggest that they may have been semi-domesticated, reared in warrens within the grounds of the manor. Rabbits seem to have been a particularly favoured delicacy of the archbishop and his retinue at Swords Castle. These animals were introduced into Ireland by the Anglo-Normans in the thirteenth century as prestige food items for the very wealthy in society (Williamson 2006). In Britain they were introduced as domesticated or semi-domesticated animals and were kept in small enclosures or warrens close to castles, monasteries or manor houses (Bailey 1988). The management of the animals was tightly controlled by powerful ecclesiastical and secular landlords, and live rabbits were bestowed as high-status gifts to others of rank setting up warrens (Creighton 2009). Rabbits were sometimes required at the table in outrageous quantities: there is a reference to a warren within the deerpark at Lopham in Norfolk providing 300 rabbits for the Countess of Norfolk's table in 1386. The fur of rabbits was also highly regarded and was commercially produced and marketed through effective management of warrens, many in the control of ecclesiastical landlords (*ibid.*). In Britain, warrens were considered as much a status-symbol as dovecotes and fishponds and were prominently displayed to be viewed by visitors as they approached the manor (Williamson 2006). Rabbits also featured prominently in medieval Christian theology and were seen to signify mankind and its salvation through Christ and the Church (Stocker and Stocker 1996). By the sixteenth century, the species that originated in southern Spain had adapted to the colder climate of northern Europe and become more widespread, as they burrowed and made their escape from the confines of warrens. After the Black Death in the late fourteenth century arable cultivation declined; with the growing demand for meat, commercial rabbit-rearing increased and rabbit gradually ceased to be viewed as a prestige foodstuff (Costello 2015). This may in part account for their decreasing numbers in the post-medieval period in Swords Castle. As late as the mid-nineteenth century the German writer Kohl noted that all the Irish estates had rabbit warrens, and there is a reference to the park at Howth Castle in 1699 having 'great stores of conies and very good fowling' (*ibid.*).

The Anglo-Normans were also responsible for the importation into Ireland of fallow deer (*Dama dama*), and high-status sites such as castles and episcopal manors enclosed vast tracts of land as game parks, where they managed and hunted red and fallow deer, wild boar, rabbits, hares and badgers (Beglane 2015b). Many British parks were located adjacent to the castle or manor house of large secular and ecclesiastical estates (Costello 2015). In Ireland, the Anglo-Normans used the emparkment of land to exert their authority over the native Irish, and the majority of the parks were located in the east and south-east of the country. Deerparks played an important role in demonstrating wealth, prestige and power, and venison consumption was confined solely to those of high rank (Malloy *et al.* 2013). The few postcranial bones found on urban sites are often attributed to the activities of poachers (Birrell 1992). During the earlier part of the medieval period, agricultural land was laid out in long strips for arable cultivation, and this open-field agricultural system survived in the archiepiscopal lands north of Dublin into the nineteenth century. Generally, there was a greater tendency in Ireland to make enclosed fields by the fifteenth century, and there are also many references to parks and enclosures (Otway-Ruthven 1951). A reference in a deed for lands at Malahide Castle in 1495 refers to a Thomas Balle being leased 'four acres more or less of tilling land to make a park' (*ibid.*). While the primary function of the deerparks was to enclose deer for hunting, the parks were also used for grazing cattle and sheep, as well as for woodland management and the procurement of firewood for the estates' large residential homes. In this respect, the absence of both red deer and fallow deer in the Swords Castle assemblage is noteworthy, as the hunting of deer and the consumption of venison are indicators of high status and generally tend to be found in relatively larger numbers at higher-status sites. Neither was wild boar established amongst the remains and it would appear that the residents of the manor were fed overwhelmingly with the results of animal husbandry from their own demesne lands.

The presence of fish and birds also highlights the domestic content of the assemblage, and these faunal groups would have supplemented the standard foodstuffs acquired through livestock farming. Domestic fowl and geese were the most common avian species and would have provided variety to the diet. Meat from immature fowl was consumed and a number of hens were raised for eggs, as suggested by the presence of medullary bone, a calcium substance laid down within long bones. Domestic geese were kept not just for meat but also as necessary providers of eggs and down, and to a lesser extent perhaps for quills. In contrast to the mammalian fauna, the wide range of bird species is suggestive of a high-status site, with evidence for numerous species of wader, gamebirds, herons, swans and doves. Doves were probably semi-domesticated and would have been encouraged to roost in dovecotes within the precinct of the manor, where they could nest and breed. Swans are present in a number of the medieval features and may have been kept in ornamental ponds on the grounds of the manor. Doves were introduced into the manorialised landscape of eastern and south-eastern Ireland by Anglo-Norman landlords (Creighton 2009). Documentary sources indicate that dovecotes were constructed in abundance in élite residences but very few survive and none have been excavated (*ibid.*). Monastic accounts show that there were several dovecotes within the grounds of abbeys and priories, and the best surviving dovecotes in Ireland are at the Augustinian priory in Ballybeg near Buttevant, Co. Cork, and the Cistercian abbey at Kilcooly, Co. Tipperary. A dovecote within a deerpark at Dunganstown, Co. Wicklow, is mentioned in an inquisition of 1333 (*ibid.*). In Britain the right to build dovecotes was a privilege of lordship, and prior to the seventeenth century these structures are found exclusively at high-status secular and ecclesiastical sites (*ibid.*). Doves were useful providers of rich manure for fertilising arable fields and as prolific breeders that provided a constant source of food for the table. Doves, swans and herons were all regarded as prestige display items to be brought to the feasting table to impress guests. Cranes and herons, because of their physical appearance, were used as centre-pieces on the banqueting table. The range of birds identified at Swords Castle is wider than at contemporary urban sites (McCarthy 2003a), which is suggestive of a socially élite community which perhaps had greater wealth than others. The presentation to the table of species such as partridge, teal, woodcock, snipe, heron and swan would certainly have impressed guests being entertained at the manor. In 1630, the Earl of Strafford found partridge so scarce around Dublin that he had to take to hawking blackbirds (Creighton 2009). Manorial records from English manor houses record that wild birds formed an important part of the diet and that they were encouraged to nest and breed in the parks next to the large residential buildings (*ibid.*). Despite the absence of raptor bones in the Swords Castle assemblage, it is possible that hawks were used to capture wild fowl and rabbits. Swans are among the other lesser-known exports to Ireland by the Anglo-Normans and they were held in high regard as prestige birds. They were semi-domesticated and would have been kept in swanneries around the precincts of important residences such as Swords Castle. There is a certain element of religious symbolism in the bird assemblage as well, through the presence of swan and dove bones. The dove is regarded as a symbol of peace, and St Columba took his name from the rock dove, *Columba livia*, the presumed ancestor of the domesticated pigeon. Swans played a prominent role in theology as symbols of purity and it is perhaps partly because of this religious association that swanneries are common features in the demesne lands of bishops' palaces (*ibid.*).

Fish appear to have made a relatively small contribution to the diet, despite this being an ecclesiastical site occupied at a time when there were many more fast days than in later centuries. The sample residues produced a moderate-sized assemblage of fish bones which indicated that marine fish resources formed a moderate part of the diet, and there is evidence for the supply of large, deep-water marine species to the manor. It might have been expected in view of the high status of the site that exotic fish species would have been present, but in general species diversity seems to have been quite limited, consisting entirely of common marine fish still caught off the east coast of Ireland. The assemblage is dominated by the bones of large marine species, including hake and several members of the cod family (Gadidae), with a few examples of flatfish and gurnard. Element distribution indicates that fish were landed intact and brought from nearby ports to the manor in a complete state. Fishponds were a common feature on high-status sites in Britain and were stocked with several species of freshwater fish to impress guests at the table. Freshwater fish were only introduced into Ireland on a large scale in the fifteenth and sixteenth centuries and this may partly explain the absence of any freshwater fish in the Swords Castle assemblage. Moreover, the proximity of the castle to the coast and to fishing ports where a regular supply of marine fish would have been landed may explain why there was no necessity for fishponds at the site.

Swords Castle was no doubt self-supporting to a large degree in terms of the provision of meat from both mammals and birds. The occupants of the manor were well provided with a variety of meats from domestic livestock, birds and fish, as well as a wide range of grains, fruit and vegetables. This was a private episcopal manor of high social rank that would have entertained guests of equal standing in society, and there are signs in the meat waste remains of this higher social status. The presence of large numbers of rabbits and a wide range of edible wild bird fauna has already been discussed. In addition, the age pattern of sheep and pigs suggests that a certain number of young lambs and suckling pigs were specifically tailored to the table, for a class of people with greater wealth than their tenant farmers and others living in the vicinity of the manor. The archbishop in residence would have practised a manorial system of farming geared towards animal husbandry and cereal cultivation, not only for immediate supply to the manor's kitchen but also for the marketing of livestock and grain into the expanding medieval and post-medieval town of Dublin not far to the south. While there is no other large corpus of contemporaneous episcopal manor fauna in Ireland, the results can be set against samples from other high-status centres such as monastic sites and castles. The faunal remains share many characteristics not only with urban sites excavated in Waterford, Dublin and Cork but also more generally with other high-status sites, such as the castle assemblages from Roscrea (McCarthy 2003b), Clogh Oughter (McCarthy 2013) and Barryscourt Castle (McCarthy 2017), and monastic sites such as Bective Abbey (Beglane 2016). The bulk of the food eaten at these sites came from a narrow resource base and the diet relied almost exclusively on domestic livestock, with the input from wild fauna, wild birds and fish being very much dependent on the geographical location of the castle or monastery. For all sites, the scarcity of pig bones seems to reflect the emphasis that was put on the economic value of cattle and sheep during the medieval and post-medieval periods, linked to the increased export of hides and wool from various Irish ports to Britain and Europe. There is consistent evidence for large-scale processing of cattle carcasses on high-status sites, which is convincing evidence of the prominent role of cattle in the supply of meat. The lands surrounding Swords Castle would have supported large herds of cattle that would have enabled the manor to have been mostly self-sufficient, feeding its permanent occupants and its guests on meat raised on the farm. There is no question that beef was by far the most common source of meat at Swords Castle in terms of volume of bone. Despite the absence of expected exotic foodstuffs such as red and fallow deer and freshwater fish, the recovered bones nevertheless suggest a socially élite class living in the manor, with a higher incidence in the assemblage of young animals reared especially for their table, such as lambs, calves and suckling pigs. The archbishop no doubt provided accommodation for visiting dignitaries who would have enjoyed not only the meat products of the farm but also an impressive range of wild bird fauna. As regards dogs, there are animals of different sizes, with large guard dogs as well as animals of a more medium size that may have been used for hunting and a smaller individual probably kept as a much-loved pet in the manor. Within the manor grounds swans and doves were reared to provide a ready and additional supplement to the larder, as well as perhaps forming centre-pieces at the feasting table. Rabbits were kept in abundance during the medieval period, probably managed in warrens on the grounds of the manor and within sight of the main residence to impress visiting guests, as these animals were then regarded as items of wealth and prestige and were important symbols of lordship. The religious link to rabbits, doves and swans is also of interest given that Swords Castle and its demesne lands were controlled by ecclesiastical landlords. A manorial system of farming directed towards animal husbandry and cereal cultivation was practised and, while a certain proportion of the produce from the land made its way into the manor's kitchen, the marketing of domestic livestock into the expanding medieval town of Dublin would also have influenced animal husbandry strategies.

Bone measurements

Table 14.5—Cattle bone measurements.

Element	Measurement	No.	Mean	Minimum	Maximum	SD*	CV*
Humerus	Bd	6	71.3	66.8	74.6	2.3	0.03
Humerus	BT	6	67.6	64.5	71.5	2.4	0.04
Radius	Bp	1	73.7	—	—	—	—
Radius	BFp	1	68.3	—	—	—	—
Radius	GL	1	38.9	—	—	—	—
Radius	Bd	3	66.5	64.3	69.7	—	—
Radius	BFd	3	62.8	58.6	66.3	—	—
Tibia	Bd	6	54.4	51	57.4	2.5	0.05
Tibia	Dd	6	40.9	37.4	45.3	2.8	0.07
Metacarpus	Bp	5	51.5	49.5	53.8	1.6	0.03
Metacarpus	Dp	5	34.1	30.2	39.9	3.9	0.11
Metacarpus	SD	1	25	—	—	—	—
Metacarpus	Bd	2	49	48.9	49.2	—	—
Metacarpus	Dd	2	29.4	27.9	30.8	—	—
Metacarpus	MDw	2	46.6	46.3	47	—	—
Metacarpus	GL	1	195.4	—	—	—	—
Metatarsal	Bp	8	42	40.1	44.1	1.3	0.03
Metatarsal	Dp	8	39.4	31.5	42.4	3.5	0.09
Metatarsal	SD	1	25	—	—	—	—
Metatarsal	Bd	7	51	47.5	55.5	2.5	0.05
Metatarsal	Dd	7	28.4	25.8	31.1	1.8	0.06
Metatarsal	MDw	5	46.3	42.9	48.4	1.9	0.04
Metatarsal	GL	1	220.5	—	—	—	—
Astragalus	GLl	11	57.4	42.1	66.1	5.9	0.1
Astragalus	Glm	11	52	40.6	55.9	4	0.08
Calcaneum	GL	5	105.2	104.3	107.1	1	0.01

SD* = standard deviation; CV* = co-efficient of variation.

Table 14.6—Pig bone measurements.

Element	Measurement	No.	Mean	Minimum	Maximum	SD*	CV*
Radius	Bp	14	26.6	23.4	29.3	1.6	0.06
Radius	Dp	14	17.4	14.4	19.2	1.4	0.08
Astragalus	GLl	3	38.4	36.1	40.9	—	—
Astragalus	GLm	3	36	32.6	40.1	—	—
SD* = standard deviation; CV* = co-efficient of variation.							

Table 14.7—Sheep/goat bone measurements.

Element	Measurement	No.	Mean	Minimum	Maximum	SD*	CV*
Humerus	Bd	28	27.1	21.3	30.9	2.2	0.08
Humerus	BT	28	25.4	15.1	29.1	2.7	0.11
Radius	Bp	11	28.3	26.3	30.4	1.5	0.05
Radius	BFP	11	25.6	23.3	28.4	1.7	0.07
Radius	Dp	11	14.1	12.3	15.9	1.1	0.08
Radius	Bd	8	25.2	23.1	27.9	1.3	0.05
Radius	BFD	8	22.7	21.1	25.1	1.4	0.06
Radius	Dd	8	17	15.2	19.2	1.4	0.08
Radius	GL	2	131.7	131.3	132.1	—	—
Tibia	Bd	23	24.2	20.1	26.1	1.4	0.06
Tibia	BFd	23	17.4	10.4	19.9	2.3	0.13
Calcaneum	GL	3	52.6	48.3	55.9	—	—
Astragalus	GLl	7	26.7	23.8	35.5	3.7	0.14
Astragalus	GLm	7	25.4	21.8	34.3	3.8	0.15
SD* = standard deviation; CV* = co-efficient of variation.							

15

Molluscs

Dr Ruth Carden, Ph.D, AIAI

INTRODUCTION

This report details the molluscan faunal remains recovered during three years of archaeological excavations (E4619) at Swords Castle, Co. Dublin (2015–17). Eighteen different molluscan species were identified, and were grouped together within five different archaeological periods. Marine gastropods dominated the early medieval assemblage relative to the marine bivalve species (71.4% and 29% respectively), whereas the marine bivalves dominated the medieval (59.4%) and post-medieval features (51.8%) relative to the marine gastropods (33.6% and 44.4% respectively for medieval and post-medieval features).

There is a lack of comparative archaeological molluscan assemblages outside of prehistoric shell middens in Ireland. The excavation and collection methods used on the site at Swords Castle therefore break new ground in redressing the lack of available molluscan material in the medieval and post-medieval periods.

METHODS

Throughout this report the vernacular names for the molluscs have been used. The Latin genus and species names have been provided in Table 15.1; these are the accepted marine species' names as designated by the World Register of Marine Species (WoRMS; www.marinespecies.org) and the terrestrial species' names as designated by the National Biodiversity Data Centre (www.biodiversityireland.ie).

The archaeological periods that were associated with features from which molluscan species were recovered were derived from a layout suggested by Christine Baker, Community Archaeologist, Fingal County Council, along with the radiocarbon dating data and three preliminary reports by Christine Baker (2016; 2017; 2018). Features were grouped into five different archaeological periods: early medieval, medieval, post-medieval, post-medieval/modern and modern. Four additional categories of features were identified: disturbed layers, topsoil, Pit A and Pit B.

The majority of the mollusc shells recovered from features were dry-sieved under the advice of Dr Meriel McClatchie, School of Archaeology, UCD. The excavated material from F19, Trench 2, was wet-sieved (retent from sample 5) and 105 countable shells (239.3g) were recovered, along with smaller uncountable fragments with a weight of 19.8g.

Highly fragmentary gastropods were counted by the number of columellae found (mainly for common whelks), but for the majority of the taxa shells were nearly complete and counted. Bivalves were counted by the number of umbones or hinges, with the addition of the adductor muscle scar in particular for European flat oyster shells. Left and right bivalve shells were counted for each bivalve species and MNI was calculated using the greater number of either left or right halves. Where a context contained only fragments (>3mm) of non-countable material, the taxa were recorded by bulk weight but not counted.

RESULTS AND DISCUSSION

Overview

A total of 2,783 (shell weight 19.97kg) countable molluscs from nineteen different species were recorded within this assemblage, along with a further 21 (7.3g) unidentified gastropod terrestrial partial remains consisting mainly of banded snails (difficult to identify and generally not eaten) and 1.9kg of small-sized (<3mm) uncountable fragmented remains. After accounting for left and right bivalves, bivalve species dominated the entire assemblage (58.5%) and nine marine species were recorded, whereas two terrestrial and eight marine gastropod species were recorded and represented 41.5% of the entire assemblage.

Feature F1 was topsoil and was identified as highly disturbed owing to gardening and agricultural activities and the presence of an orchard on site. The findings from F1 were summarised in their own section.

The distribution of the recorded species is presented in Table 15.2. Across all periods and categories, common cockle and the European flat oyster dominated the assemblage at 27% and 26.1% MNI respectively, followed by the common periwinkle (21.4% MNI). These species are edible marine molluscs, found on rocky and sandy seashores and intertidal zones.

Table 15.1—List of the vernacular and Latin names of the gastropod and bivalve species identified at Swords Castle.

Gastropods		Bivalves	
Marine		*Marine*	
Common periwinkle	*Littorina littorea*	Blue mussel	*Mytilus edulis*
Flat periwinkle	*Littorina obtusata*	Blunt tellin	*Arcopagia crassa*
Rough periwinkle	*Littorina saxatillis*	Common cockle	*Cerastoderma edule*
Needle shell	*Bittium reticulatum*	European flat oyster	*Ostrea edulis*
Common whelk	*Buccinum undatum*	Grooved carpet shell	*Ruditapes decussatus*
Dog whelk	*Nucella lapillus*	Iceland cyprina	*Arctica islandica*
Netted dog whelk	*Tritia reticulata*	King scallop	*Pectin maximus*
Common limpet	*Patella vulgata*	Razor shell	*Ensis* sp.
		Saddle oyster	*Anomia ephippium*
Terrestrial			
Garden snail	*Cornu aspersum*		
Grove snail	*Cepaea nemoralis*		

Table 15.2—Distribution of the identified shellfish from Swords Castle across all periods and categories. L = left valve; R = right valve; E. Medieval = early medieval; P.Med./Modern = post-medieval/modern.

	E. Medieval	Medieval	Post-Medieval	P. Med/Modern	Modern	Pit A	Pit B	Topsoil	Disturbed layers	Total MNI	% MNI
Bivalves											
Blue mussel		50R 51L	4R 4L			2R 5L		1R 1L	9R 12L	73	4.0
Blunt tellin		3R 3L	1R 3L					1L	1R	8	0.4
Common cockle	9R 10L	280R 294L	96R 92L	1R 3L	4R 7L	14R 19L		13R 21L	42R 37L	492	27.0
European flat oyster	11R 17L	279R 327L	30R 52L	3R 7L	6R 8L	7R 5L	3R 1L	14R 17L	46R 40L	484	26.1
Grooved carpet shell		2R	2R 1L					2L	2L	8	0.4
Iceland cyprina								1L		1	0.1
King scallop			1L					2L		3	0.2
Saddle oyster		3R 2L	1L							4	0.2
Razor shell		6R 7L	1R 2L						3L	12	0.6
Gastropods											
Common periwinkle	54	225	71	4	2	8	2	24	7	397	21.4
Rough periwinkle	7	53	15		2			8		85	4.6
Flat periwinkle	9	70	44	2	3			26	3	157	8.5
Common whelk		34	5			2		2	14	57	3.1
Dog whelk		1	2					1		4	0.2
Netted dog whelk								1		1	0.1
Common limpet		4	1							5	0.3
Needle shell		1							1	2	0.1
Garden snail		22	10	2	1	3		3	14	55	3.0
Grove snail		4	2	2						8	0.4
Total MNI	97	1101	311	20	23	44	5	110	145	1856	

Early medieval

Five features were recorded as early medieval: F85, F88, F93, F97 and F101. A total of 70 countable molluscs were identified from these features. The marine gastropod taxa dominated (71.4%), while bivalves constituted 29% of the material from this archaeological period (Table 15.2). Overall, the shell remains were largely intact and preserved, suggesting that these areas were their primary disposal location. No organisms (e.g. sponge boring holes, traces of marine polychaete worms etc.) that affect the external shell morphology were recorded.

The common periwinkle dominated, with 54 individuals recorded. Other periwinkles were also recorded but in much smaller numbers: flat periwinkle (nine individuals) and rough periwinkle (seven individuals). All periwinkle species recorded are edible and occur ubiquitously on rocky shorelines of Ireland. The smaller flat periwinkle adheres to seaweeds on the shoreline and may have been brought to the site while attached to seaweed or along with the other species.

Deliberate breakages were recorded on the aperture shell in eighteen of the common periwinkles and four each of the rough and flat periwinkles recovered. This activity is associated with the forceful removal of the animal from its shell with a hand tool, thereby indicating that these species were collected/transported from the rocky shoreline and eaten by the people inhabiting Swords Castle.

The MNI for the bivalves totalled ten common cockles (F85, F93, F97) and seventeen European flat oysters (F85, F88, F93, F97, F101). As in the case of the gastropods, deliberate breakages of certain sections of the lateral margins of the bivalves were recorded; of the ten left common cockle bivalves recorded in this period, seven displayed such damage. The common cockle is a widespread species of marine clam. Cockles bury themselves in the sand and soft sediment in 'beds'. Raking the beds is an effective way of collecting cockles. The shell, consisting of a left and a right bivalve, can be prised open with a suitable tool such as a short knife, and the flesh scooped out with a blunt knife or similar implement. The common cockle reaches adult stages at 18+ months of age and a length of approximately 15–20mm. The length measurements recorded within this assemblage for the early medieval period range from 26mm to 32mm and are of good sizes for harvesting.

The European flat oyster inhabits the lower intertidal area of the sea foreshore and sublittoral areas down to 30m. They grow on a range of substrates (sandy mud to fine gravel) and occupy 'oyster beds'. Beds can be raked and tilled to ensure the removal of silt and create suitable substrates (cultch) for the attachment of the juvenile stages. The growth rate is slow and over-harvesting may affect long-term future stocks. The recorded oyster shells were of a reasonable 'market' size, typically 63–90mm in length and 70–105mm in width in this assemblage (market sizes are 62–64mm+ in width; Stroud, n.d.). The recorded sizes are indicative of 3–7-year-old oysters.

V-shaped damage and lateral damage to the ventral and lateral margins of the European flat oyster shells were recorded on six of the seventeen individuals. This indicates that these edible species were opened using a small knife or similar tool, resulting in the shell damage observed, and contributed to the overall diet of the people inhabiting the castle and immediate area.

Shellfish dietary contribution
The estimated meat and calorific contributions by shellfish to the diet of people at Swords Castle (after Evans and Spencer 1976–7; Winder 1980) are presented in Table 15.3. Results indicate that the combined shellfish return in terms of calories within the early medieval diet at Swords Castle was quite minimal, considering that approximately 2,700 calories are required daily per adult male (Evans and Spencer 1976–7). Shellfish were not an important part of the early medieval diet at this site. In particular, the small numbers of oysters would have been an expensive luxury collected and brought in from the coast to the castle residents.

Table 15.3—Estimated meat and calorific shellfish returns at Swords Castle for the early medieval period.

Taxa	Average meat weight per shellfish (g)	No. in sample	Estimated meat weight (g)
Periwinkle	1.01	70	70.7
Cockle	1.73	10	17.3
Oyster	7.5	17	127.5

0.22kg = 143 calories

Medieval

Fifty-four medieval features contained fourteen marine and two terrestrial molluscan species. A total of 1,101 countable molluscs, with a weight of 13.1kg, were identified from these features. Overall, the shell remains were largely intact and preserved, suggesting that these areas were their primary disposal location. The bivalve species dominated the medieval features, accounting for 59.4% of the total.

Bivalve taxa, namely blunt tellin, grooved carpet shell, saddle oyster and razor shell, were infrequent finds and probably represent species brought in as by-catch with the more dominant bivalve species present in the assemblage (common cockle, European flat oyster and blue mussel). Blunt tellin, grooved carpet shell and razors all inhabit sandy soft sediments, as does the common cockle. Saddle oysters require a substrate to attach to, similar to the European flat oyster.

Marine gastropods contribute 33.6% of the countable molluscans in these medieval features. The predominant taxa identified include the edible winkles (common periwinkle, rough periwinkle and flat periwinkle) and the common whelk. Just one dog whelk shell was found (F84), one needle shell (F74) and four common limpets (F77 and F84). These taxa appear to be by-catch, probably collected on the rocky seashore along with other rocky/intertidal species.

Two species of terrestrial gastropods were identified—the common garden snail and the grove snail. These are not usually considered edible species and were likely buried with the features' deposits.

Table 15.4—Summary of the taxa identified from the medieval features and MNI (R = right, L = left).

Taxa	R valve	L valve	Gastropod	Total MNI	%MNI*
Bivalves				**687**	**59.4**
Blue mussel	50	51		51	4.4
Blunt tellin	3	3		3	0.3
Common cockle	280	294		294	25.4
European flat oyster	279	327		327	28.3
Grooved carpet shell	2			2	0.2
Saddle oyster	3	2		3	0.3
Razor shell	6	7		7	0.6
Marine gastropods				**388**	**33.6**
Common periwinkle			225	225	19.5
Rough periwinkle			53	53	4.6
Flat periwinkle			70	70	6.1
Common whelk			34	34	2.9
Dog whelk			1	1	0.1
Needle shell			1	1	0.1
Common limpet			4	4	0.3
Terrestrial gastropods				**26**	**2.2**
Garden snail			22	22	1.9
Grove snail			4	4	0.3
Total MNI	742	414		1156	

*of medieval assemblage

A number of shells were affected by various organisms—e.g. sponge boring holes, traces of marine polychaete worms (*Polydora* sp.) etc.—that cause damage to the external shell morphology (Table 15.5). A total of 91 shells displayed evidence of damage—a relatively small number given the size of the assemblage from the medieval features, which overall were generally healthy and edible. Very few boring holes caused by the carnivorous common whelk species were recorded, on the European flat oyster, common periwinkle and common cockle shells.

Bivalves

After accounting for numbers of left and right valves, the bivalve taxa (64.2%) dominated the medieval features relative to the gastropod taxa (33.6% marine, 2.2% terrestrial) (Tables 15.2 and 15.4). The most frequent bivalve taxa recorded were the European flat oyster (*n* = 327), the common cockle (*n* = 294) and the blue mussel (*n* = 51). The majority of the European flat oysters were found in F3 (*n* = 27), F77 (*n* = 24) and F71 (*n* = 21), with fewer found in the other features. The common cockles were found in F19 (*n* = 50), F146 (*n* = 39), F3 (*n* = 28), F77 (*n* = 28), F13 (*n* = 15) and F146.2 (*n* = 15). Further features contained more infrequent numbers of common cockles. Most of the blue mussels were found in F3 (*n* = 18), nine in F37 and seven in F126, with fewer infrequent finds in nineteen other features.

Table 15.5—Incidences of marine organisms negatively affecting the recorded shells of marine molluscan taxa in the medieval features.

Taxa	Carnivorous boring holes	*Polydora hoplura*	*Polydura ciliata*	Calcareous tube worms (*Pomatoceros triqueter*)	Barnacles on exterior	Sponge holes (*Cliona celata*)	Total
Bivalves							*76*
Common cockle	1						1
European flat oyster	3	34	5	21	3	9	75
Marine gastropods							*15*
Common periwinkle	3	5	2				10
Rough periwinkle		2					2
Common whelk				3			3
Total	**7**	**41**	**7**	**24**	**3**	**9**	**91**

Shell damage associated with the deliberate opening of valves

Other damage recorded on the shells of the common cockle and European flat oyster was associated with the deliberate opening or separation of the left and right valves to get at the meaty flesh within the shell. The blue mussel shells were too fragmentary to discern such damage.

Three types of damage marks were recorded from the cockle and oyster shells: (1) a V-shaped notch on the ventral or lateral edges, (ii) a W-shaped notch on ventral and/or lateral edges, and (iii) a lateral or ventral straight-line break. These types of notches and damage were not mutually exclusive of each other. A short knife is traditionally used to open oysters and cockles and this can leave tell-tale nicks (breakages) in the shells. Both V-shaped and lateral/ventral line damage types were recorded from 150 common cockle shells, indicating that these shells were forcefully opened with a suitable tool.

Damage associated with deliberate opening using a suitable tool such as a short knife was more frequently recorded from the European flat oyster shells, 197 of which displayed V-shaped and/or W-shaped notches and the lateral/ventral margins sustained line breakages. Lateral/ventral margin line breakages were the most frequently observed and prevented measurements from being recorded from these valves. The oysters were collected from their beds below the rocky seashore and brought to the castle for exploitation.

Sizes of the common cockle and European flat oyster
The common cockles recorded in the medieval features were greater than 15mm in length and thus represented adult stages. Large cockles were greater than 15mm in length and cockles found in the medieval features were generally large, with a few larger outliers (Fig. 15.1). These larger sizes represented larger modern market cockles (>22mm in length). Their difference in size from the main group may suggest that the outliers were cockles collected from different regions or seabeds, or had undergone abnormal growth owing to various environmental factors. Since the two valves of the European flat oyster are distinctly different to one another—the left is the largest valve and in modern times the meaty flesh is left in this valve for presentation and eating, while the right valve is much flatter and is smaller in overall size—the scatterplots of each of the left and right valve sizes (height by length) were plotted to examine the size ranges of these shells recorded from the medieval features.

Both recorded valve measurements showed good size ranges. The left valve typically ranged from 50mm to 122mm in length. There were a few outliers, which could be a result of abnormal growth associated with overcrowding on the oyster beds or the collection of immature specimens with respect to the smaller-sized oysters. The right valves typically ranged in size from *c.* 30mm to 110mm. Again some outliers were present, some smaller than average and some with larger than average lengths and heights. Market sizes are generally considered to be 62–64mm+ in length, and generally the larger left valves recovered from the medieval

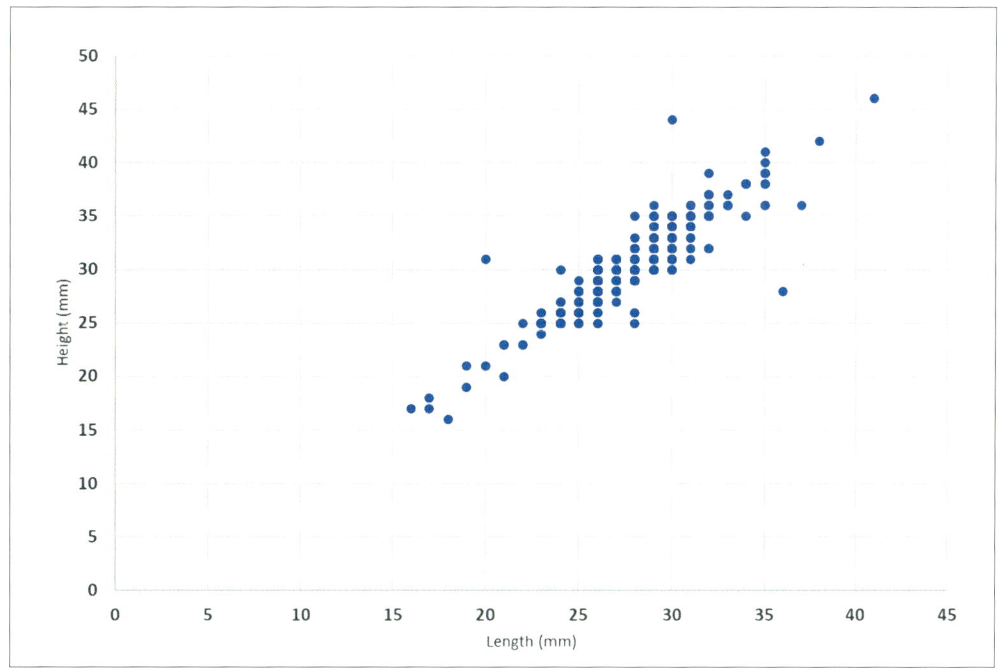

Fig. 15.1—Distribution of common cockle sizes (height by length (mm)) in medieval features.

features were indicative of market sizes and larger. The recorded sizes were indicative of oysters 2–7+ years old. The recorded measurements of the medieval oysters represented the typical ontogenetic growth of oysters rather than large differences in sizes with gaps, as might occur if the oysters were collected from different oyster beds in different geographical areas. It is therefore probable that the oysters recovered from the medieval features were all collected from the same oyster bed.

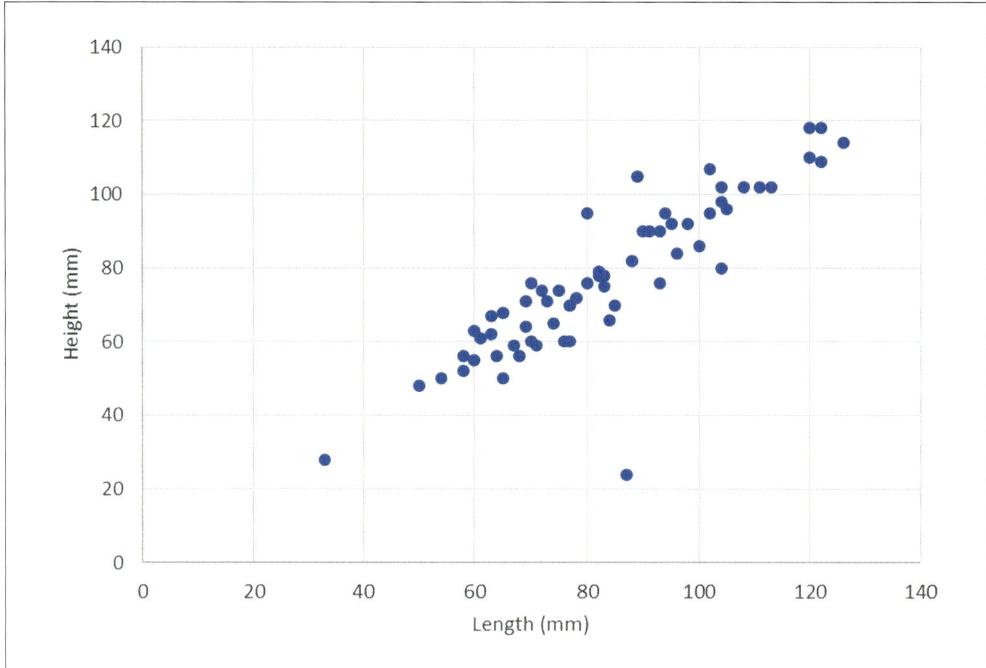

Fig. 15.2—Size distribution of left valves of the European flat oyster (height by length (mm)) in medieval features.

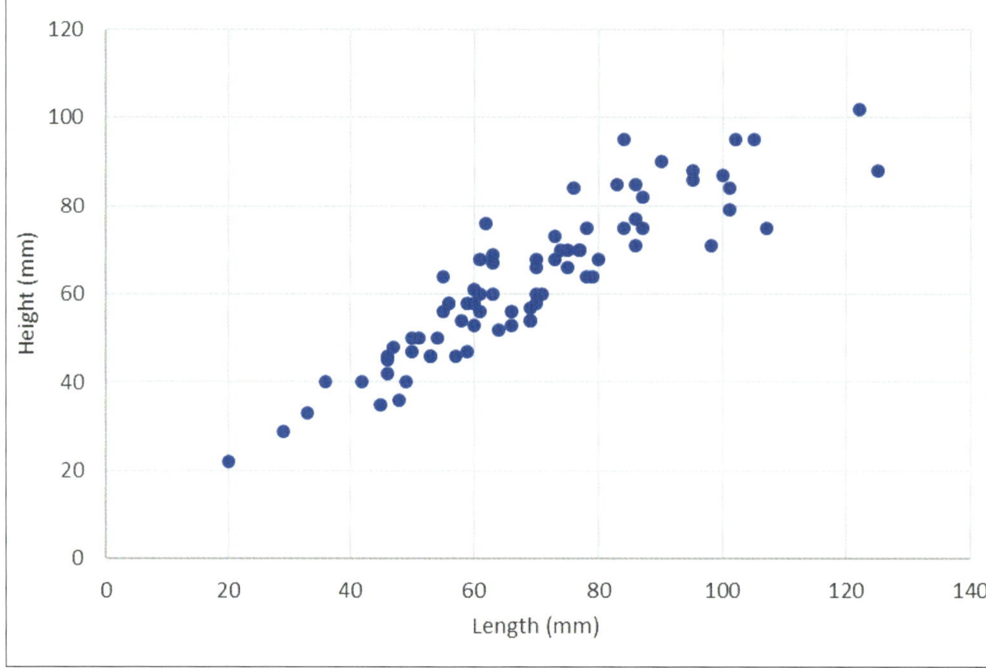

Fig. 15.3—Size distribution of right valves of the European flat oyster (height by length (mm)) in medieval features.

Gastropods

The most frequent gastropod taxa recorded from the medieval features were the edible periwinkle species, of which the common periwinkle was the most frequently recorded with 225 (Table 15.2). The most frequent finds of this species came from F3 (*n* = 24), F21 (*n* = 21) and F20 (*n* = 19), with numerous other features recording varying numbers of common periwinkles. There were 62 common periwinkles that showed damage on the aperture margin resulting from forcible removal of the meaty flesh with a suitable implement. There were only seven occurrences of damage to the common periwinkle shells by marine polychaetes, *Polydora hoplura* (*n* = 5) and *Polydura ciliata* (*n* = 2).

Seventy flat periwinkles were recorded from the medieval features. This marine species occurs on fucoidal seaweeds on the rocky seashore and subsequently may have come to the site attached to these seaweeds (which were used for fertiliser). None of the shells showed damage by external organisms, but the apertures of ten examples displayed evidence of damage caused by using an implement to pick out the flesh. This suggests that the 38 recorded individuals in F3 may have been deliberately collected and contributed to the residents' diet. Other features had infrequent occurrences of the flat periwinkle.

A total of 52 edible rough periwinkles were recorded infrequently from various medieval features at Swords Castle. Thirteen of these gastropods had apertures that were damaged by the removal of the flesh from the shell. The exteriors of only two of the shells showed evidence of marine polychaete activity (*Polydora hoplura*). The rough periwinkles were probably collected along with the common periwinkles, as they both have similar shell morphology—the rough periwinkle has small, concentric raised ridges on its shell surface, whereas the common periwinkle has a smooth shell surface (with or without colour bands). Both are edible species.

Thirty-four common whelks were recorded from fourteen different features. Three of the shells had calcareous tube worm (*Pomatoceros triqueter*) casts still attached to the surfaces. The common whelks are a carnivorous but edible species, boring holes into the shells of other gastropods and bivalves. This species inhabits the lower shore and below. The common whelks were likely to have been brought ashore and to the site along with the harvested bivalve species. A single dog whelk was found in F84. One needle shell was recorded in F74, and three common limpet shells were recorded in F77 and another in F84. These species were likely brought to the site along with the harvested edible mollusc species.

Twenty-two garden snail shells were found in twelve features. This species is commonly found across Ireland and likely inhabited the site rather than being brought in from elsewhere. The same is probably true of the four common terrestrial grove snail shells found in four features (F77, F124, F142 and F150).

Shellfish dietary contribution

The estimated meat and calorific returns to the diet from shellfish (cockles, oysters and periwinkles) from the medieval features recorded at Swords Castle (after Evans and Spencer 1976–7; Winder 1980) are presented in Table 15.6. Results indicated that the combined shellfish contribution in terms of calories to the diet of the medieval inhabitants of Swords Castle was minimal. Approximately 2,700 calories are required daily per adult male (Evans and Spencer 1976–7), and the combined total derived from the recorded shellfish from the medieval features was only 2,153 calories. It is likely that the shellfish represented luxury items consumed on a small number of occasions by certain residents of the castle.

Table 15.6—Estimated meat and calorific shellfish returns at Swords Castle for the medieval period.

Taxa	Average meat weight per shellfish (g)	No. in sample	Estimated meat weight (g)
Periwinkle	1.01	348	351.48
Cockle	1.73	294	508.62
Oyster	7.5	327	2452.5
	3.31kg = 2,153.2 calories		

Post-medieval

After accounting for right and left bivalves, the bivalve taxa (51.8%) marginally exceeded the gastropod taxa (marine species 44.4%) in overall numbers. The most frequent bivalve taxon recorded was the common cockle (*n* = 96), followed by the European flat oyster (*n* = 52) (Table 15.7). The recorded molluscan shells from the post-medieval features totalled 1.9kg in weight. Overall, the shell remains were largely intact and preserved, suggesting that these areas were their primary disposal location.

The majority of the common cockles were found in F117 and F65, with smaller numbers recorded from the other features. Most of the European flat oysters were found in F65 and F64, and fewer in the remaining features (F63, F66, F76 and F117). The periwinkles (common, flat and rough) made up the majority of the recorded marine gastropods, with most of these species recorded from F63, F64 and F65. Other marine gastropods—common whelk, dog whelk and common limpet—were recorded infrequently, indicating that they were brought to the shore as by-catch during harvesting of the other edible marine species. This may also be the case for the infrequent numbers of recorded marine bivalves—blue mussel, blunt tellin, grooved carpet shell, king scallop, saddle oyster and razor shell. Two terrestrial gastropod species were recorded, and these are common all over Ireland.

No boring holes from carnivorous gastropod species were recorded from the post-medieval shell remains. There were two incidences of damage caused by the marine polychaete (*Polydora hoplura*) on two common periwinkle shells and two incidences of damage caused by *Polydura ciliata* on two European flat oyster shells. Calcareous tube worm casts were recorded on two European flat oyster shells, one saddle oyster shell and one common whelk shell. Sponge (*Cliona celata*) boring holes were noted on three European flat oyster shells.

Shell damage associated with the deliberate opening of valves
V-shaped and W-shaped nicks and line breakages recorded on the shell margins were associated with the opening of the valves to gain access to the meaty flesh within. The periwinkle species—common (*n* = 40), rough (*n* = 5) and flat (*n* = 11)—displayed damage to their apertures, commonly associated with attempts to pick the meaty flesh from the shell.

Table 15.7—Summary of the taxa identified from the post-medieval features and MNI (R = right, L = left).

	R valve	L valve	Gastropod	Total MNI	% MNI
Blue mussel	4	4		4	1.3
Blunt tellin	1	3		3	1
Common cockle	96	92		96	31
European flat oyster	30	52		52	16.7
Grooved carpet shell	2	1		2	0.6
King scallop		1		1	0.3
Saddle oyster		1		1	0.3
Razor shell	1	2		2	0.6
Common periwinkle			71	71	22.8
Rough periwinkle			15	15	4.8
Flat periwinkle			44	44	14.1
Common whelk			5	5	1.6
Dog whelk			2	2	0.6
Common limpet			1	1	0.3
Garden snail			10	10	3.2
Grove snail			2	2	0.6
Total MNI	**161**	**150**		**311**	

This damage was recorded in five of the seven post-medieval features.

Fifty-nine cockles displayed evidence of deliberate opening/separation of the valves to gain access to the flesh: five V-shaped nicks, one W-shaped nick and 53 line-type breakages of the shell. The majority of this damage was recorded in F117, where most of the cockles were found. This shell damage to the lateral and ventral shell margins was also recorded in F63, F65 and F76.

Various types of damage were also recorded from European flat oyster valves: V-shaped (n = 8) and W-shaped (n = 5) nicks on the ventral and lateral margins, and seventeen line-type breakages on lateral/ventral margins. The majority of this shell damage was recorded in F65 and infrequently in F64, F76 and F117.

Sizes of the common cockle and European flat oyster
The common cockles ranged in length from 24mm to 41mm and were of typical adult market size and larger. There was one outlier, which may have been due to abnormal growth of the shell owing to damage during the growth phase (Fig. 15.4). The pattern observed indicated that the cockles were collected from the same area (soft sandy sediment on the foreshore) and brought to the castle for eating.

The European flat oysters ranged in length from 41mm to 97mm (left valves), and about a third of the recorded measurements were smaller than modern market sizes (62–64mm+) (Fig. 15.5). These smaller sizes may have been due to previous over-harvesting, which reduced overall population numbers and average population ages of the oyster beds. Thus people harvesting the oyster beds were collecting sub-adult sizes, as these were the only oysters available.

Fig. 15.4—Distribution of common cockle sizes (height by length (mm)) in post-medieval features.

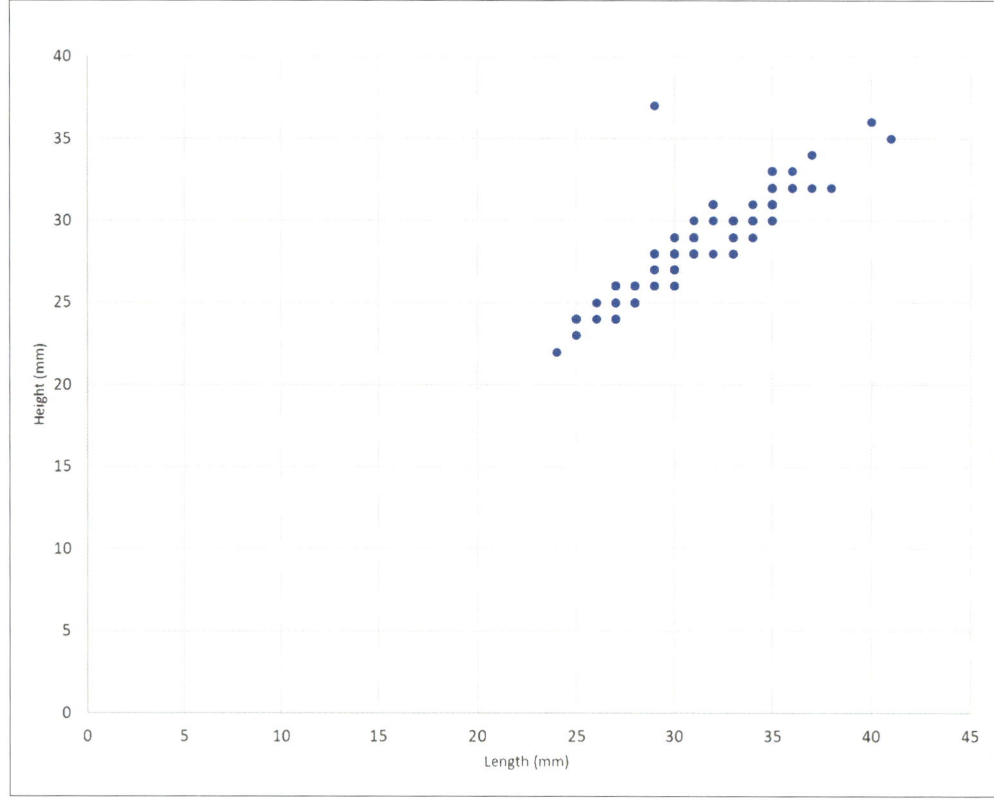

Fig. 15.5—Distribution of sizes of the left valves of the European flat oyster (height by length) (mm) in post-medieval features.

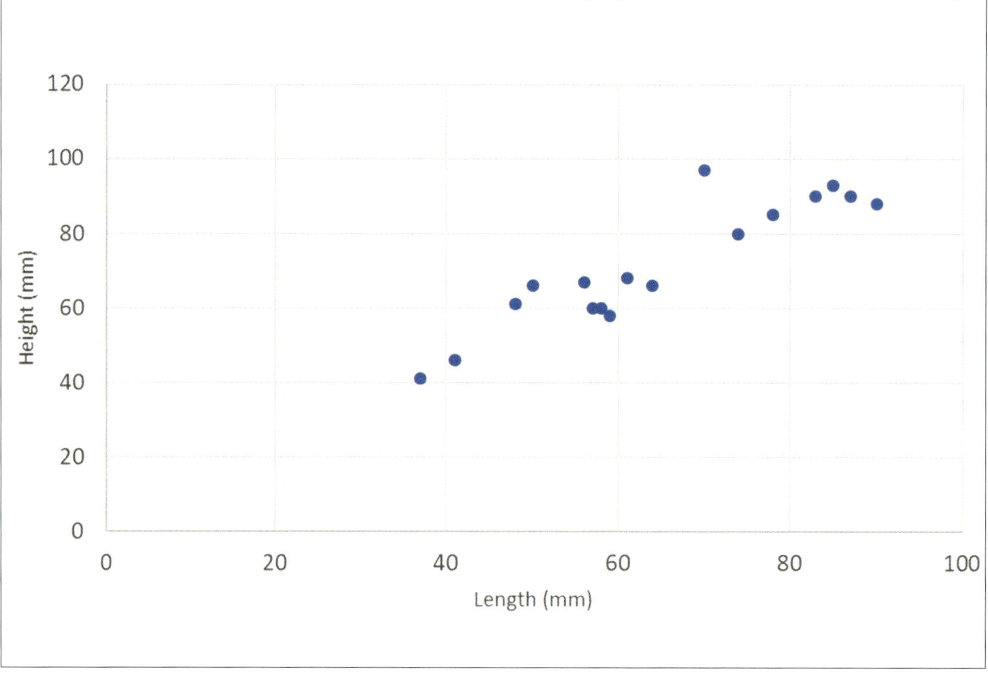

Nevertheless, the oysters collected, albeit in smaller sizes and numbers, represented luxurious and opulent food for the castle residents on occasion during the post-medieval period.

Shellfish dietary contribution

The estimated meat and calorific returns from shellfish (cockles, oysters and periwinkles) from the post-medieval features recorded at Swords Castle (after Evans and Spencer 1976–7; Winder 1980) are presented in Table 15.8. Results indicated that the combined shellfish contribution in terms of calories to the diet at Swords Castle in this period was minimal—a mere 449 calories, around a sixth of the daily requirement of an adult male (Evans and Spencer 1976–7). It is likely that the shellfish represented very occasional luxury items for certain residents of the castle.

Table 15.8—Estimated meat and calorific shellfish returns at Swords Castle for the post-medieval period.

Taxa	Average meat weight per shellfish (g)	No. in sample	Estimated meat weight (g)
Periwinkle	1.01	130	131.3
Cockle	1.73	96	166.08
Oyster	7.5	52	390
	0.69kg = 448.5 calories		

Post-medieval/modern

A total of ten marine bivalves, six marine gastropods and four terrestrial gastropods (total weight 0.33kg) were recorded from post-medieval/modern features (Table 15.9). None of these shells displayed any damage to their exterior shell surfaces caused by external organisms. A single oyster shell in F70 displayed a V-shaped nick in the ventral margin as well as the line-type damage on the lateral margin caused by a short knife used to pry open the valves. Two common cockles, three European flat oysters and three periwinkles in F70 all displayed

Table 15.9—Summary of the taxa identified from the post-medieval/modern features and MNI (R = right, L = left).

Taxa	R valve	L valve	Gastropod	Total MNI	%MNI
Bivalves				*10*	*50.0*
Common cockle	1	3		3	15.0
European flat oyster	3	7		7	35.0
Marine gastropods			*6*	*6*	*30.0*
Common periwinkle			4	4	20.0
Flat periwinkle			2	2	10.0
Terrestrial gastropods			*4*	*4*	*20.0*
Garden snail			2	2	10.0
Grove snail			2	2	10.0
Total MNI		*10*	*10*	*20*	

evidence of deliberate damage on their marginal/ventral shell margins (line-type damage) associated with retrieval of the meaty flesh. An additional common periwinkle in F73 also displayed this damage to the shell aperture.

Modern features

Five features were associated with the modern period: F67, F83, F116, F121 and F122. A total of 33 shells from 25 individual molluscs were recorded (Table 15.10).

Table 15.10—Summary of the taxa identified from the modern features and MNI (R = right, L = left).

Features and taxa		R valve	L valve	Gastropod	Total MNI
F67	*subtotal*	*2*	*3*	*5*	*8*
Common cockle		1	2		2
European flat oyster		1	1		1
Common periwinkle				1	1
Flat periwinkle				3	3
Garden snail				1	1
F83	*subtotal*	*4*	*7*		*7*
Common cockle		2	4		4
European flat oyster		2	3		3
F116	*subtotal*			*2*	*2*
Common periwinkle				1	1
Rough periwinkle				1	1
F121	*subtotal*	*3*	*1*		*3*
European flat oyster		3	1		3
F122	*subtotal*	*1*	*4*	*1*	*5*
Common cockle		1	1		1
European flat oyster			3		3
Rough periwinkle				1	1
	Total MNI	*17*		*8*	*25*

Pit A

Two features in Pit A contained six different molluscan species (Table 15.11) with a total weight of 0.32kg. The majority of the remains were recorded in F24, where 31 individual molluscs from five marine and one terrestrial species were recorded. Eleven individual molluscs were recorded in F26 and these were from three marine bivalve and one marine gastropod species. Marine polychaete species (*Polydura hoplura* and *P. ciliata*) affected two shells in F24, namely a European flat oyster shell and a common periwinkle shell. These two polychaete species both affected the same European flat oyster shell in F26. No external damage by organisms was recorded on other shells.

One European flat oyster shell from F24 displayed a V-shaped nick on the shell margins. One oyster shell from F26 displayed a V-shaped nick, and two others from the same feature bore W-shaped nicks. An additional common cockle shell and oyster shell displayed the straight line type of damage. These types of damage to the shell margins are associated with the deliberate opening of the valves with a short blunt knife or similar implement to gain access to the meaty flesh.

Table 15.11—Summary of the taxa identified from Pit A features and MNI (R = right, L = left).

Features & taxa		R valve	L valve	Gastropod	Total MNI	MNI %
F24	*subtotal*	**15**	**19**	**12**	**31**	**67.4**
Blue mussel		1	5		5	10.9
Common cockle		9	12		12	26.1
European flat oyster		5	2		5	10.9
Common periwinkle				8	8	17.4
Common whelk				1	1	2.2
Garden snail				3	3	6.5
F26	*subtotal*	**8**	**10**	**1**	**11**	**24**
Blue mussel		1			1	2.2
Common cockle		5	7		7	15.2
European flat oyster		2	3		3	6.5
Common whelk				1	1	2.2
	Total MNI	33		13	46	

Pit B

One feature, F35, was recorded in Pit B. Six shells in total, including three individual European flat oysters and two common periwinkles, were recorded from this feature, with a combined weight of 26.4g. One of the oyster shells and a common periwinkle shell showed evidence of exterior damage by the marine polychaete species *Polydura ciliata*. One oyster shell displayed both W-shaped nicks and straight line damage, incurred when the valves were pried apart by a short blunt knife or other suitable tool to gain access to the edible flesh.

Disturbed layers

Six features were recorded as disturbed layers: F106, F108, F109, F112, F118 and F127. A total of 231 shells (with a combined weight of 2.32kg) from 105 individual molluscs were recorded from these features (Table 15.12). Owing to the uncertainty regarding how these features were disturbed, no further comments were made other than to report the summary of the taxa identified per feature.

Topsoil feature (F1)

F1 was designated as topsoil and this sediment was highly disturbed through gardening and agricultural activities, along with the presence of an orchard on the site. A total of 138 shells (combined weight of 0.73kg) from 110 individual molluscs (Table 15.13) were recorded from this feature. The marine shells could be a mixture of archaeological and modern intrusions. No further comments were made on this sample.

CONCLUSIONS

Across the three archaeological periods, marine bivalve species dominated the medieval (59.4%) and post-medieval (51.8%) assemblages while the marine gastropods (71.4%) dominated the early medieval period. The cause of this change in the predominant species is unclear, but it may be simply due to the lack of available common cockle and European flat

Table 15.12—Summary of the taxa identified from the disturbed layers and MNI (R = right, L = left).

Features & taxa		R valve	L valve	Gastropod	Total MNI
F106	*subtotal*	*51*	*46*	*22*	*78*
Blue mussel		6	8		8
Blunt tellin		1			1
Common cockle		23	21		23
European flat oyster		21	14		21
Grooved carpet shell			1		1
Razor shell			2		2
Common periwinkle				5	5
Flat periwinkle				1	1
Common whelk				5	5
Needle shell				1	1
Garden snail				10	10
F108	*subtotal*	*2*	*2*		*3*
Common cockle			1		1
European flat oyster		2	1		2
F109	*subtotal*	*5*	*6*		*6*
Blue mussel			1		1
European flat oyster		5	5		5
F112	*subtotal*	*17*	*19*	*8*	*27*
Blue mussel		2	2		2
Common cockle		11	11		11
European flat oyster		4	5		5
Razor shell			1		1
Common periwinkle				2	2
Flat periwinkle				2	2
Garden snail				4	4
F118	*subtotal*	*18*	*19*	*9*	*28*
Blue mussel		1	1		1
Common cockle		4	4		4
European flat oyster		13	13		13
Grooved carpet shell			1		1
Common whelk				9	9
F127	*subtotal*	*5*	*2*		*6*
Common cockle		4			4
European flat oyster		1	2		2
	Total MNI	*109*		*39*	*148*

oyster beds on the foreshore near Swords Castle during the early medieval period, or to a dietary preference for gastropods.

The overall contribution of the edible marine shellfish to the diet of the castle residents is quite minimal in terms of overall calorific input. The cockles and oysters are generally of typical market size and larger in terms of overall size. There were relatively few incidences of damage associated with marine organisms to the external shell surfaces (e.g. boring holes by common whelk, the presence of burrows of marine polychaete worms etc.) and such damage did not spoil or affect the gastropod body within the shell (i.e. the flesh was still edible).

At all periods the shellfish appears to have been a luxury item, adding an occasional degree

Table 15.13—Summary of the taxa identified from F1 (topsoil) and MNI (R = right, L = left).

Features & taxa		R valve	L valve	Gastropod	Total MNI	MNI %
F1	*subtotal*	*28*	*45*	*65*	*110*	*100*
Blue mussel		1	1		1	0.9
Blunt tellin			1		1	0.9
Common cockle		13	21		21	19.1
European flat oyster		14	17		17	15.5
Grooved carpet shell			2		2	1.8
Iceland cyprina			1		1	0.9
King scallop			2		2	1.8
Common periwinkle				24	24	21.8
Rough periwinkle				8	8	7.3
Flat periwinkle				26	26	23.6
Common whelk				2	2	1.8
Dog whelk				1	1	0.9
Netted dog whelk				1	1	0.9
Garden snail				3	3	2.7
	Total MNI		*45*	*65*	*110*	

of opulence to the residents' dining. The terrestrial gastropod species recorded in the features—the garden snail, the grove snail and unidentified banded snail species—likely inhabited the site rather than being brought in from elsewhere.

There is a lack of comparative molluscan material available from archaeological sites in Ireland other than shell middens from the prehistoric periods. The Swords Castle assemblage (with the exception of the topsoil F1 shells) takes an important step towards redressing this lack, especially as regards the medieval and post-medieval periods.

16

Analysis of non-wood plant macro-remains

Dr Meriel McClatchie

INTRODUCTION

Thirty-eight soil samples from the excavation were analysed to investigate whether non-wood plant macro-remains were present. Typical non-wood plant macro-remains include cereal grains and chaff, weed seeds, fruit stones and nutshell. A very large quantity of food remains was recorded, all of which was preserved by charring. The material mainly consisted of cereal grains—predominantly wheat, with some oat and barley. Other cultivated crops included peas and beans. Occasional fruit and nut remains were also present, as well as weeds. The plant remains discovered at Swords Castle are typical of the types of plants grown in early medieval to medieval Ireland, particularly in the east of the island. The quantity of material recovered is, however, very unusual. More than 16,000 plant components were found, most of which were cereals, emphasising the important role that food played in activities at Swords Castle.

METHODS

Processing of soil samples

The volume of each soil sample was *c.* 20 litres in most cases. Following on-site training from McClatchie, the soil samples were processed by the excavation team using conventional flotation methods. This process involved soaking each sample in a bucket of water to disaggregate the sediment matrix. The water, including any suspended organic material (the flot), was poured into a sieve with mesh aperture measuring 300μm. Residual material that did not float remained at the bottom of the bucket. This process was repeated several times until no further material was seen to float in the water. The residue was then wet-sieved through a 500μm mesh sieve, being washed thoroughly in a concentrated flow of water. The flots and retents were dried prior to microscopic examination by McClatchie.

Identification of remains

Examination of the flots was carried out using a stereo microscope, with magnifications ranging from x6.3 to x40. The archaeobotanical material was identified by comparison to reference material in McClatchie's collection of modern diaspores and drawings from various seed keys (e.g. Beijerinck 1947; Katz *et al.* 1965; Cappers *et al.* 2006). Botanical and common names follow the nomenclature of *New flora of the British Isles* (Stace 2010).

Table 16.1—Examined deposits.

Trench/Pit	Feature	Sample	Description
Trench 1	8	3	Layer, possibly *in situ* burning
	14	4	Wall
	15	2	Fill of subcircular pit cut into consolidation layer F3
	23	10	Layer
	39	15	Fill of pit
	43	16	Layer
Trench 2	19	5	Fill of pit
Trench 3	21	8	Stony consolidation layer
	22	6	Upper fill of pit F28, possibly extending beyond cut
	27	20	Fill of small oval hearth
	28	14 19	Basal fill of shallow subrectangular pit
	31	12 (F31, c.2) 18 (F31, c.1) 17 (F31, c.1) 21 (F31, c.3)	Steep-sided pit containing 4 fills: basal fill F31, c.3, overlain by redeposited layer F29, overlain by F31, c.1, overlain by upper fill F31, c.2
	33	13	Fill of pit
Pit A	30	11	Burnt layer and stone setting (hearth?)
Trench 4	80	24 (subsamples 1–3) 24 (subsamples 4–6) 24 (subsamples 7–8) 25 28	Extensive layer

Table 16.1 (cont.)—Examined deposits.

	101	36	Fill of two large stone-packed post-holes within foundation trench
		39	
	103	41	Fill of oval pit (*in situ* burning)
Trench 5	85	35	Fill of linear ditch (possible enclosure or boundary ditch)
		40 (base)	
Trench 6	89	30	Shell-rich layer
	93	34	Primary fill of pit F95
		34B	
Trench 7	126:1	42	Occupation floor (upper)
	126:3	54	Occupation floor (basal)
	146	2	Basal fill of northern bowl of kiln F143
	161:1	66	Basal fill of kiln flue (kiln F143)
	161:2	65	Upper fill of kiln flue (kiln F143)
Trench 8	129	57	Upper layer abutting medieval wall F123
	159	64	Upper layer abutting medieval wall F123

Preservation of remains

All of the recorded plant remains were preserved by charring. It should be noted that this method of preservation is often biased in favour of plants more likely to come into contact with fire. Cereal grains, for example, may be exposed to fire when dried before storage or during cooking. Such plants are therefore more likely to be represented in charred assemblages when compared with plants more often eaten raw or boiled, such as fruits and vegetables. It is likely that the people who undertook activities at this site would have made use of a wider range of plants than those represented in the examined deposits.

NON-WOOD PLANT MACRO-REMAINS RECORDED

Trench 1

Trench 1, in the north-eastern area within the curtain wall at Swords Castle, revealed several structural elements, including a wall (F14) and foundation trench cut into the natural subsoil. Several layers were also recorded, as well as a metalled surface with a hearth setting (F45, F44) overlain by a series of fish-bone-rich layers (F41, F42, F43) that were truncated by a post-medieval pit (F38). All of this activity was overlain by a consolidation layer (F3). A possible bread wheat grain from layer F8 (S3) was radiocarbon-dated to the tenth–twelfth centuries (UBA-32453; AD 997–1187, 2σ). A possible bread wheat grain from another layer (F43, S16) was radiocarbon-dated to the thirteenth–fifteenth centuries (UBA-32454; AD 1298–1411, 2σ).

Six deposits were presented for archaeobotanical analysis, all of which contained relatively small quantities of charred plant macro-remains that are likely to date from the early medieval to medieval period (Table 16.2). The largest quantity of remains was recorded in layer F23, which contained a total of 30 plant components. Cereals included grains of *Triticum* cf. *aestivum* (possible bread wheat) and *Avena* spp (oat). Twenty-five grain fragments of Cerealia (indeterminate cereal) were also present. The wheat can be placed in the *Triticum aestivum/durum/turgidum* category; these are types of free-threshing wheat—bread wheat, durum wheat and rivet wheat. The morphology of the wheat grain in F23 suggests bread wheat. The identification of wheat species by grain alone, however, is generally unreliable (Hillman *et al.* 1996), and well-preserved chaff (such as rachis fragments, spikelet forks and glume bases) is instead a more reliable indicator of wheat species. Wheat chaff was absent from any deposit in Trench 1, although it was found elsewhere at Swords Castle. As a result, the presence of bread wheat in Trench 1 deposits cannot be confirmed. In addition to the cereals, a large seed of the Fabaceae family (pea family) was present in F23. Large seeds in the Fabaceae family include cultivars such as peas and beans, as well as vetches and wild legumes. It is unclear whether the legume seed in F23 represents a cultivated or a wild variety.

A layer dated to the tenth–twelfth centuries, F8, contained a similar assemblage, comprising a grain of possible bread wheat, indeterminate cereal grain fragments and a large seed from the Fabaceae family. F8 also contained a pod of *Raphanus raphanistrum* (wild radish), which is likely to reflect an arable weed. Arable weeds would have been growing alongside the cereals and were sometimes inadvertently harvested.

A layer dated to the thirteenth–fifteenth centuries, F43, also contained grains of possible bread wheat and oat, as well as indeterminate cereal grain fragments. A small seed of the Fabaceae family was present in F43 and, given its size, is likely to represent a wild legume rather than a cultivar. Wild legumes can be found growing in a variety of environments.

Cereal grains were also present in two pits from Trench 1. F39 contained possible bread wheat grains and indeterminate cereal grain fragments, while F15 produced indeterminate cereal grain fragments only. A deposit from a suspected medieval wall (F14) also contained possible bread wheat grains and indeterminate cereal grain fragments.

Trench 2

Trench 2 was located in the eastern area within the curtain wall at Swords Castle. Features included a pit (F19) cut into the natural subsoil, layers and a roughly metalled surface (F5).

Table 16.2—Plant macro-remains from Trenches 1 and 2.

		Trench	1	1	1	1	1	1	2
		Feature	8	14	15	23	39	43	19
		Sample	3	4	2	10	15	16	5
Botanical name	**Common name**	**Component**							
FABACEAE									
Fabaceae	Pea family	Seed >2mm	1	…	…	…	…	…	…
Fabaceae	Pea family	Seed fragment >2mm	…	…	…	1	…	…	…
Fabaceae	Pea family	Seed <2mm	…	…	…	…	…	1	…
Fabaceae	Pea family	Seed fragment <2mm	…	…	…	…	…	…	2
BRASSICACEAE									
Raphanus raphanistrum L.	Wild radish	Pod	1	…	…	…	…	…	3
POLYGONACEAE									
Persicaria maculosa Gray	Redshank	Achene	…	…	…	…	…	…	…
Rumex acetosa L.	Common sorrel	Achene	…	…	…	…	…	…	…
Rumex spp	Docks	Achene	…	…	…	…	…	…	2
Polygonaceae	Knotweed family	Achene fragment	…	…	…	…	…	…	2
RUBIACEAE									
Galium spp	Bedstraws	Seed	…	…	…	…	…	…	1
PLANTAGINACEAE									
Plantago lanceolata L.	Ribwort plantain	Seed	…	…	…	…	…	…	1
CYPERACEAE									
Cyperaceae	Sedge family	Achene	…	…	…	…	…	…	1
POACEAE									
Avena spp	Oat	Grain	…	…	…	2	…	3	6
Hordeum spp	Barley	Grain	…	…	…	…	…	…	5
Triticum cf. *aestivum* L.	cf. Bread wheat	Grain	1	3	…	1	3	4	29
Cerealia	Indeterminate cereal	Grain fragment	17	13	8	25	3	7	100
Poaceae	Grass family	Seed	1	…	…	1	…	…	20
INDETERMINATE									
Indeterminate	Indeterminate	Seed	…	…	…	…	1	…	…
		Total	**21**	**16**	**8**	**30**	**7**	**15**	**172**
		% of sample examined	100	100	100	100	100	100	100
		Converted total	21	16	8	30	7	15	172

A possible bread wheat grain from pit F19 (S5) was radiocarbon-dated to the ninth–eleventh centuries (UBA-32455; AD 894–1019, 2σ).

One deposit was presented for archaeobotanical analysis (Table 16.2). F19 was a ninth–eleventh-century pit fill, and it contained a variety of cereals and weeds. Almost 30 grains of possible bread wheat were recorded, in addition to occasional grains of oat and *Hordeum* spp (barley). A large number of indeterminate cereal grain fragments were also present. Wheat chaff, which would assist in confirming the species of wheat, was again absent.

A wide variety of weed seeds was recorded in F19 when compared with deposits in Trench 1. Wild radish and small Fabaceae seeds were present in F19, in addition to seeds of *Rumex* spp (docks), Polygonaceae (knotweed family), *Galium* spp (bedstraws), *Plantago lanceolata* (ribwort plantain) and Cyperaceae (sedge family). Wild radish is likely to represent an arable weed. Species of the sedge family can be found growing on wet ground. Ribwort plantain may have been growing nearby on field margins and in grassy places. Docks, bedstraws and species of the knotweed family will thrive in a wide variety of habitats.

Trench 3

Trench 3 was located in the western area within the curtain wall at Swords Castle. A large pit (F31) was cut into the subsoil. Human bone from fill F29 of this pit was radiocarbon-dated to the eleventh–twelfth centuries (UBA-32452; AD 1018–1154, 2σ). A possible bread wheat grain from the basal fill (S21) of the same pit was also radiocarbon-dated to the eleventh–twelfth centuries (UBA-32457; AD 1021–1186, 2σ). Another pit (F33) was recorded in Trench 3, as well as a metalled surface (F50) and a hearth (F27), both of which were cut by a pit (F28). A possible bread wheat grain from the upper fill (F22, S6) of pit F28 was radiocarbon-dated to the eleventh–thirteenth centuries (UBA-32456; AD 1032–1217, 2σ). This concentration of pits was overlain by a stony layer (F21), which was overlain in turn by compacted layers and a stone concentration.

Ten deposits were presented for archaeobotanical analysis, all of which contained charred plant macro-remains, sometimes in very large quantities (Table 16.3). All of the deposits are likely to date from the early medieval to medieval period. The largest quantity of remains was recorded in F22 (eleventh–thirteenth century), the upper fill of pit F28. F22 also extended beyond the cut of the pit. F22 contained more than 10,000 plant components, which is an extraordinarily large quantity of remains. Approximately 300 components were identified to provide a representative subsample (van der Veen and Fieller 1982; McClatchie and OCarroll 2015).

A large quantity of wheat grains was recorded in F22, all of which may be bread wheat. Chaff is a much better indicator of wheat species than grain alone, and the recovery of bread wheat rachis fragments confirms that bread wheat is definitely present here. Most, if not all, of the wheat grains are therefore likely to be bread wheat. A small number of oat and barley grains were also recorded, as well as a rachis fragment of six-row barley. Indeterminate cereal grain fragments were present, as well as culm (stem) fragments of Poaceae (grass family), which may represent cereal straw.

As well as cereals, cultivated legumes were present in F22. A small number of seeds of *Pisum sativum* (garden pea) and *Vicia faba* (broad bean) were recorded. A seed of *Vicia sativa* (common vetch) was also present. Common vetch may have been cultivated as a fodder crop or perhaps grew wild along field borders and in waste places. Small and large seeds of the

		Trench	3	3	3	3
		Feature	21	22	27	28
		Sample	8	6	20	14
Botanical name	**Common name**	**Component**				
RANUNCULACEAE						
Ranunculus acris L.	Meadow buttercup	Achene	…	…	…	…
FABACEAE						
Vicia sativa L.	Common vetch	Seed	…	1	…	…
Vicia faba L.	Broad bean	Seed	…	2	…	…
Vicia faba L.	Broad bean	Seed fragment	…	2	…	…
cf. *Vicia faba* L.	cf. Broad bean	Seed fragment	1	…	…	…
Pisum sativum L.	Garden pea	Seed	…	1	…	…
cf. *Pisum sativum* L.	cf. Garden pea	Seed	…	…	…	1
Fabaceae	Pea family	Seed >2mm	…	5	1	4
Fabaceae	Pea family	Seed frag. >2mm	3	2	…	6
Fabaceae	Pea family	Seed <2mm	…	5	4	…
Fabaceae	Pea family	Seed frag. <2mm	…	…	1	…
ROSACEAE						
Rubus spp	Brambles	Nutlet	…	…	…	1
BETULACEAE						
Corylus avellana L.	Hazel	Nutshell	…	…	…	1
EUPHORBIACEAE						
Euphorbia helioscopia L.	Sun spurge	Seed	…	…	…	…
BRASSICACEAE						
Raphanus raphanistrum L.	Wild radish	Pod	1	1	…	…
POLYGONACEAE						
Persicaria maculosa Gray	Redshank	Achene	1	…	…	…
Rumex acetosa L.	Common sorrel	Achene	…	2	…	1
Polygonaceae	Knotweed family	Achene fragment	…	…	…	…
CARYOPHYLLACEAE						
Agrostemma githago L.	Corn-cockle	Seed	…	…	…	…
Agrostemma githago L.	Corn-cockle	Seed fragment	…	…	…	…
AMARANTHACEAE						
Chenopodium album L.	Fat hen	Utricle	…	…	…	…
Chenopodium/Atriplex spp	Goosefoots/oraches	Utricle	1	…	…	…
RUBIACEAE						
Galium aparine L.	Cleavers	Seed	…	…	…	…
BORAGINACEAE						
Lithospermum arvense L.	Field gromwell	Nutlet	…	…	…	…
PLANTAGINACEAE						
Plantago lanceolata L.	Ribwort plantain	Seed	…	…	…	…
ASTERACEAE						
Anthemis cotula L.	Stinking chamomile	Achene	…	…	…	…
Glebionis segetum (L.) Fourr.	Corn marigold	Achene	…	…	…	…
POACEAE						
Avena spp	Oat	Grain	3	6	…	9
Avena spp	Oat	Grain fragment	…	…	…	…
Hordeum spp six-row	Six-row barley	Rachis fragment	…	1	…	…
Hordeum spp	Barley	Rachis fragment	…	…	…	…
Hordeum spp	Barley	Grain	3	1	…	4
cf. *Hordeum* spp	cf. Barley	Grain	…	…	1	…
Triticum aestivum L.	Bread wheat	Rachis fragment	…	7	…	1
Triticum cf. *aestivum* L.	cf. Bread wheat	Grain	68	201	2	101
Cerealia	Indeterminate cereal	Grain fragment	97	67	6	176
Poaceae	Grass family	Seed	1	1	…	6
Poaceae	Grass family	Seed fragment	2	…	…	…
Poaceae	Grass family	Culm fragment	…	5	…	…
INDETERMINATE						
Indeterminate	Indeterminate	Vegetative frag.	3	11	…	…
		Total	**184**	**321**	**15**	**311**
	% of sample examined		100	3	100	80
		Converted total	184	10700	15	389

3	3	3	3	3	3	Pit A
28	31	31	31	31	33	30
19	12	17	18	21	13	11
…	…	…	…	1	…	…
…	…	…	…	1	1	…
…	…	…	…	…	…	…
…	…	…	…	…	…	…
…	…	1	…	…	…	…
…	…	1	…	…	…	…
…	…	…	…	…	…	…
1	4	10	3	2	1	
2	2	…	2	1	…	4
…	…	4	5	…	…	3
…	…	2	2	…	1	…
…	…	…	…	…	…	…
…	…	…	…	…	…	…
…	1	…	…	…	…	…
…	…	…	1	…	…	…
…	…	…	…	…	…	…
…	2	5	…	…	1	4
…	…	…	1	1	…	1
…	…	…	1	…	…	…
…	1	…	…	…	…	…
…	…	…	…	…	2	…
…	…	…	1	…	1	…
…	…	…	1	…	…	…
…	1	1	2	…	…	…
…	…	1	…	…	…	…
…	…	…	…	…	1	…
…	1	…	…	…	…	…
1	14	13	5	5	1	1
…	…	…	3	…	…	…
…	…	…	…	…	…	…
…	…	…	…	1	…	…
…	…	…	…	…	…	…
…	…	…	2	1	…	…
…	1	9	3	…	…	…
16	180	171	119	95	4	185
66	124	86	162	181	72	120
3	4	4	4	17	3	…
…	…	…	…	…	…	…
…	1	3	2	…	…	…
…	…	1	2	…	…	…
89	**336**	**312**	**321**	**306**	**88**	**318**
100	90	30	80	90	100	20
89	373	1040	401	340	88	1590

Table 16.3—Plant macro-remains from Trench 3 and Pit A.

Fabaceae family were also recorded. The presence of wild radish in F22 is likely to represent an arable weed, while *Rumex acetosa* (common sorrel) can be found growing in grassy places.

Several thousand plant components were found in F31, an eleventh–twelfth-century pit. Four samples were taken from three pit fills. The basal fill (S21) contained possible bread wheat grains, oat grains, barley rachis, a possible barley grain and indeterminate cereal grain fragments. Common vetch, *Ranunculus acris* (meadow buttercup), Fabaceae seeds and knotweeds were also present. The Fabaceae seeds may represent cultivated or wild legumes, and the common vetch may also reflect fodder or weeds. Knotweeds can be found growing in a variety of environments, while meadow buttercup is associated with grasslands.

The main fill of F31 (S17, S18) contained bread wheat rachis, possible bread wheat grains, oat grains, possible barley grains and indeterminate cereal grains. The presence of grass culm fragments may represent cereal straw. A garden pea and a possible broad bean were also present, as well as large and small Fabaceae seeds. Possible arable weeds included wild radish, *Agrostemma githago* (corn-cockle), *Galium aparine* (cleavers) and *Lithospermum arvense* (field gromwell). Common sorrel and ribwort plantain may have been growing nearby in grassy places, while knotweed and *Chenopodium/Atriplex* spp (goosefoots/oraches) can be found in a variety of environments.

The upper fill of F31 (S12) contained bread wheat rachis, possible bread wheat grains, oat grains, indeterminate cereal grains and possible cereal straw. Large and small seeds of the Fabaceae family were recorded, which may represent cultivated or wild legumes. Possible arable weeds included *Euphorbia helioscopia* (sun spurge), corn-cockle, field gromwell and *Glebionis segetum* (corn marigold). Common sorrel may have been growing nearby in grassy places.

Two samples from the basal fill of a pit (F28) contained several hundred plant components. Cereal remains included bread wheat rachis, possible bread wheat grains, oat grains, barley grains and indeterminate cereal grain fragments. A possible garden pea was recorded, as well as large seeds of the Fabaceae family. Potentially gathered resources included *Rubus* spp (brambles) and *Corylus avellana* (hazelnut). Common sorrel may have been growing nearby in grassy places.

The remaining three deposits from Trench 3 contained a smaller quantity of remains. A stony consolidation layer (F21) produced grains of possible bread wheat, oat, barley and indeterminate cereal. A possible broad bean and large seeds of the Fabaceae family were also present. Potential arable weeds included wild radish and *Persicaria maculosa* (redshank). Species of the goosefoots/oraches genera can be found growing in a variety of environments.

A fill from pit F33 contained grains of possible bread wheat, oat and indeterminate cereal. Common vetch may represent fodder or a wild plant growing locally. Large and small seeds of the Fabaceae family were also present. Potential arable weeds included *Chenopodium album* (fat hen) and *Anthemis cotula* (stinking chamomile). Common sorrel may have been growing nearby in grassy places.

A fill from a small hearth (F27) contained a very small quantity of remains, including grains of possible bread wheat, possible barley and indeterminate cereal, as well as large and small seeds from the Fabaceae family.

Pit A

Pit A, a test pit located at the junction of the north-eastern mural tower and the curtain wall at Swords Castle, contained wall features (F49 and F48), various layers, two apparently *in situ* medieval floor tiles and a possible hearth (F26 and F30). A possible bread wheat grain from fill S11 of possible hearth F30 was radiocarbon-dated to the fifteenth–seventeenth centuries (UBA-32458; AD 1419–1616, 2σ), reflecting relatively late activity at Swords Castle.

One deposit from Pit A was presented for analysis (Table 16.3): a possible hearth (F30) dating from the fifteenth–seventeenth centuries. This deposit contained more than 1,500 plant components. Although a large quantity of material was recorded, there was less variety when compared with deposits from Trench 3. Possible bread wheat grains were dominant, with oat and indeterminate cereal also present. Small and large seeds of the Fabaceae family were recorded. Common sorrel may have been growing nearby in grassy places.

The preservation of plant remains from F30 was unusually excellent—far superior to that encountered in other trenches. This may indicate that the plant remains in F30 were subject to different taphonomic effects, or it may perhaps be because they are significantly later in date than other examined deposits.

Trench 4

Trench 4 was located over geophysical anomalies on high ground 0.5m west of Trench 1, to investigate whether the walls identified in Trench 1 continued westwards and to assess what appeared to be a significant structural anomaly on the geophysical survey. Large post-holes within a foundation trench (F101) and a fire-pit (F103) were cut into natural subsoil. A series of metalled surfaces (F100 and F86) were overlain by stone (F84) and bone-rich (F80) layers. This activity was truncated along the northern baulk by the insertion of a nineteenth-century stone drain, trench and modern pit insertions. All of this activity was overlain by a transitional layer (F65), topsoil (F1) and sod. An oat grain from a fill (S41) of fire-pit F103 was radiocarbon-dated to the eleventh–twelfth century (UBA-34519; AD 1029–1159, 2σ). A grain of possible bread wheat from layer F80 (S24) was radiocarbon-dated to the thirteenth–fourteenth century (UBA-34516; AD 1299–1413, 2σ). Eight deposits were presented for archaeobotanical analysis (Table 16.4).

The largest quantity of plant remains from Trench 4 deposits was recorded in F103, the fill of an eleventh–twelfth-century oval pit containing *in situ* burning. Cereal grains were dominant, consisting mainly of oat. The presence of a floret base of *Avena sativa* L. confirms the presence of common (cultivated) oat. Oat lemma fragments were also recorded, as well as a grass culm fragment (possible cereal straw) and a barley grain. Potential arable weeds included redshank, fat hen and possible cleavers. A hazelnut shell fragment and a stone of *Prunus spinosa* L. (sloe) were present, reflecting species that may have been growing locally on woodland margins or rough ground and whose fruits and nuts were gathered for consumption. Seeds of *Carex* spp (sedges) were also recorded; species from this genus are usually found growing in wet ground.

Five samples were examined from an extensive layer, F80, dating from the thirteenth–fourteenth century. A similar variety of remains was recorded in both S24 and S25, consisting mainly of cereal remains. Possible bread wheat grains were dominant, and the presence of a rachis fragment confirms the presence of bread wheat. A smaller number of oat and barley

Table 16.4—Plant macro-remains from Trench 4.

		Trench	4	4	4	4	4	4	4	4
		Feature	80	80	80	80	80	101	101	103
		Sample	24 (1–3/8)	24 (4–6/8)	24 (7&8/8)	25	28	36	39	41
Botanical name	**Common name**	**Component**								
FABACEAE										
Pisum sativum L.	Garden pea	Seed	…	…	…	2	…	…	…	…
Fabaceae	Pea family	Seed frag. >2mm	1	1	…	…	…	…	…	…
Fabaceae	Pea family	Seed <2mm	…	1	1	2	…	…	…	…
Fabaceae	Pea family	Seed frag. <2mm	1	1	1	…	…	…	…	…
ROSACEAE										
Prunus spinosa L.	Blackthorn (sloe)	Stone	…	… …	…	…	…	…	…	1
BETULACEAE										
Corylus avellana L.	Hazel	Nutshell	…	…	…	1	…	…	…	1
POLYGON-ACEAE										
Persicaria maculosa Gray	Redshank	Achene	…	…	…	…	…	…	…	2
AMARANTHA-CEAE										
Chenopodium album L.	Fat hen	Utricle	…	…	…	…	…	…	…	3
RUBIACEAE										
Galium aparine L.	Cleavers	Seed	…	…	…	…	…	…	1	…
Galium cf. *aparine* L.	cf. Cleavers	Seed	…	…	…	…	…	…	…	1
CYPERACEAE										
Carex spp	Sedges	Achene	…	…	…	…	…	…	…	6
POACEAE										
Avena sativa L.	Common oat	Grain and floret base	…	…	…	…	…	…	…	1
Avena spp	Oat	Grain	2	1	3	1	…	17	4	76
Avena spp	Oat	Grain fragment	…	…	…	…	…	…	…	43
Avena spp	Oat	Lemma fragment	…	…	…	…	…	…	…	2
Hordeum spp	Barley	Grain	…	…	1	…	…	…	…	1
Triticum aestivum	Bread wheat	Rachis fragment	1	…	…	…	…	…	…	…
Triticum cf. *aestivum* L.	cf. Bread wheat	Grain	68	14	15	29	11	1	…	…
Cerealia	Indeterminate cereal	Grain fragment	69	43	38	49	23	35	8	67
Poaceae	Grass family	Seed	…	1	1	…	1	…	…	…
Poaceae	Grass family	Culm fragment	…	…	…	…	…	…	…	1
		Total	142	62	60	84	35	53	13	205
		% of sample examined	100	100	100	100	100	100	100	100

grains were recorded. These samples also contained seeds of the Fabaceae family—including a cultivated species (garden pea) and possible wild varieties (<2mm in diameter)—as well as a fragment of hazelnut shell and grass seeds. Another sample (S28) from layer F80 contained a smaller quantity and variety of remains, suggesting heterogeneity in deposition practices. This latter sample contained mainly indeterminate cereal grains, as well as occasional possible bread wheat grains and a grass seed. F101 was interpreted as the fill of two large, stone-packed post-holes within a foundation trench. Two samples from this feature were analysed (S36 and S39) and contained similar remains, comprising oat grains, indeterminate cereal grains and a possible bread wheat grain. A seed of cleavers was also present.

Trench 5

Trench 5 was located in an area that had not produced significant geophysical results. It was excavated to determine the accuracy of the geophysical survey and the level of activity between the structural remains in Trench 1 and the yard surface in Trench 3. Cut into natural was a large ditch (F85) and the possible terminus of a small gully (F104). Most deposits within Trench 5 consisted of very compact stone layers and deposits. An oat grain from a fill (S40) of ditch F85 was radiocarbon-dated to the tenth–eleventh century (UBA-34517; AD 975–1037, 2σ). Two deposits were presented for archaeobotanical analysis (Table 16.5).

Two deposits were examined from the tenth–eleventh-century linear ditch, F85. Both deposits contained a small number of oat grains and hazelnut shell fragments. One sample (S35) also produced a possible bread wheat grain and a seed of the knotweed family. Knotweed will thrive in a variety of environments.

Trench 6

Trench 6 was located at a right angle to the previous season's Trench 3 to investigate whether the yard surface extended southwards and whether there was any boundary present that might define the burials identified by Fanning further south towards the Chapel. Two intercutting pits (F95, F92) were cut into natural, and another (F97) was identified in the northern section of the trench. These pits had been sealed beneath two metalled surfaces (F72, F82), above which was a consolidation layer (F63), topsoil (F1) and sod. An oat grain from the fill (F93, S34B) of pit F95 was radiocarbon-dated to the eleventh–twelfth century (UBA-34518; AD 1023–1154, 2σ). Three deposits were presented for archaeobotanical analysis (Table 16.5).

Two samples from F93, the primary fill of eleventh–twelfth-century pit F95, were analysed. Cereal grains were dominant, consisting mainly of oat, with occasional grains of hulled barley, barley and possible bread wheat. The presence of bread wheat was confirmed by the recovery of a rachis fragment, and a rachis fragment of six-row barley was also recorded. The presence of hazelnut shell reflects a species that may have been gathered for consumption. A variety of wild plants were also present. Common sorrel may have been growing in grassy places. Potential arable weeds included wild radish, fat hen, stinking chamomile and corn marigold. A seed of the Fabaceae family (possibly wild variety) was also present.

A shell-rich layer, F89, contained a smaller quantity of remains, including barley and oat grains, a seed of the Fabaceae family (possible wild variety) and seeds of *Rumex crispus* L. (curled dock). Curled dock can be found growing on field boundaries, waste and cultivated ground.

Table 16.5—Plant macro-remains from Trenches 5 and 6.

		Trench	5	5	6	6	6
		Feature	85	85 (base)	89	93	93
		Sample	35	40	30	34	34B
Botanical name	**Common name**	**Component**					
FABACEAE							
Fabaceae	Pea family	Seed <2mm	…	…	1		1
BETULACEAE							
Corylus avellana L.	Hazel	Nutshell	7	1		3	3
BRASSICACEAE							
Raphanus raphanistrum L.	Wild radish	Pod	…	…	…	1	…
POLYGONACEAE							
Rumex acetosa L.	Common sorrel	Achene	…	…	…	…	2
Rumex crispus L.	Curled dock	Achene	…	…	6	…	…
Polygonaceae	Knotweed family	Achene fragment	1	…	…	…	…
AMARANTHACEAE							
Chenopodium album L.	Fat hen	Utricle	…	…	…	1	…
ASTERACEAE							
Anthemis cotula L.	Stinking chamomile	Achene	…	…	…	1	…
Glebionis segetum (L.) Fourr.	Corn marigold	Achene	…	…	…	1	…
POACEAE							
Avena spp	Oat	Grain	1	3	2	32	11
Avena spp	Oat	Grain fragment	…	…	…	6	…
Hordeum spp six-row	Six-row barley	Rachis fragment	…	…	…	1	…
Hordeum spp	Hulled barley	Grain	…	…	…	2	1
Hordeum spp	Barley	Grain	…	…	5	2	1
Triticum aestivum L.	Bread wheat	Rachis fragment	…	…	…	1	…
Triticum cf. *aestivum* L.	cf. Bread wheat	Grain	1	…	…	2	3
Cerealia	Indeterminate cereal	Grain fragment	28	10	25	146	…
		Total	38	14	39	199	22
		% of sample examined	100	100	100	100	100

Trench 7

Trench 7 was located in the north-eastern corner of the castle precinct to investigate a geophysical anomaly, a breach in the curtain wall and internal walls of the northern mural tower. A flagged floor was discovered, and a layer sealing the flagged floor contained a silver groat coin dating from 1569. A possible oat grain from layer F126:3 (S54) above the flagged floor was radiocarbon-dated to the fifteenth–seventeenth centuries (UBA-38837; AD 1461–1636, 2σ). Intense burning was recorded at the northern limit of the floor, also evident in nearby Pit A (excavated in 2015), from which a possible bread wheat grain (F30, S11) was radiocarbon-dated to the fifteenth–seventeenth centuries (UBA-32458; AD 1419–1616, 2σ). An opening in the curtain wall that may have acted as a drain (F149) was found at the eastern end of the flagged floor. A kiln (F143) was cut through the flagged floor; it had been cleaned out and backfilled. A barley grain from the basal fill (F146:2, S59) of the northern bowl of the kiln was radiocarbon-dated to the fifteenth–sixteenth century (UBA-38839; AD 1451–1528, 2σ).

Five deposits were presented for archaeobotanical analysis (Table 16.6), four of which contained relatively small quantities of charred plant macro-remains. A basal layer (F126:3) overlying the flagged floor and radiocarbon-dated to the fifteenth–seventeenth centuries contained an oat grain that showed traces of germination. A grass culm node fragment (which may represent cereal straw) and indeterminate cereal grains were also present, as well as large and small seeds of Fabaceae. An upper layer (F126:1) overlying the flagged floor contained cereal grains, most of which were possible naked wheat, with occasional possible oat. The upper layer also contained a small number of seeds of vetch, Fabaceae family and bedstraw. Vetch may represent fodder or a wild plant growing locally. The Fabaceae family include cultivars such as peas and beans, as well as vetches and wild legumes. It is unclear whether the seeds in F126 represent cultivated or wild varieties. Bedstraw can be found growing in a variety of environments.

The kiln contained surprisingly few cereal remains, suggesting that it was either very well cleaned out or used primarily for activities other than drying cereals. A lower fill from the kiln flue (F161:1) only contained a small number of indeterminate cereal grains, and plant remains were absent from an upper fill (F161:2). A larger quantity of material was recorded in a basal fill (F146:2) of the northern bowl of the kiln, dated to the fifteenth–sixteenth century, but remains were often fragmented. Most of the cereal grains could not be identified to genus. Where they were identifiable, possible bread wheat was dominant, with occasional oat. Legumes were also present, including possible pea and vetch, as well as occasional Fabaceae and bedstraw seeds.

Trench 8

Trench 8 was opened on the eastern side of the castle precinct (along the inner edge of the curtain wall) to investigate a geophysical anomaly and to uncover the return wall of the 'Great Hall'. The remains of a substantial east–west wall were found, as well as burnt layers. A possible bread wheat grain from an upper layer (F129; S57) abutting the wall was radiocarbon-dated to the thirteenth–fourteenth century (UBA-38838; AD 1298–1372, 2σ).

Two deposits were presented for archaeobotanical analysis (Table 16.6); both contained relatively small quantities of charred plant macro-remains. An upper layer (F129) abutting the wall, radiocarbon-dated to the thirteenth–fourteenth century, contained cereal grains, including possible naked wheat, barley, *Secale cereale* L. (rye) and possible oat. This is the only trench at Swords Castle that contained rye. A seed of possible *Cirsium* sp. (thistle) was also present. Thistles can be found growing in a variety of environments. A lower layer (F159) contained a larger quantity of remains. Cereals were again dominant, mainly possible naked wheat, with some oat and barley. Seeds of the Poaceae family were also present; these were narrow and/or small, possibly reflecting wild grasses. Vetch seeds were recorded, which may represent fodder or a wild plant growing locally. A small seed of possible *Malus sylvestris* (L.) Mill. (crab-apple) was also present. Crab-apple may have been gathered locally.

Table 16.6—Plant macro-remains from Trenches 7 and 8.

		Trench	7	7	7	7	8	8
		Feature	6:1:0	6:3:0	2:2:0	17:1:0	129	159
		Sample	42	54	59	66	57	64
Botanical name	**Common name**	**Component**						
FABACEAE								
Vicia spp	Vetches	Seed >2mm	1	…	…	…	…	1
Vicia spp	Vetches	Seed <2mm	…	…	1	…	…	7
cf. *Pisum sativum* L.	cf. Garden pea	Seed	…	…	1	…	…	…
Fabaceae	Pea family	Seed >2mm	1	…	2	…	…	…
Fabaceae	Pea family	Seed frag. >2mm	…	3	10	…	…	…
Fabaceae	Pea family	Seed frag. <2mm	…	2	1	…	…	…
ROSACEAE								
cf. *Malus sylvestris* (L.) Mill.	cf. Crab-apple	Seed	…	…	…	…	…	1
RUBIACEAE								
Galium spp	Bedstraws	Seed fragment	1	…	2	…	…	…
ASTERACEAE								
cf. *Cirsium* spp	cf. Thistles	Seed	…	…	…	…	1	…
POACEAE								
Avena spp	Oat	Grain	…	1	2	…	…	7
Avena spp	Oat	Grain fragment	…	…	…	…	…	1
cf. *Avena* spp	cf. Oat	Grain	3	…	3	…	3	…
Hordeum spp	Barley	Grain	…	…	…	…	1	1
Triticum cf. *aestivum* L.	cf. Bread wheat	Grain	22	…	23	…	12	21
Triticum spp	Wheat	Grain	6	…	…	…	…	2
Secale cereale L.	Rye	Grain	…	…	…	…	1	…
Cerealia	Indeterminate cereal	Grain fragment	26	2	52	3	19	13
Poaceae	Grass family	Seed	…	…	…	…	…	12
Poaceae	Indeterminate cereal	Culm node fragment	…	1	…	…	…	…
		Total	60	9	97	3	37	66
		% of sample examined	100	100	100	100	100	100

DISCUSSION

The archaeological excavation at Swords Castle has uncovered a very large quantity of charred cereal grains dating from the early medieval to medieval period, as well as cereal chaff, cultivated legumes, weed seeds, and fruit and nut remains. Bread wheat was the dominant cereal in many deposits, with smaller quantities of oat, barley and rye recorded. Very large quantities of cereals were recorded in deposits dating from the eleventh to thirteenth centuries—the transition between the early medieval and medieval periods—and later. There are only a few medieval sites where comparably large assemblages have been recorded, including Bective Abbey, Co. Meath (Lyons 2015). While several early medieval sites have produced large cereal assemblages (McClatchie *et al.* 2015), few are dated to as late as the eleventh/twelfth century (the end of the early medieval period).

All of the plant remains from Swords Castle were preserved by charring. The cereals may have come into contact with fire and become charred during cooking associated with domestic activity at Swords Castle, with the debris eventually making its way into pits and other layers. Indeed, the early fourteenth-century description of Swords Castle in Archbishop Alen's register mentions a kitchen and bakehouse. Occupation of the site before construction of the archbishop's residence may also have included cooking structures and features. Alternatively, the cereals may represent the remnants of crops that were kiln-dried and later stored at Swords Castle. When crops are being kiln-dried, some can become accidentally burnt, and it is only these burnt remains that will survive in the archaeological record. Cereals are known to have been stored at Swords Castle during the medieval period—Archbishop Alen's register mentions the presence of a granary. Furthermore, Swords Castle was the headquarters of a medieval manorial estate that was a substantial agricultural enterprise (Murphy and Potterton 2010), and large supplies of grain would have been accumulated. In the centuries before and after the establishment of the manor, it appears that the site was also the focus for cereal-based activities, perhaps including storage.

Cereals were recorded in almost all examined deposits from Swords Castle, from the ninth–eleventh centuries up to the fifteenth–seventeenth centuries, highlighting the importance of cereals over several centuries at this location. One of the largest quantities of cereals was found in eleventh–thirteenth-century deposits in Trench 3, suggesting that this area was a focus for food storage, processing or preparation, or perhaps for the dumping of food waste. Large quantities of fragmented cereal grains were found in several deposits, perhaps reflecting significant movement and abrasion of the grains prior to their final deposition. A large quantity of cereal remains was also found in a fifteenth–seventeenth-century deposit in Pit A, perhaps reflecting a time when Swords Castle had fallen into ruin (known to have occurred from the sixteenth century) but suggesting that the location was still being used for cereal-related activities.

The importance of cereals in early medieval and medieval Ireland is reflected in the wide variety of historical and archaeological evidence for arable activity (McClatchie 2003; McClatchie *et al.* 2015; Murphy and Potterton 2010). Cereals would have been cultivated for their food value; grains could have been used in a variety of food products, including breads, gruels and porridges, as well as in brewing and as animal fodder (Kelly 1997; Sexton 1998; McClatchie 2003; Murphy and Potterton 2010). Nearby mills would have been used to grind the cereal grains to produce fine flour or coarse meal. Cereal straw and chaff would have been utilised in structures, roofing, bedding, baskets, mats and hen-roosts (Kelly 1997, 111, 240). According to an Irish early seventeenth-century document, 'in the heart of the best walled towns, cities and boroughs, there stand many poor cottages of straw, chaff and clay' (O'Brien 1923, 36). Cereals could also have been used as a form of currency, for example in food-rent (Kelly 1997, 219, 333).

Bread wheat was the main cereal recovered at Swords Castle, although oat was dominant in several eleventh–twelfth-century deposits from Trenches 4 and 6. Wheat and oat are often considered to be the primary crops of medieval Ireland (Murphy and Potterton 2010), with wheat particularly dominant in eastern and south-eastern regions. Bread wheat is a naked or free-threshing form of wheat. While it was certainly grown in early medieval Ireland, it was rarely the dominant crop on any individual site (McClatchie *et al.* 2015). The cultivation of bread wheat became much more significant after the arrival of the Anglo-Normans in Ireland (Monk 1986, 34), related in part to the introduction of new farming techniques such as crop rotation. The cultivation of bread wheat requires an increased input of labour and a better quality of soil than other cereals. Wheat was used in the production of bread. The superior quality of wheaten flour, when carefully processed, produces pleasant, light and fine-textured bread, compared to the heavy, coarse and dark breads of oat, barley and rye flours (Sexton 1998, 79). Wheat was also consumed in the form of other foodstuffs, including gruels and ale. During the harvest at Clonkeen (now Dean's Grange), Co. Dublin, in 1344, provision was made to give the workers wheat for malting in return for work carried out (Mills 1890–1, 62). Large wheat assemblages have previously been found at several medieval sites in Ireland, for example at Kilferagh, Co. Kilkenny (Monk 1987), and Bective Abbey, Co. Meath (Lyons 2015).

Oat began to be cultivated in north-west Europe during the Iron Age and early medieval periods (Stika and Heiss 2012, 362). It became one of the most important cereals in early medieval Ireland, and its importance continued into the medieval period, particularly in areas of Gaelic control (McClatchie 2003; McClatchie *et al.* 2015). Oat was used to make bread shaped as a broad, flat cake, in addition to porridge and oatmeal pastes (Sexton 1998, 79). Ale was often brewed using oats rather than barley, a custom that sometimes offended English travellers of the seventeenth century: 'scarce anywhere outside Dublin and some few other towns will you meet with any good beer or any reasonable bread for your money, only you may have some raw, muddy, unwholesome ale, made solely of oats' (O'Brien 1923, 35). Ale could have been viewed not just as a drink but also as food, its nourishing content providing a liquid alternative to what would usually be considered food. Indeed, a seventeenth-century English traveller in Ireland believed that the ale was brewed in this way to verify the proverb that 'Good drink is meat, drink and cloth' (*ibid.*, 87). The presence of a germinated oat grain in Trench 7 may reflect the production of ale (cereals are germinated as part of the brewing process), but only a single germinated grain was recorded and it is possible that it began to germinate simply because it became damp. Oat was also used in animal feed. Langdon (1982, 32) notes that oats were fed to horses and oxen in medieval England during winter, when animals could not graze in pasture.

Barley has been an important crop in Ireland since the introduction of farming in the centuries after 4000 BC (McClatchie *et al.* 2014). During the early medieval and medieval periods, barley was consumed in the form of breads, porridge and meal pastes, in stews and pottages, and also as animal fodder. Barley bread was still being eaten in certain districts in the nineteenth century, especially in County Wexford, at a time when wheaten bread had generally superseded oatcakes to become the most popular bread (Lysaght 1986, 81). The unsatisfactory baking qualities of barley makes it more likely, however, that it was combined with wheat in the production of maslin, or mixed cereal, foods. Barley was also commonly used in the production of ale. The barley cultivated in a district in south County Dublin in the fourteenth century, beyond what was required for seed, was all malted for brewing (Mills 1890–1, 61). Interestingly, while wheat and oat are mentioned in medieval documentary sources relating to agricultural production for the manor at Swords Castle (Murphy and Potterton 2010), barley is not mentioned. Its presence in the archaeological deposits from Swords Castle indicates, however, that it may also have been a feature in agricultural systems here.

Like oat, rye began to be cultivated in north-west Europe during the Iron Age and early medieval periods (Stika and Heiss 2012, 362). Rye seems to have been grown on a limited scale in medieval Ireland (only a single grain was found at Swords Castle) and is associated with environments that may not have had the potential to support wheat and barley in terms of soil texture and nutrients. The Civil Survey of 1654–6 states that an area of Longford had soils 'which are fitt only for rye and oates' (Simington 1961, 45–6), emphasising the association of rye with areas of limited agricultural productivity. In common with other cereals, rye would have been incorporated into a variety of foodstuffs, including breads, gruels and ales, as well as being used in fodder and structures. The straw of rye is very suitable for thatching, as the stems are tall, growing to around 1.5m in height.

Two types of cultivated legume were recorded in deposits at Swords Castle: garden pea and broad bean. Recent research by Lyons and McClatchie (unpublished) indicates that legumes began to be cultivated in early medieval Ireland but extensive cultivation did not occur until the medieval period. At Swords Castle, cultivated legumes were found in deposits dating from the eleventh–twelfth century and later. Pea and bean have been recorded in medieval deposits elsewhere, including Kilferagh, Co. Kilkenny (Monk 1987), and Bective Abbey (Lyons 2015). Legumes are important not just as foodstuffs but also owing to their ability to fix nitrogen in soils, thus making cultivation plots more productive. The presence of legumes and the dominance of bread wheat at Swords Castle is striking: bread wheat requires a better quality of soil than other cereals, and it is possible that legumes formed part of a crop-rotation system to improve soil quality. Farmers in medieval England recognised this potential, which led to legumes becoming an important component of intensive cropping regimes (Green 1984, 107). There is no documentary evidence that these intensive systems were employed in Ireland (Murphy and Potterton 2010, 314). Substantial information for legume cultivation and use in medieval Ireland can be found, however, in administrative records associated with large estates and demesnes, particularly those located in the east of the island. The accounts of food liveries from Swords Castle, Clonkeen and Grangegorman document the production of legumes for human and animal consumption as an important component of the domestic economy (*ibid.*, 315). As well as being fed harvested legumes, animals were sometimes left to graze on standing legume crops, the stumps of which were subsequently ploughed back into the soil along with animal dung to further enhance soil quality (*ibid.*, 314). Pea is mentioned in medieval documentary sources relating to agricultural production for the manor at Swords Castle but bean is not. Its presence in the archaeological deposits from Swords Castle suggests, however, that bean may also have been a feature in agricultural systems here.

Occasional vetch seeds were recorded at Swords Castle. Vetch is often considered to have been utilised in foods, whether for humans or animals. Gerard (1633, 1226) acknowledged its use in times of famine. Green (1984, 107) maintains that vetches were grown in medieval England as a field crop and often mixed with cereals, while other commentators have suggested that vetch was deliberately harvested for its use in animal fodder (Greig 1991, 323). There is no documentary evidence for the cultivation of vetches in medieval Ireland (Murphy and Potterton 2010, 314–16). By contrast, there is extensive documentary evidence for the cultivation of vetches in medieval England, principally as fodder and also as famine food—such evidence can be found in manorial accounts associated with seigniorial estates and smallholdings (Campbell 2000, 228–30). In the case of Swords Castle, it is difficult to decide whether vetch remains similarly represent cultivated produce or instead represent weeds growing locally or in arable fields, perhaps gathered for consumption but not actually cultivated.

It is believed that a medieval garden existed at Swords Castle, but there are no historical records for an orchard here before the eighteenth century. The recovery of a small quantity of crab-apple, bramble, sloe and hazelnut remains could reflect trees and shrubs growing in a medieval garden here. While cereals are more likely to have been cultivated in fields outside the castle grounds, legumes can thrive in small garden plots and may also have been a feature of local horticulture here.

Small quantities of weed seeds were present in many deposits. The low levels of weed seeds and cereal chaff at Swords Castle indicate that the cereals and legumes had been almost completely cleaned of contaminants and were ready for final storage or use. Several of the weeds are likely to represent arable weeds, including corn-cockle, redshank, fat hen, sun spurge, wild radish, cleavers, field gromwell, stinking chamomile and corn marigold. Corn-cockle is an interesting weed because it is somewhat poisonous and would have affected the colour and taste of flour (Tierney and Hannon 1997, 888–9). It is now largely extinct in Ireland but would have been a noxious and troublesome weed of arable fields during the medieval period. Weeds from grassy and damp environments (including common sorrel, meadow buttercup and ribwort plantain) may indicate the use of meadow and wetland grasses and plants in roofing and other structures.

Several of the 'weeds' present may also have been gathered as leafy greens. A traveller in Ireland during the seventeenth century observed that the Irish 'gladly eat raw herbs' (Falkiner 1904, 320), while another traveller in 1672–4 noted that the Irish consumed some 'roots' with their flat oatcakes (Buckley 1904, 95). The texture and taste of these oatcakes are compared to horses' hooves in a twelfth-century poem, *Aislinge Meic Con Glinne*, and it seems that there may have been a preference for the use of condiments with such foods (Sexton 1998, 83). Many of these condiments may not have been important in terms of nutrition but, used in conjunction with other foods, they could have been vital for palatability. In early medieval documents, common sorrel is mentioned as being used as such a condiment (*ibid.*). Gerard's late medieval *Herball* described how common sorrel provided a 'profitable sauce in many meats' and was 'pleasant to the taste' (Gerard 1633, 398). Lucas (1960, 137) notes that sorrel was considered to be one of the 'curious salads' consumed by the Irish. It is even suggested that 'weeds' such as fat hen were not just gathered but also managed, perhaps since the prehistoric period (Stokes and Rowley-Conwy 2002). Indeed, fat hen was sold by hawkers and eaten as a leafy vegetable (similar to spinach) until the eighteenth century in Dublin (Geraghty 1996, 37). Wild radish is also believed to have been consumed in Viking Dublin to add variety to the diet (Mitchell 1987, 26; Geraghty 1996, 35). Plants gathered for medicinal use are difficult to identify, as many different plant species have had medicinal uses attributed to them in the past. Several documentary sources provide evidence for the use of plants for their medicinal benefits (Keogh 1735; Gerard 1633; Salmon 1710), but it is difficult to demonstrate that these plants were actually used for medicinal purposes on the basis of their presence in archaeological deposits. It can be similarly difficult to provide definite archaeobotanical evidence for the use of plants in cloth-processing and dyeing. Sorrel, for example, is known to have been used as a mordant in dyeing garments (Moloney 1919, 39). While it can be difficult to demonstrate the use of these 'weeds', their potential should nonetheless be considered.

CONCLUSIONS

An archaeological excavation at Swords Castle, Co. Dublin, has uncovered a substantial assemblage of plant remains dating from the early medieval to the medieval period. Swords Castle was a manorial centre that controlled significant agricultural production in the region. The excavation also revealed evidence for activity here in the centuries prior to establishment of the manor. A variety of crops were recovered, including plants that are not mentioned in existing medieval manorial records. Bread wheat was the dominant crop, with smaller quantities of oat, barley, rye, pea and bean also present. Occasional fruit and nut remains were recorded, as well as weeds.

The species represented in the plant remains from Swords Castle have been found at many other early medieval and medieval sites in eastern Ireland. The quantity of remains recorded here is, however, very unusual. More than 16,000 plant components were observed, mainly consisting of cereal grains. It appears that food-related activities played an important role at Swords Castle, emphasising its importance as the centre of a vast agricultural enterprise.

17

Charcoal report

Dr Ellen OCarroll

INTRODUCTION

This report presents the results of the analysis of six charcoal fragments sampled from medieval occupation layers and a kiln at Swords Castle, Co. Dublin. The analysis presented here concentrates on species identification, species selection and the composition of the local woodland during the medieval/later medieval period in the immediate environs of Swords Castle.

METHODS

Wood, whether it is charred, dried or waterlogged, is identified by comparing the anatomical structure of samples with known comparative material or keys (Schweingruber 1990). A wood reference collection from the Botanical Gardens in Glasnevin, Dublin, was also used.

The identification of charcoal material involves breaking the charcoal piece along its three sections (transverse, tangential and radial) so that clean sections of the wood pieces can be obtained. Each piece of charcoal was examined and orientated first under low magnification (10x–40x) before being broken to reveal its transverse, tangential and longitudinal surfaces. Pieces were mounted in plasticine and examined under a binocular microscope with dark ground light and magnifications generally of 200x and 400x. The charcoal species are determined by close examination of the micro-anatomical features of the samples. Identification was undertaken to the highest taxonomic level possible (usually that of genus) according to the anatomical characteristics described by Schweingruber (1990), with nomenclature according to Stace (1991). Individual taxa were quantified (mature and twig separated) and the results tabulated.

Quantifying charcoal samples can be difficult, as many wood species can be affected by heat in different ways and hence become fragmented into an arbitrary number of fragments. Fragment count was low from some of the samples (sample nos 2 and 66). Owing to the potential for a very high number of charcoal fragments from the samples, a representative sample of 50 charcoal fragments (Keepax 1988) were randomly chosen from larger samples for identification and analysis. In the case of smaller samples, all charcoal fragments within were identified. The charcoal fragments of each species were also identified, counted, weighed (grams) and bagged according to species.

The general age group of each taxon per sample is recorded, as well as the diameters of the charcoal fragments. The ring curvature was also noted where applicable from each charcoal fragment. Weakly curved annual rings suggest the use of trunks or larger branches, while strongly curved annual rings indicate the burning of smaller branches or twigs.

RESULTS AND ANALYSIS

A total of nine taxon types were identified from the charcoal sampled from the excavations. Oak (*Quercus* sp.) was the dominant taxon, followed by ash (*Fraxinus excelsior*), hazel (*Corylus avellana*), willow (*Salix* sp.), birch (*Betula* sp.), blackthorn (*Prunus spinosa*), holly (*Ilex aquifolium*), Pomoideae (apple/pear/hawthorn and mountain ash) and furze *(Ulex europaeus)* (Fig. 17.1; Table 17.1).

When the data are plotted by feature type, we see oak dominating within both types (layers and kilns). Other taxa present in the kiln are blackthorn and furze. Ash and hazel were relatively common from the layers, with lesser counts of blackthorn, birch, holly, Pomoideae, willow and furze also present (Fig. 17.1).

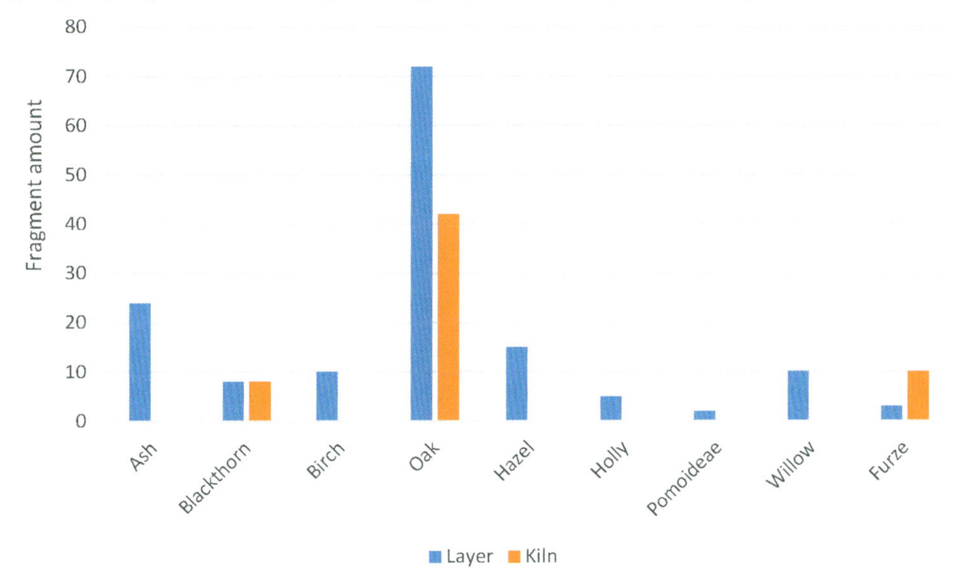

Fig. 17.1—Taxa identified by feature type.

DISCUSSION: WOOD SELECTION, USE AND FUNCTION

A total of 209 charcoal fragments with a combined weight of 64.75g were analysed from occupation layers and a kiln dating from the medieval/late medieval periods (Fig. 17.1; Table 17.1).

One of the principal motivations for charcoal analysis is the general hypothesis that firewood will be collected as close to a site as possible and thus will reflect the local wooded environment. It is likely, however, that abandoned structural timbers or wood brought to the site for other uses would also have been reused as firewood. Thus charcoal identifications

Table 17.1—Analysis of charcoal fragments.

Context no.	Sample no.	Context type	Date	Wood species	No. of fragments	Charcoal weight (grams)	Size of fragments (mm)	No. of growth rings	Comment
F126:1	42	Upper level—occupation floor		*Fraxinus excelsior* (ash)	20	1.8	3–8	5–10	
				Quercus sp. (oak)	12	1.1	3–7	3–10	
F126:3	2	Lower level — occupation floor	AD 1461 –1636	*Corylus avellana* (hazel)	5	0.3	3–6	2–4	All identifiable fragments identified
				Betula sp. (birch)	4	0.1	2–8	3–8	
				Ulex europaeus (furze)	3	0.1	3–6	2–6	
F129	5	Layer—AD 1298–1372	AD 1298–1372	*Betula* sp. (birch)	6	0.4	2–9	3–10	All identifiable fragments identified
				Salix sp. (willow)	10	0.9	2–7	3–6	
				Fraxinus excelsior (ash)	4	0.2	3–8	2–3	
				Corylus avellana (hazel)	10	0.9	2–8	3–6	
				Prunus sp. (blackthorn)	8	0.3	4–8	4–8	
				Ilex aquifolium (holly)	5	0.5	2–7	2–5	
				Quercus sp. (oak)	10	0.25	3–7	3–10	
				Pomoideae	2	0.2	3–6	4–6	
F159	64	Layer		*Quercus* sp. (oak)	50	54	5–45	5–43 years	
F161:1	66	Flue connecting fire-pit and bowl of kiln		*Quercus* sp. (oak)	10	1.3	5–15	3–28	Very small charcoal fragment
F161: 2	65			*Quercus* sp. (oak)	32	1.8	5–15	3–28	Some furze brushwood

represent the various modes of collection and selection of woods used as fuel at the site, and go some way towards interpreting (although not exhaustively) the local woodland dynamics of an area over time.

A mosaic of woodlands were present around Swords Castle in the medieval periods. The charcoal identified from the samples suggests the selection of wood from mixed woodlands (oak, ash, hazel and holly) or scrub-type woodland (furze, hazel, holly, blackthorn and Pomoideae). Pomoideae includes apple, pear, hawthorn and mountain ash and cannot be differentiated microscopically. Birch and willow prefer wetter ground, which indicates the presence of some wetter terrain close to the castle.

Oak charcoal was identified in larger quantities from most features, and in particular from the kiln. Charcoal was particularly important to activities that required heat, as it burned hotter and cleaner than wood and was considered a superior fuel. The heavier and denser the wood, the higher its calorific value. Oak can burn for a considerable period of time and can reach the extremely high temperatures necessary for the production of metal objects and smelting, as well as cremations (O'Donnell 2007). It is not unreasonable to conclude, therefore, that the wood used in the layers and in particular within the kiln was deliberately selected from oak woodlands when a high temperature was required.

Thus the firewood/charcoal associated with the kiln would have been deliberately selected for industrial use. While other charcoals present may have been deliberately selected for certain purposes, the functionality of those recovered from the layers remains ambiguous, making the determination of woodland selection more difficult for these features. Charcoal from these deposits and layers may represent firewood and extraneous waste from various activities at the site.

Pollen analysis by Cole and Mitchell (2003) at Liffey Head Bog, Co. Wicklow, and All Saints Bog, Co. Offaly, indicates that there was considerable woodland cover in the midland and eastern areas of Ireland from the eighth century through to the fifteenth century, and possibly later. Similar tangible evidence from charcoal studies is highlighted in recent research that shows a shift to a dominant use of oak in kilns from the tenth century onward, which is also reflected more broadly in structures, ditches and pits (Lyons 2018). These results are mirrored at Swords Castle, where oak is dominant in most of the post-tenth-century archaeological features. Lyons also postulates that over-exploitation in the seventh and eighth centuries would have resulted in a decline in the quality and quantity of mature oak available. This in turn necessitated the management (possibly coppiced) and strict control of the oak woodlands required for medieval and later medieval towns such as Swords.

SUMMARY AND CONCLUSIONS

Six charcoal samples were examined from occupation layers and a kiln dating from between the thirteenth and sixteenth centuries at Swords Castle, Co. Dublin. Taxa identified (in order of representation) were oak (*Quercus* sp.), ash (*Fraxinus excelsior*), hazel (*Corylus avellana*), willow (*Salix* sp.), birch (*Betula* sp.), blackthorn (*Prunus spinosa*), holly (*Ilex aquifolium*), Pomoideae (apple/pear/hawthorn and mountain ash) and furze (*Ulex europaeus*). Identifications were dominated by oak, which is present in high quantities from nearly all features analysed as well as from burning activities associated with the kiln. Results indicate that oak woods may still have been a major component of the woodland landscape surrounding Swords after the tenth century and may have been managed to ensure a consistent supply of wood and charcoal for metalworking activities and construction. Ash, also a woodland canopy-forming tree, was used frequently as firewood in association with activities at the castle.

Scrub-type woodland (furze, hazel, Pomoideae and holly) was also present in the area, and species from these woodlands were selected for burning at the castle site. Willow and birch prefer wetter ground, which implies selection of wood from a wetter landscape. Along with the oak wood, it can be proposed that furze wood may have been deliberately selected, as it is highly inflammable and has been identified from medieval oven fills at Glanworth Castle, Cork, and Danesfort 4, Co. Kilkenny.

18

Radiocarbon dates

The following radiocarbon dates (see overleaf) were produced by the [14]CHRONO Centre, Queen's University Belfast. All samples are fraction-corrected using AMS $\partial^{13}C$. The radiocarbon calibration program used is CLAIBREV6.0.0 (© 1986–2010, M. Stuiver and P.J. Reimer), in conjunction with Stuiver and Reimer 1993. For calibration datasets see Stuiver and Reimer 1993.

Lab. code	Dated material and context	Year BP	Calibrated date 2σ
UBA-34515	Fragment of human cranium (aged 45±) retrieved from the base of the eastern post-hole F101	1089 ± 28	AD 893–933 (35%)
			AD 936–1013 (65%)
UBA-32455	Charred wheat (possible bread wheat) from oval pit F19	1076 ± 33	AD 894–931 (27%)
			AD 937–1019 (73%)
UBA-38842	SK15	980 ± 37	AD 994–1059 (45%)
			AD 1064–1154 (55%)
UBA-38841	SK14	982 ± 27	AD 995–1053 (52%)
			AD 1079–1152 (48%)
UBA-34517	Charred oat seed from basal fill, enclosure ditch F85	1021 ± 25	AD 975–1037
UBA-38840	SK01	954 ± 47	AD 996–1185
UBA-32453	Charred wheat (possible bread wheat) from burnt deposit F8	952 ± 46	AD 1011–1187 (98%)
UBA-32452	Human seventh cervical vertebra from redeposited clay F29	966 ± 29	AD 1018–1059 (35%)
			AD 1065–1154 (65%)
UBA-32457	Charred wheat (possible bread wheat) from basal fill of pit F31	935 ± 40	AD 1021–1186
UBA-34518	Charred oat seed from F93, primary fill of pit F95	953 ± 29	AD 1023–1154
UBA-34519	Charred oat seed from pit F103	934 ± 28	AD 1029–1159
UBA-32456	Charred wheat (possible bread wheat) from a deposit, F22, which contained more than 10,000 plant components	898 ± 42	AD 1032–1217
UBA-32454	Charred wheat (possible bread wheat) from lower (F43) of series of thin layers	595 ± 32	AD 1298–1373 (72%)
			AD 1377–1411 (28%)
UBA-38838	Charred wheat seed from heat-affected soil F129	601 ± 28	AD 1298–1372 (75%)
			AD 1377–1407 (25%)
UBA-34516	Charred wheat (possibly bread wheat) from untrammelled ground surface F80	589 ± 31	AD 1299–1371 (70%)
			AD 1379–1413 (30%)
UBA-32458	Charred wheat (possible bread wheat) from heat-affected deposit (F30) in Pit A	432 ± 33	AD 1419–1512
UBA-38839	Charred barley grain from the basal fill (F146:2) of the kiln	361 ± 29	AD 1451–1528 (52%)
			AD 1544–1634 (48%)
UBA-38837	Charred oat seed from basal layer F126:3, overlying flagged floor	348 ± 31	AD 1461–1636

Bibliography

Albion Archaeology 2013 *La Grava: The archaeology and history of a royal manor and alien priory of Fontevrault* [dataset]. Archaeology Data Service [distributor] (http://archaeologydataservice.ac.uk).

Allen, L. (n.d.) Chapter 15. Medieval and post-medieval metalwork in Framework Archaeology. In *Excavations at Stansted Airport* (http://www.framearch.co.uk/stansted; accessed August 2018).

Apel, W. 1953 *The notation of polyphonic music, 900–1600*. Medieval Academy of America, Cambridge, Mass.

Atkinson, D. and Oswald, A. 1969 London clay tobacco pipes. *Journal of the Archaeological Association* (3rd ser.) **32**, 171–227.

Aufderheide, A.C. and Rodríguez-Martín, C. 1998 *The Cambridge Encyclopedia of Human Paleopathology.* Cambridge University Press, Cambridge.

Aultman, J. and Grillo, K. 2012 *DAACS cataloging manual: Buttons* (http://daacs.org/wp-content/uploads/buttons.pdf).

Ayto, E.G. 1987 *Clay tobacco pipes.* Shire Publications, Aylesbury.

Bailey, M. 1988 The rabbit and the medieval East Anglian economy. *Agricultural History Review* **36** (1), 1–20.

Baker, B.J., Dupras, T.L. and Tocheri, M.W. 2005 *The osteology of infants and children.* Texas A&M University Press, College Station, Texas.

Baker, C. 2010 Occam's Duck: three early medieval settlement cemeteries or ecclesiastical enclosures? In C. Corlett and M. Potterton (eds), *Death and burial in early medieval Ireland in the light of recent archaeological excavations*, 1–22. Wordwell, Dublin.

Baker, C. 2015 Swords Castle: Digging History. *Archaeology Ireland* **29** (4), 41–4.

Baker, C. 2016 Archaeological excavation preliminary report. Season 1: August–September 2015. Swords Castle, Swords, Co. Dublin. Consent no.: C450. Excavation ref.: E004619. Unpublished technical report prepared for Fingal County Council.

Baker, C. 2017 Archaeological excavation preliminary report. Season 2: August–September 2016. Swords Castle, Swords, Co. Dublin. Consent no.: C450. Excavation ref.: E004619. Unpublished technical report prepared for Fingal County Council.

Baker, C. 2018 Archaeological excavation preliminary report. Season 3: August–September 2017. Swords Castle, Swords, Co. Dublin. Consent no.: C450. Excavation ref.: E004619. Unpublished technical report prepared for Fingal County Council.

Baker, C. 2020 Archaeological excavation final report. Swords Castle 2015–17, Swords, Co.

Dublin. Consent no.: C450. Excavation ref.: E004619. Unpublished technical report prepared for Fingal County Council.

Basford, J.L. 2012 A commodity of good names: the branding of products, *c.* 1650–1900. Unpublished Ph.D thesis, University of York (accessed at http://etheses.whiterose. ac.uk/2754/7/7_Chapter_Five_Final_Corrected.pdf).

Bass, W.M. 1995 *Human osteology: a laboratory and field manual.* Missouri Archaeological Society, Columbia, Miss.

Beglane, F. 2014 Theatre of power: the Anglo-Norman park at Earlspark, Co. Galway, Ireland. *Medieval Archaeology* **58**, 307–17.

Beglane, F. 2015a Behind stone walls in Loughrea. *Archaeology Ireland* **29** (2), 33–6.

Beglane, F. 2015b *Anglo-Norman parks in medieval Ireland.* Four Courts Press, Dublin.

Beglane, F. 2016 The faunal remains from Bective Abbey. In G. Stout and M. Stout, *The Bective Abbey Project, Co. Meath: excavations 2009–12*, 126–70. Wordwell, Dublin.

Beijerinck, W. 1947 *Zadenatlas der Nederlandsche Flora.* H. Veenman & Zonen, Wageningen.

Bergmann, T.F., Hyde, T.E. and Yochum, T.R. 2002 Active or inactive spondylolysis and/or spondylolisthesis. *Journal of the Neuromusculoskeletal System* **10**, 70–8.

Berry, H.F. 1910 *Statute rolls of the Parliament of Ireland: reign of King Henry the Sixth.* HMSO, Dublin.

Betts, I.M. and Cromwell, T.G. 2011 Windsor Castle Governor's House (Norman Gate, South Tower, first floor). Survey record and interpretation of a medieval tiled floor: archaeological report. English Heritage Research Department unpublished report series, no. 26 (https://doi.org/10.5284/1033727).

Bhreathnach, E. 1999 Columban churches in Brega and Leinster: relations with the Norse and the Anglo-Normans. *Journal of the Royal Society of Antiquaries of Ireland* **129**, 5–18.

Binder, M., Berner, M., Krause, H., Kucera, M. and Patzak, B. 2016 Scientific analysis of a calcified object from a post-medieval burial in Vienna, Austria. *International Journal of Paleopathology* **14**, 24–30.

Birrell, J. 1992 Deer and deer farming in medieval England. *Agricultural History Review* **40** (2), 112–26.

Blair, J. and Ramsay, N. (eds) 1992 *English medieval industries.* Hambledon Press, London.

Blake, H. and Davey, P. (eds) 1983 *Guidelines for the processing and publication of medieval pottery from excavations.* Department of the Environment Directorate of Ancient Monuments and Historic Buildings, London.

Bliss, A.J. 1965–6 The inscribed slates at Smarmore. *Proceedings of the Royal Irish Academy* **64**C, 33–60.

Boessneck, J. 1969 Osteological differences between sheep and goat. In D.R. Brothwell and E. Higgs (eds), *Science in archaeology: a survey of progress and research*, 331–58. Thames and Hudson, London.

Bolton, J. 2016 Swords Castle mortar report. Unpublished report for Fingal County Council.

Bourke, E. 1997 The glass. In M.F. Hurley and O.M.B. Scully, *Late Viking Age and medieval Waterford: excavations 1986–1992*, 381–9. Waterford Corporation, Waterford.

Bradley, J. 1998 The medieval boroughs of County Dublin. In C. Manning (ed.), *Dublin and beyond the Pale: studies in honour of Patrick Healy*, 129–44. Wordwell, Bray.

Brassey, R. 1991 Clay tobacco pipes from the site of the Victoria Hotel, Auckland, New Zealand. *Australian Historical Archaeology* **9**, 27–30.

Brenan, J. 1998 Furnishings. In G. Egan, *The medieval household: daily living* c. *1150–c. 1450*, 65–87. Medieval Finds from Excavations in London 6. The Stationery Office, London.

Brewer, J.S. and Bullen, B.W. (eds) 1868–73 *Calendar of the Carew manuscripts preserved in the archiepiscopal library at Lambeth* (6 vols). Public Record Office, London.

Brook, S.T. and Suchey, J.M. 1990 Skeletal age determination based on the os pubis: a comparison of the Acsádi–Nemeskéri and Suchey–Brook methods. *Human Evolution* **5**, 227–38.

Brothwell, D.R. 1981 *Digging up bones: the excavation, treatment and study of human skeletal remains.* British Museum (Natural History), London.

Brothwell, D. and Zakrzewski, S. 2004 Metric and non-metric studies of archaeological human bone. In M. Brickley and J.I. McKinley (eds), *Guidelines to the standards for recording human remains*, 27–33. Institute of Field Archaeologists Paper No. 7. BABAO and IFA, Southampton and Reading.

Buckley, J. 1904 A tour in Ireland in 1672–4. *Journal of the Cork Historical and Archaeological Society* **10**, 85–100.

Buckley, L. and Conway, C. 2010 Early medieval settlement and burial ground at Faughart Lower, Co. Louth. In C. Corlett and M. Potterton (eds), *Death and burial in early medieval Ireland in the light of recent archaeological excavations*, 49–60. Wordwell, Dublin.

Buckley, L., Murphy, E. and Ó Donnabháin, B. 1999 *The treatment of human remains: technical paper for archaeologists.* Dublin. [Reprinted by the Institute of Archaeologists of Ireland, 2004.]

Buikstra, J.E. and Ubelaker, D.H. 1994 *Standards for data collection from human skeletal remains: proceedings of a seminar at the Field Museum of Natural History, organized by Jonathan Haas.* Arkansas Archeological Survey, Fayetteville.

Campbell, B.M.S. 2000 *English seigniorial agriculture, 1250–1450.* Cambridge University Press, Cambridge.

Campbell, K. 2007 The floor tiles. In M. Clyne, *Kells Priory, Co. Kilkenny: archaeological excavations by T. Fanning and M. Clyne*, 234–60. Stationery Office, Dublin.

Cappers, R.T.J., Bekker, R.M. and Jans, J.E.A. 2006 *Digital seed atlas of the Netherlands.* Barhuis, Groningen.

Chamberlain, A.T. and Witkin, A. 2000 Human skeletal remains from Cloghermore Cave, County Kerry, Ireland. Unpublished report for client.

Channing, J. 1995 Swords Castle, Swords, Co. Dublin. In I. Bennett (ed.), *Excavations 1994.* Wordwell, Bray.

Clark, J. 1995 *The medieval horse and its equipment, c.1150–c.1450.* Medieval Finds from Excavations in London, 5. HMSO, London.

Clark, M.A., Worrell, M.B. and Pless, J.E. 1997 Postmortem changes in soft tissue. In W.D. Haglund and M.H. Sorg (eds), *Forensic taphonomy: the postmortem fate of human remains*, 151–64. CRC Press, Boca Raton.

Cole, E.E. and Mitchell, F.J.G 2003 Human impact on the Irish landscape in the late Holocene inferred from palynological studies at three peatland sites. *The Holocene* **13**, 507–15.

Commissioners of Public Works 1938 *106th Annual Report for the year ended 31st March 1938.* Stationery Office, Dublin.

Costello, V. 2015 *Irish demesne landscapes 1660–1740.* Four Courts Press, Dublin.

Cowgill, J. 1987 Manufacturing techniques. In J. Cowgill, M. de Neergaard and N. Griffith,

Knives and scabbards, 8–50. Medieval Finds from Excavations in London, 1. HMSO, London.

Cox, A. 1996 Post-medieval dress accessories from recent urban excavations in Scotland. *Tayside and Fife Archaeological Journal* **2**, 52–9.

Creighton, O.H. 2009 *Designs upon the land: elite landscapes of the Middle Ages.* Boydell Press, Suffolk.

Crowley, C., Hallinan, F., MacMahon, S., McClatchie, M. and Mullee, A. 2020 *All Bread is Made of Wood: This Dirt*—a public art intervention at Swords Castle. In C. Baker (ed.), *Partnership & participation: community archaeology in Ireland*, 201–10. Wordwell, Dublin.

Curtin, N. 2019 Pottery production in twelfth–fifteenth-century Ireland as an indicator of cultural, social and economic relationships. *Journal of Irish Archaeology* **28**, 139–60.

D'Arcy, G. 1981 *The guide to the birds of Ireland.* Irish Wildlife Publications, Dublin.

Dalton, J. 1838a *The history of the county of Dublin.* Dublin.

Dalton, J. 1838b *The memoirs of the archbishops of Dublin.* Dublin.

de Neergaard, M. 1987 The use of knives, shears, scissors and scabbards. In J. Cowgill, M. de Neergaard and N. Griffiths, *Knives and scabbards*, 51–61. Medieval Finds from Excavations in London, 1. HMSO, London.

Dempsey, E. and O'Clery, M. 1993 *The complete guide to Ireland's birds.* Gill and Macmillan, Dublin.

Di Folco, J. 1985 A survey of medieval floor tiles in St Andrews Cathedral Museum and the Abbot's House, Arbroath Abbey. *Proceedings of the Society of Antiquaries of Scotland* **115**, 289–95.

Doherty, C. 1985 The monastic town in Ireland. In H.B. Clarke and A. Simms (eds), *The comparative history of urban origins in non-Roman Europe: Ireland, Wales, Denmark, Germany, Poland and Russia from the ninth to the thirteenth century*, 55–63. British Archaeological Reports, International Series 255. BAR, Oxford.

Duco, D. 2004 *The* Crowned L, *a famous trade mark from Gouda, Holland.* Pijpenkabinet Foundation, Amsterdam (accessed at http://www.pijpenkabinet.nl/Artikelen/L gekroond/art-E-L gekroond.html).

Duffy, S.G. 2010 Bone and antler artefacts from Kilkenny Courthouse. Unpublished report for Arch-Tech Ltd.

Duffy, S.G. 2011a Glass objects from Kilkenny Courthouse. Unpublished report for Arch-Tech Ltd.

Duffy, S.G. 2011b Ceramic objects from Kilkenny Courthouse, 08E0462. Unpublished report for Arch-Tech Ltd.

Duffy, S.G. 2011c Metal artefacts from Kilkenny Courthouse. Unpublished report for Arch-Tech Ltd.

Duffy, S. 2016 Analysis of animal bone for Swords Castle enabling works. Unpublished report for Fingal County Council.

Dunlevy, M. 1988a *Ceramics in Ireland.* National Museum of Ireland, Dublin.

Dunlevy, M. 1988b A classification of early Irish combs. *Proceedings of the Royal Irish Academy* **88**C, 341–422.

Durham, B. 1977 Archaeological investigations in St Aldates, Oxford. *Oxoniensia* **42**, 83–203.

Eames, E. 1992 *Medieval craftsmen: English tilers.* British Museum Publications, London.

Eames, E. and Fanning, T. 1988 *Irish medieval tiles.* Royal Irish Academy, Dublin.

Eames, E. and Keen, L. 1972 Some line-impressed tile mosaic from western England and Wales. *Journal of the British Archaeological Association* **34**, 66–70.

Egan, G. 1998 *The medieval household: daily living, c. 1150–c. 1450.* Medieval Finds from Excavations in London, 6. The Stationery Office, London.

Egan, G. 2005 *Material culture in London in an age of transition: Tudor and Stuart period finds c. 1450–c. 1700 from excavations at riverside sites in Southwark.* MoLAS Monograph 19. Museum of London Archaeology Service, London.

Egan, G. and Pritchard, F. 1991 *Dress accessories, c. 1150–c. 1450.* Medieval Finds from Excavations in London, 3. HMSO, London.

Egan, P.M. 1894 *History, guide and directory of the county and city of Waterford.* Waterford.

Emery, A. 2006 *Greater medieval houses of England and Wales. Volume 3: Southern England.* Cambridge University Press, Cambridge.

Evans, J.G. and Spencer, P. 1976–7 The Mollusca and environment, Buckquoy, Orkney. In G. Ritchie, 'Excavation of Pictish and Viking-age farmsteads in Buckquoy, Orkney', 215–19. *Proceedings of the Society of Antiquaries of Scotland* **108**, 174–227.

Falkiner, C.L. 1904 *Illustrations of Irish history and topography, mainly of the seventeenth century.* Longmans, Green and Co., London.

Fanning, T. 1975 An Irish medieval tile pavement: recent excavations at Swords Castle, County Dublin. *Journal of the Royal Society of Antiquaries of Ireland* **105**, 47–82.

Fay, D., Kramers, G., Zhang, C., McGrath, D. and Grennan, E. 2007 *Soil geochemical atlas of Ireland.* Teagasc and the Environmental Protection Agency, Wexford.

Fernie, E. 2000 *The architecture of Norman England.* Oxford University Press, Oxford.

Fibiger, L. 2010 The human skeletal remains from Ratoath, Co. Meath. In C. Corlett and M. Potterton (eds), *Death and burial in early medieval Ireland in the light of recent archaeological excavations***, 117–37. Wordwell, Dublin.

Fibiger, L. and Knüsel, C. 2005 Prevalence rates of spondylolysis in British skeletal populations. *International Journal of Osteoarchaeology* **15**, 164–74.

Fingal County Council 2014 *Swords Castle Conservation Plan* (http://www.fingal.ie/ planning-and-buildings/architectural-conservation/conservationplansandreports/).

Fingal County Council 2015 *Swords Castle Cultural Quarter Masterplan* (http://www. fingalcoco.ie/planning-and-buildings/swordsculturalquartermasterplan/).

Forbes, S. 2021 'Always rowdy, violent and colourful'? Eighteenth century elections in the borough of Swords, Co. Dublin (https://thehistoryofparliament.wordpress.com/ 2021/01/19/).

Ford, B. 1987 Lead alloy objects. In P. Holdsworth (ed.), *Excavations in the medieval burgh of Perth, 1979–81*, 130. Society of Antiquaries of Scotland, Edinburgh.

Ford, B. and Walsh, A. 1987 Horseshoe nails/iron nails. In P. Holdsworth (ed.), *Excavations in the medieval burgh of Perth, 1979–81*, 137–9. Society of Antiquaries of Scotland, Edinburgh.

Fraser, R. 1801 *General view of the agriculture and mineralogy, present state and circumstances of the County Wicklow [etc.].* Dublin.

Gaunt, J.D. 2002 Stone counter: comments. In P. Ottaway and N. Rogers, *Craft, industry and everyday life: finds from medieval York*, 2950–1. The Archaeology of York 17/15. Council for British Archaeology, York.

Geraghty, S. 1996 *Viking Dublin: botanical evidence from Fishamble Street.* Royal Irish Academy, Dublin.

Gerard, J. 1633 *The herball or generall historie of plantes: very much enlarged and amended by Thomas Johnson.* Islip and Norton & Whitakers, London.

Gerrard, C.M., Gutiérrez, A., Hurst, J.G. and Vince, A.G. 1995 A guide to Spanish medieval pottery. In C.M. Gerrard, A. Gutiérrez and A.G. Vince (eds), *Spanish medieval ceramics in Spain and the British Isles*, 281–95. British Archaeological Reports, International Series 610. BAR, Oxford.

Giacometti, A. and McGlade, S. 2015 Archaeological report: James and Thomas Street QBC Dublin 8. Unpublished report for Wills Bros Ltd/Dublin City Council (https://archaeologyplan.files.wordpress.com › 2011/05).

Giacometti, A. and Rico, A. 2010 Clay pipes from Kilkenny Courthouse 04E1286. Unpublished report for Arch-Tech Ltd.

Gilbert, J.T. (ed.) 1885 *Tenth report of the Royal Commission on Historical Manuscripts. Appendix 5: Archives of the Municipal Corporation of Waterford.* Eyre and Spottiswoode, London.

Gładykowska-Rzeczycka, J.J. and Nowakowski, D. 2014 A biological stone from a medieval cemetery in Poland. *PLoS One* **9** (10), e109096 (doi:10.1371/journal.pone.0109096).

Goodall, I.H. 2005 Iron objects. In M. Biddle, *Nonsuch Palace: the material culture of a noble Restoration household*, 373–411. Oxbow Books, Oxford.

Grant, A. 1975a The animal bones. In B. Cunliffe (ed.), *Excavations at Portchester Castle, Vol. 1: Roman*, 378–408. Society of Antiquaries of London, London.

Grant, A. 1975b Appendix B: The use of tooth wear as a guide to the age of domestic animals. In B. Cunliffe (ed.), *Excavations at Portchester Castle, Vol. 1: Roman*, 437–50. Society of Antiquaries of London, London.

Grant, A. 1983 *North Devon pottery: the seventeenth century.* University of Exeter, Exeter.

Green, F.J. 1984 The archaeological and documentary evidence for plants from the medieval period in England. In W. van Zeist and W.A. Casparie (eds), *Plants and ancient man: studies in palaeoethnobotany*, 99–114. Balkema, Rotterdam.

Greig, J. 1991 The British Isles. In W. van Zeist, K. Wasylikowa and K.-E. Behre (eds), *Progress in Old World palaeoethnobotany*, 299–334. Balkema, Rotterdam.

Griffith, M.C. 1991 *Calendar of Inquisitions.* Stationery Office, Dublin.

Gwynn, A. and Hadcock, R.N. 1970 *Medieval religious houses: Ireland.* Longman, London.

Halpin, E. 1999 Archaeological impact assessment & finds retrieval & section recording exercise, Bridge Street, Swords (99E0320). Unpublished report for ADS Ltd.

Hamilton-Dyer, S. 2016 Bird and fish bones from Bective Abbey. In G. Stout and M. Stout, *The Bective Abbey Project, Co. Meath: excavations 2009–12*, 170–9. Wordwell, Dublin.

Hammond, P. 1986 Points arising…. *Society for Clay Pipe Research* **11**, 27–8.

Hayden, A. 2011 *Trim Castle, Co. Meath: excavations 1995–8.* Archaeological Monograph Series 6. Stationery Office, Dublin.

Hayden, A. 2020 St Sepulchre's palace: new perspectives from recent excavations. In S. Duffy (ed.), *Medieval Dublin XVIII*, 283–324. Four Courts Press, Dublin.

Hayden, A. and Moore, M. 1997 Stone objects. In C. Walsh, *Archaeological excavations at Patrick, Nicholas and Winetavern Streets, Dublin*, 156–8. Brandon, Dingle.

Hencken, H.O'N. 1950 Lagore crannog: an Irish royal residence of the 7th to 10th centuries AD. *Proceedings of the Royal Irish Academy* **53**C, 1–247.

Henderson, G. 1974 Saints and kings at medieval Melrose Abbey. *Liturgical Review* **4**, 36–44.

Higgins, D.A. 2009 National clay pipe summaries: England. *Journal of the Académie Internationale de la Pipe* **2**, 41–50 (http://www.academia.edu/9652697/National_Clay_Pipe_Summaries_England).

Higgins, D.A. (n.d.) Southampton French Quarter 1382 Specialist Report Download F2: Clay tobacco pipes (https://library.thehumanjourney.net/48/1/SOU_1382_Specialist_report_download_F2.pdf).

Hillman, G.C., Mason, S., de Moulins, D. and Nesbitt, M. 1996 Identification of archaeological remains of wheat: the 1992 London workshop. *Circaea* **12**, 195–220.

Hillson, S. 1986 *Teeth*. Cambridge University Press, Cambridge.

Hillson, S. 1996 *Dental anthropology*. Cambridge University Press, Cambridge.

Hoare, P.G. and Sweet, C. 2002 The orientation of early medieval churches in England. *Journal of Historical Geography* **26** (2), 162–73.

Horning, A. 2004 Marbles and balls. In E. Fitzpatrick, M. O'Brien and P. Walsh, *Archaeological investigations in Galway City, 1987–1998*, 460–2. Wordwell, Bray.

Humphrey, R.V. 1969 Clay pipes from Old Sacramento. *Historical Archaeology* **3**, 12–33.

Hunter-Mann, K. 2008 *York Archaeological Trust Report 2008/1* (accessed at http://www.york.gov.uk/download/).

Hurl, D.P., Sandes, C. and Buckley, L. 2002 The excavation of an Early Christian cemetery at Solar, County Antrim, 1993. *Ulster Journal of Archaeology* **61**, 37–82.

Hurley, M.F. 1997a Artefacts of skeletal material. In M.F. Hurley and O.M.B. Scully, *Late Viking Age and medieval Waterford: excavations 1986–1992*, 650–702. Waterford Corporation, Waterford.

Hurley, M.F. 1997b Artefacts of skeletal material. In D.C. Twohig, *Skiddy's Castle and Christ Church, Cork: excavations 1974–77*, 239–73. Tower Books, Cork.

Hurley, M.F. 1997c Bone and antler artefacts. In M.F. Hurley, *Excavations at the North Gate, Cork, 1994*, 144–8. Cork Corporation, Cork.

Hurley, M.F. 2003 Artefacts of skeletal material. In R.M. Cleary and M.F. Hurley (eds), *Excavations in Cork City, 1984–2000*, 329–46. Cork County Council, Cork.

Hurley, M.F. 2004 Bone artefacts. In E. Fitzpatrick, M. O'Brien and P. Walsh, *Archaeological investigations in Galway City, 1987–1998*, 463–76. Wordwell, Bray.

Hurley, M.F. and McCutcheon, S.W.J. 1997 Wooden artefacts. In M.F. Hurley and O.M.B. Scully, *Late Viking Age and medieval Waterford: excavations 1986–1992*, 553–634. Waterford Corporation, Waterford.

Hurst, J.G., Neal, D.S. and van Beuningen, H.J.E. 1986 *Pottery produced and traded in north-west Europe 1350–1650*. Museum Boymans-van Beuningen, Rotterdam.

Jackson, R., Jackson, P. and Price, R. 1983 *Ireland and the Bristol clay pipe trade*. Self-published, Bristol.

Jennings, S. 1981 *Eighteen centuries of pottery at Norwich*. Norwich Survey and Norfolk Museums Service, Norwich.

Jope, E.M. 1961 Cornish houses 1400–1700. In E.M. Jope (ed.), *Studies in building history*, 192–222. Odhams Press, London.

Joyce, P.W. 1920 *The origin and history of Irish names of places*, vol. 3. Educational Company of Ireland, Dublin.

Katz, N.J., Katz, S.V. and Kipiani, M.G. 1965 *Atlas and keys of fruits and seeds occurring in the Quaternary deposits of the USSR*. Nauka, Moscow.

Keepax, C.A. 1988 Charcoal analysis with particular reference to archaeological sites in Britain. Unpublished Ph.D thesis, University College London.

Kelly, F. 1997 *Early Irish farming*. Dublin Institute for Advanced Studies, Dublin.

Keogh, J. 1735 *Botanalogia universalis Hibernica or a general Irish herbal*. Harrison, Cork.

Lancaster, R. 1975 Northolt Manor. *The London Archaeologist* **2** (13), 339–42.

Lane, S. 1995 Clay pipes. In M.F. Hurley, *Excavations at the North Gate, Cork, 1994*, 102–5. Cork Corporation, Cork.

Lane, S. 1997 The clay pipes. In M.F. Hurley and O.M.B. Scully, *Late Viking Age and medieval Waterford: excavations 1986–1992*, 366–74. Waterford Corporation, Waterford.

Langdon, J. 1982 The economics of horses and oxen in medieval England. *Agricultural History Review* **30** (1), 31–40.

Larsen, C.S. 1997 *Bioarchaeology: interpreting behavior from the human skeleton*. Cambridge University Press, New York.

Leask, H.G. 1941 *Irish castles and castellated houses*. Dundalgan Press, Dundalk.

Lieverse, A.R. 1999 Diet and aetiology of dental calculus. *International Journal of Osteoarchaeology* **9**, 219–32.

Lovejoy, C.O., Meindl, R.S., Pryzbeck, T.R. and Mensforth, R.P. 1985 Chronological metamorphysis of the auricular surface of the ilium: a new method for the determination of the adult skeletal age at death. *American Journal of Physical Anthropology* **68**, 15–28.

Lucas, A.T. 1960 Irish food before the potato. *Gwerin* **3** (2), 1–36.

Lynch, G., Roundtree, S. and Shaffrey Associates Architects 2009 *Bricks: a guide to the repair of historic brickwork*. Department of the Environment, Heritage and Local Government Advice Series. Stationery Office, Dublin.

Lynch, L.G. 2016a Osteoarchaeological report on the disarticulated human skeletal remains excavated at Swords Castle, Swords, Co. Dublin (Season 1, 2015). Consent No.: C450. Excavation Ref.: E4619. Unpublished report for client.

Lynch, L.G. 2016b Osteoarchaeological report on the disarticulated human skeletal remains excavated at Swords Castle, Swords, Co. Dublin (2015, 2016). Consent No.: C450. Excavation Ref.: E4619. Unpublished report for client.

Lyons, S. 2015 Appendix X: The environmental remains: archaeobotanical and charcoal analysis (https://bective.files.wordpress.com/2015/08/bective00lyonsappendix2.pdf, accessed April 2016).

Lyons, S. 2018 Pioneering new approaches to woodland ecology and human activity in medieval Ireland (*c.* 500–1550 AD): an investigation using archaeological charcoal. Unpublished Ph.D thesis, University College Cork.

Lysaght, P. 1986 Continuity and change in Irish diet. In A. Fenton and E. Kisbán (eds), *Food in change: eating habits from the Middle Ages to the present day*, 80–9. John Donald, Edinburgh.

McCartan, S.B. 2004 Stone artefacts. In E. Fitzpatrick, M. O'Brien and P. Walsh (eds), *Archaeological investigations in Galway City, 1987–1998*, 530–40. Wordwell, Dublin.

McCarthy, M. 1988 Animals in the economy of medieval and post-medieval Cork. Unpublished MA thesis, University College Cork.

McCarthy, M. 1995 Faunal remains. In C. Power, 'Excavations at St Augustine Street/Church

Street, Dungarvan'. *Tipperary Historical Journal* (1995), 202–6.

McCarthy, M. 2003a The faunal remains. In R.M. Cleary and M. Hurley (eds), *Cork City excavations 1984–2000*, 375–91. Cork City Council, Cork.

McCarthy, M. 2003b Faunal report. In C. Manning (ed.), *Excavations at Roscrea Castle*, 110–13. Archaeological Monograph Series 1. Stationery Office, Dublin.

McCarthy, M. 2013 The faunal remains. In C. Manning, *Clogh Oughter Castle, Co. Cavan: archaeology, history and architecture*, 185–91. Archaeological Monograph Series 8. Stationery Office, Dublin.

McCarthy, M. 2015 The animal bones from the Gatehouse, Swords Castle. Unpublished report for Irish Archaeological Consultancy Services.

McCarthy, M. 2017 The faunal remains. In D. Pollock, *Barryscourt Castle, Co. Cork: archaeology, history and architecture*, 216–28. Archaeological Monograph Series 11. Stationery Office, Dublin.

McClatchie, M. 2003 The plant remains, Cork city excavations. In R.M. Cleary and M.F. Hurley (eds), *Cork city excavations 1984–2000*, 391–413. Cork City Council, Cork.

McClatchie, M. and OCarroll, E. 2015 *National Roads Authority palaeoenvironmental sampling guidelines: retrieval, analysis and reporting of plant macro-remains, wood, charcoal, insects and pollen from archaeological excavations*. National Roads Authority, Dublin.

McClatchie, M., Bogaard, A., Colledge, S., Whitehouse, N., Schulting, R., Barratt, P. and McLaughlin, R. 2014 Neolithic farming in north-western Europe: archaeobotanical evidence from Ireland. *Journal of Archaeological Science* **51**, 206–15.

McClatchie, M., McCormick, F., Kerr, T. and O'Sullivan, A. 2015 Early medieval farming and food production: a review of the archaeobotanical evidence from archaeological excavations in Ireland. *Vegetation History and Archaeobotany* **24**, 179–86.

McCormick, F. 1996 The animal bones. In M.F. Hurley and O.M.B. Scully, *Late Viking Age and medieval Waterford: excavations 1986–1992*, 819–53. Waterford Corporation, Waterford.

McCorry, M. 1997 Roof tiles: a petrological report. In C. Walsh, *Archaeological excavations at Patrick, Nicholas and Winetavern Streets, Dublin*, 153–4. Brandon, Dingle.

McCutcheon, C. 2000 Medieval pottery in Dublin: new names and some dates. In S. Duffy (ed.), *Medieval Dublin I*, 117–25. Four Courts Press, Dublin.

McCutcheon, C. 2006 *Medieval pottery from Wood Quay, Dublin*. Medieval Dublin Excavations 1962–81, Ser. B, Vol. 7. Royal Irish Academy, Dublin.

McCutcheon, S. 1997 The stone artefacts. In M.F. Hurley and O.M.B. Scully, *Late Viking Age and medieval Waterford: excavations 1986–1992*, 404–32. Waterford Corporation, Waterford.

McGarry, D. 2001 Swords Castle, the geophysical survey. Unpublished report for Heritage International Ltd.

McGlade, S. 2017 Excavation report, Old Schoolhouse, Church Road, Swords, Co. Dublin. Unpublished report for Archaeology Plan Ltd.

MacGregor, A. 1985 *Bone, antler, ivory and horn: the technology of skeletal materials since the Roman period*. Croom Helm, London.

MacGregor, A. 1989 Bone, antler and horn industries in the urban context. In D. Serjeantson and T. Waldron (eds), *Diet and crafts in towns: the evidence of animal remains from the Roman to the post-medieval periods*, 107–28. British Archaeological Reports, British Series 199.

BAR, Oxford.

McLoughlin, G. 2019 Test excavation, Windmill Lands and Townparks, Swords, Co. Dublin. Unpublished report for Courtney Deery Ltd.

McNeill, C. (ed.) 1950 *Calendar of Archbishop Alen's Register* c. *1172–1534*. Royal Society of Antiquaries of Ireland, Dublin. [Extra volume of the *Journal of the Royal Society of Antiquaries of Ireland* for 1949.]

MacShamhráin, A. 2016 Swords and district: the political and ecclesiastical background, fifth to twelfth centuries. In S. Duffy (ed.), *Medieval Dublin XV*, 39–63. Four Courts Press, Dublin.

Maginn, C. 2011 Note on an Elizabethan coin found at Terryland Castle, Galway. *Journal of the Galway Archaeological and Historical Society* **63**, 71–2.

Malloy, K., Hall, D. and Oram, R. 2013 Prestigious landscapes: an archaeological and historical examination of the role of deer at three medieval Scottish parks. *Eolas: the Journal of the American Society of Irish Medieval Studies* **6**, 66–87.

Mann, R.W. and Murphy, S.P. 1990 *Regional atlas of bone diseases: a guide to pathologic and normal variation in the human skeleton.* Charles C. Thomas, Springfield, IL.

Maresh, M.M. 1970 Measurements from roentgenograms. In R.W. McCammon (ed.), *Human growth and development*, 157–200. Charles C. Thomas, Springfield, IL.

Mays, S. 1998 *The archaeology of human bones.* Routledge, London.

Mays, S., Fysh, E. and Taylor, G.M. 2002 Investigation of the link between visceral surface rib lesions and tuberculosis in a medieval skeletal series from England using ancient DNA. *American Journal of Physical Anthropology* **119**, 27–36.

Mills, J. 1890–1 Tenants and agriculture near Dublin in the fourteenth century. *Journal of the Royal Society of Antiquaries of Ireland* **21**, 54–63.

Mitchell, G.F. 1987 *Archaeology and environment in early Dublin.* Royal Irish Academy, Dublin.

Moloney, M.F. 1919 *Irish ethno-botany and the evolution of medicine in Ireland.* Gill, Dublin.

Monk, M.A. 1986 Evidence from macroscopic plant remains for crop husbandry in prehistoric and early historic Ireland: a review. *Journal of Irish Archaeology* **3**, 31–6.

Monk, M.A. 1987 Appendix II: Charred seeds and plant remains. In M.F. Hurley, 'Kilferagh, Co. Kilkenny', 98–9. In R.M. Cleary, M.F. Hurley and E.A. Twohig (eds), *Archaeological excavations on the Cork–Dublin Gas Pipeline (1981–82)*, 88–100. Department of Archaeology, University College Cork, Cork.

Monk, M.A. and Kelleher, E. 2005 An assessment of the archaeological evidence for Irish corn-drying kilns in the light of the results of archaeological experiments and archaeobotanical studies. *Journal of Irish Archaeology* **14**, 77–114.

Moorhouse, S. 1988 Documentary evidence for medieval ceramic roofing materials and its archaeological implications: some thoughts. *Medieval Ceramics* **12**, 33–5.

Moorrees, C.F.A., Fanning, E.A. and Hunt Jr, E.E. 1963a Age variation of formation stages for ten permanent teeth. *Journal of Dental Research* **42**, 1490–502.

Moorrees, C.F.A., Fanning, E.A. and Hunt Jr, E.E. 1963b Formation and resorption of three deciduous teeth in children. *American Journal of Physical Anthropology* **21**, 205–13.

Moraghan, M., McIlreavy, D., Toibin, M. and Scully, S. 2016 Archaeological excavation report, Swords Castle (C450/E4376). Unpublished report for Fingal County Council.

Morrin, J. 1861 *Calendar of the patent and close rolls of Chancery in Ireland*, vol. 1. Stationery Office, Dublin.

Morrisey, J.F. (ed.) 1939 *Statute rolls of the parliament of Ireland—13th to the 21 and 22nd years of the reign of Edward VI*, part II. Stationery Office, Dublin.

Moss, R. 2006 Permanent expressions of piety: the secular and the sacred in later medieval stone sculpture. In R. Moss, C. Ó Clabaigh and S. Ryan (eds), *Art and devotion in late medieval Ireland*, 72–97. Four Courts Press, Dublin.

Mould, Q., Carlisle, I. and Cameron, E. 2003 *Craft, industry, and everyday life: leather and leatherworking in Anglo-Scandinavian and medieval York.* The Archaeology of York 17/6. Council for British Archaeology, York.

Moxon, J. 1703 *Mechanick exercises: or the doctrine of handy-works. Applied to the arts of smithing, joinery, carpentry, turning, bricklaying.* London (http://www.hathitrust.ort/ access_use#pd).

Munby, J. 1993 *Stokesay Castle.* English Heritage, York.

Murphy, M. 1989 Ecclesiastical censures: an aspect of their use in thirteenth century Dublin. *Archivium Hibernicum* **44**, 89–97.

Murphy, M. and Potterton, M. 2010 *The Dublin region in the Middle Ages: settlement, land-use and economy.* Discovery Programme Monograph 10. Four Courts Press, Dublin.

Nicholls, J. 2011 Geophysical survey report: Bremore Castle & Swords Castle Conservation Plan (Licence no. 11R038). Unpublished report for Fingal County Council.

Nicholls, K.W. 1994 *The Irish fiants of the Tudor sovereigns*, vol. 1 [1521–58] and vol. 2 [1558–86]. Edmund Burke, Dublin.

Nikolova, S. and Toneva, D. 2012 Frequency of metopic suture in male and female medieval cranial series. *Acta Morphologica et Anthropologica* **19**, 250–2.

Nikolova, S., Toneva, D., Georgiev, I. and Lasarov, N. 2019 Relation between metopic suture persistence and frontal sinus development. In T.-C. Wang (ed.), *Challenging issues on paranasal sinuses* (DOI: 10.5772/intechopen.79376, accessed 16 October 2019).

Noël Hume, I. 1969 *A guide to the artifacts of Colonial America.* University of Pennsylvania Press, Philadelphia.

Norton, J. 1986 Points arising… . *Society for Clay Pipe Research Newsletter* **12**, 29–30.

Norton, J. 1997 Clay pipes. In C. Walsh, *Archaeological excavations at Patrick, Nicholas and Winetavern Streets, Dublin*, 183–4. Brandon, Dingle.

Norton, J. 2004 Clay pipes. In E. Fitzpatrick, M. O'Brien and P. Walsh (eds), *Archaeological investigations in Galway City, 1987–1998*, 427–47. Wordwell, Dublin.

Norton, J. 2013 Pipe dreams: a directory of clay tobacco pipe-makers in Ireland. *Archaeology Ireland* **27** (1), 31–6.

Norton, J. and Lane, S. 2007 Clay tobacco-pipes in Ireland, *c.* 1600–1850. In A. Horning, R. Ó Baoill, C. Donnelly and P. Logue (eds), *The post-medieval archaeology of Ireland, 1550–1850*, 435–52. Irish Post-Medieval Archaeology Group Proceedings 1. Wordwell, Dublin.

O'Brien, D. 2014 The importation of building and other stone into Ireland *c.* 1142–1400. Unpublished MPhil. thesis, University College Cork.

O'Brien, G. (ed.) 1923 *Advertisements for Ireland.* Royal Society of Antiquaries of Ireland, Dublin.

O'Carroll, F. 2008 Excavation, Church Lane, Swords, Co. Dublin. Unpublished report (https://excavations.ie/report/1998/Dublin/0003391/).

O'Donnell, L. 2007 Environmental archaeology: identifying patterns of exploitation in the Bronze Age. In E. Grogan, L. O'Donnell and P. Johnson (eds), *The Bronze Age landscapes of the Pipeline to the West: an integrated archaeological and environmental assessment*, 27–101.

Wordwell, Bray.

O'Donovan, D. 2003 English patron, English building? The importance of St Sepulchre's archiepiscopal palace, Dublin. In S. Duffy (ed.), *Medieval Dublin IV*, 253–78. Four Courts Press, Dublin.

O'Donovan, E. 2009 Archaeological excavations on Mount Gamble Hill: stories from the first Christians in Swords. In C. Baker (ed.), *Axes, warriors and windmills: recent archaeological discoveries in North Fingal*, 64–75. Fingal County Council, Dublin.

O'Donovan, E. and Geber, J. 2010 Excavations on Mount Gamble Hill, Swords, Co. Dublin. In C. Corlett and M. Potterton (eds), *Death and burial in early medieval Ireland in the light of recent archaeological excavations*, 227–38. Wordwell, Dublin.

Ó Floinn, R. 1988 Handmade medieval pottery in SE Ireland—'Leinster Cooking Ware'. In G. Mac Niocaill and P. Wallace (eds), *Keimelia: studies in medieval archaeology and history in memory of Tom Delaney*, 325–49. Galway University Press, Galway.

O'Keeffe, T. 2015 *Medieval Irish buildings 1100–1600.* Maynooth Research Guides for Irish Local History. Four Courts Press, Dublin.

O Rahilly, C. 1998 A classification of bronze stick-pins from the Dublin excavations 1962–72. In C. Manning (ed.), *Dublin and beyond the Pale: studies in honour of Patrick Healy*, 23–33. Wordwell, Bray.

O'Sullivan, E. 2001 Archaeological report on the removal of overburden at Swords Castle, Bridge Street, Swords, Co. Dublin, Phase II. Unpublished report by ADS Ltd for Fingal County Council.

Ortner, D. 2003 *Identification of pathological conditions in human skeletal remains.* Academic Press, Amsterdam.

Ortner, D.J. and Putschar, W.G.J. 1981 *Identification of pathological conditions in human skeletal remains.* Smithsonian Institution Press, Washington.

Oswald, A. 1975 *Clay pipes for the archaeologist.* British Archaeological Reports, British Series 14. BAR, Oxford.

Ottaway, P. and Rogers, N. 2002 *Craft, industry and everyday life: finds from medieval York.* The Archaeology of York 17/15. Council for British Archaeology, London.

Otway-Ruthven, J. 1951 The organisation of Anglo-Irish agriculture in the Middle Ages. *Journal of the Royal Society of Antiquaries of Ireland* **81** (1), 1–13.

Pearce, D. (n.d.) *Spot the furniture: a mini-guide to English furniture design.* National Trust, London.

Pearce, J.E., Vince, A.G. and Jenner, M.A. 1985 *A dated type series of London medieval pottery part 2: London-type ware.* London and Middlesex Archaeological Society, London.

Philpotts, C. 1999 The metropolitan palaces of medieval London. *The London Archaeologist* **9**, 47–53.

Prummel, W. and Frisch, H.-J. 1986 A guide for the distinction of species, sex and body size in bones of sheep and goat. *Journal of Archaeological Science* **13**, 567–77.

Pugh, R.B. (ed.) 2002 *A history of the county of Cambridge and the Isle of Ely*, vol. 4. Victoria County History, London.

Rahtz, P. 1969 Upton, Gloucestershire, 1964–1968. Second report. *Transactions of the Bristol and Gloucestershire Archaeological Society* **88**, 74–126.

Rajic, M. (n.d.) The glass. In A. Giacometti, 'Final excavation report, Vol. II, New Street South, Dublin 8, 04E1286', 66–76 (https://archaeologyplan.com/other-sites/).

RCAHMW 2000 *An inventory of the ancient monuments in Glamorgan, Vol. 3.1. Medieval secular monuments: (b) the later castles, from 1217 to the present.* HMSO, Cardiff and London.

Reeners, R. (ed.) 2014 *Swords Castle Conservation Plan.* Fingal County Council, Swords.

Reeves, W. 1970 *A lecture on the antiquities of Swords delivered in Swords, … Sept. 12, 1860.* Dublin.

Roberts, C.A. and Buikstra, J.E. 2003 *The bioarchaeology of tuberculosis: a global view on a reemerging disease.* University Press of Florida, Gainesville.

Roberts, C.A. and Manchester, K. 1995 *The archaeology of disease.* Cornell University Press, Ithaca, NY.

Roberts, C., Lucy, D. and Manchester, K. 1994 Inflammatory lesions of the ribs: an analysis of the Terry Collection. *American Journal of Physical Anthropology* **95**, 169–82.

Rogers, J. and Waldron, T. 1995 *A field guide to joint disease in archaeology.* Wiley, Chichester.

Salmon, W. 1710 *Botanologia: the English herbal.* Rhodes and Taylor, London.

Samson, R. 1982 Finds from Urquhart Castle in the National Museum, Edinburgh. *Proceedings of the Society of Antiquaries of Scotland* **112**, 465–76.

Şarbak, A., Çirak, M.T. and Çirak, A. 2017 Osteoarchaeological investigations of metopic suture in the Late Roman period in Spradon. *Mediterranean Archaeology and Archaeometry* **17**, 27–38.

Savage, C. 2015 *Introduction to post medieval coins and identification guide for archaeologists.* BAJR Practical Guide Series no. 38 (downloadable reference article available at bajr.org).

Savage, G. and Newman, H. 2000 *An illustrated dictionary of ceramics.* Thames and Hudson, London.

Schaefer, M., Black, S. and Scheuer, L. 2009 *Juvenile osteology: a laboratory and field manual.* Elsevier, Amsterdam.

Scheuer, L. and Black, S. 2000 *Developmental juvenile osteology.* Academic Press, San Diego, CA.

Schofield, J. 2013 London waterfront tenements: a project summary [available from colat.org.uk]. The City of London Archaeological Trust.

Schofield, J. and Vince, A.G. 2003 *Medieval towns: the archaeology of British towns in their European setting.* Leicester University Press, Leicester.

Schweingruber, F.H. 1990 *Microscopic wood anatomy* (3rd edn). Swiss Federal Institute for Forest, Snow and Landscape Research, Birmensdorf.

Scott, B.G. 2013–14 Lead cloth seals from Carrickfergus, County Antrim, and a London seal in the National Museum of Ireland. *Ulster Journal of Archaeology* (3rd ser.) **72**, 220–6.

Scott, G. 1974 Some shop tickets countermarked and engraved on copper coins at the end of the eighteenth century. *British Numismatic Journal* **44** (9), 78–80.

Scott, G. 1980 Some unpublished countermarks on copper coins. *British Numismatic Journal* **50** (13), 137–9.

Scott, S.M. 2010 *Toys and American culture: an encyclopedia.* ABC-CLIOLLL, Santa Barbara.

Scully, O.M.B. 1997a Late medieval and stone houses. In M.F. Hurley and O.M.B. Scully, *Late Viking Age and medieval Waterford: excavations 1986–1992*, 190–227. Waterford Corporation, Waterford.

Scully, O.M.B. 1997b Metal artefacts. In M.F. Hurley and O.M.B. Scully, *Late Viking Age and medieval Waterford: excavations 1986–1992*, 438–89. Waterford Corporation, Waterford.

Seaby, P. 1970 *Coins and tokens of Ireland.* Seaby's Standard Catalogue Part 3. B.A. Seaby Ltd, London.

Serjeantson, D. 2009 *Birds.* Cambridge University Press, Cambridge.

Sevastopulo, G. 2014 Analysis of three samples of stone. In Fingal County Council, *Swords Castle Conservation Plan*, Appendix D (http://www.fingal.ie/planning-and-buildings/architectural-conservation/conservationplansandreports/).

Sexton, R. 1998 Porridges, gruels and breads: the cereal foodstuffs of early medieval Ireland. In M.A. Monk and J. Sheehan (eds), *Early medieval Munster: archaeology, history and society*, 76–86. Cork University Press, Cork.

Shaw, H. 1988 *The Dublin Pictorial Guide & Directory of 1850.* Friar's Bush Press, Belfast.

Silver, I.A. 1971 The ageing of domestic animals. In D.R. Brothwell and E. Higgs (eds), *Science in archaeology: a survey of progress and research*, 250–68. Thames and Hudson, London.

Simington, R.C. (ed.) 1961 *The Civil Survey 1654–6. Vol. 10: Miscellanea.* Irish Manuscripts Commission, Dublin.

Smiles, S. 1889 *The Huguenots: their settlements, churches, and industries in England and Ireland.* John Murray, London.

Smith, B.H. 1984 Patterns of molar wear in hunter-gatherers and agriculturalists. *American Journal of Physical Anthropology* **63**, 39–56.

Smith, B.H. 1991 Standards of human tooth formation and dental age assessment. In M.A. Kelley and C.S. Larsen (eds), *Advances in dental anthropology*, 142–68. Wiley–Liss, New York.

Stace, C. 1991 *New flora of the British Isles.* Cambridge University Press, Cambridge.

Stace, C. 2010 *New flora of the British Isles.* Cambridge University Press, Cambridge.

Stalley, R. 1987 *The Cistercian monasteries of Ireland.* Yale University Press, New Haven.

Stalley, R.A. 2006 The archbishop's residence at Swords: castle or country retreat? In S. Duffy (ed.), *Medieval Dublin VII*, 152–76. Four Courts Press, Dublin.

Steane, J. 1985 *The archaeology of medieval England and Wales.* Taylor and Francis, Abingdon.

Stika, H.P. and Heiss, A.G. 2012 Plant cultivation in the Bronze Age. In H. Fokkens and A. Harding (eds), *The Oxford handbook of the European Bronze Age*, 348–69. Oxford University Press, Oxford.

Stocker, D. and Stocker, M. 1996 Sacred profanity: the theology of rabbit breeding and the symbolic landscape of the warren. *World Archaeology* **28** (2), 265–72.

Stokes, P. and Rowley-Conwy, P. 2002 Iron Age cultigen? Experimental return rates for fat hen (*Chenopodium album* L.). *Environmental Archaeology* 7, 95–9.

Stokes, W. 1905 *The Martyrology of Oengus the Culdee.* Henry Bradshaw Society, London.

Stopford, J. 2005 *Medieval floor tiles of northern England. Pattern and purpose: production between the 13th and 16th centuries.* Oxbow Books, Oxford.

Stout, G. and Stout, M. 2008 *Excavation of a secular cemetery at Knowth Site M, County Meath, and related sites in north-east Leinster.* Wordwell, Dublin.

Stroud, G.D. (n.d.) (https://www.fao.org/3/x5954e/x5954e01.htm).

Stuart-Macadam, P. 1991 Anaemia in Roman Britain: Poundbury Camp. In H. Bush and M. Zvelebil (eds), *Health in past societies: biocultural interpretations of human skeletal remains in archaeological contexts*, 101–13. British Archaeological Reports, British Series 567. BAR, Oxford.

Stuiver, M. 1993 A note on single-year calibration of the radiocarbon time scale, AD

1510–1954. In M. Stuiver, A. Long and R. S. Kra (eds), 'Calibration 1993'. *Radiocarbon* **35**(1), 67–72.

Stuiver, M. and Reimer, P.J. 1993 *CALIB User's Guide Rev. 3.0.* University of Washington Quaternary Isotope Laboratory.

Sullivan, E. 2001 Archaeological report on the removal of overburden at Swords Castle, Bridge Street, Swords, Co. Dublin (Phase II). Unpublished report by ADS Ltd for Fingal County Council.

Swan*,* D.L. 1983 Enclosed ecclesiastical sites and their relevance to settlement patterns of the first millennium AD. In T. Reeves-Smyth and F. Hamond (eds), *Landscape archaeology in Ireland*, 269–80. British Archaeological Reports, British Series 116. BAR, Oxford.

Swan, L. 1994 The Pound Licensed Premises, Bridge St., Swords. In I. Bennett (ed.), *Excavations 1993*. Wordwell, Bray.

Sweetman, H. 1875–86 *Calendar of documents relating to Ireland: preserved in Her Majesty's Public Record Office, London, 1171–1307* (5 vols). Longman, London. [Vol. I, 1172–1251 (1875); vol. II, 1252–84 (1877); vol. III, 1285–92 (1879); vol. IV, 1293–1301 (1881); vol. V, 1302–7 (1886).]

Sweetman, P.D. 1978 Archaeological excavations at Trim Castle, Co. Meath, 1971–74. *Proceedings of the Royal Irish Academy* **78**C, 127–98.

Sykes, N. and Curl, J. 2010 The rabbit. In T. O'Connor and N. Sykes (eds), *Extinctions and invasions: a social history of British fauna*, 116–26. Windgather, Oxford.

Symonds, H. 1917 The Elizabethan coinages for Ireland. *Numismatic Chronicle and Journal of the Royal Numismatic Society* (4th ser.) **17**, 97–125.

Thurely, S. 2009 The cloister and hearth. *Journal of the British Archaeological Association* **162**, 179–95.

Tierney, J. and Hannon, M. 1997 Section 22: Plant remains. In M.F. Hurley and O.M.B. Scully, *Late Viking Age and medieval Waterford: excavations 1986–1992*, 854–93. Waterford Corporation, Waterford.

Tierney, J. and Johnston, P. 2009 Archaeological excavation report, N25 Rathsillagh to Harristown Realignment, Harristown Little. *Eachtra* **4**.

Tobin, M. 2015 Osteological analysis of human remains from Swords Castle, Swords, Co. Dublin (E4376, C450). Unpublished report for Irish Archaeological Consultancy.

Tsaliki, A. 2008 Unusual burials and necrophobia: an insight into the burial archaeology of fear. In E.M. Murphy (ed.), *Deviant burial in the archaeological record*, 1–16. Oxbow Books, Oxford.

Turell, S. 2013 Final report of monitoring of groundworks at Swords Castle. Unpublished report by ADS Ltd for Fingal County Council.

van der Veen, M. and Fieller, N. 1982 Sampling seeds. *Journal of Archaeological Science* **9**, 287–98.

Van Leeuwen, T. 2011 *The language of colour: an introduction*. Routledge, London.

Vince, A. 1977 The medieval and post-medieval ceramic industry of the Malvern region: the study of a ware and its distribution. In D.P.S. Peacock (ed.), *Pottery and early commerce: characterization and trade in Roman and later ceramics*, 257–305. Academic Press, London.

Von den Driesch, A. 1976 *A guide to the measurement of animal bones from archaeological sites*. Peabody Museum Bulletin 1. Peabody Museum of Archaeology and Ethnography, Harvard University, Cambridge, Mass.

Waldron, T. 2009 *Palaeopathology.* Cambridge University Press, Cambridge.

Walker, P.L., Bathurst, R.R., Richman, R., Gjerdrum, T. and Andrushko, V.A. 2009 The causes of porotic hyperostosis and cribra orbitalia: a reappraisal of the iron-deficiency anemia hypothesis. *American Journal of Physical Anthropology* **139**, 109–25.

Walsh, C. 2000 Archaeological excavations at the abbey of St Thomas the Martyr, Dublin. In S. Duffy (ed.), *Medieval Dublin I*, 185–202. Four Courts Press, Dublin.

Walsh, C. 2002 3 Main Street, Swords. In I. Bennett (ed.), *Excavations 1998*. Wordwell, Bray.

Walsh, R. 1888 *Fingal and its churches: a historical sketch of the foundation and struggles of the Church of Ireland in that part of the County Dublin which lies to the north of the River Tolka.* William McGee, Dublin.

Walton, P. 1991 Textiles. In J. Blair and N. Ramsay (eds), *English medieval industries: craftsmen, techniques and products*, 319–54. Hambledon Press, London.

Waterman, D.M. 1970 Somersetshire and other foreign building stone in medieval Ireland. *Ulster Journal of Archaeology* (3rd ser.) **33**, 63–75.

Webb, D.A. 1977 *An Irish flora.* Dundalgan Press, Dundalk.

Wheeler, A. 1978 *Key to the fishes of northern Europe.* Frederick Warne, London.

Wheeler, A. and Jones, A.K.G. 1989 *Fishes.* Cambridge University Press, Cambridge.

White, C.L. 2005 *American artifacts of personal adornment, 1680–1820: a guide to identification and interpretation.* AltaMira Press, Lanham.

White, T.D. and Folkens, P.A. 1991 *Human osteology.* Academic Press, San Diego.

Whiteford Geosciences 2000 Geophysical survey at Swords Castle, Dublin. Unpublished report on behalf of Archaeological Development Services Ltd.

Whitehead, R. 1996 *Buckles: 1250–1800.* Greenlight Publishing, Chelmsford.

Whitty, Y. and Gill, E. 2004 Johnstown 1: archaeological excavation of a multi-period burial, settlement, and industrial site. In N. Carlin, L. Clarke and F. Walsh (eds), *The archaeology of life and death in the Boyne floodplain: the linear landscape of the N4*, CD Appendix. NRA Scheme Monographs 2. National Roads Authority, Dublin.

Wilbur, A.K., Farnbach, A.W., Knudson, K.J. and Buikstra, J.E. 2008 Diet, tuberculosis, and the paleopathological record. *Current Anthropology* **49**, 963–91.

Williamson, T. 2006 *The archaeology of rabbit warrens.* Shire Archaeology 88. Shire Publications, Princes Risborough.

Winder, J.M. 1980 *Southampton Archaeological Research Committee Report 1.* CBA Report 33. Council for British Archaeology, London.

Wood, M.E. 1965 *The English medieval house.* Phoenix House, London.

Woodfield, C. and Woodfield, P. 1981–2 The palace of the archbishops of Lincoln at Lyddington. *Transactions of the Leicestershire Archaeological and Historical Society* **57**, 1–16.

Woods, H. 1982 Excavations at Eltham Palace 1975–9. *Transactions of the London and Middlesex Archaeological Society* **33**, 214–66.

Woodward, M. and Walker, A.R.P. 1994 Sugar consumption and dental caries: evidence from 90 countries. *British Dental Journal* **176**, 297–302.

Wren, J. 1987 Crested ridge tiles from medieval urban sites in Leinster 1200–1500. Unpublished MA thesis, University College Dublin.

Wren, J. 1997 The roof tiles. In M.F. Hurley and O.M.B. Scully (eds), *Late Viking and medieval Waterford: excavations 1986–1992*, 361–5. Waterford Corporation, Waterford.

Wren, J. 2006 Medieval and post-medieval roof tiles. In C. McCutcheon, *Medieval pottery from Wood Quay, Dublin*, 177–95. Medieval Dublin Excavations 1962–81, Ser. B, Vol. 7. Royal Irish Academy, Dublin.

Wren, J. 2007 The roof tiles. In M. Clyne, *Kells Priory, Co. Kilkenny: archaeological excavations by T. Fanning and M. Clyne*, 225–33. Stationery Office, Dublin.

Wren, J. 2010 Roof tiles. In A. Lynch, *Tintern Abbey, Co. Wexford: Cistercians and Colcloughs. Excavations 1982–2007*, 138–44. Stationery Office, Dublin.

Wren, J. (forthcoming) Clay building materials. In M. Moraghan, *Excavations at Swords Castle.*

Yalden, D.W. and Albarella, U. 2009 *The history of British birds*. Oxford University Press, Oxford.

Zori, D. 2007 Nails, rivets, and clench bolts: a case for typological clarity. *Archaeologia Islandica* **6**, 32–7.

Internet sources

Blowing bubbles in paintings: http://www.artistsandart.org/2010/06/blowing-bubbles-in-painting.html (accessed 1 December 2015 and 3 November 2016).

Boettcher, D. (2016): http://www.vintagewatchstraps.com/watchmovement.php (accessed January 2017).

www.british-history.ac.uk.

British Farthings (2007–18)—*Coins of England: William III (farthing)*: http://www.britishfarthings.com/Royal/3/All_William_III.html (accessed September 2018).

British Museum—The Portable Antiquities Scheme Database: https://finds.org.uk/ (accessed 2016, 2017 and 2018).

British Museum—Fifteenth-century mazer, Museum no. AF 3116: http://www.britishmuseum.org/research/collection_online/search.aspx?searchText=mazer (accessed February 2016).

Cambridge Archaeology Field Group (November 2012)—*Evolution of clay tobacco pipes in England*: http://www.cafg.net/docs/articles/claypipes.pdf.

Carrara: http://www.webmineralshop.com/articoli/carrara_eng.htm (accessed 14 December 2015).

Catalogue c. 1885 for Jan Prince & Cie, Gouda: http://www/claypipes.nl/19e-eeuw/jan-prince/catalogus/.

Census of Ireland, 1901 and 1911: http://census.nationalarchives.ie/ (accessed 20 November 2015 and 3 November 2016).

Coleman, H. (2015)—*The art and archaeology of clay pipes*: http://www.dawnmist.org/gallery.htm (accessed 13 November 2015 and 30 October 2016).

Elections: https://thehistoryofparliament.wordpress.com/2021/01/19/always-rowdy-violent-and-colourful-eighteenth-century-elections-in-the-borough-of-swords-co-dublin/.

Elton, S.F. (2011)—*The Bagseal Gallery*: http://www.bagseals.org/gallery/main.php?g2_itemId=31&g2_page= (accessed August 2018).

Farber & Associates LLC (2015–16)—*Vintage toy cap guns*: http://vintagetoycapguns.com (accessed January 2017).

Find of the Month—Early 19th-century gilt buttons: https://thepragmaticcostumer.wordpress.com/2016/10/25/find-of-the-month-early-19th-century-gilt-buttons/ (accessed September 2018).

George II halfpenny, 1727–60 (image): http://www.coins-of-the-uk.co.uk/pics/halfp.html#g2

(accessed January 2017).

Gilt buttons with decoration (image): http://www.buttoncountry.com/Metals2.html (accessed September 2018).

Hargaden, M. (2005)—*The Ballygahan and Ballymurtagh Mines*: http://www countywicklowheritage.org/page/mining_in_west_avoca (accessed February 2016).

Irish Congress of Trade Unions: http://www.irishlabourhistorysociety.com/pdf/ICTU.pdf (accessed 23 November 2015 and 3 November 2016).

Jones, F. (2010)—*Counterstamped coins—twice the history*: https://numistories.com/537/ counterstamped-coins-twice-the-history/ (accessed September 2018).

Laning, C. (2007–9)—*Paternoster-Row: researching historical rosaries—Gauds or marker beads*: http://paternoster-row.medievalscotland.org/ (accessed 3 December 2015).

McIvor, B.—*17th century British tokens*: http://www.thecoppercorner.com/history/ (accessed January–February 2016).

McIvor, B.—*18th century provincial tokens ('conder' tokens)*: http://www.thecoppercorner.com/ history/18thC_hist.html (accessed January 2016).

Market Street Media (2007–17)—*Vintage cap guns*: http://www.collectorsweekly.com/ toys/cap-guns (accessed January 2017).

Milkmaid mark: http://www.claypipes.nl/merken/afb-natuur-personen/melkmeid.

Pair of 1883 Victorian Metal Pencil Sharpeners (image): http://www.ebay.ie/itm/Vtg-Pair-of-1883-Victorian-Metal-Pencil-Sharpeners-Marked-SO-Tiny-Oldies-/182283418501 (accessed January 2017).

Prince family of Gouda: http://www.goudapipes.nl/books/meulen/catalog/db/.

Samford, P. (2008)—*Writing slate.* Diagnostic artifacts in Maryland: https://www.jefpat.org/CuratorsChoiceArchive/2008CuratorsChoice/Sep2008-WritingSlate.html.

Samford, P.—*Marbles.* Diagnostic artifacts in Maryland: https://www.jefpat.org/ diagnostic/SmallFinds/Marbles/index-marbles.html (accessed 29 May 2018).

Slate pencils: http://www.officemuseum.com/pencil_history.htm.

Smith, M. (1998)—*Some Anglo-Irish copper mining tokens of the late eighteenth century*: http://www.mining-memorabilia.co.uk/AIMC.htm (accessed January–February 2016).

Stafford-Langan, J. (1994–2014)—*Irish milled coinage (1660–1823)*: http://www irishcoinage.com/MILLED.HTM#jas2 (accessed January 2016).

Stub-stemmed pipes: http://www.pijpenkabinet.nl./Pijpenkabinet/00-E frame.html.

The Buttonmonger (2011)—Gilded buttons. *The Buttonmonger* **1** (7): http://www. thebuttonmonger.com/content/July2011.pdf (accessed January 2017).

The woollen cloth trade in Exeter: http://clothtrade.co.uk/index.php/processes/burling/ (accessed February 2016).

Thom's Almanac and Official Street Directory for the year 1862: http://www. libraryireland.com/Dublin-Street-Directory-1862/Home.php (accessed 21 November 2015 and 30 October 2016).

Thurston, Albert—*History and tradition*: http://www.albertthurston.com/history2. cfm?catid=4 (accessed January 2016).

Trowbridge Museum (2011)—*Cleaning and mending cloth*: http://trowbridgemuseum.co. uk/finishing-the-cloth-2/ (accessed February 2016).

van Oostven, J. (2013)—*Seals typology*: https://kleipijp.home.xs4all.nl/metaal.htm (accessed August 2018).